THE
CARIBBEAN
...LIKE A LOCAL

Waveland Beach, Jamaica. Photo: © Christian Heeb/hemis.fr

THE CARIBBEAN...LIKE A LOCAL

Chief Contributing Editor	Peter Greenberg
General Manager	Cynthia Clayton Ochterbeck
Editorial Manager	Jonathan P. Gilbert
Editor	Gwen Cannon
Principal Writers	Claire Boobbyer, Paul Crask, Zain Deane, Glenn Michael Harper, Oliver Hill, Russell Maddicks, Steven Olsen, Sandra Phinney, Megan E. Smith
Production Manager	Natasha G. George
Cartography	Peter Wrenn
Photo Editor	Yoshimi Kanazawa
Photo Researcher	Chris Bell
Proofreader	Sean Cannon
Interior Design	Chris Bell
Layout	Nicole D. Jordan, Natasha G. George
Cover Design	Chris Bell
Cover Layout	Michelin Travel and Lifestyle North America
Peter Greenberg Editorial Team	Sarika Chawla, Lily J. Kosner, Alyssa Caverley, Adriana Padilla
Contact Us	Michelin Travel and Lifestyle North America One Parkway South Greenville, SC 29615 USA travel.lifestyle@us.michelin.com www.michelintravel.com
	Michelin Travel Partner Hannay House 39 Clarendon Road Watford, Herts WD17 1JA, UK ✆01923 205240 travelpubsales@uk.michelin.com www.ViaMichelin.com
Special Sales	For information regarding bulk sales, customized editions and premium sales, please contact us at Travel.Lifestyle@us.michelin.com www.michelintravel.com

HOW TO USE THIS GUIDE

INTRODUCTION
The Welcome section at the front of the guide explores the region's nature and geology, history, art and architecture, literature and the Caribbean today. It includes a section of full-color photographs representative of the region's sights, fesitvals, activities, resorts, food and other themes.

PLANNING YOUR TRIP
The Planning Your Trip section gives you ideas for your trip and practical information to help you organize it. You'll find tours, practical information, a host of outdoor activities, a calendar of events, information on shopping, sightseeing, kids' activities and more.

DISCOVERING
The Discovering section features Principal Sights by region, featuring the most interesting local Sights, Walking Tours, nearby Excursions, and detailed Driving Tours. Admission prices shown are normally for a single adult.

ADDRESSES
We've selected the best hotels, restaurants, cafes, shops, nightlife and entertainment to fit all budgets. See the Legend on the cover flap for an explanation of the price categories.

STAR RATINGS★★★
Michelin has given star ratings for more than 100 years. If you're pressed for time, we recommend you visit the ★★★, or ★★ Sights first:

★★★ Highly recommended
★★ Recommended
★ Interesting

MAPS
ⓢ Principal Sights map.
ⓢ Region maps.
ⓢ Town maps.
All maps in this guide are oriented north, unless otherwise indicated by a directional arrow. A complete list of the maps found in the guide appears at the back of this book.

LIKE A LOCAL... FEATURES
Full page features give you the low-down on the best little things that make each area of the Caribbean special.

ASK PETER...
One-on-one Q&A sessions with Peter answer your worries so that you can enjoy your visit.

Travel Tips: Peter's Travel Tips give you the inside track on local deals, tricks and techniques that you might otherwise miss.

SIDEBARS
Throughout this guide you will find short sidebars with lively anecdotes, detailed history and background information.

CONTENTS

THE CARIBBEAN IN PICTURES

WELCOME TO THE CARIBBEAN

PLANNING YOUR TRIP

DISCOVERING THE CARIBBEAN

WELCOME TO
THE CARIBBEAN

BEACHES

Where else but the Caribbean can you find not only powdery white-sand beaches, but pink-, golden- and even black-sand beaches? The Bahamas' Pink Sand Beach and Barbados' pale-pink Crane Beach lie off the Atlantic. Forged by volcanic eruptions, black-sand beaches edge Vieques and St. Kitts. Silky white sands line Anguilla's Rendezvous Bay and St. John's Salomon Bay. Golden sands grace Puerto Rico's Rincon Beach and Tobago's Bloody Bay Beach. But the waves, not the sand, of Dominican Republic's Cabarete Beach and Aruba's Hadicurari Beach attract windsurfers.

1 Seven Mile Beach, Grand Cayman. Though actually 5.5 miles long, this beach draws swimmers and snorkelers to its blue-green waters and popular hotels. *See p148.*

2 Catamarans on Rendezvous Bay Beach, Anguilla. This crescent-shaped, peaceful stretch of white sand is surrounded by salt marshes begging to be explored. *See p211.*

3 Baby Beach, Aruba. With shallow, lake-calm waters averaging 4 feet deep, this small beach is ideal for families with children. *See p284.*

4 Wallilabou Bay, St. Vincent and the Grenadines. The Soufrière volcano created St. Vincent's rugged black-sand beaches. *See p62*.

5 Pink Sands Beach at dusk, Harbour Island, Eleuthera. Red conch shells mixed with white sand to create the rosy tint of this alluring Bahamian beach. *See p120*.

6 Coconut palms on Magens Bay Beach, St. Thomas, US Virgin Islands. Enjoy a picture-perfect mile of fine white sand lined with palm trees. *See p190*.

7 Fishing boats on Boston Bay Beach, Jamaica. Come for a swim and stay for lunch at a Jamaican jerk beach shack. *See p160*.

FESTIVALS

Say "Caribbean" and Carnival springs to mind. Trinidad's 2-day blitz brings elaborate costumes, calypso, steel pans, parades and street dancing. No longer limited to Easter, Carnivals elsewhere happen February to August. Other festivals celebrate Latin films, literary works, pirates, gospel, conchs, Christmas—the list is endless. Jive to jazz fests in Jamaica, St. Lucia, Puerto Rico, Curaçao and Martinique, or listen to local sounds at Aruba's Soul Beach Music Festival, Dominica's World Creole Music Festival and Jamaica's Reggae Sumfest, to name a few. Make your reservations early.

1 Carnival, Saint-Martin. Celebrate in late April with creative costumes, calypso, dancing and a parade *See p75.*

2 Pirate ship, Pirates Week, George Town, Grand Cayman. Join sea-faring scoundrels for parades and mock invasions. *See p78.*

3 Scintillating adornments of Trinidad's Carnival. Be bowled over by baubles, beads, sequins and feathers at the oldest and liveliest of Caribbean Carnivals. *See p74.*

4 Emancipation Festival, British Virgin Islands. Brightly costumed, stilt-dancing *mocko jumbies* trace their origin to 13C West Africa. *See p193.*

5 Junkanoo Parade, Nassau, Bahamas. This flashy day parade moves down Bay Street December 26 and again New Year's Day. *See p78.*

6 Street parade, Holetown Festival, Barbados. Musicians and onlookers commemorate Barbados' First Settlement. *See p76.*

SPORTS AND RECREATION

What better playground than the Caribbean for a round of golf, an island cycle or a horseback ride on the beach? Lush rain forests, smoldering volcanoes, miry mangrove swamps, limestone cliffs and clear-blue waters set the stage for catamaran sailing, snorkeling, deep-sea fishing, cliff-diving, spelunking, hiking and zip-lining. Windsurf Dominican Republic's waves, kiteboard along St. Barts' shores, reel in a big one off St. Lucia and behold exotic birds in Belize and Tobago. Roatán and the Caymans offer coral formations and shipwrecks. Cheer on cricket in Antigua, polo in Barbados and even croquet in Saba.

1 Catamaran on Cancún's waters.
Mexico's Riviera Maya is an ideal launch for a seafaring adventure. *See p293.*

2 Dominica's Aerial Tram.
The canopy rides soar within and above a tropical jungle for more than an hour. *See p72.*

3 Terre-de-Haut, Les Saintes, Guadeloupe. Cycling is a great way to exercise while taking in the island at your own pace. *See p68.*

4 Four Seasons Resort, Nevis. Swing a golf club at one of the many luxuriant golf courses in the Caribbean islands. *See p70.*

5 Roatán Island's underwater thrills. The Mesoamerican Barrier Reef is the second-largest living reef in the world. *See p300.*

6 Harrison's Cave, Barbados. Watch as spectacular stalactites and stalagmites come into view on a train ride in this limestone cavern. *See p270.*

13

ARCHITECTURE

Nowadays the Caribbean conjures up brightly painted wooden houses awash in bold pastels. Mexico, Belize and Honduras boast ancient Maya remains. In the early 16C, the Spanish imported their Spanish-Colonial style, seen today in Havana, San Juan, Santo Domingo and Cartagena. The French infused Guadeloupe, Martinique and St. Lucia with an 18C Creole style. The British built Georgian-style homes and sturdy forts. Danish styles still grace St. Croix, and the Dutch brought gables to Curaçao. Contemporary Caribbean style relies on durable materials for hotels and houses.

1 Catedral de San Cristóbal, Havana, Cuba. Though Neo-classical inside, this grand cathedral steals the attention with its undulating Cuban-Baroque style facade. *See p136.*

2 Chattel House Village, St. Lawrence Gap, Barbados Plantation workers' houses converted to shops show off bright colors. *See p270.*

3 Greenwood Great House, Jamaica. This former 18C sugar estate mansion near Falmouth can be toured today. *See p164.*

4 Mayan ruins, Tulum, Mexico.
This centuries-old defensive tower helped
Tulum earn its name: "wall" in Maya.
See p294.

**5 Ciudad Amurallada, Cartagena,
Columbia.** The old walled city is a treasure
trove of 16C Spanish-Colonial architecture.
See p306.

**6 Santo Domingo, Dominican
Republic.** This UNESCO World Heritage
city holds many Spanish-Colonial buildings
like this arcaded one. *See p172.*

**7 Castillo San Felipe
del Morro, San Juan,
Puerto Rico.** This
massive fortress—
towers, dungeons,
ramparts and all—has
repelled enemy fire
since 1595. *See p178.*

EXOTIC CREATURES

A wonderful bonus of a Caribbean vacation is the host of wildlife. Unexpected encounters might include a rock iguana in Turks and Caicos, a green sea turtle in the Caymans or a 1,500-pound leatherback on St. Lucia. Divers *expect* to see tropical fish, rays, octopus and nurse sharks. Dolphin encounters are a tourist staple in Jamaica, Paradise Island and Xcaret. Belize protects black howler monkeys, Barbados and Trinidad harbor agoutis, Isla Holbox has pink flamingos, Belize has toucans. Add to those the singular Cayman Brac parrot and near-extinct Puerto Rican Amazon parrot.

1 **Grenada Mona Monkey.** Spot these now-native monkeys, once transported here with slaves from West Africa, in Grand Étang National Park. *See p264.*

2 **Caribbean Flamingo, Curaçao.** North America's only native flamingo thrives in coastal waters throughout the Caribbean. *See p69.*

3 **Stingray City, Grand Cayman.** Don't miss an opportunity to swim in shallow waters teeming with graceful rays. *See p56, p146.*

4 Blackbar soldierfish, Belize. The many cays along the Mesoamerican Barrier Reef shelter rich, diverse sealife. *See p294.*

5 Rock Iguana, Little Water Cay, Turks and Caicos. These endangered iguanas are protected at this beach by the islands' National Trust. *See p128.*

6 Hummingbird, Asa Wright Nature Centre, Trinidad. Exotic birds and other wildlife intermingle at this former plantation estate. *See p277.*

1 Boiling Lake, Dominica. A 3-hour hike gives access to the second-largest lake of its kind, located in Morne Trois Pitons National Park. *See p61.*

2 Balata Gardens, Martinique. Some 3,000 tropical plants flourish in these gardens on this "island of flowers." *See p241.*

3 Petit Piton, St. Lucia. Seasoned hikers can climb one of the island's two iconic peaks. *See p252.*

4 Parque de las Cavernas del Río Camuy, Puerto Rico. These winding caves were river-carved 1,000 years ago. *See p69.*

Expecting only white-sand beaches and turquoise waters? You may be surprised by the topographical diversity here, from lush cloud forests, tropical jungles and marshy mangrove swamps to dry, low-lying deserts. A day's exploration can include hiking mountains, exploring caves and navigating volcanoes as well as swimming in the sea. Dominica, St. Lucia and Belize, among others, have been designated World Heritage Sites for biological uniqueness. Thankfully, environmental groups are working to restore and preserve the islands' natural assets.

5 St. Margaret Falls, Grenada. Also known as the Seven Sisters Falls, they cascade down along a hiking trail in Grenada's Grand Étang National Park. *See p264.*

6 The Baths, Virgin Gorda, British Virgin Islands. House-size granite boulders crowd the beach, concealing sunlit grottoes. *See p203.*

7 Turk's-head cactus, Providenciales, Caicos. This cactus, with its fez-like top, gave the Turks islands their name. *See p124.*

FOOD AND DRINK

Mix the ingredients of indigenous, Spanish, French, English, Dutch and African dishes, and the result is boldly sauced, well spiced Caribbean cuisine. Meat is seasoned with jerk (Scotch bonnet peppers plus spices) in Jamaica, stewed in Cuba and Antigua, or simmere with coconut milk in Barbados and Grenada. Offshore's bounty of tasty options means Bahamian conch fritters, Caymans turtle stew and fried fish at Bajan Friday fests. Sides mean plantains, yams, cassava, or heaping servings of white or yellow rice topped with red or black beans. Enjoy tropical fruit right off the tree or in a rum-spiked cocktail.

1 Fried grouper, The Caymans.
A local favorite, grouper is plentiful in the sea—and on plates throughout the Cayman Islands. *See p153.*

2 Blue Mountain Coffee, Jamaica. Jamaica's famous brew is grown atop its cool, misty mountain ranges. *See p163.*

3 Lechón, Puerto Rico. Of Spanish origin, lechón is suckling pig roasted, rotisserie style, over charcoal. *See p182.*

4 Green mangoes, St. Lucia. Growing wild in Caribbean jungles, mangoes feature in both sweet and savory local dishes. *See p255.*

5 Punch bottles, local market, Guadeloupe. Food shopping is fun at local markets selling spices, rum punch and other treats. *See p232.*

Oma's Bake and Shark

6 Food shack, Maracas Bay, Trinidad. Seasoned fried shark stuffed in fried dough, with condiment options, is a perennial beach-food favorite. *See p63.*

7 Conchs, Conch World, Caicos. The Providenciales' farm produces about a million conchs, the Turks and Caicos' main export. *See p130.*

1 Shop signs, Gustavia, St. Barts.
The "Paris of the Caribbean," St-Barthélemy abounds in duty-free, upscale boutiques stocked with the latest fashions. *See p220.*

2 Tourist trolley, Willemstad, Curaçao.
Caribbean tours can be taken by boat, bus, taxi, horse-drawn carriage, airplane, aerial tram, and even trolley. *See p66.*

3 Fruit market, Kingstown, St. Vincent and the Grenadines. Mingle with the locals and sample authentic dishes at outdoor markets found in most towns. *See p232.*

ACTIVITIES

Countless activities away from the beach await Caribbean visitors. Tours take in a St. Lucia cacao plantation, a coffee estate in Guadeloupe, Puerto Rico's rum distillery and a cigar factory in Havana. Rent a car for scenic drives on St. Croix, Curaçao or St. Kitts. Cook or chat with locals in Jamaica's and Bahamas' meet-the-people programs, at Angelica's Kitchen in Curaçao or Miss June's in Nevis. Shop for spices in Grenada, crafts at Nassau's Straw Market, art in Jamaica, jewelry in St. Thomas. One evening, go to a casino in Sint Maarten, Aruba or Paradise Island.

4 Knife sharpener, Cancún. Seek out the skills and crafts of local residents in Cancún and other Caribbean destinations. *See p292.*

5 Street musicians, Callejón de Hamel, Havana. This tiny alley fills with Sunday crowds for live rumba, music popular in the region. *See p56.*

6 Jeep Safari, Barbados. Explore the wilds of the island on an organized tour and spot animals. *See p271.*

7 Horseback Tour, Samaná Peninsula, Dominican Republic. Ecotours, hiking, horse-riding and cycling tours open up off-the-beaten path settings. *See p67.*

23

RESORT LIFE

Hammock-strung huts, dreamy villas, romantic cottages, colonial mansions, comfortable casas, high-rise hotels, expensive yachts, mega-resorts: Caribbean lodgings come in all shapes and sizes. Uber-resorts extend every amenity and activity. Humble eco-cabins promise simplicity and seclusion. Most rooms typically offer large balconies and open floor plans to let in sea breezes and afford sweeping views. Honeymooners love the privacy of Tensing Pen's cottages in Jamaica and Grenada's Villa Sankofa. Families love Dominican Republic's Villa Taina and Antigua's Curtain Bluff.

1   Jungle Bay Resort Hotel, Dominica. Rustic yet elegant cottages are nestled amid forest and beach settings. *See p248.*

2   Jack Sprat Restaurant, Jake's Hotel, Jamaica. Art-filled villas and two restaurants grace Jake's lodging complex. *See p168.*

3   Anse Chastanet Resort, St. Lucia. Original art decorates tree house-like villas at the resort's jungle setting with a stunning beach. *See p255.*

4 Atlantis Resort, Bahamas. This mammoth complex offers gambling, spa treatments, beach bars, lagoons, themed water slides—you name it. *See p122.*

5 Restaurant, Cotton House, Mustique.
This elegant, former 18C sugar plantation is the private island's only hotel. *See p260.*

6 Anthony's Key Resort, Roatán, Honduras. Diving sites and dolphin encounters lie near these stilt-held huts over water. *See p302.*

7 True Blue Bay Resort, Grenada. Relaxed, airy rooms and villas encircle the clear waters of True Blue Bay. *See p266.*

25

1 Horse-drawn carriage, Walled Town, Cartagena. Step back in time to leisurely explore Centro Histórico's charms. *See p306.*

3 Decorative street donkey, Jamaica. Though a tourist attraction, these beasts of burden help farmers, rather than serve as people transport. *See p154.*

2 Moored boats, Admiralty Bay, Bequia. Board a yacht, sailboat or cruise ship from this scenic bay in the Grenadines. *See p258.*

4 Ferry, Xunantunich National Park, Belize. Ferries, even hand-pulled, carry visitors to off-the-path sights as well as between islands. *See p100.*

A trip to the Caribbean calls for scenic walks on cobblestone streets in colonial towns and strolls down wide sandy beaches. To make it happen, hop among islands on sea-bound ferries or short plane flights. Cars are readily available to rent, or you can easily hire a taxi with driver. Many islands have regular bus transport, like Puerto Rico, Saint-Martin, Barbados and Aruba. Or opt for local flair: Havana's yellow coco-taxis or vintage American vehicles, horses for hire for rides along Mustique's or Jamaica's beaches, or boats for charter in Turks and Caicos and the Grenadines.

Modern-day rickshaws, Samaná Peninsula, Dominican Republic. Local transport avoids the hassle of car rental and usually takes in more scenery. *See p173.*

St. Kitts Scenic Railway. These double-decker coach cars offer scenic rides along the island's coastline. *See p222.*

7 Havana's coco-taxis. Yellow 3-wheel vehicles carry tourists through Havana's busy streets, but at a higher cost than regular taxis—for the novelty of it. *See p137.*

The Caribbean Today

Few places inspire us to indulge and escape as much as the Caribbean. The siren call of sun-splashed beaches, wondrous reefs, swaying hammocks, coconut palms and tropical beats is hard to ignore. For 500 years, the world's playground has lured plunderers and playboys, swashbucklers and sunbathers to its shores. The happy hordes keep coming, and the Caribbean greets them with a long, curved smile. More than 30 countries ring the Caribbean Sea, each with unique traditions, customs, artistic expressions and geographic diversity. Its residents total some 40 million people—an ethnic melting pot of native Indians, Africans, Europeans and recent minorities from around the globe speaking four major languages and numerous local dialects. Its territory has been claimed at one point or another by no less than five global superpowers, each of whom has left an indelible footprint on its respective colonial outposts. Such is the colorful mix that is the Caribbean. Welcome. You're on island time.

Geography

The Caribbean's more than **7,000 islands**, reefs, and keys stretch southeast from Cuba in an arc reaching south to Venezuela. Many straddle the Atlantic Ocean and the Caribbean Sea. Often lumped with the Caribbean islands, the Bahamas and Turks and Caicos are entirely surrounded by the Atlantic. Collectively, the archipelago spans some 2,500 miles. Beyond the islands, the Caribbean's southern boundaries include Colombia, Honduras, Belize, and Mexico's famed Riviera Maya.

Visitors are often astounded to find such a diverse **topography** in the Caribbean, from subtropical rain forests, karst cliffs and waterfalls to arid desert and active volcanoes just a few miles from dazzling beaches. The region's geographic cornucopia traces its origin to nature's ancient landscaping. Roughly 50 to 70 million years ago, violent underwater **volcanic eruptions** pushed a submarine mountain chain to the surface; evidence of this activity can be found today in the volcanic black-sand beaches sprinkled about the Caribbean and in the jagged mountain ranges of Cuba, Puerto Rico, and Saint Thomas, to name a few. By contrast, the relatively flat Cayman Islands, Bahamas, and Saint Croix do not have volcanic origins.

The region is geographically broken into **island clusters**. The largest of these, the **Greater Antilles**, lie to the north and west and comprise close to 90 percent of the landmass: namely,

TRAVEL ...LIKE A LOCAL

When most people travel through the Caribbean, it's easy to get caught up in the confines of the resort or cruise experience, but given a choice, why would you go from buffet to planned excursion and back again? Why would you do that when you can travel like a local? Traveling like a local means getting a real feel for a country instead of following the crowds from one contrived spot to another. Here are my top five tips for how to have the local experience:

Tip One: Get off the computer

If you're like me, you are more or less addicted to your need for connectivity. But that can be expensive. On a cruise ship, there are no cell towers, and connecting via satellite will rack up astronomical charges. In some more remote parts of the islands, forget about getting a signal. Take this opportunity to embrace being disconnected.

Tip Two: Eat like a local

The Caribbean is set up to accommodate every palate, but don't limit yourself to food made for tourists. Fine dining is not the way to go. Caribbean culture is heavily influenced by West African, European and even Indian cultures, and each island has a specialty dish or event celebrating food. Want a foodie adventure with the locals? How about a Bahamas Fish Fry? In Arawak Cay, you'll find local shacks serving up the island's best seafood. In Trinidad, you want to get a specialty called bake and shark at Richards.

Tip Three: Visit residential neighborhoods on Turks and Caicos, instead of the tourism centers on the south side of the island.

Instead of hanging with the herds in Providenciales, go to the residential north side where more locals live and you'll find one of the best places to watch the sunrise.

Tip Four: Make your own excursions

Cruise ships and resorts make a healthy business partnering with outside vendors and upselling their guests on excursions. Don't see the islands from a tour bus. Instead, book yourself a car and driver, or connect directly with the tour operator to get a better deal. Renting a car on St. Vincent lets you drive on the Leeward and Windward highways and see both the Caribbean and Atlantic coasts. It's a beautiful trip. Just remember that the roads can be narrow and windy, and that the locals drive on the left side of the road.

Tip Five: Visit local hot spots

Don't go to Senor Frogs, Margaritaville or any other tourist-heavy party spot. Instead, look for local music. And trust me, it's more than tired old reggae covers. In Turks and Caicos, you'll hear ripsaw music, which feature instruments like goatskin drums, handsaws and hand accordions. Find a bar or street festival with ripsaw music and you're sure to be partying like a local.

Cuba, Jamaica, Haiti, Hispaniola, and Puerto Rico.

The **Lesser Antilles**, in the southeast, are younger volcanic or coral islands divided into three groups: the **Windward Islands** to the southeast (Barbados, Grenada, Martinique, St. Lucia, St. Vincent and the Grenadines, Trinidad and Tobago), the Leeward Islands to the north (including Anguilla, Antigua, Barbuda, Dominica, Guadeloupe, Nevis, Saba, Saint-Barthélemy, Sint Eustatius, St. Kitts, Saint-Martin, and the US and British Virgin Islands), and the **Leeward Antilles** off Venezuela, including the Dutch ABC Islands. The Bahamas do not fall under the Antilles groups.

People and Population

The Caribbean's more than 40 million people are testimony to its rich and often turbulent history. The majority of the population today claims **African origins**, but the region as a whole befits a genetic forging of native Amerindians, European colonizers and African slaves. Some indigenous peoples have been nearly eradicated, or were assimilated through conquest, disease and colonization, notably the Arawak, or Taíno Indians of Cuba, Jamaica and Puerto Rico, and the Bahamas' Lucayans (a branch of the Taíno). The Caribs, for whom the region is named, have dwindled but survived through the ages; they maintain small communities in Dominica, Colombia, Belize and elsewhere.

African slaves have fared better than island natives. Today, most of the Bahamas's 300,000 people claim **West African** descent. The same can be said of more than 90 percent of Jamaica's 2.8 million residents, and populations of numerous Caribbean islands. It is interesting that descendents of African slaves form a significant minority in continental nations with a Caribbean coastline, such as Mexico and Colombia.

No colonial power has left a deeper footprint in the Caribbean than Spain. Predominantly **Hispanic populations** in the region include Cuba, Colombia, Dominican Republic, Mexico and Puerto Rico. By contrast, the Dutch, English and French form a distinct minority in the region, although their cultural contributions have been significant. The Caribbean has seen an influx of Chinese, Indian, Lebanese, American and European settlers adding to the racial melting pot.

The islands of the Caribbean vary greatly by **size** and demographics. The largest is Cuba, with a population of more than 11 million. The Dominican Republic, Puerto Rico, and Jamaica also rank among the most populated islands (with 4 million residents, Puerto Rico is considered one of the most densely populated territories in the world). On the other end of the spectrum, the British Virgin Islands are home to a mere 19,000 people, and the Dutch island of Saba has yet to eclipse 2,000.

HURRICANES AND INSURANCE

Hurricane season comes every year and runs from June 1 through November in the Atlantic. In recent years, the Caribbean has been hit hard by Irene, Dean and Felix. If you're traveling to the Caribbean or taking a cruise during hurricane season, you are not without recourse. First off, you can purchase travel insurance, which offers you some protection if your travels are interrupted or canceled due to unforeseen circumstances. But unforeseen means you need to book in advance. Once a hurricane is named by the National Hurricane Center, it's no longer an unforeseen circumstance. so don't wait too long to purchase a policy, especially if you're traveling to hurricane-prone areas during the season. Insurance also doesn't mean your costs are covered if it rains on your vacation or if you choose to cancel after long flight delays. And if there are heavy storms or dangerous conditions, don't expect compensation if your cruise line skips some—or all—of the ports on your itinerary.

Government

The Caribbean is a **microcosm** of the world's political systems. Within its borders lie a communist state in Cuba, a constitution-al monarchy in Jamaica, the commonwealth of Puerto Rico, and a mix of sovereign democratic republics and territories owned and governed by their colonizing nations (Britain, France, The Netherlands and the US). Even its independent nations boast a variety of political models. The Bahamas is a parliamentary de-mocracy; Trinidad and Tobago is a republic with a two-party sys-tem; the Dominican Republic is a representative democracy.

One cannot discuss **politics** in the Caribbean without men-tioning the continuing role of the **international powers** that stay claim to the region.

On the one hand, there are the pure "David vs. Goliath" conflicts such as Cuba thumbing its nose at its gargantuan neighbor to the north, and Puerto Rico's ideological struggle to accept its commonwealth status (imparted by said neighbor). On the other, there is the prominent influence of American and Euro-pean politics in the region, ranging from aid and investment, to tax havens for US corporations and trade benefits offered by EU nations to the Caribbean's European territories.

Economy

The Caribbean is relatively poor in natural resources. Through-out its history, its main commercial value was **agricultural**, and a wide variety of agricultural products continue to be its main

export. Among the more well-known crops are coffee, tobacc
bananas, spices, sugar and its infamous by-product, rum. Hov
ever, agriculture has been losing ground as many Caribbean n
tions push for market diversification.

Many nations have taken positive steps to **diversify** the
economies. The Dominican Republic has successfully investe
in telecommunications and free trade zones. Recent growth
Trinidad and Tobago has been attributed to investments in li
uefied natural gas, petrochemicals and steel. Puerto Rico ar
Trinidad and Tobago have invested heavily in industrial growt
Other niche industries advanced in the region include offsho
banking, petroleum refining, fisheries and pharmaceuticals

For most islands, **tourism** has become the most profitab
industry, which in turn has boosted related industries such
construction. As an example, tourism accounts for 70 perce
of the GDP of the US Virgin Islands. Numerous islands hav
jumped on the **ecotourism** bandwagon. Antigua, Barbado
Cuba, the Dominican Republic and Mexico have tapped in
the multibillion dollar **medical tourism** niche market.

However, the Caribbean faces critical **economic challenge**
Its relatively high cost of doing business and poor infrastru
ture, as well as cheaper products from emerging markets, ha'
made it increasingly difficult for its economies to compete on
global scale. To combat this reality, efforts have been made '
promote regionalism and economic solidarity. Numerous asse
ciations, such as the Caribbean Common Market and Comm
nity (CARICOM), the Association of Caribbean States (ACS), ar
the Organisation of Eastern Caribbean States (OECS), have bee
established to foster greater economic and governmental c
operation in the region. OECS members share a common cu
rency, the Eastern Caribbean Dollar, following the EU's exampl
Similarly, the CARICOM Single Market and Economy is expecte
to introduce a single currency by 2015.

Language

A major roadblock to a unified Caribbean might just be la
guage. There are no less than four **major languages** spoke
in the region: Spanish in the west and central Caribbean; En
lish in the north, central, and east; French in the central ar
east; and Dutch on the Dutch islands in the southeast. Thes
languages are supplemented by **local dialects** including P'
piamento (hybrid of Portuguese and Creole), Patois, Creole, ar
indigenous languages. (For example, "hammock," "canoe" ar
"potato" are just three examples of Taíno words that have bee
adopted into the modern lexicon.)

To add more linguistic flavor, many islands draw from a healtr

Medjet keeps me in the game.

Jim Furyk

Medical emergencies don't play games.

So whether I am on the Tour or vacationing with my family I make sure Medjet is there with me. It's priceless peace of mind.

If you become hospitalized 150 miles or more from home, Medjet will arrange medical transfer to the hospital of your choice. All you pay is your membership fee.

Best of all, with Medjet memberships starting at $99 you don't have to be a PGA Tour winner to travel like one.

Jim Furyk: 16-Time PGA Tour Winner & Medjet Member

Jim Furyk

MedjetAssist.
Take trips. Not chances.
Annual Family Membership

MedjetAssist. | Medjet.com | 800.527.7478

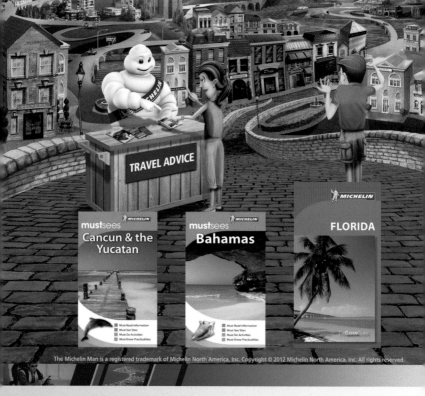

repertoire of local **slang**. And that's not even including the lilting brogue prevalent in so many Caribbean nations (or even the markedly different Spanish intonations; Puerto Ricans, for example, tend to casually leave out or substitute letters, particularly "r"s and "l"s). Here are a few examples:

Bill – "Chill out" in Jamaica

Bol' Face – Pushy, loud and obnoxious in Trinidad

Bon Bini – "Welcome" in the Dutch ABC Islands

Brutal – "Awesome" in Puerto Rico

Ganja or *Collie* – "Marijuana" in Jamaica

Gussy Mae – A chubby Bahamian girl

Heba – "Chick" or "Gal," usually to denote an attractive girl, in Cuba

Liming – "Hanging out" in the British Virgin Islands

Religion and Beliefs

When the Spaniards arrived in the Caribbean, they found inhabitants whose religion was based on ancestral continuity. The **Caribs**, responsible for a reputation as "cannibals," kept the bones of their ancestors because of their religious significance. The less bellicose **Arawaks** worshipped a pantheon of nature spirits and gods whom they represented as carved wooden figures called *zemís*. As in Mexico, and throughout the Spanish colonies, **Catholicism** quickly won converts by force but also by its adaptability to the tribal ritual calendar and practice of idolatry. Saints were superimposed on existing deities and their respective festivities. Africans brought as slaves also added to religious syncretism. In Cuba, the Yoruba tradition of Nigeria became **Santería** when it fused African deities called *orishas* with Roman Catholic saints. Throughout the islands, a spiritist tradition known as Obeah, Myal or Kumina, thought to be of West African origin, earned a reputation as **black magic**. In fact, the men and women who practice this magic call on ancestral spirits for good or bad purposes. The ritual possessions employed for healing are achieved through music and dance, and involve communication with the spirits of ancestors. These practices partially merged with Baptist beliefs into **Revivalism** in the mid-19C, and with the region's Pentacostal churches in recent years. Spain's erstwhile colonies remain predominantly Catholic. In Anglophone areas, **Protestantism** prevails.

In Jamaica an informal religious movement called **Rastafari** grew in the slums of Kingston in the 1920s. Basing it on their belief in the Judeo-Christian God, the movement's rastas, or practitioners, recognize the crowning of Ethiopian emperor Haile Selassie I in 1930 as the return of Christ to earth. Rastas gained international attention thanks to Bob Marley and his reggae music in the 1970s. Generally, Rastas promote their ancestral lands of Africa as God's promised paradise. Purists are vegetarian and wear their hair in dreadlocks. The movement is well known for its ritual use of cannibas, for which Biblical consent is cited.

Food and Drink

Blending indigenous, African, and colonial traditions with hybrid island culture, Caribbean plates also fuse the food groups. **Jamaican jerk** is meat rubbed in spices and Scotch bonnet peppers, then fired in barrels. *Sancocho* is a thick Dominican meat and vegetable stew similar to Cuban *ajiaco*. Another Cuban classic, *ropa vieja*, simmers leftover shredded meat with tomato, and is scrambled with eggs in Mexico. In Antigua legend has it that a *pepperpot*—yielding a bittersweet meat stew—will not spoil as long as cassareep (sweet cassava concentrate) is added proportionally with new meat to the boil. In Grenada and Barbados an *oil down* simmers meat in coconut milk. West Indian wraps, *roti* are meat- and/or vegetable-filled flatbread.

The Bahamas and Turks and Caicos are famous for abundant **conch**, eaten cracked or in fritters. In the Antilles eat salted fish, and in St. Lucia ask for it with green figs—boiled green plantains. The Caribbean **spiny lobster** is usually grilled and washed down with a fresh mango daiquiri. The lobster-bearing reefs surrounding Anegada in the British Virgin Islands have long supplied these tasty crustaceans to many Caribbean islands. The Caymans serve up a hearty **turtle stew**, and in Dominica the legs of the world's largest frog—now endangered—come fried and doused in gravy.

Starches include plantains, African yams, and native tubers like cassava. The cassava-based *bammy* is a Jamaican flatbread in the tradition of the Mesoamerican tortilla. Cornmeal and okra gruel are savored as *fungi* in the Virgin Islands and *coo coo* in Barbados. *Pastechis* are tasty Aruban breakfast pastries, stuffed with meat or cheese, then fried. Throughout the islands, particularly in Cuba, rice and red or black **beans** are constant. The rice may be yellow, like a *pelau* in Trinidad. It may join *glandules* (pigeon peas), roast pork and a *piña colada* in Puerto Rico. In the French Isles it will come alongside *colombo*, a curry-like blend of all the Caribbean staples.

Tropical **fruits** like soursop, anona, passion fruit and papaya abound. In the Grenadines roasted breadfruit is served with fried Jack fish. In Trinidad and the Virgin Islands *callaloo* is boiled-down, saucy green leaves, used like gravy. Fresh tropical fruit juices and coconut milk quench **thirst**, along with soda-like bittersweet Maubi. The Caribbean is the birthplace of rum, citrusy Curaçao, and myriad mixed drinks.

History

Migration, conquest and exploitation sum up Caribbean history. Long before the conquistadors showed up, disparate peoples moved in, and were driven out. When the Old World collided with the New, the Caribbean became a battleground, a treasure chest, and a plantation. Only in the 20C did it become today's playground in the sun.

The Earliest Inhabitants

Archaeological findings place the first human settlements in the Caribbean before 3,000 BC. The Stone-Age **Ciboneys**, a peaceful society of hunter-gatherers, were followed by **Arawaks**, a seafaring people from northern Brazil and Venezuela. Around 1200 AD, the Arawaks were displaced in violent fashion by the warlike Caribs, who scattered them as far as Cuba and the Bahamas. The **Taíno**, relatives of the Arawak, settled in Cuba, the Bahamas, Hispaniola and Puerto Rico. One of the world's great pre-Hispanic civilizations, the **Maya** inhabited the coastal Caribbean from the Gulf of Mexico to Nicaragua. After their Golden Age (250–900 AD) came mysterious collapse, then rebirth in the 10C.

On October 12, 1492, Columbus reached the East Bahamas' island of San Salvador, or so it was believed. New findings in 1986 claim that Columbus arrived 60 miles southeast of San Salvador, in Samana Cay (now Atwood Cay). When Columbus gazed at this alien shore and saw a gentle tribe who announced themselves as **Lukku-cairi**, or "island people," he concluded that he had discovered a new trade route to the East Indies, and called them "Indians."

Columbus' arrival ushered in more than 300 years of **Spanish rule** in the New World. Lured by riches, Europe's maritime powers joined Spain in exploiting the Americas. Together, they nearly obliterated the native peoples, imported generations of African slaves, and fundamentally altered the diet of the entire Western hemisphere. The indigenous tribes were decimated by war and disease—particularly smallpox. To replace the labor force, the Spanish imported **African slaves** to work mines and plant crops. Demand for slave labor set up a triangular trading system linking Europe, Africa and the New World. These lucrative trade routes did not go unnoticed. Spain faced near-continuous threats of foreign invasion, uprising and piracy. To protect Spain's interests, the conquistadors built heavily fortified military strongholds in Cuba, Puerto Rico, Cartagena and other settlements.

European Colonization

It didn't take long for the rest of Europe to follow Spain's lead. From the 1620s to the 1800s and beyond, the Dutch, British, French, Danes, and briefly the Swedish, planted their flags all over the Caribbean. The **colonies** became valuable spoils of war in the ongoing battles among their European owners, with one monarch's flag displacing another after a victory. St. Lucia underwent no less than 14 regime changes. Many islands faced a **revolving door of ownership** until well into the 18C, when revolutionary fervor swept through both the New and Old Worlds. One important consequence was the **emancipation of slaves** in the 1800s, which in turn led to an influx of immigrant indentured servants into the Caribbean.

Independence Movements

The American and French Revolutions fomented **uprisings** of oppressed against oppressor across the Americas. In 1804 Haiti became the first Caribbean nation to win its independence. In South America, the Spanish had to contend with the brilliance and determination of Venezuelan-born **Simón Bolívar**, El Libertador (The Liberator). Following a succession of military victories, on September 7, 1821, Bolívar became president of the newly minted **Gran Colombia**, a territory comprising most of modern-day Colombia, Ecuador, Panama, Venezuela, and parts of Peru and Brazil. Though this loose federation was not to endure, Bolívar and fellow freedom fighter **José de San Martín** would ultimately help liberate most of Spanish America.

Mexico's centuries-long quest for independence actually lasted a full century, beginning September 16, 1810, when a Catholic priest named Miguel Hidalgo issued his **Grito de Dolores** (cry of Dolores) in the village of Dolores in Guanajuato. Mexico's revolutions were bloody affairs that engendered a pantheon of heroes and legends. In the Yucatán Peninsula, tensions between Spanish hacienda owners and the labor classes (in which natives were the bottom rung) led to the **Caste War**, a conflict that continued until the Mexican Revolution in 1910—and claimed more than 300,000 lives.

By 1825 Spain's hold in the region had dwindled to two islands: Puerto Rico and Cuba. Neither was particularly happy with the status quo. Tensions between Spain and Cuba escalated in the 1850s. The last straw broke in 1867, when Spain increased taxes on the island yet again. On October 10, 1868, landowner **Carlos Manuel de Céspedes** jump-started the **Ten Years' War**, which ended with Cuba's gaining neither freedom nor independence. Eventually, a renewed struggle for independence began under **José Martí**, who founded the Cuban Revolutionary Party

n 1892, and helped ignite a second war in February 1895. In 1898 the US intervened, sending the USS *Maine* into Havana Bay to protect its considerable economic interests on the island. The explosion of the *Maine* under mysterious circumstances on February 15, 1898, was the catalyst that plunged the US into the war. On December 10, 1898, Spain signed the **Treaty of Paris**, giving Cuba its independence. The island immediately found itself under US military occupation.

Puerto Rico's history followed a similar course. Puerto Ricans were divided about their future: some wanted total separation from Spain, others preferred self-rule without autonomy. The tipping point occurred on September 23, 1868, when a physician named **Ramón E. Betances** led a revolt in the town of Lares. **El Grito de Lares**, or "The Cry of Lares," lasted only one day, but it became a rallying call that signaled a sea change in the mood of the people. In 1870 Puerto Rico established its first political parties. In 1897 the island was granted political and administrative authority, and an independent government was installed on February 9, 1898. The Spanish American War brought US forces to the island that same year, and the Treaty of Paris turned Puerto Rico into America's first commonwealth.

Cuba spent much of the 1900s suffering under corrupt puppet governments that secured and defended US interests. **Fidel Castro Ruz** and Argentinian **Ernesto "Che" Guevara** sowed the seeds of revolution in the 1950s, which culminated in the ouster of dictator **Fulgencio Batista** on December 31, in 1958, and the introduction of Castro's regime on January 1, 1959.

Castro wasted little time in confronting "the imperialist giant." In October 1960, the US responded by imposing an embargo on North American products to Cuba. Framed against the backdrop of the Cold War, relations between Communist Cuba and the US further disintegrated. On April 17, 1961, CIA-backed Cuban exiles reached the **Bay of Pigs** in what would be a failed mission to overthrow the communist regime. Castro's victory effectively terminated all economic dealings between Cuba and the US, and tensions between the nations peaked the following year. October 1962 gave the world a nuclear scare in what became known as the **Cuban Missile Crisis**. The US discovered that Cuba had Soviet nuclear missiles pointing at Florida and responded with a naval blockade of the island. Facing the impending threat of nuclear war, the Soviet Union agreed to remove the missiles in exchange for a US guarantee not to invade Cuba. The stalemate between the Castro brothers and the US continues today, despite the exodus of Cubans into exile in the US and the severe economic hardships the island has suffered.

In the 1950s and 60s, many islanders pushed for liberation from foreign control. From 1958 to 1962, the majority of the British colonies in the Caribbean formed the **West Indies Federation**, a first stab at independence. Jamaica, Trinidad and Tobago, and Barbados achieved independence in the 1960s. The Bahamas, Dominica, Grenada and St. Lucia followed suit in the 1970s.

Today and Beyond

The Caribbean today comprises mostly independent islands, or autonomous territories within a commonwealth. Despite being a cultural and political melting pot, the region has collectively relished its role as one of the world's favorite playgrounds. Yet economic and political uncertainties continue to pose serious threats to its long-term fortunes. Its **economic malaise** is indicative of larger problems, including poor infrastructure, increasing reliance on industries that depend on a healthy global economy, economic debt (Jamaica alone has the fourth highest public debt in the world on a per capita basis), and lack of development.

To better compete in the world market, there has been a strong push toward creating an economically integrated single market in the Caribbean. The most advanced of these efforts is the Caribbean Community, or **CARICOM**. But the EU model has yet to crystallize in the region, as political infighting and lack of a cohesive integration plan has hindered CARICOM's efforts.

For the foreseeable future, however, the hopes of the Caribbean rest on **tourism**. The sum of its history—a seesaw of colonization and trade—makes the Caribbean one of the most distinctive regions of the world. Its islands continue to welcome the world with open arms, a tropical melody and enchanting hospitality.

EVOLVING CRUISE SHIPS

The Caribbean is one of the most popular cruise ports and destinations, but did you know that the modern cruise ship can trace its origin back to the steam engine? It was steam technology that made transatlantic travel possible. First in 1849 British White Star Lines built luxury transatlantic liners that broke the mold. Ships include the Olympic, the Britannic and the Titanic. Then in 1900, the Hamburg American Line built the first ship that was intended mainly for cruising, the Prinzessin Victoria Luise. Today cruise ships have more than your standard buffet and shuffleboard. Modern ships can hold more than 5,000 passengers and have rock-climbing walls, water parks and university-style lectures and much more.

Architecture

The palm-thatched wood dwellings Columbus saw in today's Dominican Republic were similar to current vernacular Caribbean architecture. The Cuban bohío is a present-day example, though corrugated metal might have replaced the palm, and walls may be made of concrete block. Thatched structures known as malocas are still used in the indigenous Kogui village in Colombia's Sierra Nevada de Santa Marta near the Caribbean Sea.

Ancient Structures

At the thinnest point in Mexico, near the Gulf coast, what is known as Mesoamerica's first civilization, the **Olmeca** ("men of rubber" in the Aztec language) established their earliest-known center. San Lorenzo Tenochtitlan, where 10 of the 17 known colossal heads were found, rests on a branch of the Coatzacoalcos River that diverges then rejoins its source downstream, forming the island of Tacamichapan. Here, the architecture of the Olmeca dots a rolling, man-made mesa, not unlike the Acropolis featured in the cities of its Maya successors. It boasts more than 200 **earthen mounds** that have revealed elaborate stone sculptures. Despite the simplicity of flattening out plazas as one builds earth up into strategic heights, these structures have stood firm since 2500 BC. Farther south, in Mexico's Chiapas and Yucatán, as well as in Guatemala and Belize, are stone remains of grand Maya cities. Palenque is an elegant, artistic token of Maya creativity. At Chichén Itzá's Castillo, an architectural and astrological phenomenon sends the feathered serpent Kukulcán slithering down the north steps each year at the spring and autumn equinox.

Colonial Imports

As the colonial powers who deposed these urban centers gained their piece of the Caribbean, they brought their distinct architecture with them, though the tropical terrain and climate demanded alterations. Heat and humidity coupled with exposure to hurricanes and consequent flooding drove new rulers to adopt some native practices, like stilts and shutters that swing up in inclement conditions and swing down to capture full breeze on a nice day.

Spanish Colonial style reigns in the military, religious, and domestic architecture of Spain's former footholds. After losing the vestiges of settlements they had left upon arrival, the Spanish immediately began building fortresses and churches when they

MAYA WORLD

One of the most evolved of all Mesoamerican cultures, the Maya, because of their numerical system, calendars and hieroglyphic writing, have attracted the attention of researchers of all kinds. Maya territory embraced the present day states of Tabasco, Chiapas and the Yucatán peninsula, as well as the neighboring countries of Guatemala, Belize, Honduras and El Salvador. Their origins are undetermined, but the archaeological record places their inception as a culture in the Formative pre-Classic period (2000 BC to 100 AD) and their fall during the post-Classic period (800–1500). In the Classic period (100–800) Maya culture, under a theocratic system, reached the peak of its glory in science and the arts, while its religion became more complex with the proliferation of gods and deities. In the post-Classic period it appears that a great drought in Mesoamerica led to political and social strife among the Maya peoples. At the same time, Toltec invaders arrived from Tula (Mexico state), perhaps also driven by a lack of water. They conquered the Maya and intermarried.

During this time the science of war flourished while the arts cultivated by the Maya languished. Recently the governments of Mexico, Guatemala, Belize, Honduras and El Salvador have developed **La Ruta Maya** or **Mundo Maya** (The Maya Route or Maya World) project to protect and promote Maya culture. The route offers the opportunity to visit this most extraordinary region; unique not only for its pre-Hispanic treasures but also because of its natural and biological riches.

returned at the turn of the 16C. In the Dominican Republic, Santo Domingo is home to a host of New World firsts, most demonstrating late-Medieval influences. The **Santa María Cathedral** was the first in the Americas. The Ozama Fortress and its Tower of Homage, built in 1503 to guard Santo Domingo's port, is a Medieval-style military structure. Cartagena, Colombia is home to South America's most extensive fortress, **Castillo San Felipe de Barajas** (begun 1536) as well as the **Convento de Santo Domingo** (1578), both emblems of Spanish Colonial military and religious architecture between the 16C and 18C. Cruciform-shape **San Juan Cathedral** (1540) in Puerto Rico bears a Spanish Colonial façade and vaulted Gothic ceilings. In Cuba several Spanish Colonial **town centers** are preserved with the help of UNESCO. The traditional colonial town was laid out on a **grid pattern** with streets intersecting at right angles. At its

heart was the **parque central**, a spacious square, often lined with palaces and official buildings; Havana's is a handsome example. As for residential buildings, the colonial house was built around a **patio**, a courtyard surrounded by arcaded galleries giving access to various rooms. In Havana, an example of a typical 17C house, which now is home to a restaurant, can be seen at the corner of Calles Bernaza and Brasil.

On French-settled islands like Guadeloupe, Martinique, the French Antilles and St. Lucia, **Creole architecture** used "*bousillage*"—a mortar made of mud mixed with animal hair or moss—to set the foundations of elegant and humble abodes alike. Such dwellings were characteristically rectangular, raised above ground level, and lined by broad front porches with thin supporting columns. While a common house contained one room in each corner, without corridors, grander estates embellished the theme with outdoor passages and wrought-iron enclosed verandas. The 18C Creole-style **Old House** in Saint- Martin once occupied by the wealthy Beauperthuy family, who owned a sugar plantation, exemplifies a grand estate. To combat the tropical climate and its damaging forces, the mansions of Martinique—like Habitation Pécoul (1760) in Basse-Pointe—adapted the model of 18C French **planter architecture**, with windows that could be completely shuttered, and an interior lined with an inner wall as an additional insulation against heat and hurricanes. In Barbados, the centerpiece of Francia Plantation is an elegant house built of coral stone by a French planter in 1913. Double-sash inclined shutters on the *demerera* windows prevent rainwater from entering, yet let air through. The surviving manor (1820) of Martinique's **Clement Estate** illustrates the luxury enjoyed by the wealthy plantation society and conveys an idea of 19C plantation-style architecture. Constructed mostly of wood, the manor features eight spacious rooms on the first floor alone.

The British imported a number of styles to the islands; many of their solidly built structures remain to this day. In the late-1700s they built **Fort Charlotte** in the Bahamas to protect Nassau's harbor; its fortified walls were carved out of solid rock and surrounded by a moat. **Brimstone Hill Fortress** in St. Kitts, completed in the 18C, includes a hospital and ammunition warehouses alongside the bastion. In Barbados, **historic Bridgetown** and its garrison demonstrate a typical British urban layout, which follows a serpentine pattern—in contrast to the Spanish grid—and even has its own version of London's Trafalgar Square. Jamaican **Georgian** architecture, popular in the 18C and 19C, also adapted its models to local standards, again raising living quarters above ground level, while still

1

ASK PETER...

Q: Why are many St. Croix buildings not air-conditioned?

A: The Danes discovered how to adapt 18C-style buildings to the West Indies to reduce heat, maximize breeze and withstand tropical storms. Before ceiling fans and cross ventilation were enhanced by rectangular-shaped buildings, trey ceilings let warm air rise. Today, many buildings and homes on St. Croix are not air-conditioned thanks to this ingenious practical design. Early buildings here were constructed from cut coral blocks and Danish bricks brought as ship ballast. Thick walls keep the interiors cool, and courtyards and arcades provide shady retreats.

maintaining its symmetrical, British appearance. The imposing Georgian-style buildings of **Nelson's Dockyard** in Antigua include the naval officer's house and a pitch-and-tar store. Loyalists fleeing America during the Revolution built wooden houses in the Bahamas, but Nassau's **Balcony House** has a feature rarely seen in 18C Loyalist structures: an overhanging balcony. The British introduced glass-paned double-hung windows to replace Spanish wood *rejas*, or open window grills, as well as the hipped roofs, dormers and clapboard upper stories seen in 18C Caribbean houses. Typical of Colonial Bahamian architecture are corner quoins placed on the dwelling's southern side, and jalousie windows, invented in the early 1900s, which stack glass or wood louvers that tilt to open and let air, but not rain, into the house.

Danish Colonial architecture can be seen in Denmark's former colonies, like today's US Virgin Islands. **Fort Christian** in St. Thomas' capital, Charlotte Amalie, was erected in red brick in 1672 when the Danish took control of the island. **Whim Plantation** on St. Croix is one of the best-preserved plantation estates in the Caribbean; it showcases a mid-18C manor, a cookhouse, a windmill among other structures. St. Croix's Danish-Caribbean flair is seen in windmills and plantation ruins dotting the countryside, and in the faded yellow buildings of its capital city, Christiansted. Dutch colonies like Aruba, Bonaire, Curaçao—the ABC Islands—include narrow alleys and wide thoroughfares, numerous plazas, and steep roofs with curvy Dutch gables, like those at **Plaza Daniel Leo** in Oranjestad, Aruba. In Curaçao, the Punda quarter of the capital is home to **Hurá Kulanda**, an area that boasts the best of 18C and 19C Dutch styles.

As urban centers grew throughout the islands, many houses and other structures were built completely of wood. Others featured brick or coral bases with wooden structures on top. Many urban centers were lost to earthquakes and their subsequent fires throughout the centuries.

Today, what has been rebuilt, regardless of the materials used, tends to be painted with bright pastels, often with contrasting trim around doors and windows. The buildings lining Aruba's waterfront in **Oranjestad** greet visitors with a mix of vibrant façades. The wooden houses of Barbados are radiant with brightly painted colors, reflective of the Barbadians colorful dress.

Modern Trends

Contemporary architecture in the Caribbean continues to be mindful of climate above all. Concrete is desirably durable. Ventilation and shade are primary considerations for building. **Jade Mountain Hotel** in St. Lucia is a modernist melding of luxury and nature. The capital of Guadeloupe, reconstructed after natural destruction in 1932, is predominantly Modernist in architectural design.

Another recent trend is the "**greening**" of the Caribbean; its new-found quest for sustainability is seen in increased use of recyclable materials, water-saving toilets and shower heads, and solar panels, particularly in the resorts and hotels crowding the islands and peninsulas of the Caribbean Sea. New hotel construction is heading in this direction as owners realize the cost savings associated with such measures in the long run. Caribbean tourism organizations are certifying more and more properties here, and even mounting related conferences to generate new ideas and practices to offset overdevelopment and its tendency toward ecological decline.

Art

From Taíno rock paintings to contemporary conceptual pieces, the art of the Caribbean is vibrant, rich and varied. The Arawak, Carib, Ciboney and Taíno left petroglyphs and carvings. Found in Cuba, the Dominican Republic, the Bahamas, Jamaica, Puerto Rico, St. Lucia, Trinidad and the Virgin Islands, the representations depict long-lost myths, creation stories and ancient histories. Mysterious Zemi sculptures are sacred figurines in wood, stone, pottery, shell and bone believed to represent ancestors, powerful gods or spirits.

Pre-Colombian

In Colombia the myth of **El Dorado** (the Golden Man) was based on a Muisca ritual on Lake Guatavita, near Bogotá. The Muisca chief would cover his body in gold dust before immersing himself in the sacred lake as an offering to the gods. Remnants of exquisite **gold artifacts** produced by the Sinu (sometimes Zenu) can be seen in Cartagena's Museo de Oro.

In Mexico, the stunning art of the Aztecs and Maya includes brightly painted murals; polychrome ceramics; obsidian, jade and gold ornaments; and intricate **hieroglyphics** carved into stone stelae and temples. No visit to the Mexican Riviera is complete without a visit to one of the nearby Maya sites or the Maya museum in Cancun.

Religious Art

The Spanish mission in the Caribbean was as much about conversion to the Catholic faith as it was about conquest. Paintings,

statues and altarpieces were shipped from Spain, but the constant demand for **religious art** to decorate churches and monasteries spawned the first Creole artisans. Colombian painter **Baltasar de Figueroa** (1629-67) developed a Baroque style influenced by the Quito and Cuzco schools, while Puerto Rican painter **Jose Campeche** (1751–1809) refined the rococo style.

Local Artists

In the 19C, local artists started to emerge on the English- and French-speaking islands. Perhaps the most famous Caribbean artist is the French Impressionist **Camille Pissarro** (1830-1903) born in Charlotte Amalie on St. Thomas. The first Hispanic Impressionist was Puerto Rican painter **Francisco Oller** (1833-1917), who studied under Gustave Courbet in Paris, taught Paul Cezanne how to paint, and returned to Puerto Rico to open an art school for women. **Michel Jean Cazabon** (1813-88) also studied in Paris before returning to his native Trinidad to execute carefully constructed watercolors and oils depicting landscapes and local scenes. Another artist drawn to the Caribbean was the French Post-Impressionist **Paul Gauguin**, who before his famous trip to Polynesia, first experimented with tropical primitivism in Martinique in 1887.

Mexico's most lasting influence on the Caribbean came with the **muralists** of the 1920s: **Diego Rivera** (1886-1957), **José Clemente Orozco** (1883-1949) and **David Alfaro Siqueiros** (1896-1974), who represented Indigenist, Marxist and revolutionary visions of Mexican history in large murals. Rivera's wife, **Frida Kahlo** (1907-54), produced smaller, introspective works, which have been equally influential in the region.

In the second half of the 20C, distinct local styles and important artists began to appear in the English- and French-speaking islands. In the 1920s the emergence of the Jamaica School of Art, founded by sculptor **Edna Manley** (1900-87), helped forge a generation of local artists who explored their African roots through painting and sculpture. Revivalist preacher turned painter and wood carver, **Mallica Reynolds** (1911-1989), better known as **Kapo**, popularized folk or naïve art in early 1930s under the banner of Intuitive Art. In Martinique, the Fwomajé group of artists, including **Victor Anicet** (b. 1938), **Rene Louise** (b.1949), and **Ernest Breleur** (b. 1945), have drawn on pre-Columbian Amerindian art, African wood carvings, local Bèlè dances and slavery to forge a post-colonial identity inspired by the writings of Aime Cesaire and the Negritude movement.

Inspired by Surrealism and Picasso's works, Cuba artist **Wifredo Lam** (1902-82) achieved world renown for his semi-abstract paintings of deities of the Afro-Cuban Santería religion.

Colombian artist **Fernando Botero** (b. 1932) is internationally famous for paintings and sculptures that portray subjects from the mountain villages of his native Medellín as grossly inflated figures. Martiniquan artist **Laurent Valere** (b. 1959) has created a moving monument of 15 large stone statues overlooking the sea at Anse Caffard, in homage to Africans who died when a slave ship sank off the coast in 1830. A similar siren-like sculpture called *Manmandlo*, submerged 33 feet in the bay of Saint Pierre, has become a magnet for divers.

On the smaller islands, a lack of dedicated exhibit space finds galleries and art shows in banks, restaurants, stores and hotels. Some artists, especially primitive or naïve artists, show their works in their homes. **Canute Caliste** (b. 1916) has artworks in international museums, but the best place to see his naïve paintings of mermaids, whales and ships at sea is in his simple house in Carriacou. Havana artist **José Fúster** (b. 1946) emblazons his house with his ceramics; it is covered with fantastical creations clearly influenced by Gaudí and the *trencadís* mosaic tradition.

Music and Dance

A bubbling musical melting pot, the Caribbean is the cradle of a dizzying array of rhythms and dance styles, with new musical hybrids being created all the time. Jamaican reggae, Puerto Rican salsa and Carnival's infectious calypso are savored the world over, but they are only one bite of the musical pie this region has baked.

Early Traditions

The Arawak and Carib peoples Christopher Columbus encountered used maracas, drums and pipes in **ritual dances** infused with smoking tobacco and a hallucinogenic snuff called *cohoba*. Mexico's Aztec and Maya incorporated more elaborate music and dance styles into their sacred calendar of dance rituals. Few of these early traditions survived the conquest, apart from **maracas**, which have become a staple of Caribbean and Latin sounds. Indigenous traditions continue, however, on the Caribbean coast of Honduras and Belize. Here the Garifuna (also known as Black Caribs) blend Carib and West African language and beats to create a distinct music known as **punta**, which uses hand drums, tortoise-shell drums, maracas and conchshell trumpets. The late Andy Palacio pioneered Punta rock, a modern version using electric instruments.

CELEBRITIES IN THE CARIBBEAN

Living like a local in the Caribbean just might mean living like a celebrity. Mustique Island, which has been known as the playground for the incredibly rich and famous, is home to Mick Jagger and David Bowie. Johnny Depp owns his own island in the Bahamas. Virgin CEO and Founder Richard Branson owns his island in the British Virgin Islands that he rents out for more than $50,000 a night. You'll also find celebrities with palatial homes on almost all of the Caribbean islands. Oprah Winfrey has a mansion in Antigua, John Travolta owns a few units in the Old Bahamas Bay Hotel, and Simon Cowell has an estate in Barbados. Bruce Willis and Donna Karan have huge vacation homes in the Turks and Caicos.

Contemporary Forms

Today's Caribbean music originated with the fusion of the waltz, polka, quadrille and mazurka of the islands' European plantation society with the West African **drumming** of slaves brought here to work the land. The French Islands of Martinique and Guadeloupe have their own West African drum traditions of **chouval bwa** and **gwo ka**, but created a Parisian dance craze in the 1930s with a jazz version of the **beguine**, which is still played on clarinet today. Trinidad is the birthplace of **steel pans**, ubiquitous tinkling drums formed of discarded oil barrels in the 1950s; today no Carnival would be without them. It is also home to **calypso**, the original music of Carnival, and the faster **soca** that has replaced it in many countries. Modern hybrids include chutney soca, sung in English and Hindi, and the grittier ragga soca. Jamaican **reggae**, dub and dancehall are now found all over the Caribbean, with Bob Marley's son Damian "Jr. Gong" Marley carrying the torch for socially aware roots music, and artists like Sean Paul crossing over into the pop charts.

Elsewhere, groups such as the Jolly Boys keep alive the music of **mento**, played on banjos, guitars and hand drums. Puerto Rico, a center for **salsa**, also has its own country music, the plaintive guitar sound of **jibaro** and the more dancible **plena**, played on tambourine-like drums. Cuba deserves a musical chapter all to itself: from the stylish **son** that inspired Buena Vista Social Club recordings and the jazzy timba to *guajiro* country music, *changui* Carnival tunes, and the politically charged **nueva trova** songs of Pablo Milanes. The Dominican Republic is another musical powerhouse, producing the singing two-step **merengue** and **bachata**, a country-style sad guitar music reinvented as a dance craze in the 1980s by Juan Luis Guerra. Bachata has been

further reinvented by R&B-style groups like Aventura into a Latin pop phenomenon. The British Virgin Islands and the US Virgin Islands have their own local calypso styles, known respectively as **fungi** and **quelbe**.

The most popular music is **zouk**, a hit in France in the 1980s for local group Kassav, which has spawned urban styles zouk R&B and ragga zouk, combining Jamaican dancehall influences. In the ABC islands, a major slave-trading post in the past, folk music **tumba** is forged from drums and cowbells, with call and response vocals sung in Papiamento, a local Creole language composed of Portuguese, Spanish, African and Dutch. **Ritmo kombina** is a fusion of reggae, R&B, salsa and jazz, reflecting the importance of these musical styles on the islands.

In the Spanish-speaking Caribbean and along the coasts of Colombia and Mexico, the slick Latin beats of salsa, merengue, reggaeton, rap, pop and rock *en español* rule supreme. Colombia is famous for its accordion-driven **cumbia** and *vallenato* dance styles, but has also produced pop stars Shakira and Juanes, and the crazy **champeta**, a popular dance from Cartagena that fuses tropical beats with the African legacy of runaway slaves from the town of Palenque de San Basilio. Mexico's coastal Riviera Maya, a major Spring Break destination, throbs to the beat of Latin party tunes, **reggaeton** and *cumbia*, but also features distinctive mariachi bands dressed in big sombreros, silver studded trousers and short jackets, who busk the streets or serenade diners at swanky restaurants.

Literature

The Caribbean, Colombia and Mexico have produced four Nobel Prize winners for literature: Colombian novelist Gabriel García Márquez (b.1927), Mexico's Octavio Paz (1914-98), the St. Lucian poet Derek Walcott (b.1930) and most recently, Trinidadian author V.S. Naipaul (b.1932).

Early Writings

The Taíno, Arawaks and Caribs did not have a writing system, but Spanish explorers and priests recorded their myths and legends. Colombus' letters and journals introduced Taíno words *hamaca* (hammock), *tabaco* (tobacco), *canoa* (canoe), *juracan* (hurricane) and others to the European lexicon. Spanish friar **Ramón Pané** wrote a detailed account of Taíno beliefs in his

Relacion acerca de las Antiguedades de los Indios (Report about the Antiquities of the Indians). **Fray Bartolomé de las Casas** defended tribal rights in his *Brevísima Relación de la Destrucción de las Indias* (A Short Account of the Destruction of the Indies), which became the basis of the Black Legend of Spanish atrocities in the New World used by Spain's Protestant enemies in the 16C and 17C to defend attacks against its colonies in the Caribbean.

The Aztec and Maya had advanced literary forms, including hieroglyphics, engravings on stone monuments known as stelae and elaborately illustrated bark-cloth books called **codices** that were produced by scribes.

Although most were destroyed by zealous priests in the 16C, three full codices as well as fragments have survived. The best preserved Maya literary work is the **Popul Vuh**, a Maya creation myth of twin brothers who travel to the underworld of Xibalba and play the Mayan ball game against the gods.

Evolving Expression

Slaves transported forcibly to the New World could carry nothing but their languages and **oral traditions**, some of which survive in today's Caribbean folk yarns. The tale of **Anansi** the spider can be traced to Ashanti stories of West Africa. Although Anansi is a trickster, he came to represent the poor black slave who outwits the more powerful slave master, symbolized by a jaguar or other dangerous animal. Brer Rabbit replaces Anansi in the American South as does Tío Conejo in Colombia, and on Creole-speaking islands, he is known as Compère Lapin.

An important Caribbean literary movement of the 1930s was **Négritude**, championed by Martiniquan poet and playwright **Aimé Césaire**, and best represented by his book *Notebook of a Return to My Native Land* (1939).

This focus on the relationship between slaves and masters in colonial society aimed at re-engaging Caribbean culture with its African roots. Contemporary Martiniquan novelists such as **Patrick Chamoiseau** (b.1953), author of *Texaco*, continue to explore the black identity of the French-speaking islands, but under the banner of **créolité** (creolism).

London emerged as a center of the Caribbean literary boom in the 1950s with the BBC radio program **Caribbean Voices**, a launching pad for writers and poets such as **George Lamming** (b.1924) and **Sam Selvon** (1923-94). Like many of his contemporaries, V.S. Naipaul, wrote his first novels only after arriving in England. Back in Barbados, the literary magazine *Bim* published short stories by poets such as Derek Walcott and **Kamau Brathwaite**. In Cuba, novelist **Alejo Carpentier** (1904-80) was inspired by French Surrealism to create his own literary genre, **magical**

WHAT TO READ

A House for Mr Biswas
V.S. Naipaul, Picador, 2011.
A carefully crafted early masterpiece by the Nobel Prize winner describing the Indo-Caribbean community of his native Trinidad.

Annie John *Jamaica Kincaid, Vintage, 1997.* The tale, set in Antigua, of a young girl's increasingly difficult relationship with her mother.

The Brief Wondrous Life of Oscar Wao *Junot Diaz, Faber and Faber, 2009.* Trujillo's dictatorship frames this comic tale of a doomed Dominican teen in modern-day New York.

Brother Man *Roger Mais, Macmillan Caribbean, 2004.* A classic of Jamaican fiction that follows a Rastafarian healer through Kingston's rude-boy run ghettos.

Conquistadora *Esmeralda Santiago, Knopf, 2011.* Inspired by tales of the conquistadors, the Spanish heroine of the novel sets sail for Puerto Rico and a sprawling colonial slave plantation.

The Death of Artemio Cruz *Carlos Fuentes, Farrar Straus Giroux, 2009.* Mexico's past and present are interwoven in this ambitious novel about power and corruption.

Havana Fever *Leonardo Padura Fuentes, Bitter Lemon Press, 2009.* The Cuban crime writer investigates Mafia ties to pre-revolutionary Havana with his detective-turned-bookseller Mario Conde.

Love in the Time of Cholera *Gabriel García Márquez, Penguin, 2007.* A sweeping story of thwarted love set in the Colombian coastal city of Cartagena.

Omeros *Derek Walcott, Faber and Faber, 2002.* The St. Lucian poet brilliantly remolds Homer's *Odyssey* in a Caribbean context.

Oxford Book of Caribbean Short Stories *Stewart Brown and John Wickham, Oxford Paperbacks, 2001.* A comprehensive collection of Caribbean short fiction, including all the major writers of the last 100 years.

Texaco *Patrick Chamoiseau, Vintage, 1998.* An imagined 150 years of Martinique's history is squeezed into this novel of slavery and emancipation.

Victoire: My Mother's Mother *Maryse Condé, Atria Books, 2010.* An historical novel about the Guadeloupean author's grandmother, who worked as a cook for a white Creole family.

Wide Sargasso Sea *Jean Rhys, Penguin Modern Classics, 2000.* A romantic masterpiece inspired by Charlotte Brontë's *Jane Eyre* and set in Jamaica's strict 1830s society.

realism, exemplified in his 1949 novel *El Reino de Este Mundo* (The Kingdom of this World). The most famous exponent of magical realism to emerge from the "Latin American boom" of the 1960s and 70s is Colombian novelist **Gabriel García Márquez** (b.1927), who achieved international acclaim for his novel *Cien años de Soledad* (A Hundred Years of Solitude).

In Mexico, **Laura Esquivel** (b.1950) applied the genre to a tale of love and lust inspired by heavenly Mexican food in her novel *Como Agua para Chocolate* (Like Water for Chocolate), which was made into a hit movie. Another landmark novel by the Nobel-Prize winning Mexican author **Carlos Fuentes** (b.1928) is *La Muerte de Artemio Cruz* (The Death of Artemio Cruz), an ambitious, epic novel of Mexican history, from the Aztecs to modern times.

Nature and Environment

While each Caribbean island has varied topographies and ecosystems, ranging from rain forests to desert lowlands, some generalizations are notable in the region. Many Caribbean islands support deciduous forests, cactus-spotted deserts, and tropical jungles with brilliant flowers. Others host mangrove swamps, seagrass meadows and coral reefs, which flourish despite general marine depletion in much of the zone. Mangroves thrive along sandy shores because their seeds are designed to float in the ocean until they reach the outskirts of land and take root there. The islands along the front of tectonic plates, like Cuba, Jamaica, Puerto Rico, Dominica, Saint Lucia and Martinique, boast impressive mountain ranges, while others like Aruba, Barbados and the Bahamas have rather flat terrain.

ASK PETER...

Q: Is there any poisonous plant to avoid?
A: Beware of residue of the shore-dwelling **Manchineel**, called the "little apple of death" by the Spanish. Blisters form when its leaves drip with rainwater onto human skin. It resembles a crab apple. Above all, do not eat its fruit, which is deadly!

Natural Features

The Yucatan Peninsula's porous **limestone** forces Mexican farmers to plant the few patches of earth found among otherwise rocky ground. Void of above-ground rivers, the peninsula holds its fresh water in deep limestone wells called **cenotes**.

Singled out by UNESCO, Dominica's Morne Trois Pitons National Park and St. Lucia's Pitons Management Area reside in a **volcanic zone** rife with hot springs and hardy flora, including some of the region's healthiest **coral reefs**. World Heritage status was bestowed on Belize's barrier reef reserve, the largest in the Northern Hemisphere, for its endangered species.

Wildlife

Fauna consists largely of birds, amphibians and reptiles. At the time of conquest, accounts of "forest demons" are thought to have referred to the now-extinct **Cuban Giant Owl**—flightless, 3ft tall, and up to 20 pounds in weight. Also long-extinct is the **giant hutia**, a rodent as large as America's black bear. Today, the nocturnal and venomous **solenodon**, an endemic mammal, is rare in Cuba; of scientific interest, it displays characteristics of primitive mammals that date back to the dinosaurs. A native species of Cuba that has retreated to remoter areas of the country, **jutias** are large, rat-like rodents related to the **agoutis** of South America (agoutis are also found in the Caribbean today). Barbados harbors the world's smallest snake. Trinidad boasts the world's largest snake: anacondas up to 30 feet in length. **Crocodiles** make their home in the Caribbean islands as well. **Monkeys** in the region include the black howler found in Belize, the red howler in Trinidad, and Grenada's mona monkey. Cuba is renowned for its painted snails called **polymitas**, which can be found mostly in the eastern part of the island.

The whole region, especially Trinidad for its location along north and south migration routes, is enlivened by cheerful **bird life**, from pelicans to roseate spoonbills. The endemic Puerto Rican Amazon Parrot, the island's once plentiful green parrot, is now critically endangered. Mexico's Isla Holbox witnesses pink flamingos as does Curaçao, and the Belize Audobon Society is active in protecting the jabiru stork.

The Caribbean's rich **marine life** includes humpback whales, Atlantic dolphins, manta rays and West Indian manatees. Many species are becoming endangered and extinct throughout the region, a tragedy attributed to human impact.

Environmental Concerns

The tropical Caribbean islands are generally sunny and warm year-round. In hurricane season (June to November) as well as winter, rainfall is heavier, but most days sunny skies and ocean breezes prevail. The southward islands of Grenada and Barbados mark the starting point of the Atlantic hurricane belt, but seasonal storms consistently rage through the region.

Current environmental concerns stem from the pandemic warming, erosion and general depletion caused by human habits and natural processes. Trinidad and Tobago's Permaculture Institute as well as the Caribbean Tourism Organization, Caribbean Alliance for Sustainable Tourism, Green Globe, and other groups are working toward a "**green shift**" to reestablish a natural balance and right some of the wrongs brought about here by rampant development.

PLANNING
YOUR TRIP TO
THE CARIBBEAN

When to Go

Seasons

Winter is the best time to travel to the Caribbean islands. **Peak season** for tourists is mid-Dec–mid-Apr. Generally, you'll find the best lodging discounts from late September until about mid-December. The months of April through July are hot and humid with many sudden showers. For most islands, the **rainy season** begins in May and ends in the fall.

For the mainland destinations, Mexico's Yucatán Peninsula is a year-round destination with average annual temperatures of 41°C/106°F; the peninsula's winter (Oct-Jan) temperatures average 21-32°C/70-90°F with precipitation of 7-20cm/3-8in. **Peak tourist season** occurs during Holy Week (Jun-Aug and Dec). Colombia's Cartagena is also a year-round destination, but the best time to visit is during the short summer (Dec-Mar), since these months are the driest. Another popular time of year is **mid-June to mid-August**, but bear in mind that these travel periods coincide with school holidays in Colombia.

Weather

On most Caribbean Islands, the weather is consistently warm and humid throughout the year, with regular northeasterly trade winds bringing moisture from the Atlantic Ocean. Air temperatures hover around 28°C/82°F in summer and 24°C/75°F in winter. The water temperature averages 28°C/82°F in summer, and 26°C/79°F in winter. Rain tends to fall in the late afternoon and early evening, often with thunderstorms.

Hurricanes normally occur from June through November; the peak month is September. Recovery efforts usually get well under way after any devastating hurricane season; for updates, check the **Caribbean Disaster Emergency Management Agency** (CDEMA) at www.cdema.org.

The weather in Colombia is strongly influenced by **altitude**. As a coastal area, Cartagena is hot and humid year-round. The coast of Mexico's Yucatán Peninsula experiences warm weather year-round.

Reservations

Advance bookings are strongly advised for all destinations during holidays and major festivals (*see CALENDAR OF EVENTS*). Because demand is higher during these periods, prices for accommodations also are generally higher. In low season (off-peak season), lower rates and even genuine bargains may be available.

Where to Go

The destinations sitting in, or along the shore of, the Caribbean Sea promise gorgeous landscapes, warm weather, diverse recreation and friendly people. Below are suggested itineraries for one or two weeks to induce you to come and see for yourself.

Bahamas★★

The Bahamas were tailor-made for island-hopping, but before you hop, take two or three days to explore **Nassau★★**, the charming capital where you can shop duty-free, encounter dolphins and visit historic buildings. Across the bridge, **Paradise Island★** holds built-to-entertain Atlantis and other resorts and the white sands of **Cabbage Beach★**. The vibe changes completely when you head to the secluded beaches and blue holes of **Andros Island**; its star attraction is the third largest **coral reef★★★** in the world. On **Grand Bahama** enjoy shopping at **Port Lucaya**, the subterranean majesty of **Lucayan National Park★★** and its 96 miles of beaches.

Spend a second week exploring the other Out Islands, including **Harbour Island's Pink Sands Beach★★★** and the tiny archipelago of **Exuma Cays**, James-Bond-worthy Thunderball Grotto, and **Exuma Cays Land and Sea Park★★**. Boating and fishing enthusiasts can devote time to big-game fishing or bonefishing in the **Berry Islands** or boating off the **Abacos Islands**.

Turks and Caicos★

These small, sandy islands are perfect for a day of snorkeling and diving or soaking up the sun. **Providenciales** (Provo, for short) is the main tourist destination and **Grace Bay Beach★★★** one of its top beaches. Don't miss the kid-favorite **Conch World★**, an enlightening look into the world of this large marine mollusk. Snorkelers should plan a trip to **Smith's Reef**, where buoys guide you to the best spots. Experienced divers should explore the **Shark Hotel★** dive site. Popular boat day trips from Provo include **Big Ambergris Cay** and the protected **Little Water Cay**, populated by rare iguanas. Grand Turk's tiny capital **Cockburn Town**, with its wandering donkeys and goats, has a heritage walk that merits an afternoon stroll past the bars on Duke Street to the National Museum, where you can learn about the history of pirates and shipwrecks.Great diving can be found at **Coral Gardens★★** and **Black Forest★**; local dive shops can organize trips. If you have more time to spare, take a ferry or boat trip to laid-back **Salt Cay★★**, a World Heritage Site that recalls the time when salt was worth more than gold.

Travel Tip: It's easier to stay within the boundaries of a resort in Turks and Caicos and any of the Caribbean islands, but there's more to do than lie on the beach. For starters, get out to the North and Middle Caicos to see the various uninhabited islands and cays, which are ideal for snorkeling, kayaking and diving. Look into daily ferry service to get off the main islands.

Cuba★★★

Explore Havana's Spanish Colonial **Old Town★★★**, especially the Baroque **Catedral de San Cristóbal★★★** and leafy **Plaza des Armas★★★** (1582), the city's oldest public square. View Cuban art at **Museo Nacional de Bellas Artes★★**, then have a cigar at **La Casa del Habano**, and watch them being made at **Fábrica de Tabacos Partagás★**. Lunch on Creole dishes at La Bodeguita del Medio, a Hemingway hangout, then hire a polished 1950s American automobile from Gran Car to drive you to arts and crafts market **Almacenes San José★★**. Dine at **La Guarida** and admire film memorabilia. In **Centro Habana**, sit on the **Malecón★★** seawall and watch *habaneros* fish, before strolling tree-lined **Prado★** to see the **Capitolio Nacional★★**, similar to the US Capitol's design. On Sunday take a yellow coco-taxi through Havana's **Chinatown** to reach **Callejón de Hamel★**, an alley where crowds groove to live rumba. Along lengthy **La Rampa★** (Calle 23), try Cuban ice cream at **Coppelia** followed by a drink at **Hotel Nacional★**, host to international celebrities. After a Cuban meal at Café Laurent, see Afro-Cuban dances by Conjunto Folklórico Nacional de Cuba. Recall Fidel Castro and Che Guevara at **Plaza de la Revolución**, then view elaborate gravestones at **Cementerio de Cristóbal Colón★★★**. Don't leave without seeing the world-famous **Tropicana** show.

Cayman Islands★★

The many attractions of **Grand Cayman★★**, the largest of the Cayman Islands, demand at least three days' exploration. Nothing on Cayman compares with the unforgettable experience of swimming in shallow waters carpeted with gentle rays at **Stingray City and Sandbar★★★**. Lined with hotels, the powdery sands of **Seven Mile Beach★★** have long lured visitors to the island. Quaint **George Town** offers duty-free shops, historic sights and an opportunity to board a pirate ship or a submarine. And the **Cayman Turtle Farm★** is a must-visit for families. One of the world's premier diving destinations, Cayman has no shortage of dive sites, and its newest has quickly become one of its most popular: nestled in shallow waters with outstanding visibility, the sunken **USS Kittiwake** can be enjoyed by both divers and snorkelers.

A one- or two-day trip to **Cayman Brac** and **Little Cayman** lets you escape to idyllic, unspoiled retreats. Divers will marvel at the teeming marine life and coral formations at Little Cayman's **Bloody Bay Marine Park★★**, while birders and nature lovers can observe red-footed residents of the **Booby Pond Nature Reserve★★** on Little Cayman, or try to spot the rare Cayman Parrot at the **Cayman Brac Parrot Reserve★**.

Jamaica★★

Must sees in **Kingston** include the **Bob Marley Museum**, the **National Gallery** and **Devon House**. Hiking, birding and coffee tours draw visitors to Jamaica's misty **Blue Mountains**. Their peak is a moderate hike offering stunning vistas. In **Port Antonio★★**, don't miss **Blue Lagoon, Winifred Beach** and **Reach Falls**. St. Ann is the "garden parish," where **Coyaba Gardens** is worth a visit; the **White River** is ideal for tubing and canoeing, despite its countless cascades. **Robin's Bay**, in St. Mary, attracts nature lovers for tours of Strawberry Fields and Green Castle Estate. Don't miss **Firefly★★**, Noël Coward's former hillside lair with its mesmerizing views.

Montego Bay spreads outwards from Sharpe Square, culminating at **Doctors Cave Beach★** and **Cornwall Beach**, its best stretches of sand. East of Montego Bay, **Rose Hall Great House★★★** and **Greenwood Great House★** have excellent tours of their handsome manor houses. Falmouth has beaches suitable for kiteboarding and windsurfing. Good Hope Plantation offers luxury accommodations and a slew of activities.

Negril boasts the country's longest beach. Negril's cliffs make the destination unique, luring visitors to jump happily into the sea. **YS Falls★★**, Appleton Estate, Black River and **Treasure Beach** are the top attractions along the South Coast. Don't miss **Little Ochie** if you enjoy seafood.

Dominican Republic★

There are lots of options to fill a week, from beach hopping, windsurfing, exploring the island's rich history and enjoying great local dishes like *locrio* and *mofongo*. **Santo Domingo★★★**, the country's capital, is a must-see, with plenty of sights in the Old City to fill a day or two. Start in **Calle de Las Damas**, the heart of this Spanish-Colonial city founded by Christopher Columbus. Another must-see is the fascinating **Museo del Hombre Dominicano★★**, whose exhibits take you back in time to the world of the pre-Columbian Taíno peoples. If you're staying in a northern resort, plan a day trip to the equally historic city of **Puerto Plata** to relive pirate days at **San Felipe Fortress★★★**, stroll along the seaside Malecón, and enjoy a tipple at the Brugal rum factory.

Just east of Puerto Plata, world-class windsurfing and kitesurfing conditions await enthusiasts at **Cabarete**; there are enough local excursions and diversions in this party town to last a week. If you're here from mid-January to mid-March, don't miss the unrivaled opportunity to get up close and personal with thousands of humpback whales that arrive in **Samaná Bay★** to breed and nurse their young.

Travel Tip: You'll find all the typical Caribbean activities in the Dominican Republic, but for a different way of experiencing this island, think up in the air. There are 14 airports on the island and many are remote. For an adventure, take a plane tour of the Northwest corner of the island and the Monte Cristo region.

Puerto Rico★★★

Begin your journey in colorful **Old San Juan★★★**, where the historic fortresses of **El Morro★★★** and **San Cristóbal★★**, the governor's mansion at **La Fortaleza★★** and the city's Colonial architecture will captivate you for at least a day or two. From here, spread out to San Juan's neighborhoods of **Condado** and **Isla Verde**, where you can sample gourmet dining at Pikayo or Budatai and shop at designer boutiques. Also worth visiting is the **Bacardi Rum Distillery★★** across the water from Old San Juan, which gives informative, interactive tours of "The Cathedral of Rum."

Many believe the real Puerto Rico exists outside San Juan. To the east lies **Balneario de Luquillo★★**, touted as one of the most stunning beaches in all of Puerto Rico. A day trip south to **El Yunque** will reward you with a verdant and unspoiled rain forest where you can hike, swim in waterfalls and generally get away from civilization. To the west of San Juan, at the island's northern end, you'll find surfer favorite **Rincon Beach★★** and world-famous **Jobos Beach★**. The quaint second-largest city of **Ponce**, with its colonial elegance, presents yet another side of island life. Or you can visit the eastern islands of **Vieques** or **Culebra**, where pristine white-sand beaches and a rustic, relaxed vibe await. Vieques also offers the glow-in-the-dark wonder of its biobay, while Culebra tempts with its **Flamenco Beach**, one of the most picture-perfect beaches in the world.

US Virgin Islands★★

Soak up the Danish heritage of USVI in its capital of **Charlotte Amalie** on **St. Thomas★** island and do some duty-free shopping at more than 300 stores. Plan a day or two on **Coki Beach**, where you can learn to snorkel while companioned by colorful fish. Make friends with locals when they ask to braid your hair, or bring you a fresh coconut or rum cocktail. Another inviting beach on St. Thomas is **Magen's Bay★★★**, a heart-shaped stretch of sand with a gift shop, grill and huge bar. For those who love to golf, St. Thomas' 18-hole **Mahogany Golf Course** has spectacular ocean views and a reliable restaurant. At night, experience the bars and restaurants in nearby **Red Hook**. Take the ferry to **St. John★★★** island to the hiking paradise of **Virgin Islands National Park★**, where **Trunk Bay★★** has been rated the most beautiful beach in the world; its diving trail winds among coral reefs. Dedicate a day to water sports and jet ski, parasail, and scuba dive around the island. End you trip in **St. Croix★★** with a visit to **Whim Plantation★★★**, one of the best-preserved sugar plantation estates in the Caribbean.

Travel Tip: Each island has its own distinct personality and different attractions to go along with the island's style. Know what kind of vacation you want before you head out. If you're looking to spend your time gambling, the US Virgin Islands have only one casino, on St. Croix. But if you're looking to scuba dive, the casino in St. Croix pales in comparison to great wreck diving.

A DAY IN THE LIFE OF PETER GREENBERG

In the Caribbean I almost always start my morning on the water. For a memorable boating experience you need constant trade winds, good anchorages and well-equipped charter companies; so you really can't do better than the British Virgin Islands.

The beauty of boating is that just because I start in one place doesn't mean I'm tied to that location for the rest of the day. For lunch, I can stop in a port that caters to local fisherman and businesses. That way I'm trying a regional specialty and not eating an overpriced chicken Caesar salad with the fanny pack set. In Puerto Rico, at Luquillo Beach, I head to one of the street kiosks that sell everything from *mofongo* to *empanadas* to *alcapurrias*. Or if I'm in Jamaica, it's off to Scotchies for some of my favorite jerk chicken.

The Caribbean sun is deceptively strong, so heading indoors in the afternoon is always a good idea. That's when you want to hit the spa, and what's cool in this region is that spas often rely on local resources. In St. Lucia, the Spa at The Jalousie Plantation uses sulfur and other minerals for some unique island-specific spa treatments.

There's nothing more magical than sunset on the beach. There are white, pink and black sand beaches in the Caribbean. The US Virgin Islands has white sand beaches as well as protected wilderness and rain forest, and you can always do a twilight nature walk. But I opt for a walk on the otherworldly black sand beaches on St. Vincent's shores.

It's still possible to go local even when splurging at an upscale restaurant. The Coal Pot in St. Lucia blends island flavors with French techniques. The marina setting is the perfect way for me to celebrate a day out on the Caribbean waters and shores.

Travel Tip: Island hopping may have some hidden costs. Several islands have imposed a visitor's tax that can catch up to you if you're island hopping. Saint-Martin, Antigua, St. Lucia, St. Vincent, Grenada and Belize all levy an airport departure tax, and those taxes can be up to $20 a piece.

British Virgin Islands★★★

If you're a sailor, charter a sailboat or catamaran for the first week, or spoil yourself and hire a captain. On the first day, take a short sail in Sir Frances Drake Channel to **Norman, Peter★** and **Cooper islands**. The best snorkeling en route is found at The Indians and The Cave; the top diving site is the **Wreck of the Rhone★★★**. On day two, visit **Trellis Bay** and go ashore to see the artisans' co-op. Spend 2 days on **Virgin Gorda★★★**, where must-sees include the **The Baths★★★**, **Gorda Peak National Park** and **North Sound★★**. On day 5 sail north to **Anegada**, known for its **coral reefs** teeming with tropical fish, its dive sites, and its lobster dinners. On day 6, cruise to the upper side of **Tortola★★** for a swim at **Cane Garden Bay★★**, followed by a lively evening on the island of **Jost Van Dyke★**. On day 7, slip into **Smuggler's Cove** for a fun day at the beach.

For week two, with your home base in Tortola, spend a day shopping and sightseeing in **Road Town**; a day making the loop around the West End (while there, see **Soper's Hole★**, **Callwood's Rum Distillery** and **Sage Mountain★**); a day looping the East End, including lunch and a swim at the Tamarind Club; and two days relaxing at the beach.

Lesser Antilles★★

Allow at least a week in **Saint-Martin★★** to relish its beaches and French cuisine, and visit the **Marigot Museum★**, **Fort Saint-Louis★** and the **Butterfly Farm**. Spend an evening in neighboring **Sint Maarten★★** in one of its Las Vegas-style **casinos**. Then hop on flights or ferries to the nearest islands of Anguilla, Saba, St. Barthélemy (affectionately St. Barths) and St. Eustatius (Statia for short). Spend a day in **Anguilla** at the white sands of crescent-shaped **Rendezvous Bay★★★**. Stay a night in **St. Barths★★** to snorkel at the **Grand Cul-de-Sac Cove★★**, and shop at deluxe boutiques in **Gustavia** or **Saint Jean**. Journey to the remote volcanic islands of **Saba★** and **Sint Eustatius** (best accessed by airplane), both ideal for hiking and diving. Drive the hairpin turns of Saba's **The Road** and hike Statia's legendary 2,000ft dormant volcano, **The Quill**.

Begin a second week on **St. Kitts★★** riding its **Sugar Train★★** and walking through **Brimstone Hill Fortress★★**. On neighboring **Nevis★★**, behold orchids and palms at its **Botanical Garden★★**. If you're a dedicated hiker, climb **Nevis Peak★★**. While on **Antigua★**, see 18C British navy haunt **Nelson's Dockyard★★** and other historic sites, as well as the beach at **Half Moon Bay★**. Then ferry-hop to **Barbuda★** and the pink sands of **Southern Beach** before admiring frigate birds at the **Bird Sanctuary★**.

French Isles★★★

The capital of **Guadeloupe★★★**, **Pointe-à-Pitre★** merits a day to see its 19C houses along **Rue Nozières** and markets like **Saint-Antoine★**. Just north, the underwater sanctuary of the **Bouillante Reserve★★★**, off western **Basse-Terre**, appeals to snorkelers and divers. Visit a coffee plantation like **La Grivelière** before you leave the region. On Grande-Terre, a day trip to see the savage beauty of **La Soufrière★★★** volcano is a must. Off the mainland in **Les Saintes★★★** archipelago, **Marie-Galante** and La Désirade deserve a look, but **Terre-de-Haut★★★** is the most spectacular of these islands. One could easily spend 3 to 4 days hiking **La Trace des Crêtes★★★** (Hilltops Trail), exploring **Fort Napoléon★★★** and discovering secluded coves.

Neighboring **Martinique★★★** is a bit of France in the Caribbean. Its capital, **Fort-de-France★**, nestles among three rivers and the Bay of Flanders. See the fine architecture of Henri Picq's eclectic **Schoelcher Library★★** and **Saint-Louis Cathedral**. Then head just north to the **Jardins de Balata★★** to see why early inhabitants called Martinique the "Island of Flowers." Nature lovers should hike the savannahs and mangroves of **Reserve Naturelle de la Caravelle★★★** on the Atlantic coast. In the south, **Presqu'ile Sainte-Anne★** has lovely beaches connected by the **Trace des Caps** hiking and bike trail.

Dominica★

While away a half day exploring the capital of **Roseau**, with its **French Quarter** and craft stalls at **Old Market Square**. Must sees on the island include **Morne Trois Pitons National Park★★**, home to rain-forest covered mountains, rivers and **Boiling Lake★**, thought to be the second largest of its kind in the world. Dominica's numerous waterfalls include **Trafalgar Falls, Sari Sari Falls** and **Victoria Falls**.

Don't miss **Soufrière Scotts Head Marine Reserve**, a volcanic seascape of pinnacles, abyssal drop-offs, pristine reefs and colorful marine creatures. Saunter amid forests to reach battlement ruins, cannons and the restored **Fort Shirley Garrison** in **Cabrits National Park** on the island's north side. In fact, hikers could spend days exploring the island's network of trails, or trekking the 200km/115mi **Waitukubuli National Trail** that meanders from the south to the island's northern tip. The **Syndicate Nature Trail** in the shadow of **Morne Diablotin**, Dominica's tallest mountain, offers the opportunity to observe endemic Amazonian parrots, the sisserou and the jaco. After all that hiking, find rejuvenation and relaxation at Dominica's hot **sulphur springs** like **Screw's**, Ti Kwen, Tia's and Papillote Wilderness Retreat, where steaming pools are surrounded by lush tropical gardens.

61

Travel Tip: Want to take a dip? The hotel pool is not an inspired choice. For a different experience, go to the northeast coast of St. Vincent, where you'll find the Owia Salt Pond. Born from volcanic eruption, the hot saltwater is credited with healing properties by locals.

St. Lucia★★

Forested peaks descend to palm-fringed sandy bays with calm child-safe waters at **Marigot Bay★★** and **Choc Beach,** perfect for a week of sunshine and seafood. They flank the capital of **Castries**, where Creole cuisine abounds in restaurants like The Coal Pot. A day trip to the **Pitons★★**, the two peaks that dominate the skyline, is a must for adventurers. The arduous climb to the top of **Gros Piton** must be done with a guide, but the rewards are great views of the island. To recover, take a day to soak in the **Soufrière Sulphur Springs★**, where you can steam away in natural rock pools. If you hanker after other healing waters with a bit of history, a nearby spa at the **Diamond Botanical Gardens** retains mineral baths used by Napoleon's wife, Josephine. Party people seeking a typical "jump up" should head to the fishing village of **Gros Islet** for its **Friday Fish Fry.** Eat your fill of lobster and jerk chicken from food vendors while sound systems pump the streets full of reggae and RnB.

St. Vincent★ and the Grenadines★★

With boat and ferry connections between the main islands and St. Vincent★, it's easy and fairly inexpensive to spend a week exploring Bequia, **Mustique★**, Canouan and Union islands. On volcanic St. Vincent, the capital, **Kingstown**, is worthy of a day's sightseeing. Don't miss the oldest botanical garden in the Caribbean and the walk up to Fort Charlotte on Berkshire Hill for the views. The best of the black-sand beaches is **Wallilabou** in the north. Spare a day and start early for the four-hour hike through rain forest and across lava formations of imposing **La Soufrière★★**, an active volcano. A day in **Bequia★** should take in the natural harbor of **Admiralty Bay★★** and lunch in the main town of **Port Elizabeth** before you head to **Friendship Bay** for an afternoon swim and snorkel. If you have time, take the ferry to **Union Island** and arrange a boat trip to the tiny isles of the **Tobago Cays★★** to enjoy their exquisite setting.

Grenada★

Must-sees include **Belmont Estate★** whose tree-to-bar process transforms organic cocoa to scrumptious chocolate; the **River Antoine Rum Distillery** whose methods and machinery for converting sugar cane to rum date to the 1700s; in **St. George's market square**, home to the spices for which Grenada is famous; **Grand Anse★**, a natural anchorage where sailboats rest and resort hotels offer self-indulgence. Hikers should trek **Grand Étang National Park** to find waterfalls, and Grand Étang itself, a serene crater lake that sits beneath the lofty peaks of Qua Qua and Fédon.

sit neighboring **Carriacou** island to see the boat yards of indward and their hand-built sloops. **Petit Martinique** nearly makes a pleasant island day-excursion.

arbados★

nown for exclusive resorts like **Sandy Lane**, Barbados beckns tourists for a week of sand and waves at its beautiful public eaches. **Sandy Lane Bay★** and **Mullins Beach★** on the west past coast attract couples and families. On the southeast shore, pinkh-hued **Crane Beach★★** lies off the Atlantic coast. The capital f **Bridgetown** can be seen in an afternoon, but set aside a day o add **Garrison Historic Area** and the **Barbados Museum**, a rmer prison that puts the island's African slave past into perpective. A must-see excursion is the mini-train ride through **arrison's Cave★** to admire spectacular stalactites.

nother popular day trip is to **Barbados Wildlife Reserve**, here you can wander through a mahogany forest and enounter local birds and animals, including the inquisitive green onkeys that roam wild. For a wild Caribbean night of your wn, head to the village of Oistins any Friday for a lively food nd music party known as the **Fish Fry**.

rinidad★ and Tobago★★

ost visitors choose party nights in **Trinidad★** or the slow pace f smaller, more rustic **Tobago★★**. Connected by ferry service, oth islands offer amazing beaches, world-class birdwatching nd rain forest treks. **Port of Spain**, Trinidad's sprawling, inustrialized capital can be seen in a day. Stroll around **Queens ark Savannah★★** to see magnificent colonial mansions.

earby, the well-kept **Botanical Gardens★** are a must-see, ith neatly labeled Caribbean shrubs and flowers in a riot of opical colors. At night, head for Ariapita Avenue, a strip of upale restaurants and clubs that play jazz, calypso and reggae. or a day trip to the island's best beach, take a tour or drive over rested hills to **Maracas Bay**, where the bake and shark is a ust-try.

or a taste of the rain forest and the island's wilder side, take a ip to the **Asa Wright Nature Centre★★**, a world-class birdatching spot aflutter with irridescent hummingbirds. Take a oat trip through mangroves filled with scarlet ibis (the national rd) and roseate spoonbills in **Caroni Bird Sanctuary★**.

you have a few days in **Tobago★★**, head for the golden ands and glistening waters of **Pirates Bay Beach★**, **Bloody ay Beach★★** and **Castara Bay Beach★★**. Plan a day at the **obago Forest Reserve**, a must-do trip into dense rain forest o see birds, plants and waterfalls.

Travel Tip: Many people will tell you that Pigeon Point on the southern tip of Trinidad is the island's most picturesque beach. While it's beautiful, it's also heavily trafficked. It's a common cruise destination, so it's often crowded. To move away from the crowds, go to the opposite end of the island to Pirate's Bay.

There's a lot of talk about travel safety and Mexico, but the bottom line is that many people continue to travel there safely—and I am one of them. Violence in Mexico is largely limited to border towns and is gang-on-gang conflict. The US State Department issues advisories if there are any safety concerns, but if you limit yourself to government reports, you're doing yourself a disservice. Read the local papers and most importantly, talk to the people actually on the ground. The worst four-letter word when it comes to travel is "fear." And fear, when it comes to travel in Mexico, is, for the most part, unwarranted.

Aruba★, Bonaire★, Curaçao★★★

There are currently no ferries operating between the island but each one has enough attractions to keep you busy for week. The focus is on the beaches in **Aruba★**, but don't mi out on the capital **Oranjestad**, with its Dutch buildings ar old colonial fort, and leave an afternoon for souvenir-hunting the swank shops of the center. Good restaurants, casinos wit musical entertainment and throbbing clubs make for a live night out. Use the island's excellent bus service to beach ho from **Palm Beach★★**, popular with the locals, to **Hadicurari** a magnet for windsurfers. Wildlife lovers should explore th cactus, caves and lava formations along the well-signed trai of **Arikok National Park**, home to the Aruban parakeet ar lots of lizards. Divers won't get bored on **Bonaire★**, a world r nowned diving destination with some 80 dive sites to choos from, many accessible from the shore.

In **Curaçao★★★**, must-sees include the quaint capital **Willemsta ★★★**, a World Heritage Site. Spend a day strolling around th floating market of Punda, and learn about the island's history slavery and Dutch colonialism at the **Museum Kurá Huland ★★★**. For the largest and best-kept beach on the island, hea to **Cas Abao★★**, which is worth the modest entry fee. A bo trip to the desert island of **Klein Curaçao★★** is a great way break up the week.

Mexico★★★, Belize★★, Honduras★

Absolute must sees in **Mexico's Yucatán Peninsula** lie alon the **Riviera Maya★★** and inland at the millennial Maya city **Chichén Itzá★★★**. Here an early morning is ideal for standin among the pyramids, so allow for at least one night betwee arriving and departing, and use the time to be pampered May style at **Hacienda Chichén**.

On the Riviera, shop till you drop, then dance the night awa along chic 5th Avenue in **Playa del Carmen★★**. Take at least days to go to diving mecca **Isla Cozumel★** by ferry. Use thos days to bask on the beach and explore underwater at **Pala car.** Swim with dolphins on a day trip to **Xcaret★★★**, the cu tural, natural theme park. Take a day for a jaunt to **Tulum★** climb ancient pyramids, then stroll to the sea for a swim. To from the airport, take a day's break in **Cancún★★** for quinte sential Caribbean beach time or world-class shopping at La Is or Kukulkan Plaza. Overnight on **Isla Mujeres★**, a famous di spot north of Cancun.

The absolute musts in Belize surround **Ambergris Caye★** From its hub, **San Pedro★★**, dive sites are accessed by boa Beginning divers should go to **Hol Chan Marine Reserve★**

Travel, Dine and Explore with Confidence

Michelin, experts in travel guides and maps for more than 100 years. Available wherever books are sold.

www.michelintravel.com

MICHELIN
A better way forward

Snorkelers, make your way to **Shark Ray Alley★★★**. Serious divers and adventurers, take a 1hr boat ride to the **Turneffe Islands★★★** to dive the enigmatic great **Blue Hole★★★** and the sunken ships of **Lighthouse Reef★★★**. Animal lovers should make the trip to **Half Moon Caye National Monument★★★** to see, if lucky, a red-footed boobie. Mayan enthusiasts must take the boat west to the Northern River, inland to the "submerged crocodile," Lamanai.

From **Belize City**, day trips to the **Belize Zoo★★**, or the Mayan sites at **Xunantinich** and **Altún Ha**, are readily arranged. If you want to climb the complex that marks the highest man-made point in Belize, Caana at **Caracol★★**, allow at least 2 days

Flights to and from **Roatán Island★★** span Saturday to Saturday. Resorts with all-inclusive dive packages offer 10 dives at the island's plethora of pristine, newly trafficked sites in one week. Above water, allow half a day for souvenir shopping at **West End Village★**, where you can also choose your own daily adventure from varied dive packages. Alternately, stock up on picnic supplies and head to **West Bay Beach** on a water taxi. If you love quiet, hire a cab for the day and ask your driver to take you to a secluded beach. On the mainland, on an overnight trip, you can raft or kayak the extreme **Río Cangrejal**. Allow at least 3 days to make the trek—be it by sea and land or by air—to the immense Mayan ruins at the magnificent **Copán★★**—out of the way, but well worth it.

Cartagena★★★

Cartagena de Indias is steeped in history. Allow at least 2 days to wander within the walls of the historic walled town **Ciudad Amurallada★★★**. Must-sees include the fine Colonial architecture of **Iglesia de San Pedro Claver★★**, the gory **Museum of the Inquisition★★** and the fascinating museum of pre-Colombian gold. **Las Bovedas** is an old barracks converted into shops and a good spot to climb atop the thick city walls.

At night take a *chiva*, a traditional wooden bus outfitted with a rum bar and band that picks you up at your hotel from about 8pm for a 4-hour tour with tropical tunes and hip-shaking hilarity. Set aside one day to visit the impressive fortifications of **Castillo San Felipe de Barajas★★★**, a UNESCO World Heritage Site just outside the town center.

For beaches, avoid the gray sands of **Bocagrande**, and follow the locals on a boat tour to Isla del Baru or **Islas del Rosario** to eat fried local fish and swim in crystalline waters. If you seek further adventure, book a tour to the **Volcán de Lodo el Totumo★**, a bubbling "mud volcano" some 32 miles outside Cartagena, where you can wallow in restorative mud baths.

Travel Tip: Cartagena takes the party bus to a whole new level. You can take a night tour of the city on a *chiva*, which will drive you through the city for three to four hours with a band playing *vallenato*. And the party's not over when the bus stops. Usually riders get let out in front of a local disco and the festivities continue late into the night.

What to See and Do

Sightseeing

Local **tourist offices** can usually supply in person and online maps, names of local tour companies and even brochures of walking or cycling tours. For exploring on your own, bicycles, mopeds and/or scooters are commonly available to rent in most towns, as are car rentals.

Another source is your **hotel concierge** or desk staff; be aware that some might try to steer you toward their own preferred services that may not be the best available. For additional **tour operators**, visit the official tourism website for each destination *(see PLANNING YOUR TRIP for tourism office websites)*. Unless otherwise stated, tours below are in English.

Here is just a sampling;
Adventure Tours

Bahamas: Day-long dolphin encounters at Blue Lagoon Island www.dolphinswims.com.

Jamaica: Barrett Adventures www.barrettadventures.com and Chukka Caribbean Adventures www.chukkacaribbean.com provide general tours of the island. Jamaica's free People to People program pairs visitors with locals to fish, garden or cook together, for example. www.bahamas.com.

Mexico: The Playa del Carmen-based Alltournative company offers adventure-filled day tours in the Yucatán Peninsula. www.alltournative.com, as does Eco Colors, Cancún, www.ecotravel-mexico.com.

Bus Tours

Barbados: Once a week the Barbados National Trust offers bus tours of historic buildings and private homes throughout the island. http://trust.funbarbados.com.

Cuba: **HabanaBusTour**, operated by Transtur (www.transtur.cu), runs daily hop-on, hop-off open-top red buses along two tourist routes through Havana. Víazul buses service tourists points farther afield. www.viazul.com.

Boat Tours

Curaçao: Mermaid Boat Trips www.mermaidboattrips.com.

St. Vincent and the Grenadines: HazECO Tours in Kingstown, St. Vincent personalize itineraries and transport customers by powerboat or catamaran. Board a 60ft catamaran from Captain Yannis Day Charter catamaran cruises from Union Island for a day excursion around the Tobago Cays www.yannissail.com.

Cycling Tours

Cuba: WoWCuba MacQueen's Island Tours rents bikes for a 3-day minimum period. www.wowcuba.com.

Puerto Rico: Bike Old San Juan with Explorer Adventure PR, Inc. www. exapr.com.

St. Lucia: Ride miles of trails in an orchid and mango-filled jungle of Anse Mamin with Bike St. Lucia. www.bikestlucia.com.

Culinary Tours

Curaçao: In Willemstad you can cook a traditional Curaçaon meal in the home of a resident islander. Angelica's Kitchen www.angelicas-kitchen.com.

Jamaica: Bellefield Great House opens to small groups for tours of its fruit and vegetable gardens followed by a buffet lunch. www.bellefieldgreathouse.com.

Nevis: Once a week Miss June brings guests into her West Indies home to dine on global dishes, including Trinidad curry. Miss June's Cuisine ☎869-469-5330.

Ecotours

Caymans: Cayman Brac has limestone caves, dive sites, rock climbing, bird watching (even bat-watching) and 35 marked hiking trails. Contact the tourism office for details.

Mexico: Ecotourismo Yucatán leads several excursions throughout the peninsula. www.ecoyuc.com.

Belize: Green Dragon Tours offers reef and rain forest adventures up to 14 days. www.greendragonbelize.com.

Guided Tours

Bahamas: See Nassau on a Segway ride. Bahamas Segway Tours www.bahamassegwaytours.com. Smiling Pat's Adventures will enhance your visit of Freeport. www.smilingpat.com.

Puerto Rico: Eco Action Tours cover all islands as well as tours of historic sites. www.ecoactiontours.com.

St. Vincent and the Grenadines: HazECO Tours in Kingstown, St. Vincent, personalizes itineraries and transports customers by luxury van or Land Rover jeep, powerboat or catamaran.

Sightseeing Tours

Bahamas: **Horse-drawn carriage** tours of Old Nassau; downtown locations and Prince George Wharf near cruise-ship terminal. Ride a **jitney** (32-seat public bus) from downtown Nassau/Bay Street to Cable Beach and to the Paradise Island bridge.

Nevis: Take a horse-drawn carriage ride in a mid-19C Creole conveyance in the island's countryside; depart from the Hermitage Inn in Gingerland ☎869-469-3477.

Puerto Rico: Atlantic San Juan Tours in air-conditioned vans www.puertoricoexcursions.com.

Grenada: Private taxis offer island tours. Here are a few: Caribbean Horizons ☏473-444-1555, www.caribbeanhorizons.com. Henry's Safari Tours ☏473-444-5313, www.henrysafari.com. Mandoo Tours ☏473-440-1428, www.grenadatours.com. Sunsation Tours ☏473-444-1594, www.grenadasunsation.com.

USVI: Charlotte Amalie's St. Thomas Skyride gives an aerial view of the city; www.paradisepointtranway.com. Rent a car (or hire a tour taxi) to drive the 72mi St. Croix Heritage Trail that encircles St. Croix island. www.stcroixheritagetrail.com.

Belize: Escorted excursions in well-equipped vehicles to Belize's interior are organized by Belize VIP Travel Services. www.belizetransfers.com. Far Horizons also offers excursions www.farhorizon.com. Natural history tours are guided by Holbrook Travel, Inc. www.holbrooktravel.com. Discovery Expeditions Belize Ltd. arranges trips from Belize City to Ambergris Caye and San Ignacio. www.discoverybelize.com.

Walking Tours

Bahamas: Walking tours of Nassau organized by Ministry of Tourism depart from Rawson Square twice Mon-Sat; ☏242-325-8687.

Jamaica: For Falmouth Heritage Walks, go online to: www.falmouthheritagewalks.com.

St. Lucia: Tours of the island's heritage, such as a working cacao plantation, are organized by communities. Access online www.heritagetoursstlucia.org.

Sports and Recreation
Biking

Caymans: Cayman Brac hotels usually have complimentary bikes for guests.

Guadeloupe: Guadeloupeans love biking. Renting a bike is a good way to meet the locals.

Birding

Bahamas: Rand Nature Centre tours. www.bnt.bs.

Barbuda: Codrington Lagoon Bird Sanctuary has the largest frigate bird colony in the West Indies. Arrange with your hotel.

Belize: Chan Chich Lodge has parrots among its 300 bird species. www.chanchich.com.

Caymans: Brac Parrot Reserve on Cayman Brac. Access www.nationaltrust.org.ky. Gore Bird Sanctuary on Grand Cayman for grassquits, moorhens, grebes, flycatchers. www.nationaltrust.org.ky.

Travel Tip: Say you want to use your vacation to learn a new sport. Whenever you're testing out new activities make sure that you're fully informed. Look into a sport program like snorkeling and water skiing to make sure they have proper equipment and certifications. At the very least, companies should offer instruction on how to use that equipment before they send you on the way. Bottom line: make sure your instructor knows your skill and fitness level and you're grouped with similar participants.

Mexico: Take a side trip to Yucatán Peninsula's **Isla Holbox** to see flamingos and swim with whale sharks.

Trinidad: Asa Wright Nature Centre (www.asawright.org) has rare oilbirds, toucans, hummingbirds, agoutis, armadillos. Caroni Bird Sanctuary (reserve tours with Winston Nanan, ☏868-645-1305) has scarlet ibis and swamps that are home to caimans and tree snakes. Caroni Swamp National Park attract pelicans, roseate spoonbills and the rare red-capped cardinals.

Tobago: Tobago Forest Reserve's rain forest is best explored with expert guide David Rooks. David Rooks Nature Tours, Scarborough ☏868-756-8594.

Boating
Bahamas: Abacos Islands are known for world-class boating and sailing. Sailboats and catamarans can be rented (often with a captain) or chartered.

British Virgin Islands: Boat charters www.b-v-i.com/charter. Some charters come with a captain.

Grenadines: Bequia attracts yachting folks to **Admiralty Bay** filled with sailboats and giant cruise ships.

Mexico: See Cozumel.

Saint Vincent and Grenadines: Learn to sail with Barefoot Yacht Charters. www.barefootyachts.com. Day-trip charters in Bequia aboard a 44ft sailing yacht through Frangipani Hotel www.frangipanibequia.com.

Turks and Caicos: Boats with a captain can be rented from Leeward Marina, Providenciales.

Kayaking and Canoeing
Kayaks and canoes can be rented, and paddled, with a guide.

Honduras: Pico Bonito National Park is the place for white-water rafting and kayaking on the Class V Río Cangrejal.

Jamaica: Ocho Rios: White River canoe paddle ends upriver with dinner and folklore on the riverbank; your hotel can make arrangements.

Rafting
Jamaica: Bamboo rafts with guide down the Rio Grande River from Rafter's Rest, 5mi west of Port Antonio; ☏876-993-2778.

Caving
Barbados: Harrison's Cave www.harrisonscave.com.

Puerto Rico: Parque de las Cavernas del Río Camuy south of Arecibo (☏787-898-3100) holds subterranean caverns carved out by the Camuy River, where visitors walk with a guide to witness 1,000-year-old stalagmites and stalactites.

Travel Tip: Always pay attention to boating safety basics. Watch what you drink; BUI, or boating under the influence, is a huge problem. Between the sun and the salty air, boating operators are likely to become impaired more quickly than a driver, drink for drink. And a personal floatation device is a must; parents, know that an adult life jacket is not appropriate for children.

Diving

Anguilla: Stoney Bay Marine Park conceals the wreck of a 1772 Spanish galleon. Shoal Bay Scuba & Watersports will take you to it. www.shoalbayscuba.ai.

Bahamas: Bahama Divers (Nassau) www.bahamadivers.com. Lucayan National Park www.bnt.bs.

Belize: Blue Hole Diving www.bluedive.com.

Bonaire: Bonaire National Marine Park www.bmp.org.

Dominica: For scuba diving trips and whale watching tours in Soufrière Scotts Head Marine Reserve, contact Anchorage Dive Centre www.anchoragehotel.dm; ALDive www.aldive.com or Dive Dominica www.divedominica.com.

Guadeloupe: For Bouillante Nature Reserve underwater sanctuary, these outfits offer dive expeditions: Les Heures Saines www.heures-saines.gp; Plaisir Plongée Karukera www.plaisir-plongée-karukera.com; and UCPA www.ucpa.com.

Mexico: These dive companies offer dives in Cozumel: Sea Robin Diving www.searobincozumel.com, Caribbean Divers www.caribbeandiverscozumel.com and Dive Palancar www.divepalancarcozumel.com. For dives in Cancún, contact Aqua Tours www.aquatours.travel or Aquaworld www.aquaworld.com.mx.

Sint Eustatius: Adive companies for Statia Marine Park include Dive Statia (℘599-318-2435); Golden Rock Dive Center www.goldenrockdive.com; Scubaqua www.scubaqua.com.

Tobago: These dive companies specialize in dives off the island's west coast: AquaMarine Dive Ltd.www.aquamarinedive.com and Man Friday Diving www.manfridaydiving.com.

Fishing

St. Lucia: Deep-sea excursions for marlin, mackerel and barracuda are offered by Castries-based Hackshaws Boat Charters and Captain Mike's Sportfishing Cruises, both accessible online at www.worldwidefishing.com.

Golf

Barbados: Championship Golf Courses include Barbados Golf Club www.barbadosgolfclub.com, Rockley Golf & Country Club www.rockleygolfclub.com, the expensive and private Sandy Lane Country Club www.sandylane.com and Royal Westmoreland www.royalwestmoreland.com.

Jamaica: Golfers have long known that Jamaica's fairways. Courses include Montego Bay's Tryall Club www.tryallclub.com and the Negril Hills Golf Club www.negrilhillsgolfclub.com.

Nevis: Four Seasons Resort Nevis Golf Course in Pinney's Beach on Nevis www.fourseasons.com/nevis.

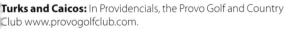

Turks and Caicos: In Providencials, the Provo Golf and Country Club www.provogolfclub.com.

USVI: Mahogany Run on St. Thomas www.mahoganyrungolf. com and Carambola Golf Club on St. Croix ✆ 340-778-5638.

Hiking

Barbados: Morning and afternoon hikes and moonlight walks through Hike Barbados www.barbados.org.

Dominica: Walk some of the island's 115 mile Waitukubuli National Trail www.waitukubulitrail.dm.

St. Lucia: Hikes to Gros Piton or Petit Piton can be arranged with your hotel concierge, Gros Piton Guides Association ✆ 758-459-9748 or SunLink Tours www.sunlinktours.com.

Sint Eustatius: One popular trail on the island is a 2,000ft climb to The Quill, a dormant volcano.

Nevis: Nevis Peak is a challenging hike on a dormant volcano. Sunrise Tours (✆ 869-469-2758) can provide local guides.

St. Vincent and Grenadines: Hire a guide (HazEco Tours ✆ 784-457-8634) for a four-hour, round-trip hike to the active volcano of La Soufrière.

USVI: Virgin Islands National Park in St. John has 22 easy-to-difficult hiking trails; www.nps.gov/viis.

Saba: Boiling House, Booby Hill, Mary's Point, Mt. Scenery and Saba's other trails vary in difficulty. Find a guide at the Saba Conservation Foundation's **Trail Shop** (✆ 599-416-3295), behind the tourist office in Windwardside.

Horseback Riding

Jamaica: Hooves Riding Stables www.hoovesjamaica.com organizes rides on the beach or in the mountains. Book through your hotel and you'll be picked up and driven to the stables.

Mustique: Mustique Equestrian Center offers trail rides that end with a gallop on the beach ✆ 784-458-4316.

Snorkeling

Barbuda: Off most of Barbuda's coast lie coral reefs with shipwrecks and great conditions for snorkeling: little or no current, warm waters and visibility up to 140ft.

Belize: Shark Ray Alley is ideal for snorkelers, in depths of only 6.5ft alongside harmless nurse sharks and rays.

St. Vincent and Grenadines: Bequia's **Friendship Bay** for swimming and snorkeling.

USVI: Buck Island Reef National Monument off St. Croix's northeast shore has an easy, marked trail for novice snorkelers. www.nps.gov/buis.

Travel Tip: Before you head out on a hike, look down at your feet. Depending on the trail and duration of your hike, you're not going to want to hike in flip flops. The number-one rule of hiking is to wear good shoes. One bad blister and you're done for the day or even the trip. Why not invest in a good pair of walking shoes or hiking boots? And be sure to break them in.

ASK PETER...

Q: What Does Duty-Free Mean?
A: "Duty-free" means that the store owner doesn't pay duties when importing merchandise to sell in his store. However the owner is not required by law to pass that savings on to customers—some do; some don't. Before you go, research the cost of jewelry, electronics, linens, liquor and other merchandise you're interested in purchasing, so you can compare prices in the islands. The term "duty-free" can be misleading and is not always a good deal in terms of price or ease of return.

Windsurfing
Dominican Republic: Playa Cabarete is a windsurfing hangout. Windsurfing lessons are available at Carib BIC Center www.caribwind.com.

Kiteboarding
St. Barts: This fairly new sport is big on St. Barts, especially off the shores of Hotel Guanahani. www.leguanahani.com.
Aruba: Hadicurari Beach, site of an annual competition.

Yoga
Bahamas: Sivananda Ashram Yoga Retreat on Paradise Island www.sivanandabahamas.org.
Tobago: Kariwak Village Holistic Haven www.kariwak.com offers tai chi, Hatha yoga or Buddhist meditation.
USVI: The Self Centre at Caneel Bay on St. John offers sessions in Thai yoga therapy. www.caneelbay.com.

Zip-lining
Dominica: Rainforest Aerial Tram has a 90min canopy ride www.rainforestadventure.com.
Jamaica: Chukka Caribbean Adventures www.chukkacaribbean.com offers zip-line rides, as does YS Falls www.ysfalls.com.
Puerto Rico: Zip-line tours with Explorer Adventure PR, Inc www. exapr.com. Toro Verde Nature Adventure Park in Orocovis ℘787-867-6606 or www.toroverdepr.com.

Spectator Sports
Baseball
Cuba: The biggest match is between Industriales of Havana and Santiago de Cuba. Hotels can arrange tickets for games. For schedules, check www.baseballdecuba.com.
Dominican Republic: Dominicans have a history of producing world-renowned baseball players. Hotels can arrange tickets for games. Schedules can be found at www.lidom.com.do.
Cricket
Official schedule of the West Indies cricket team (known as "the Windies") and ticket information at www.windiescricket.com.
Antigua: To see a match, contact Antigua Cricket Association in St. John's ℘268-462-9089.
Barbados: The Kensington Oval is a historic cricket ground that hosts matches. Stadium ticket office ℘246-274-1109.
Croquet
Saba: Games on Sunday afternoons, with white-attired players, are played outside the Harry L. Johnson Museum. Check with the tourism office for times ℘599-416-2231.

Horse races
Barbados: The Barbados Turf Club hosts races on various Saturdays during the year. www.barbadosturfclub.org.
Jamaica: Caymanas Park in St. Catherine hosts about 80 races per year.
Nevis: Indian Castle Race Track, Gingerland, has races one Sunday a month. www.ntajc.com.

Activities for Kids
Adventures
Bahamas: Atlantis Resort's Discovery Channel Camp for children ages 4-12. www.atlantis.com.

Animals
Bahamas: Ardastra Gardens and Zoo features Caribbean flamingos, monkeys, reptiles. www.ardastra.com.
Belize: Belize Zoo has more than 150 animals, including jaguars, in open spaces. www.belizezoo.org.
Cayman Islands: Hand-feed stringrays at Stringray Sandbar on Grand Cayman's North Sound; your hotel can book a tour for you. Cayman Turtle Farm has turtles on view. www.turtle.ky.
Curaçao: Curaçao Sea Aquarium lets children feed sea turtles, dolphins, nurse-shark pups and many other sea creatures. www.curacao-sea-aquarium.com. The Curaçao Ostrich and Game Farm in Groot St. Joris West has more than 500 ostriches and baby chicks, as well as a kids' menu at the on-site restaurant.
Jamaica: See iguanas, eels and turtles at Dolphin Cove. www.dolphincovejamaica.com. Feed birds at Rocklands Bird Feeding Station near Anchovy, south of Montego Bay. ☏876-952-2009.
Turks and Caicos: Conch World offers tours of conch farming in Grand Turk and Providenciales. www.conchworld.com.

Classes and lessons
USVI: Caneel Bay Resort on St. John offers children's classes in island drumming at The Self Centre. www.caneelbay.com.

Museums
Bahamas: Pirates of Nassau Museum will entertain kids of all ages. www.pirates-of-nassau.com
Puerto Rico: Arecibo Observatory (www.naic.edu), west of San Juan, has the world's largest radio telescope. Old San Juan has the Children's Museum (Museo del Niño). ☏787-722-3791.
Saint-Martin: The Butterfly Farm in Quartier d'Orléans has caterpillars and exotic winged creatures. www.thebutterfly-farm.com.

Calendar of Events

Below is a selection of the Caribbean's most popular annual events. Dates may vary. For details, contact the Caribbean Tourism Organization (*US & Canada:* ℘ *212-635-9530, www.caribbean travel.com; UK:* ℘ *0208-948-0057, www.caribbean.co.uk*).

January

Spice Island Billfish Tournament
3-day fishing tournament with cash prizes.
℘473-435-3842; www.sibtgrenada.com
Grenada Yacht Club, Marina St. George's, Grenada

Jamaica Jazz & Blues Festival
3-day festival with local and international acts.
℘876-929-9200; www.jamaicajazzandblues.com
Trelawny, Jamaica

St-Barths Music Festival
Fortnight of classical, opera, ballet and jazz.
℘650-464-7222; www.stbartsmusicfestival.org
Various locations, St-Barthélemy

February

Cartagena International Film Festival
Colombian and other Latin films in city venues.
℘575-664-2345; http://ficcifestival.com
Cartagena, Colombia

Holetown Festival
Week-long concerts and fairs to celebrate the First Settlement.
℘246-427-2623; www.visitbarbados.org
Holetown, Barbados

Aruba Carnival
Street parades and burning of "King Momo."
℘297-582-3777; www.aruba.com
San Nicolas and Oranjestad, Aruba

Dominica Carnival
Month's worth of events culminating in Ash Wednesday.
℘767-448-2045; www.dominicacarnival.com
Various locations, Dominica

Trinidad and Tobago Carnival
Most vibrant and energy-filled of Caribbean Carnivals.
℘868-627-1357; www.ncctt.org
Port of Spain, Trinidad

March

BVI Spring Regatta and Sailing Festival
4-day festival followed by a 3-day Regatta.

Travel Tip:

In Trinidad there are two seasons: Carnival and preparing for Carnival. To get with the party there, contact the National Carnival Commission to join one of the many bands that participate in the parade. You'll spend a few hundred dollars but you get a costume for the float and unlimited food and drinks during the two-day celebration. If you're going to celebrate Carnival in Trinidad, you may as well be a part of the festivities and not a spectator.

📞 284-541-6732; www.bvispringregatta.org
Nanny Cay Marina, Tortola, British Virgin Islands
La Ruta Maya Belize River Challenge
4-day canoe race San Ignacio to Belize City.
📞 501-824-3075 (fax); www.larutamayabelize.com
San Ignacio, Belize

April
Antigua Sailing Week
5-day regatta with participants from the world over.
📞 268-725-4692; www.sailingweek.com
St. John's, Antigua and Barbuda
Carriacou Maroon & String Band Music Festival
3 days of string bands, smoked food and dancing.
📞 473-443-7948; www.carriacoumaroon.com
Carriacou Island, Grenada
Roatán Carnival
April 12 commemoration of Garifuna people's arrival.
📞 504-222-2124; http://tourismroatan.com
Roatán, Honduras
Semana Santa (Holy Week)
Re-enactments and street processions for Easter.
📞 52-998-881-2745; http://cancun.travel/en
Cancún, Mexico
Sint Maarten Carnival
A fortnight of events with parade on April 30.
📞 599-522-0509; www.stmaartencarnival.net
Philipsburg, Sint Maarten

May
Gospelfest
8 days of performances by top international Gospel artists.
📞 246-426-5128; www.barbadosgospelfest.com
Various locations, Barbados
Soul Beach Music Festival
6-day festival with international acts.
📞 297-582-3777; www.soulbeach.net
Various locations, Aruba
St. Lucia Jazz Festival
A renowned annual festival mixing fusion jazz with R&B.
📞 758-452-4094; www.stluciajazz.org
Pigeon Island National Park, St. Lucia
St. Thomas Carnival
Month-long celebration culminating in Street Mas.
📞 800-372-8784; www.vicarnival.com
St. Thomas, US Virgin Islands

June

International Shrimp Festival
A 2-day music festival with reggaeton acts.
📞 504-96-60-96-63; www.roatanshrimpfest.com
Roatán, Honduras

Puerto Rico Heineken JazzFest
4-day festival with Latin, Brazilian and big-band jazz.
📞 787-294-0091; www.prheinekenjazz.com
San Juan, Puerto Rico

Saint-Martin Billfish Tournament
5-day tournament with dockside entertainment.
📞 590-690-61-63-30; www.billfish-tournament.com
Marigot Waterfront, Saint-Martin

Vincy Mas
Fortnight of events include Mardi Gras Parade of Bands.
📞 784-457-2580; www.carnivalsvg.com
Kingstown, St. Vincent

July

Crop Over Festival
5 weeks of steel-pan parades, art shows and performances.
📞 246-427-2623; www.barbadoscropoverfestival.com
Bridgetown, Barbados

Havana Carnival
Street parades with Afro-Cuban musical groups in Havana.
📞 1-416-362-0700, www.gocuba.ca (Canada)
📞 0207-240-6655, www.travel2cuba.co.uk (UK)

Reggae Sumfest
Week-long festival of reggae, ska, dub and dancehall music.
📞 876-953-2933; www.reggaesumfest.com
Montego Bay, Jamaica

Saba Carnival
Week-long Carnival with dancing, music and parades.
📞 599-416-2231; www.sabatourism.com; The Bottom, Saba

Santo Domingo Festival of Merengue
3-day festival with Latin merengue acts.
809-221-4660; www.godominicanrepublic.com
Santo Domingo, Dominican Republic

St. John Festival
Month's worth of events ending with July 4th Parade.
📞 800-372-8784; www.usvitourism.vi
Cruz Bay, St. John, US Virgin Islands

Tobago Heritage Festival
2-week festival celebrating Tobago's music and culture.
📞 868-639-5016; http://tobagoheritagefestival.com
Scarborough, Tobago

August
Anguilla Summer Festival
10-day Caribbean beach party, first Monday in August.
☎ 264-497-2759; www.axasummerfestival.com
Landsome Bowl in the Valley, Anguilla
Festival of Women Cooks
Parade of cooks with a feast Saturday closest to August 10.
☎ 590-590-82-09-30; www.lescuisinieresdelaguadeloupe.fr
Pointe-à-Pitre, Guadeloupe
International Costa Maya Festival
4 days of beauty pageants and musical acts from around
Central America.
☎ 501-227-2420; www.internationalcostamayafestival.com
San Pedro, Belize
Spicemas
5 weeks of Carnival events ending the first week of August.
☎ 473-435-2839; www.spicemasgrenada.com
Various locations, Grenada

September
Cayman Madness Fall Dive Events
6-week diving festival of treasure hunts and evening parties.
☎ 345-949-0623; www.divecayman.ky
George Town, Grand Cayman Island
Curaçao North Sea Jazz Festival
Dutch jazz festival over two nights.
☎ 599-9-522-2583; www.curacaonorthseajazz.com
Piscadera Bay, Curaçao
Grito de Dolores (Cry of Dolores)
Commemoration of Mexican independence.
☎ 52-998-881-2745; http://cancun.travel/en
Cancún, Mexico

October
Bonaire International Sailing Regatta and Festival
Windsurfing, fishing boat and microboat competitions
held over 3 days.
☎ 599-785-0333; www.bonaireregatta.org
Bay of Kralendijk, Bonaire
World Creole Music Festival
3-night festival with prominent Creole musicians.
☎ 767-448-4833; www.wcmfdominica.com
Roseau, Dominica

Travel Tip: Caribbean festivals are a ton of fun, but remember to stay alert in the crowds and keep your eyes open for pick pocketers. Only bring a limited amount of cash, one credit card and a copy of your passport—leave the real one at your hotel in a secure spot. Never keep all your valuables together in one purse or backpack. And avoid using a hip pouch, which is a sure sign that you're a tourist.

November
Day of the Dead
November 1st and 2nd bring performances, gatherings and famed calavera decorations.
𝒫 52-998-881-2745; www.dayofthedead.com
Cancún, Mexico
Martinique Jazz Festival
A biennial, two-week festival that attracts local and international jazz talent.
𝒫 0596-70-79-29; www.cmac.asso.fr
Island-wide, Martinique
Pirates Week
Cayman's national festival with 11 days of street parades and mock pirate invasions.
𝒫 345-949-5078; www.piratesweekfestival.com
George Town, Grand Cayman Island
Statia Day
Week of celebrations culminating on November 16.
𝒫 599-318-2433; www.statiatourism.com
Various locations, St. Eustatius
Turks and Caicos Conch Festival
Weekend of beach-side events and entertainment.
𝒫 649-331-6832; www.conchfestival.com
Providenciales, Turks and Caicos

December
Crucian Christmas Festival
Street parades, beauty pageants and fireworks.
𝒫 340-719-3379; www.stxfestival.com
St. Croix, U.S. Virgin Islands
Foxy's Old Year's Night
Renowned New Year's Eve party.
𝒫 284-495-9258; www.foxysbar.com
Jost Van Dyke, British Virgin Islands
Junkanoo Festival
Day street parade day after Christmas and New Year's Day
𝒫 246-427-2623; www.bahamas.com
Nassau, New Providence Island, The Bahamas
The Junkanoo Festival is also held in June and July in Nassau.
St. Kitts and Nevis National Carnival
Festivities culminate in a queen pageant December 27.
𝒫 869-467-1539; www.stkittsneviscarnival.com
Basseterre, St. Kitts and Nevis

Know Before You Go

Useful Websites (www.)

caribbeantravel.com Caribbean Tourism Organization
visitcentroamerica.com Central America Tourism Agency
colombiaespasion.com Colombia's official website
sectur.gob.mx Mexico Secretary of Tourism
http://travel.state.gov US Dept. of State's travel advisory

Tourism Offices

Contact these organizations to obtain maps and information.

Anguilla

Anguilla Tourist Board
Coronation Ave., The Valley, Anguilla, AI-2640
British West Indies
264-497-2759; http://ivisitanguilla.com
Canada & US 1-800-553-4939
UK 0207-736-6030

Antigua and Barbuda

Antigua & Barbuda Tourism Authority
ACB Financial Centre, High Street
St. John's, Antigua, West Indies
268-562-7600; www.antigua-barbuda.org
Canada 416-961-3085
UK 01245-707-471
US 1-888-268-4227

Aruba

Aruba Tourism Authority
L.G. Smith Blvd. 8
Eagle, Aruba
Dutch Caribbean
297-582-3777; www.aruba.com
Canada & US 1-800-862-7822
UK 0207-928-1600

Bahamas

The Bahamas Ministry of Tourism
George Street, Nassau, Bahamas
242-302-2000; www.bahamas.com
Canada & US 1-800-224-2627
UK 0207-355-0800

Barbados

Barbados Tourism Authority
Harbour Rd., Bridgetown, Barbados, West Indies
246-427-2623; www.visitbarbados.org
Canada & US 1-800-744-6244
UK 0207-299-7175

Travel Tip: On the subject of resources, check out my website, PeterGreenberg.com, which has up-to-the-minute travel news, travel videos, even more of my travel tips, and coverage of travel destinations beyond the Caribbean and all around the world. It's not just about travel destinations, but also about the process of travel.

Belize
Belize Tourism Board
64 Regent Street, Belize City, Belize
501-227-2420; www.travelbelize.org
Canada & US 1-800-624-0686
UK 0207-723-3603 (Belize High Commission in London)

Bonaire
Tourism Corporation Bonaire
Kaya Grandi #2, Kralendijk, Bonaire, Dutch Caribbean
599-717-8322; www.tourismbonaire.com
Canada & US 1-800-266-2473
Europe 0031-23-543-0705

British Virgin Islands
British Virgin Islands Tourist Board
De Castro Street, Road Town, Tortola VG1110, BVI
284-494-3134; www.bvitourism.com
Canada & US 1-800-835-8530
UK 0207-355-9585

Cayman Islands
Cayman Islands Department of Tourism
Grand Cayman, KY1-1102, Cayman Islands
345-949-0623; www.caymanislands.ky
Canada 1-800-263-5805
UK 0207-491-7771
US 1-877-422-9626

Colombia (Cartagena)
Muelle Turístico La Bodeguita Piso 2
Cartagena, Colombia
57-5-655-0211 (Cartagena Office); www.colombia.travel/en
Nearest Colombian Consulate or Embassy:
Canada 613-230-3760
UK 0207-927-7123
US 202-387-8338

Cuba
Cuba Tourist Board in Canada
1200 Bay Street, Suite 305, Toronto, ON. M5R 2A5
1-416-362-0700; www.gocuba.ca
Cuba Tourist Board in the UK
154 Shaftesbury Avenue, London WC2H 8HL, UK.
0207-240-6655; www.travel2cuba.co.uk

Curaçao
Curaçao Tourist Board
Pietermaai 19, Curaçao
5999-434-8200; www.curacao.com
Canada & US 1-800-328-7222
Europe 0031-10-414-2639

Dominica
Discover Dominica Authority
Financial Centre, Roseau, Commonwealth of Dominica
767-448-2045; www.dominica.dm
Canada & US 1-866-522-4057
UK 0207-928-1600

Dominican Republic
Ministry of Tourism of the Dominican Republic
Calle Cayetano Germosen, esquina avenida Gregorio
Luperón, Santo Domingo, Dominican Republic.
809-221-4660; www.godominicanrepublic.com
Canada 1-800-563-1611
UK 0207-242-7778
US 1-888-374-6361

Grenada
Grenada Board of Tourism
Burns Point, St. George's, Grenada, West Indies
473-440-2279; www.grenadagrenadines.com
Canada 416-595-1339
UK 0208-328-0650
US 1-800-972-9554

Guadeloupe
Tourist Board Council of the Guadeloupe Islands
5, square de la Banque, B.P. 555, 97166 Pointe-à-Pitre,
Guadeloupe cedex, FWI
590-590-82-09-30; www.go2guadeloupe.com
Canada & US 1-888-932-2582
Europe 033-14-296-7064

Honduras
Col. San Carlos, Edificio Europa, Apodo. Postal N° 3261
Tegucigalpa, Honduras
504-222-2124; www.letsgohonduras.com
Canada & US 1-800-410-9608
Europe 0034-91-571-6257

Jamaica
Jamaica Tourist Board
64 Knutsford Blvd., Kingston 5, Jamaica, West Indies
876-929-9200; www.visitjamaica.com
Canada 1-800-465-2624
UK 0207-225-9090
US 1-800-526-2422

Martinique
Le Comité Martiniquais du Tourisme
Immeuble "Le Beaupré," Pointe de Jaham, 97233 Schoelcher
596-596-61-6177; www.martinique.org
Canada 1-800-361-9099

UK 09068-244-123 (Maison de la France, London branch)
US 212-838-6887

Mexico

Consejo de Promoción Turística de México
Viaducto Miguel Aleman 105 Col. Escandón D.F. C.P 011800
México 52-78-4200; www.visitmexico.com
Canada & US 1-800-446-3942
Europe 00800-1111-2266

Puerto Rico

Puerto Rico Tourism Company
La Princesa Bldg. #2 Paseo La Princesa
San Juan, Puerto Rico, PR 00902
Canada & US 1-800-866-7827
UK 0207-367-0982
www.seepuertorico.com

Saba

Saba Tourist Bureau
Windwardside, Saba, Dutch Caribbean
599-416-2231; www.sabatourism.com
Canada & US 786-866-0480
UK 0207-539-7950 (Netherlands Tourism & Convention)

St-Barthélemy

Saint Barts Tourist Board Council
Rue Gén. de Gaulle 97133 St-Barthélemy
590-27-87-27; www.st-barths.com
Canada 514-288-2026 (Maison de la France)
UK 09068-244-123 (Maison de la France)
US 514-288-1904 (Maison de la France)

Sint Eustatius

Sint Eustatius Tourism Development Foundation
Fort Oranje, Oranjestad, Sint Eustatius, Netherlands Antilles
599-318-2433; www.statiatourism.com
Canada & US 786-866-0480
UK 0207-539-7950 (Netherlands Tourism & Convention)

St. Kitts and Nevis

St. Kitts Tourism Authority
Pelican Mall, Basseterre, St. Kitts
869-465-4040; www.stkittstourism.kn
Nevis Tourism Authority
Main Street, Charlestown, Nevis, W.I.
869-469-7550; www.nevisisland.com
Canada 416-368-6707
UK 0207-376-0881
US 1-800-582-6208

St. Lucia
St. Lucia Tourist Board
Sureline Building, Vide Bouteille, Castries, St. Lucia
758-452-4094; www.stlucia.org
Canada & US 1-800-456-3984
UK 0207-341-7000

Saint-Martin
Saint-Martin Tourism Office
Route de Sandy Ground, Marigot, 97150 Saint-Martin
590-590-87-57-21; www.stmartinisland.org
Canada & US 1-646-227-9440

Sint Maarten
Sint Maarten Tourist Bureau
Vineyard Office Park, WG Buncamper Road 33, Philipsburg,
Sint Maarten, Netherlands Antilles
599-542-2337; www.vacationstmaarten.com
Canada 514-288-8500
Europe 0031-71-5622002
US 516-594-4100

St. Vincent and the Grenadines
St. Vincent & The Grenadines Tourism Authority (SVGTA)
NIS Building, Upper Bay Street, Kingstown
St. Vincent and The Grenadines
784-456-6222; http://discoversvg.com
Canada 1-866-421-4452
UK 0207-937-6570
US 1-800-729-1726

Trinidad and Tobago
Tourism and Industrial Development Company Ltd.
Maritime Centre, 29 Tenth Avenue, Barataria
Trinidad, West Indies
868-675-7034; www.gotrinidadandtobago.com
Canada & US 1-800-816-7541
UK 0800-804-8787

Turks and Caicos
Turks and Caicos Tourist Board
Front St., Grand Turk, Turks and Caicos Islands, BWI
649-946-2321; www.turksandcaicostourism.com
Canada 1-866-413-8875
UK 0207-034-7845
US 1-800-241-0824

US Virgin Islands
USVI Division of Tourism; www.visitusvi.com
78-123 Estate Contant, Charlotte Amalie, USVI 00802
Canada 905-235-9091
UK 0208-948-0057 US 1-800-372-8784

International Visitors
Foreign Consulates
Foreign ministry websites provide up-to-date travel advice.
Canada: http://www.international.gc.ca
UK: http://www.fco.gov.uk   US: http://travel.state.gov
For after-hours emergencies, Canadian citizens are advised to call collect the **Emergency Operations Centre of the DFAIT at 613-996-8885 / 613-944-1310 (TTY), or toll free to Ottawa: 001-800-514-0129 (Mexico), 1-888-772-6448 (Puerto Rico), 1-866-600-0184 (US Virgin Islands)**. For consular help when you are at your destination, call or email the following contact points:

Anguilla
Canada (represented in Barbados): 246-629-3550; bdgtn@international.gc.ca; UK (Governor's Office): 264-497-2621; contactusanguilla@fco.gov.uk; US (represented in Barbados): 246-227-4399; BridgetownACS@state.gov

Antigua and Barbuda
Canada (represented in Barbados): 246-629-3550; bdgtn@international.gc.ca; UK (Honorary Consul): 268-561-5046; robert.wilkinson-honcon@fconet.fco.gov.uk; US (represented in Barbados): 246-227-4399; BridgetownACS@state.gov

Aruba
Canada (represented in Curaçao): 5999-466-1115 or 466-1121; joe.vandongen@mcb-bank.com; UK (represented in Curaçao): 5999-461-3900; britconcur@cura.net; US (represented in Curaçao): 5999-461-3066 or for after-hours emergency 5999-510-6870; ACSCuracao@state.gov

Bahamas
Canada (represented in Jamaica): 876-926-1500; kngtn@international.gc.ca; UK (represented in Jamaica): 876-936-0700; Kingston.Consular@fco.gov.uk; US: 242-328-3496 or for after-hours emergency 242-322-1181 ext. 9; ACSN@state.gov

Barbados
Canada: 246-629-3550; bdgtn@international.gc.ca; UK: 246-430-7800; ukinbarbados@fco.gov.uk; US: 246-227-4399; BridgetownACS@state.gov

Belize
Canada (Honorary Consul): 501-223-1060; cdncon.bze@btl.net UK: 501-822-2717; consular.belize@fco.gov.uk; US: 501-822-4011 after-hours emergency 501-610-5030; embbelize@state.gov

Bonaire

Canada (represented in Curaçao): 5999-466-1115 or 466-1121; joe.vandongen@mcb-bank.com; UK (represented in Curaçao): 5999-461-3900; britconcur@cura.net; US (represented in Curaçao): 5999-461-3066, after-hours emergency 5999-510-6870; ACSCuracao@state.gov

British Virgin Islands

Canada (represented in Barbados): 246-629-3550; bdgtn@international.gc.ca; UK (Governor's Office): 284-394-0009; govoffice.tortola@fco.gov.uk; US (represented in Barbados): 246-227-4399; BridgetownACS@state.gov

Cayman Islands

Canada (represented in Jamaica): 876-926-1500; kngtn@international.gc.ca; UK (Governor's Office): 345-925-4307; Melenie.Mylrea@fco.gov.uk; US: 345-945-817, after-hours emergency 876-702-6000; consagency@candw.ky

Colombia

Canada: 57-1-657-9800 (in Bogotá), 57-5-665-5838 (Honorary Consul in Cartagena); bgota@international.gc.ca; UK (Consulate in Cartagena): 57-5-664-7590; consulat.cartagena@fco.gov.uk; US (Consulate in Barranquilla): 5-353-2001/2182; ACSbogota@state.gov.

Cuba

Canada: 53-7-204-2516; havan@international.gc.ca; UK: 53-7-214-2200 or 53-7-204-1771; embrit@ceniai.inf.cu; US Interests Section: 53-7-833-3551(through to 3559), after-hours emergency 53-7-833-2302; havanaconsularinfo@state.gov

Curaçao

Canada: 5999-466-1115 or 466-1121; joe.vandongen@mcb-bank.com; UK: 5999-461-3900; britconcur@cura.net; US: 5999-461-3066, after-hours emergency 5999-510-6870; ACSCuracao@state.gov

Dominica

Canada (represented in Barbados): 246-629-3550; bdgtn@international.gc.ca; UK (Honorary Consul): 767-275-7800; justina.alexander-honcon@fconet.fco.gov.uk; US (represented in Barbados): 246-227-4399; BridgetownACS@state.gov

Dominican Republic

Canada: 809-262-3100 (Santo Domingo), 809-586-5761 (Puerto Plata), 809-455-1730 (Puerto Cana); sdmgo.consul@ international.gc.ca; UK: 809-472-7111 (Santo Domingo), 829-726-0757 (Puerto Plata), 829-726-0750 (Punta Cana); brit.emb. sadom@codetel.net.do; US: 809-221-2171 (Santo Domingo); 809-586-8017 (Puerto Plata), conspplata@codetel.net.do

Grenada

Canada (represented in Barbados): 246-629-3550; bdgtn@ international.gc.ca; UK (Honorary Consul): 473-405-8072; ukinbarbados@fco.gov.uk; US: 473-444-1173/4/5; usemb_gd@spiceisle.com

Guadeloupe

Canada (represented in Barbados): 246-629-3550; bdgtn@ international.gc.ca; UK (Honorary Consul): 590-590-825-757; public.paris@fco.gov.uk; US (represented in Barbados): 246-227-4399; BridgetownACS@state.gov

Honduras

Canada (in Tegucigalpa): 504-2232-4551; tglpa@international. gc.ca; UK (Honorary Consul in Roatan): 504-2455-7568; Matthew.JohnHarper-HonCon@fconet.fco.gov.uk; US (in Tegucigalpa): 504-2236-9320; usahonduras@state.gov

Jamaica

Canada: 876-926-1500; kngtn@international.gc.ca; UK: 876-936-0700; Kingston.Consular@fco.gov.uk; US: 876-702-6450, after-hours emergency 876-702-6000; kingstonacs@state.gov

Martinique

Canada (represented in Barbados): 246-629-3550; bdgtn@ international.gc.ca; UK (represented in Paris): 0033-144-51-31-00; public.paris@fco.gov.uk; US (represented in Barbados): 246-227-4399; BridgetownACS@state.gov

Mexico

Canada (Mexico City): 01-55-5724-7900; mxico@international. gc.ca; UK (Honorary Consul in Cancun): 52-998-881-0100; consular.mexico@fco.gov.uk; US (Consulate in Merida): 01-999-942-5700; meridacons@state.gov

Puerto Rico

Canada: 787-759-6629; miami-td@international.gc.ca
UK: 787-850-2400; http://ukinusa.fco.gov.uk/miami

Saba
Canada (represented in Curaçao) 5999-466-1115 or 466-1121; joe.vandongen@mcb-bank.com; UK (represented in Curaçao): 5999-461-3900; britconcur@cura.net; US (represented in Curaçao): 5999-461-3066, after-hours emergency 5999-510-6870; ACSCuracao@state.gov

St-Barthélemy
Canada (represented in Barbados): 246-629-3550; bdgtn@international.gc.ca; UK (represented in Paris): 0033-144-51-31-00; public.paris@fco.gov.uk; US (represented in Barbados): 246-227-4399; BridgetownACS@state.gov

Sint Eustatius
Canada (represented in Curaçao) 5999-466-1115; joe.vandongen@mcb-bank.com; UK (represented in Curaçao): 5999-461-3900; britconcur@cura.net; US (represented in Curaçao): 5999-461-3066, after-hours emergency 5999-510-6870; ACSCuracao@state.gov

St. Kitts and Nevis
Canada (represented in Barbados): 246-629-3550; bdgtn@international.gc.ca; UK (Honorary Consul): 869-764-4677; Sarah.Percival-HonCon@fconet.fco.gov.uk; US (represented in Barbados): 246-227-4399; BridgetownACS@state.gov

St. Lucia
Canada (represented in Barbados): 246-629-3550; bdgtn@international.gc.ca; UK: 758-452-2484/5; britishhc@candw.lc; US (represented in Barbados): 246-227-4399; BridgetownACS@state.gov

Saint-Martin
Canada (represented in Barbados): 246-629-3550; bdgtn@international.gc.ca; UK (represented in Paris): 0033-144-51-31-00; public.paris@fco.gov.uk; US (represented in Barbados): 246-227-4399; BridgetownACS@state.gov

Sint Maarten
Canada (represented in Barbados): 246-629-3550; bdgtn@international.gc.ca; UK (represented in Curaçao): 5999-461-3900; britconcur@cura.net; US (represented in Curaçao): 5999-461-3066, after-hours emergency 5999-510-6870; ACSCuracao@state.gov

St. Vincent and the Grenadines

Canada (represented in Barbados): 246-629-3550; bdgtn@
international.gc.ca; UK (Honorary Consul): 784-457-6860;
donald.browne-honcon@fconet.fco.gov.uk; US (represented
in Barbados): 246-227-4399; BridgetownACS@state.gov

Trinidad and Tobago

Canada (in Port of Spain, Trinidad): 868-622-6232; pspan@
international.gc.ca; UK (in Port of Spain, Trinidad): 868-350-
0444; ConsularEnquiries.tnt@fco.gov.uk; US (in Port of Spain,
Trinidad): 868-622-6371; acspos@state.gov

Turks and Caicos

Canada (represented in Jamaica): 876-926-1500; kngtn@
international.gc.ca; UK (Governor's Office): 649-946-2309;
governorgt@fco.gov.uk; US (represented in the Bahamas):
242-328-3496, after-hours emergency 242-322-1181 ext. 9;
ACSN@state.gov

US Virgin Islands

Canada (represented in Miami): 305-579-1600, miami@
international.gc.ca; UK (represented in Puerto Rico): 787-850-
2400; http://ukinusa.fco.gov.uk/miami

Entry requirements

Before you travel, contact your destination's tourist office for
entry requirements. Information is also available from the **Caribbean Tourism Organization**, 80 Broad St., Suite 3200, New
York, NY 10004; 212-635-9530; www.caribbeantravel.com.

Tourists must hold a **valid passport** (with a minimum validity
of normally six months prior to entry) to enter destinations in
the Caribbean. Visas are not normally required, but an onward
or return transportation ticket is mandatory, along with pre-
booked accommodations. A stay of more than 30 days in Belize
may require a **visa**; consult a Belizean consulate.

Travelers to Cuba must have a valid passport, and a **tourist card**
available from the nearest Cuban consulate or through tour operators. The Cuban government allows US citizens to visit, but
the US prohibits American citizens from spending money (in
any currency) relating to Cuban travel unless they are licensed
by the US Department of the Treasury **Office of Foreign Assets Control**, or are Cuban Americans with close relatives in
Cuba. For information, access www.treasury.gov.

All visitors to Mexico who plan to remain more than 72 hours
require a **tourist card**, available from Mexican government
tourist offices, travel agents and airline companies.

US citizens only need show a valid government photo ID to enter the US Virgin Islands or Puerto Rico.

British and Canadian tourists to the Dominican Republic require a **tourist card**, available from the nearest Dominican Consulate or upon arrival at the airport. British travelers to Puerto Rico or the US Virgin Islands may enter under the Visa Waiver Program via the Electronic System for Travel Authorization (*https://esta. cbp.dhs.gov*) at least 72hrs prior to their journey. Canadian travelers to Puerto Rico or US Virgin Islands must hold a valid passport or be a NEXUS card holder (*http://www.getnexus.com*).

Several countries collect an **exit tax** payable in cash at the airport, and in some cases at the port, upon your departure. Insure that you have sufficient funds for this tax when departing.

Customs

Check in advance with the tourist office of your destination for items you can bring into the Caribbean for personal use. Regarding tortoise-shell jewelry or other articles made from threatened or endangered animal species (whalebone or ivory, skins or fur), contact the US Fish and Wildlife Service (*www.fws. gov; 1-800-344-9453*). Keep **receipts** for all purchases.

Travelers to countries in the **Caribbean Basin Initiative** (CBI) generally have a $600 duty-free exemption on their return to the US (CBI countries included in this guide: Antigua and Barbuda, Aruba, the Bahamas, Barbados, Belize, British Virgin Islands, Dominica, Grenada, Jamaica, Netherlands Antilles, St. Kitts and Nevis, St. Lucia, St. Vincent and the Grenadines, Trinidad and Tobago). For US citizens returning from the US Virgin Islands, the duty-free exemption is $1,600. For information on what you can bring back to the US, contact US Customs Service (*1-877-227-5511; www.cbp.gov*). For Canadian citizens who have been out of Canada a minimum 7 days, the Canada Border Services Agency (*1-800-461-9999; www.cbsa.gc.ca*) allows a duty-free limit of $750 Canadian dollars. In the UK, travelers are allowed to bring in goods worth up to £270 from non-EU countries before tax and duty applies. HM Revenue & Customs (*0845-010-9000; www.hmrc.gov.uk*) publishes *A Guide for Travellers,* which lists customs regulations and duty free allowances.

Health

All travelers should have comprehensive travel insurance before departure. While no **vaccinations** are required to enter most of the countries, you should ensure that yours are up-to-date before traveling. For Cuba, health insurance, with provision for emergency repatriation, is compulsory for all visitors, who must carry **proof of health insurance**, or face fines. For infor-

Travel Tip: Here's something to consider before jumping into a hotel pool. Even crystal-clear waters can be deceptive. Bacteria that can cause diarrhea can live for several days even in chlorinated waters. There was even a study that showed that you may want to avoid moonlight dips—bacteria levels seem to rise during full moons, presumably because lunar tides are churning up the waters.

mation on recommended vaccinations and diseases that may be encountered, check the page for your respective destination on the website of the Center for Disease Control (*www.cdc.gov*). Malaria is present in some areas of Belize below 400m/1,312ft. All prescription drugs should be clearly labeled; it is recommended that you carry a copy of the prescription and always pack urgent medications in your carry-on baggage. In addition, don't assume that medications available in the US, UK or Canada will be as easy to obtain in the Caribbean.

HEALTH PRECAUTIONS

Nothing can derail a trip faster than a health crisis. Emergencies happen, but the key is to prepare yourself before you even leave the house. Most traditional health insurance plans won't work outside the US. In Cuba, it's actually a requirement that visitors have health insurance with provision for emergency repatriation. The good news: A growing number of comprehensive travel insurance policies include medical coverage.

It's up to you to ask the tough questions: If you get sick or injured on the road, it's not always wise to get treated in the nearest facility. Does the policy include medical evacuation and repatriation? Will you be transported to the hospital or clinic of your choice, or theirs? Do they have English-speaking employees on the ground to vet medical facilities and be your advocate?

If you're traveling to a country with endemic diseases, like yellow fever in Trinidad and Tobago, have a travel medicine doctor vet your itinerary at least 4 to 6 weeks before your trip. Carry prescription medication in the original bottles, and get prescriptions for both the brand name and the generic name of the medication, in case you need an emergency refill. Bring along a small first-aid kit that includes: alcohol-based antibacterial hand gel, a topical antibiotic, hydrocortisone cream, pain relievers, antacids, an antihistamine, and anti-diarrhea medication.

Mosquito-born diseases like dengue fever are endemic to parts of the Caribbean, so pack an insect repellent with at least 30 percent DEET. And last, but certainly not least, carry a laminated copy of all your emergency contacts—including your primary healthcare provider—and list current medical conditions.

Accessibility

Except for major international hotel chains, businesses and attractions in the Caribbean have little or no accommodations for disabled travelers. Puerto Rico and the US Virgin Islands are the exception, since they must adhere to US federal law regarding access for the disabled. National parks in Puerto Rico and the US Virgin Islands have facilities for the disabled. For more information, check the National Park Service website (*www.nps.gov*).

Getting There

By Airplane

The majority of flights from the US to the Caribbean depart from Atlanta, Georgia; Charlotte, North Carolina; and Miami, Florida, often with a transfer in San Juan, Puerto Rico.

Major Caribbean airports

The following chart excludes chartered flights. Thomson Airways is the British arm of TUI Group and is a charter airline, but the routes listed here are scheduled services.

Airport	from Canada	from UK	from US
Anguilla Clayton Lloyd Int'l Airport (AXA) www.gov.ai/airport.php; 264-497-3510		from Antigua, LIAT	from San Juan, Cape Air
Antigua and Barbuda V.C. Bird Int'l (ANU), St. John's www.antigua-barbuda.org/Agtsp01.htm; 268-462-0358	Air Canada	British Airways Virgin Atlantic	American Airlines Delta Air Lines United Airlines US Airways
Aruba Queen/Reina Beatrix Int'l Airport (AUA) Oranjestad www.airportaruba.com; 297-524-2424	Air Canada Sunwing Airlines	Thomson Airways	AirTran Airways American Airlines Delta Air Lines JetBlue Airways Spirit Airlines United Airlines US Airways
Bahamas Lynden Pindling Int'l Airport (NAS) www.nas.bs; 242-702-1010 Grand Bahama Int'l Airport (FPO) www.freeportcontainerport.com; 242-350-8000	Air Canada Sunwing Airlines	British Airways	American Airlines AirTran Airways Delta Air Lines JetBlue Airways Spirit Airlines United Airlines US Airways

Barbados Grantley Adams Int'l Airport (BGI) Bridgetown www.barbados.org; 246-428-7101	Air Canada	British Airways Thomson Airways Virgin Atlantic	American Airlines JetBlue Airways US Airways
Belize Philip S. W. Goldson International Airport (BZE) Belize City; www.pgiabelize.com; 501-225-2045	American Airlines		American Airlines Delta Air Lines United Airlines US Airways
Bonaire Flamingo International Airport (BON) www.bonaireinternationalairport.com; 599-717-5600			Delta Air Lines United Airlines
British Virgin Islands Terrence B. Lettsome International Airport (EIS),Tortola www.bvitouristboard.com; 284-494-3701	from Barbados, BVI Airways	from San Juan, Air Sunshine, Cape Air	
Cayman Islands Owen Roberts Int'l Airport (GCM) Grand Cayman Gerrard Smith Int'l Airport (CYB) Cayman Brac www.caymanislands.ky; 345-949-7811	Air Canada	British Airways	American Airlines Delta Air Lines United Airlines US Airways
Colombia Rafael Núñez Int'l Airport (CTG) Crespo, Cartagena www.sacsa.com.co; 57-5-656-9200	Air Transat		Spirit Airlines
Cuba José Martí International Airport (HAV); 537-266-4644	Air Canada Air Transat Sunwing Airlines	Thomson Airways Virgin Atlantic	
Curaçao Curaçao Int'l Airport (CUR) Willemstad www.curacao-airport.com; 5999-839-1000	Air Canada		American Airlines United Airlines
Dominica Canefield Airport (DCF), Roseau Melville Hall Airport (DOM), near Marigot www.ndcdominica.dm; 767-449-1199	from Barbados, LIAT, BVI Airways	from San Juan, LIAT American Eagle	
Dominican Republic Las Américas International Airport (SDQ) www.aerodom.com/app/do/lasamericas.aspx. 809-947 -2225; Punta Caucedo, 24km/15mi E of Santo Domingo Gregorio Luperón International Airport (POP) Puerto Plata; 809-291-0000. www.aerodom.com/ app/do/aeropuertos__puertoplata.aspx	Air Canada Air Transat Sunwing Airlines	British Airways Thomson Airways	American Airlines AirTran Airways Delta Air Lines JetBlue Airways LAN Airlines PAWA Dominicana Spirit Airlines United Airlines US Airways

Grenada Maurice Bishop Int'l Airport (GND) St. George's www.mbiagrenada.com; 473-444-4555	Air Canada	British Airways Virgin Atlantic	American Airlines Delta Air Lines
Guadeloupe Point-à-Pitre Le Raizet Int'l Airport (PTP) Point-à-Pitre www.guadeloupe.aeroport.fr; 590-21-71-71	Air Canada		
Honduras (Roatán) Juan Manuel Gálvez Int'l Airport (RTB)	Sunwing Airlines		Delta Air Lines United Airlines
Jamaica Norman Manley Int'l Airport (KIN), Kingston www.nmia.aero; 876-924-8452-6 Sangster International Airport (MBJ), Montego Bay www.mbjairport.com; 876-952-3124	Air Canada Air Transat American Airlines Sunwing Airlines	British Airways Thomson Airways Virgin Atlantic	American Airlines AirTran Airways Delta Air Lines JetBlue Airways Spirit Airlines United Airlines US Airways
Martinique Int'l Lamentin Airport (FDF), Lamentin www.martinique.org/transportation.htm 596-42-16-00	Air Canada		
Mexico (Yucatán) Cancún Int'l Airport (CUN), Cancún. www.cancun-airport.com; 52-998-848-7200	Air Canada Air Transat American Airlines Sunwing Airlines	British Airways Thomson Airways Virgin Atlantic	American Airlines AirTran Airways Delta Air Lines Spirit Airlines JetBlue Airways United Airlines US Airways Virgin America
Puerto Rico Luis Muñoz Marín Int'l Airport (SJU), San Juan Rafael Hernandez http://welcome.topuertorico.org/tinfo.shtml; 787-319-9262	Air Canada Sunwing Airlines	British Airways	American Airlines AirTran Airways Delta Air Lines JetBlue Airways Spirit Airlines United Airlines US Airways
Saba Juancho E. Yrausquin Airport, Flat Point www.sabatourism.com/gettosaba.html 599-4-62255	from Sint Maaten, Winair	from Sint Maaten, Winair	
St-Barthélemy Aéroport de St-Barthélemy (SBH) Bale de St. Jean www.st-barths.com; 590-27-65-41	from Sint Maaten, Winair	from Sint Maaten, Winair	
Sint Eustatius Franklin D. Roosevelt Airport (EUX) Concordia. www.statiatourism.com; 599-318-288	from Sint Maaten, Winair	from Sint Maaten, Winair	

St. Kitts and Nevis Robert L. Bradshaw Int'l Airport (SKB) Basseterre, St. Kitts www.stkitts-tourism.com/DiscoverSK/Airlines.asp 869-465-8972 Newcastle Airport (NEV)Newcastle, Nevis 869-469-9040	Air Canada American Airlines	British Airways	American Airlines Delta Air Lines US Airways
St. Lucia Hewanorra Int'l Airport (UVF), Vieux Fort www.slaspa.com; 758-454-6355 George F. L. Charles Airport (SLU), Castries 758-452-1156	Air Canada Air Transat Sunwing Airlines	British Airways Virgin Atlantic	American Airlines Delta Air Lines JetBlue Airways US Airways
Saint-Martin and Sint Maarten Princess Juliana Int'l Airport (SXM) Philipsburg, Sint Maarten www.pjiae.com; 599-546-7542	Air Canada Air Transat		American Airlines Delta Air Lines JetBlue Airways Spirit Airlines United Airlines US Airways
St. Vincent and the Grenadines E. T. Joshua Airport (SVD) Arnos Vale, St. Vincent http://discoversvg.com; 784-458-4685	from Barbados, LIAT	from San Juan, LIAT	
Trinidad and Tobago Piarco Int'l Airport (POS) Port of Spain, Trinidad. www.tntairports.com; 868-669-4868 A.N.R. Robinson Int'l Airport (TAB) Crown Point, Tobago www.tntairports.com; 868-639-8547	British Airways	Virgin Atlantic	American Airlines United Airlines
Turks and Caicos Islands Providenciales Int'l Airport (PLS) Providenciales. www.visitprovidenciales.com; 649-946-4420	Air Canada	British Airways	American Airlines Delta Air Lines JetBlue Airways United Airlines US Airways
US Virgin Islands Cyril E. King International (STT) 4mi/6km E of Charlotte Amalie, St. Thomas Henry E. Rohlsen Airport (STX) 9mi/14km SW of Christiansted, St. Croix			American Airlines Delta Air Lines Spirit Airlines United Airlines US Airways

Airlines serving the Caribbean

Aerocaribbean
www.fly-aerocaribbean.com
Aerogaviota
*www.aerogaviota.com(in
Spanish)*
Aerolíneas Mas
*http://aerolineasmas.com
(in Spanish)*
Aeroméxico
www.aeromexico.com
Air Antilles Express
www.flyairantilles.com
Air Canada
www.aircanada.com
Air Caraïbes
www.aircaraibes-usa.com
Air France
www.airfrance.com
Air Jamaica
www.airjamaica.com
Air Sunshine
www.airsunshine.com
AirTran Airways
www.airtran.com
Air Transat
www.airtransat.com
Air Turks and Caicos
www.flyairtc.com
American Airlines
www.aa.com
Aserca Airlines
*www.asercaairlines.com (in
Spanish)*
Avianca
www.avianca.com
Bahamasair
http://bahamasair.com
British Airways
www.ba.com
BVI Airways
www.gobvi.com
Caribbean Airlines
www.caribbean-airlines.com
Cape Air
www.flycapeair.com
Cayman Airways
www.caymanairways.com

Conviasa
*www.conviasa.aero (in
Spanish)*
Corsairfly
www.corsairfly.com
Cubana
www.cubana.cu
Delta Air Lines
www.delta.com
Direct Air
www.visitdirectair.com
Divi Divi Air
www.flydivi.com
Dutch Antilles Express
http://flydae.com
E-Liner Airways
www.e-liner.net
Frontier Airlines
www.frontierairlines.com
Insel Air
www.fly-inselair.com
JetBlue Airways
www.jetblue.com
KLM
www.klm.com
LAN Airlines
www.lan.com
LIAT (Leeward Islands Air
Transport)
www.liatairline.com
Maya Island Air
www.mayaislandair.com
Mustique Airways
www.mustique.com
PAWA Dominicana
www.pawad.com.do
REDjet
www.flyredjet.com
Seaborne Airlines
www.seaborneairlines.com
St. Barth Commuter
www.stbarthcommuter.com
Spirit Airlines
www.spirit.com
Sun Country Airlines
www.suncountry.com

Sunwing Airlines
   www.flysunwing.com
Surinam Airways
   www.slm.firm.sr
SVG Air
   www.svgair.com
TACA Airlines
   www.taca.com
Tiara Air
   www.tiara-air.com
Thomson Airways
   www.thomsonfly.com
United Airlines
   www.united.com
US Airways
   www.usairways.com

USA3000 Airlines
   www.usa3000.com
Virgin Atlantic
   www.virgin-atlantic.com
Virgin America
   www.virginamerica.com
Vision Airlines
   www.visionairlines.com
WestJet
   www.westjet.com
Western Air
   www.westernairbahamas.com
Winair
   www.fly-winair.com

By Cruise Ship

The following English-speaking cruise lines operate in the Carib bean. For additional information, visit Cruise Lines Internation Assn. at: www.cruising.org. Departure cities shown below in the U include Galveston, Texas; Miami, Florida; Port Canaveral, Florida. the Caribbean: San Juan, Puerto Rico and Bridgetown, Barbados.

Azamara Club Cruises

A premium boutique branch of Royal Caribbean Cruises wit an emphasis on overnight port stays and multi-day excursior Azamara operates one- and two-week cruises, departing M ami, San Juan or Bridgetown Nov-Mar. Gratuities are include *Canada & US 1-877-999-9553. UK 0800-018-2525. www.azamar clubcruises.com*

Carnival Cruise Lines

The world's most popular cruise line serving 4 million pa sengers per year (est. 2011), Carnival is known for Las Vega style entertainment and amenities. One-week cruises depa several locations year-round, including Galveston, San Jua Bridgetown and Florida. *Canada & US 1-800-764-7419. UK 084 351-0556. www.carnival.com*

Celebration Cruise Line

Celebration offers a 2-day budget cruise and shore excursior in the Bahamas, departing every other day throughout the ye from Palm Beach, Florida. *Canada & US 1-800-314-7735. www bahamaships.com*

Celebrity Cruises

A premium subsidiary of Royal Caribbean International with upscale dining and passenger service, Celebrity offers one-to two-week cruises departing various US locations such as Bayonne (New Jersey), Fort Lauderdale, Miami as well as San Juan Dec-Apr. Beverage packages available on non-chartered sailings. *Canada & US 1-800-647-2251. UK 0844-493-2043. www.celebritycruises.com*

Costa Cruises

Offering a full complement of North American-style services with an Italian flavor, this line operates various cruises in the Caribbean, departing Savona, Italy, La Romana, Dominican Republic, or Miami Nov-Apr. Service charges are added at the end of the cruise. *Canada & US 1-800-462-6782. UK 0845-351-0552. www.costacruise.com*

Cruise and Maritime Voyages

This British-based company offers a 45-night, traditional-style cruise departing London's Port of Tilbury every January. The route includes Portugal's Azores and Brazil's Amazon coast before visiting Grenada, Barbados, St. Lucia and Antigua. Onboard currency is British sterling. *UK 0845-430-0274. www.cruiseandmaritime.com*

Crystal Cruises

Japanese-owned luxury line offers fortnight cruises departing Los Angeles, New York, Miami, Costa Rica, Buenos Aires or Barcelona Oct-Mar. All-inclusive bookings available. Canada & US 1-888-722-0021. UK 0207-287-9040. www.crystalcruises.com

Cunard Line

This prestigious line operates the Queen Elizabeth, Queen Victoria and Queen Mary 2. Two- to three-week cruises depart New York, Los Angeles (via the Panama Canal) or Fort Lauderdale. One-month cruises depart Southampton, England. Cruises run Nov-Feb. *Canada & US 0-800-728-6273. UK 0845-678-0013. www.cunard.com*

Disney Cruise Line

Catering to families, Disney offers 6- to 8-night cruises around the Western and Eastern Caribbean departing Port Canaveral and Galveston. Supervised activity centers, live shows and Disney characters keep young ones entertained, while adults enjoy spas, whirlpools and cocktail lounges. *Canada & US 1-888-325-2500. UK 0800-028-3179. www.disneycruise.com*

Travel Tip: When
the cruise ship docks
for the day, instead
of being trapped
into some package
excursion, you can
be ahead of the
game, and save up
to 50 percent if you
book in advance
with an independent
company. In the
Cayman Islands, you
can arrange your
own snorkeling,
horseback riding and
other excursions.
Look for independent
companies online,
then vet them by
confirming their
license and insurance
are up to date and
finding out whether
there have been
any recent safety
violations.

Fred Olsen Cruise Lines

Operating smaller ships with a decidedly British atmosphere,
Fred Olsen offers cruises of two to six weeks departing Southampton and Dover, England; Bridgetown, Barbados; or Montego Bay, Jamaica, Nov-Apr. On-board currency is British sterling.
*Canada 1-866-760-1987. UK 01473-746-175. US 1-800-843-0602.
www.fredolsencruises.com*

Holland America Line

This line operates traditional-style cruises on smaller ships
departing Fort Lauderdale and Tampa, Florida; Southampton,
England; and Rotterdam, The Netherlands, Oct-Apr. *Canada &
US 800-577-1728. UK 0845-351-0557. www.hollandamerica.com*

MSC Cruises

This Italian-style cruise line offers 4-day to 14-day cruises departing Port Everglades, Florida, Nov-Mar. *Canada & US 1-877-
665-4655. UK 0844-561-7412. www.msccruises.com*

Norwegian Cruise Line

A pioneer of free-style cruising with informal dining options and
a wealth of evening entertainment, Norwegian offers 7-night to
14-night cruises departing New York; New Orleans, Louisiana;
Port Canaveral and Tampa, Florida Oct-Apr. *Canada & US 800-
327-7030. UK 0845-201-8900. www.ncl.com*

Oceania Cruises

A luxury line known for itineraries aimed at discerning travelers,
Oceania offers cruises departing New York, Miami and Los Angeles Nov-Mar. Caribbean cruises via the Panama Canal depart
San Francisco, California and Lima, Peru in May. *Canada & US
800-531-5658. UK 01344-772-334. www.oceaniacruises.com*

P&O Cruises

Britain's leading line catering to a variety of budgets and tastes
offers 11-night to 35-night cruises departing Southampton and
Barbados Sept-Apr. *Canada & US 1-877-828-4766. UK 0845-678-
0014. www.pocruises.com*

Princess Cruises

Offering liberal dining times and a variety of adult entertainment, Princess operates one- to three-week cruises around the
Caribbean departing Fort Lauderdale, Los Angeles, Galveston,
New York and San Juan. *Canada & US 800-774-6237. UK 0845-
075-0031. www.princess.com*

Regent Seven Seas Cruises
A luxury line featuring cocktail parties, performances of opera and talks by notable scientists, Regent offers all-inclusive packages on cruises departing Fort Lauderdale, Miami and San Francisco Oct-Apr. *Canada & US 877-505-5370. UK 02380-682-280. www.rssc.com*

Royal Caribbean International
Offering a wealth of onboard entertainment and activities as well as shore excursions, Royal's gargantuan ships depart various locations including New York, Florida, San Juan and Cartagena, Colombia Oct-Apr. *Canada & US 800-327-6700. UK 0844-493-4005. www.royalcaribbean.com*

Saga
Focusing on travelers over the age of 50, this British tour company offers 4- and 5-week cruises departing Southampton. Two-week cruises depart Bridgetown, Barbados; Havana, Cuba; and Caldera, Costa Rica; Charter flights are provided from London's Gatwick Airport. *UK 0800-096-0078. http://travel.saga.co.uk*

Seabourn Cruise Line
This luxury small-ship line offers 2- to 18-day cruises departing Fort Lauderdale, Philipsburg (Sint Maarten), Charlotte Amalie (St. Thomas, US Virgin Islands) and Bridgetown Nov-Mar. *Canada & US 866-755-5619. UK 0845-070-0500. www.seabourn.com*

SeaDream Yacht Club
This upscale company with attentive staff but a limited capacity offers 1-week cruises Nov to early Feb departing San Juan, Charlotte Amalie, Bridgetown and other Caribbean ports. *Canada & US 800-707-4911. UK 0800-783-1373. www.seadream.com*

Silversea Cruises
Operating smaller capacity ships with personalized amenities, Silversea offers 1- to 2-week cruises departing New York, Fort Lauderdale, San Diego (California), San Juan and Bridgetown Oct-Apr. *Canada & US 800-722-9955. UK 0844-251-0837. www.silversea.com*

Star Clippers
Re-created 19C clipper ships make 7- to 11-night inter-island cruises in the Eastern Caribbean Nov-Apr from Sint Maarten, Barbados and other departure points. *Canada & US 800-442-0551. UK 0845-200-6145. www.starclippers.com*

Thomson Cruises

This branch of the UK-based package tour operator and part of the TUI Travel group, Thomson operates cruises mainly to Barbados, St. Lucia and Antigua Dec-Apr departing Bridgetown and Santa Cruz, Tenerife. *UK 0871-230-2800. www.thomson.co.uk*

Windstar Cruises

This line of luxury sailing yachts schedules few activities onboard in order to maintain tranquility. Cruises depart Sint Maarten and Barbados Dec-Mar. *Canada & US 1-800-258-7245. UK 0207-292 2387. www.windstarcruises.com*

Getting Around

Island Hopping

For interisland air carriers, check the website of your destination's airport (see chart above). Some island airlines offer fares for flights among several islands in a specific time period.

The Bahamas Out Islands – Departing from Potters Cay (under Paradise Island bridge) in Nassau, Bahamas, **ferries** (*242-323-2166; www.bahamasferries.com*) service Harbour Island/Spanish Wells, Andros, the Exumas, the Abacos and Eleuthera. Mail boats ("slow boats") also depart from Potters Cay (for schedules contact the dock master's office 242-393-1064).

Cayman Islands – There is no ferry service from island to island, only **air service**. Island Air Cayman Islands BWI offer charter flights to Little Cayman from Grand Cayman (*345-949-5252; http://islandair.ky*).

French Isles – **Ferries** run regularly between Guadeloupe of Martinique and Dominica and between Guadeloupe and the southern islands of Les Saintes and Marie-Galante.

Grenada's Out Islands – A **ferry** departs Saint George's for Carriacou 5 days weekly; return ferry departs 4 days a week.

Lesser Antilles – **Ferries** from Saint-Martin service Saba and Saint-Barthélemy. Basse-Terre (*Bay Rd.*), St. Kitts is connected by ferry to Charlestown, Nevis.

Trinidad and Tobago – A once-daily (*except Sun*) **ferry** departs Port of Spain, Trinidad for Scarborough, Tobago (*an approx 5-hour crossing*).

Virgin Islands – **Ferries** from St. Thomas in the US Virgin Islands depart Charlotte Amalie and Red Hook for the British Virgin Island's (BVI's) Tortola and Virgin Gorda islands. Ferries from St. John (USVI) service BVI's Tortola, Jost Van Dyke and Virgin Gorda islands. Ferries from Tortola serve Peter Island. Check with the tourism office about other boat services.

Bay Islands of Honduras – A 2hr **ferry** ride connects Safeway Dock in Roatán and the port of La Ceiba (*www.safewaymaritime. com*). Also twice-daily service between La Ceiba and Utila on the Utila Princess (*504-2425-3390*).

On-Island Transport

By Car – Cars can be rented at most Caribbean airports. Rates are often higher than the US; a credit-card deposit may be required.

Driving in the Caribbean – A **US driver's license** is valid on some, but not all, Caribbean islands. Check in advance with the tourism office of your destination. Inquire about **international driver's licenses** at the American (*800-463-8646; www.aaa. com/vacation/idpf.html*) and Canadian (*613-247-0117; www.caa. ca/travel/travel-permits-e.cfm*) Automobile Associations.

UK driving licenses are valid for 90 days in the Bahamas and Belize. For other countries, UK drivers may apply for an International Driving Permit from either the AA (*0870-600-0371; www.theaa. com/motoring_advice/overseas/idp-requirements-by-country. html*), the RAC (*0800-550-055; www.rac.co.uk/driving-abroad/ international-driving-permit*) or the post office (*08457-223-344; www2.postoffice.co.uk/counter-services/licences-vehicle-tax/in- ternational-driving-permits*).

Some islands require a local permit, obtainable from rental-car companies. Drivers must carry **vehicle registration** and/or rental contract, and proof of automobile insurance at all times. Gasoline is usually sold by the gallon (1 US gallon=3.8 liters or 0.83 Imperial gallon) and is generally expensive (about $4.75 or £3 per US gallon). Vehicles are driven on the left side of the road in British Commonwealth countries and the US Virgin Islands.

By Public Transportation – **Puerto Rico** has extensive bus service throughout the island; a free trolley runs within Old San Juan. **Saint-Martin** operates mini-buses daily between Grand-Case, Marigot, and Philipsburg (on the Dutch side); mini-buses also operate in Dominica. **St. Thomas** in the US Virgin Islands, **Barbados** and **Aruba** offer regular bus service. Contact the tourism office of your destination for specific information.

CAR RENTAL
The following are some of the major rental-car agencies with locations in the Caribbean:

Alamo	www.alamo.com	1-877-222-9075
Budget	www.budget.com	1-800-472-3325
National	www.nationalcar.com	1-877-222-9058
Hertz	www.hertz.com	1-800-654-3001

By Taxi – Travel by taxi is common in the Caribbean. In mos
cases, taxis are regulated and fares are established by the gov
ernment; many drivers carry a fare chart. Agree on a rate and
the type of currency with the driver before you enter the cab.
*See specific destinations in Discovering the Caribbean section fo
additional modes of transportation.*

Basic Information

Communications
Area codes
To call between the French Isles, dial 0 and the area code and
the 6-digit number. To call between Saint-Martin and Sin
Maarten, dial 00 + area code + local number. Except in Puerto
Rico (dial 1 + area code + number) and the French Isles, it i
not necessary to dial the area code to make a local call in the
Caribbean. For the most part, this guide shows the area code fo
telephone numbers given.

International calls
Country codes: United Kingdom 44; US and Canada 1.
Caribbean islands: Most Caribbean countries adhere to the
North American Numbering Plan (NANP).
- To phone NANP Caribbean countries from Canada and the
  US: Dial 1 + country code + the local number.
- To phone NANP Caribbean from the UK: Dial 00 + country
  code + the local number.

Anguilla 264
Antigua 268
Aruba 297
Bahamas 242
Barbados 246
Belize 501
Bonaire 599 7
British Virgin
Islands 284
Cayman Islands
345
Colombia 57
Cuba 53
Curaçao 599 9
Dominica 767

Dominican
Republic 809, 829
and 849
Grenada 473
Guadeloupe 590
Honduras 504
Jamaica 876
Martinique 596
Mexico 52
Puerto Rico 787
or 939
Saba 599 4
Saint-Barthélemy
590

Sint Eustatius
599 3
St. Kitts and Nevis
869
Saint Lucia 758
Saint-Martin 590
Sint Maarten 599 ９
St. Vincent and the
Grenadines 784
Trinidad and
Tobago 868
Turks and Caicos
649
US Virgin Islands
340

The international access code in most of the region is 011.

- To make an international call from the Caribbean: Dial 011 + country code + local number.
- From non-NANP countries: Dial 011+ the country code + the local number.

The following destinations use 00 as their international access code: Aruba, Belize, ABC Islands, Guadeloupe, Honduras, Martinique, St-Barthélemy, and Saint-Martin.

Other exceptions to this are: **Cuba** (Dial 119 + country code + the local number), **Colombia** (Dial 009 + country code + the local number) and **Mexico** (Dial 98 + country code + the local number.) To call the **US** and **Canada** from Mexico: dial 001+ country code + area code + number.

Cell/mobile phones

Some US and UK mobile phones will work in the Caribbean as there are GSM network providers throughout the region. If not, many hotels will arrange cell/mobile phone coverage for you during your stay and even help you rent a paid phone.

Electricity

Voltage in Anguilla is 110 volts AC 60 Hz, which is the same as the US and Canada. Additionally, voltage in Puerto Rico, the Cayman and the Virgin Islands is 120 volts AC 60 Hz, which is compatible with the 110 V voltage used in the US and Canada. On other Caribbean islands, it can range from 110 volts to 230 volts. Foreign-made appliances may need AC adapters and North American flat-blade plugs.

Emergencies

For emergency telephone numbers, please *see the Practical Information in individual destinations in the Discovering the Caribbean section.*

Health

For medical services, please see the Practical Information in the individual destinations in the Discovering the Caribbean section. *See also Health in the International Visitors section above.*

Languages

English is spoken on most of the islands described in this guide. English is the official language of all US- and British Commonwealth-affiliated islands in the Caribbean. French is the official language in the French isles, and Dutch is the official language of the Netherland Antilles.

Travel Tip: To be a smarter traveler, just look at your smartphone. The US Department of State has released its own app. The Smart Traveler app gives you up-to-date access to the State Department's country information, travel alerts, travel warnings, maps, US embassy locations and more.

Measurement Equivalents									
Degrees Farenheit	95	86	77	68	59	50	41	32	23
Degrees Celsius	35	30	25	20	15	10	5	0	-5
1 inch = 2.5 centimeters				1 foot - 30.48 centimeters					
1 mile = 1.6 kilometers				1 pound = 0.45 kilograms					
1 US quart = 0.9 liters				1 US gallon = 3.78 liters					

Money
Currency
Unless otherwise noted, all prices shown in this guide are in US dollars. US dollar bills are accepted on many Caribbean islands. For the local currency, please see the Practical Information in individual destinations in the Discovering the Caribbean section.

Currency exchange
Currency can be exchanged at most banks and airports; in some destinations, like Cuba, all major hotels have currency exchange desks on-site. For up-to-date rates, it is best to check with a currency conversion website such as www.xe.com before you arrive.

Credit cards and traveler's checks
Banks, some stores, large restaurants and major hotels usually accept traveler's checks with photo identification. Credit cards are generally accepted in larger establishments but not in small or rural shops or markets; small restaurants accept cash payment only. Credit cards and traveler's checks drawn on US banks are not honored in Cuba. To report a lost or stolen credit card: **American Express** (*1-800-528-4800; www.americanexpress.com*); **Diners Club** (*1-303-799-1504; www.dinersclubinternational.com*); **MasterCard** (*1-636-722-7111; www.mastercard.com*); **Visa** (*1-303-967-1096; www.visa.com*); **Discover** (*1-801-902-3100; www.discovercard.com*). For cash transfers, contact **Western Union** (*1-800-325-6000; www.westernunion.com*).

ATMs
Automatic Teller Machines (ATMs) are common throughout the Caribbean islands and the mainland destinations described in this guide, but cash dispensed is in the local currency. ATMS can be found at airports, hotel lobbies and banks.
Most ATMs impose a limit on the amount of funds withdrawn and all apply transaction fees.

Taxes and Tips

All the Caribbean countries included in this guide impose a hotel or occupancy tax of 6 percent or higher (10 percent is common). In Mexico, the federal Value Added Tax applied to goods and services is 16 percent. Some governments tax meals and alcoholic beverages, as well as rental cars. Except in the US Virgin Islands, a **departure tax** (*usually $20US or higher*) is charged at the airport; it's advisable to have enough cash on hand to pay this tax when you depart. Many Caribbean hotels, cruise lines and resorts automatically add a service charge (the average is 10 percent to 15 percent) to your bill.

Tips are expected for hotel maids (*$2 to $5US a day*) and bellhops (*$1US per bag*), but tips are usually included at all-inclusive resorts. It is customary to tip taxi drivers 10 percent and tour guides $2 or more US dollars. If a service charge is added to your bill at restaurants, no tip is necessary; otherwise 10-20 percent is a good rule for waitstaff providing satisfactory service.

Time Zones

The Yucatán Peninsula and Belize observe **Central Time** (GMT -6 hours). Islands in the Western Caribbean (*see map inside front cover*) observe **Eastern Time** (GMT -5 hours). Islands in the Eastern Caribbean (*see map inside back cover*) observe **Atlantic Time** (GMT -4 hours).

Water

In most of the islands, the water is potable at major resorts and hotels, and restaurants in the major cities. You may prefer to drink **bottled water**, which is generally available at convenience stores and hotels.

In Cuba, it is highly recommended that you drink only bottled water, which is for sale at most tourist restaurants, bars and shops. Avoid consuming street food and beverages containing water. Be wary of ice, even in the finest hotels. Ask if the water served has been boiled.

In Colombia drinking water from the tap is reasonably safe. Colombia's Agua Manantial (mineral water) is inexpensive and widely available for visitors not wanting to risk the tap water. In Mexico most **tap water** is unpurified. Only bottled water should be used for drinking, brushing teeth and rinsing contact lenses. Avoid ice cubes and all foods that have to be washed (salads, fruits).

DISCOVERING
THE CARIBBEAN

3 DISCOVERING
BAHAMAS★★

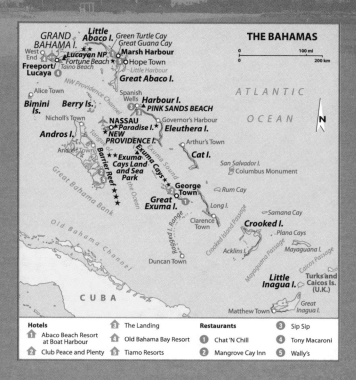

THE BAHAMAS

Hotels		The Landing	Restaurants		Sip Sip
1	Abaco Beach Resort at Boat Harbour	4 Old Bahama Bay Resort	1	Chat 'N Chill	4 Tony Macaroni
2	Club Peace and Plenty	5 Tiamo Resorts	2	Mangrove Cay Inn	5 Wally's

The Commonwealth of the Bahamas is a chain of 700 islands, cays and uninhabited islets in the Atlantic Ocean. Not long after Christopher Columbus landed here in 1492, the original inhabitants, the Lucayans, were wiped out by the Spaniards. British settlers arrived in the mid-1600s. Slave trade with Africa and piracy both benefited from nearby shipping routes. The Bahamas became a British colony in 1783 during the American Revolution and gained independence in 1973. New Providence is the most populated island, with its capital city of Nassau. Grand Bahama lies closest to the US and has large swaths of natural land, though its tourist activity is concentrated in Freeport and Lucaya. The more remote Out Islands may just be dots on a map, but comprise some

PETER'S TOP PICKS

CULTURE

Get a personal lesson on island lifestyle and culture by taking advantage of the free People-to-People program, which connects visitors with local hosts. Contact the Tourism Ministry to be matched up with an ambassador. (p **113**)

HISTORY

Most all of the Bahamian islands have a rich and colorful past, but the Abacos islands' history is especially unique. They were settled by British loyalists who fled the US after the American Revolution. For a time, there was even a movement to keep the Abacos under British rule after independence. (p **118**)

STAY

Atlantis Resort on Paradise Island is enormous in almost every way. It has the largest resort in the Caribbean, a series of aquariums and an open-air marine habitat, and a 141-acre water park, Aquaventure. Oh, and it has almost 3,500 rooms, from standard hotel rooms to private family-friendly villas. (p **122**)

SHOP

Port Lucaya Marketplace is the nerve center of Grand Bahama, with an open-air market selling every kind of island-made handicraft and duty-free item imaginable. Nassau, on New Providence Island, has the best shopping in the country, and a stroll along Bay Street will take you past duty-free designer boutiques, shopping arcades and souvenir shops. (p **116**)

EAT

In Arawak Cay on New Providence Island, the Fish Fry is a collection of casual, waterside eateries where all the locals hang out. These pastel-colored restaurants have some of the best seafood on the island. (p **123**, Goldies)

of the most idyllic getaways, including the Exumas, the Abacos and Bimini. The sailing capital of the Bahamas, the Abacos are a cluster of dreamy isles. The largest island in the Bahama chain, and least-charted, Andros is a haven for underwater adventurers who come to explore the 140mi offshore coral reef. The Berry Islands are known for bonefishing. The Biminis are the Bahamas' big-game fishing capital. Cat Island is known for friendly locals and Mount Alvernia. Crooked Island boasts 45mi of barrier reefs. Eleuthera is famous for its beaches and pineapples. Neighboring Harbour Island is considered the most beautiful. The Exumas lay claim to the most shades of blue water. Little Inagua attracts pink flamingos.

ASK PETER...

Q: What is Junkanoo and how can I see it?
A: Junkanoo, quite simply, is a colorful masquerade parade. Locals dance in the street clad in brilliantly elaborate costumes and headdresses made from layers of cardboard, crepe and beads. Its origins date back more than 200 years when, under British law, slaves were allowed three days off around Christmas. Legend has it they would steal away under the cover of night to celebrate their African heritage, which eventually grew into Junkanoo. The largest event takes place on Bay Street in Nassau after midnight on Christmas Day (Boxing Day) and on New Year's Day. On Grand Bahama Island, there's a Junkanoo Summer Festival.

Nassau★★ *and Vicinity*

The capital of the Bahamas, Nassau lies along the northeast coast of New Providence Island, fronting Nassau Harbour. Nassau is the island's vibrant commercial, political, and historic hub. Occupying a mere 25 blocks, this charming colonial city has a long and colorful history. Settled by the British in the late 1600s, the city today welcomes more than half of all travelers to the Bahamas. Nassau Harbour is one of the principal ports of call for cruises to the islands. The city's main tourist zone is bounded by Bay Street in the north, East Hill Street in the south, Elizabeth Avenue in the east and West Street in the west.

Christ Church Cathedral★

George St. ℰ242-322-4186. http://christchurchcathedral bahamas.com. Open Mon–Fri 8:30am–5pm, Sat 8:30am–4pm.
Nassau wasn't officially a city until 1684, when Christ Church was completed. The stately Gothic structure, made of local limestone blocks, is the fourth cathedral on this site; previous iterations fell victim to the Spanish and termites. Note the stained glass windows and the Garden of Remembrance on the south side.

Fort Charlotte★

West Bay St., across from Arawak Cay. ℰ242-322-7500. Open daily 8am–4pm; $5.
Of the three forts in Nassau, Fort Charlotte is the largest and most impressive. Perched on a hill with sweeping views of Nassau, the harbor and Paradise Island, the fort covers 100 acres. Built in 1788 by Lord Dunmore to protect the harbor, it was named after the wife of King George III. Its 42 cannons have never seen military action, and its dungeons and passageways remain in pristine condition. Tour guides, dressed in period costume and working for tips, will happily show you around.

Straw Market★

Northwest end of Bay St. Open daily 9am–4pm.
Straw vending is one of the oldest crafts in the Bahamas, and Nassau's venerable Straw Market is its most famous venue.
Under a massive white tent, hundreds of vendors hawk a cornucopia of straw products, many of which are actually made in Taiwan (the vendors do sew on the raffia work).
Expect to be loudly courted, and enter with your best ready-to-bargain face. You'll also find T-shirts, souvenirs, and fake designer bags here.

WHEN TO GO
The Bahamas' coolest months are Sept–May; even "cold" **winters** here reach a balmy 21°/70°F. Temperatures the rest of the year average 80°F-90°F with high humidity. Expect a drop of 5-7 degrees at night, and cooler temperatures in the northern islands. While it can rain at any time on the islands, May and Jun see the heaviest **rainfall**. The northern islands tend to get twice the rainfall of the southern islands. Many Bahamas hotels offer a hurricane cancellation policy. **Peak tourist season** is Dec to Apr.

GETTING AROUND
BY BUS – For **jitneys**, a type of minibus, fares start at $1.25; you'll need exact change.
BY TAXI – Taxis can be flagged down. Taxis bearing a Bahamas host decal are specially trained and endorsed. Fares are metered and fixed by law. A 5mi ride will cost roughly $12 for one to two passengers. Each additional passenger $3. Grand Bahama Taxi Union (✆242-352-7101/7859) and Jermaine's Taxi and Tours (✆242-425-1789, http://jermainstaxiandtours.com).
BY CAR – Most major rental car companies have offices in Nassau, Grand Bahamas, and at the airports.On the smaller Out Islands, local shops offer rentals. About $60 per day and up; minimum rental age is 25.
BY FERRY – Bahamas Ferries (✆242-323-2166/394-9700; www.bahamasferries.com) offers air-conditioned inter-island service. Albury's Ferry (✆242-367-0290) services the Abaco Islands.

Other transport – Scooters cost around $40 a day. Call ahead to reserve a **golf cart** in the smaller Out Islands. D&P Rentals in Abaco (✆242-365-4655) or Dolphin's Golf Cart Rental in Bimini (✆242-464-5704 or ✆242-347-3407).

VISITOR INFORMATION
Main tourism office: George Street, Nassau. ✆242-302-2000, 1-800-Bahamas (toll-free).
Important numbers
Emergency (24hrs): 919 or 911
Police: ✆242-322-4444
Medical Services:
Princess Margaret Hospital, Nassau: ✆242-322-2861
Rand Memorial Hospital, Grand Bahama: ✆242-352-6735
Emergency Medical Services: ✆242-502-1400
Accommodations
For a selection of lodgings, *see Where to Stay* at the end of this chapter.

MONEY/CURRENCY
The official currency is the Bahamanian dollar, which has the same value as the US dollar. But American dollars are accepted everywhere on the islands. Because the Bahamian dollar a restricted currency, it is illegal to leave the country with more than $200 Bahamian dollars.
Major credit cards, most debit cards, and internationally recognized traveler's checks in dollar denominations are widely accepted. You can also use your ATM card to withdraw cash, although fees do apply.

Bahamas Segway Tours
✆242-467-8764, 888-411-0553. www.bahamassegwaytours.com.
3 tours daily, Mon from 8:30am, Tue–Sun from 9:30am.
$65 if booked online.
Among the most popular tours in the Bahamas, these guided tours will teach you how to operate (and stay balanced on) an X2 Offroad Segway before you take a three-in-one tour through a nature preserve, the beach, and the city. The tours run about three hours, including pickup and drop-off.

Diving Sites

Bahama Divers, East Bay St. ☎ *242-393-5644, 800-398-3483. www.bahamadivers.com. Stuart Cove's Dive Bahamas, South Ocean, Nassau.* ☎ *242-362-4171. www.stuartcove.com.*

Nassau's coast offers an underwater playground of coral reefs, marine life, and sunken wrecks (including **Twin Sisters**, two 200ft oil tankers mired 70ft deep; and **Tears of Allah**, which was featured in the James Bond movie *Never Say Never Again*). For a real thrill, go on a **shark dive** and swim with these majestic creatures (no cages!). Check out Stuart Cove's dives and shark awareness programs. Novice divers might prefer **Schoolhouse Reef**, a living aquarium just 15ft below the surface.

Dolphin Encounters

Blue Lagoon Island. ☎ *242-363-1003. www.dolphinencounters.com Daily departures 8:30am. $90 and up.*

This popular attraction rose from humble beginnings in 1989 to boast 18 dolphins (three of which starred in the 1996 movie *Flipper*), 6 sea lions and a staff of some 150 today on **Blue Lagoon Island**, north of Nassau.. There are a variety of programs and encounters.

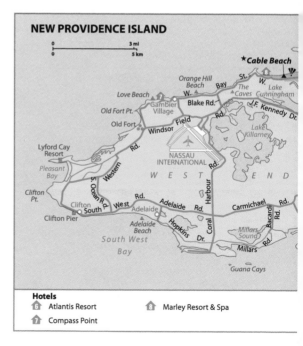

Paradise Island★

It's hard to believe this place was once called Hog Cay, or that it was uninhabited only 40 years ago. The 680sq mi island, connected to Nassau by bridge or a $6 water taxi ride, has been transformed into a resort enclave. Among its cluster of high-end hotels, none looms larger than the sprawling **Atlantis** (*see Where to Stay*). Many resorts here are full-service destinations offering every amenity and activity. Some of the best beaches around Nassau are beyond their gates. When the sun goes down, Paradise gets going, thanks to its clubs, casinos, and weekend Junkanoo.

Cabbage Beach★

There are really two beaches on this two-mile stretch of sand: the west attracts parasailers, swimmers, sunbathers, and water-sports enthusiasts; farther east, the crowds fall back. Swimmers should watch for drop-offs in the water level away from shore, as well as undertows during winter months. For those without direct hotel access, two walkways lead to Cabbage Beach; one east of the Riu Hotel, the other west of Ocean Club Estates.

Travel Tip: People-to-People is a free program organized by the Ministry of Tourism that brings together tourists with local ambassadors. Your host may bring you home for a meal, show you their favorite sights around the island, and share their family's history to give you a unique perspective on their culture.

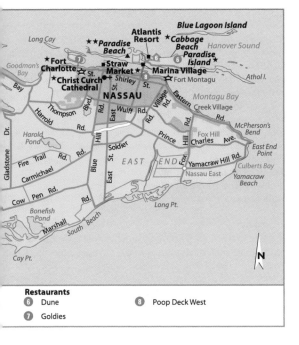

Restaurants
- ⑥ Dune
- ⑦ Goldies
- ⑧ Poop Deck West

ASK PETER...

Q: Can I island-hop in the Bahamas?

A: There are several ways to get from island to island in the Bahamas, depending on your time constraints and starting point. Traveling between Nassau and Paradise Island is as easy as getting in a cab or a water taxi. High-speed ferries connect Nassau with Harbour Island, Exuma, Andros and Eleuthera. Getting from Nassau to Freeport on Grand Bahama is easiest on Bahamasair, the national airline. If you've really got a sense of adventure and plenty of time (and a good supply of motion-sickness pills), you may be able to get on an inter-island mail boat. Just keep in mind these vessels don't just carry mail; you might be spending the night with livestock.

Atlantis Casino

Atlantis. ☎ *242-363-3000, 800-528-7155. www.atlantis.com. Main casino open 24/7.*

At 50,000 square feet, the **Atlantis** easily sports the largest casino in the Caribbean. The floor comfortably accommodates more than 850 slot machines, 90 table games (Roulette, Craps, Blackjack, Mini-Baccarat and Baccarat, Caribbean Stud Poker and Let It Ride), and a race and sports book. Dale Chihuly sculptures lend an elegant touch to the casino's Temple of the Moon and Temple of the Sun rooms. High rollers have their own secluded section, and newcomers can take free lessons daily.

Junkanoo at Marina Village

Marina Village. Fri & Sat 9:30pm.

For many years, a traveler's only chance to see Junkanoo Festival was December 26 and January 1. Fortunately, Paradise Island has its own troupe of Junkanoo performers, who rush through Marina Village Friday and Saturday, their drums banging and their cow bells ringing. The spectacle may not be as grand as the Bay Street parades, but it's a much easier show to catch.

Grand Bahama Island

Originally home to Lucayan Indians, Grand Bahama is known as the "Second City" of the Bahamas. The island sits just 55mi east of Florida, but despite its proximity, size (at 530sq mi, the fourth-largest Bahamian island) and popularity (second only to Nassau), Grand Bahama hasn't quite lived up to its grand expectations. What this island does have, however, is beaches: 96 miles of them. The island comprises three distinct areas: West End, official capital of Grand Bahama, a laid back fishing village; Freeport/Lucaya, the island's largest city; and East End, a largely undeveloped stretch of quaint communities. Grand Bahama Highway, the island's main artery, leads to the incomparable Lucayan National Park and rustic settlements.

Freeport

Grand Bahama's administrative and commercial center, the country's second most-populous city is a designated free-trade zone. Designed to serve tourists, the city was crippled by hurricanes Jeanne and Frances in 2004, and parts of it have never recovered. Similarly, its **International Bazaar** has seen better days, but **Rand Nature Centre★** remains a pristine natural sanctuary, and its snorkeling and diving rank among the best.

BAHAMIAN SHIPWRECKS

The shipwrecks around the Bahamas represent centuries of maritime history in this region. Unpredictable weather and dangerous reefs were a deadly combination for early seafarers, and piracy was a constant threat to ships along this popular trade route. Bahamians made wrecking a way of life centuries ago, salvaging treasure from sunken ships. Today, more modern underwater structures have made this area one of the premier wreck-diving sites in the world. There are wrecks ranging from a shallow 15 feet down to 100 feet all around Nassau/Paradise Island, Grand Bahama, and several of the Out Islands. Divers will come from all over the world to explore some of the more notable wrecks. The James Bond Wrecks are actually made from movie props, including a tugboat called "The Tears of Allah" that appeared in the film, *Never Say Never Again*, and the Vulcan bomber from *Thunderball*.

Shark lovers will have fun diving among the *Bahama Mama*, a former party boat, and the *Ray of Hope*, a cargo ship that the government sunk in 2003. Farther out, near Eleuthera, is the notable *Arimoroa*, also known as the Egg Island wreck. This Lebanese freighter caught on fire, and the captain ran it straight into the nearest land, the uninhabited Egg Island. Today, the sunken ship is home to a population of tropical fish that makes it an underwater photographer's paradise.

Lucaya

People often lump Freeport and Lucaya together, the former being the institutional hub and the latter an oceanfront residential and resort community catering to tourists, with a large casino, championship golf courses and a fantastic beach. **Port Lucaya** is the nerve center of tourist life on the island.

Lucayan National Park★★

Grand Bahama Highway. ✆ 242-352-5438. www.bnt.bs. Open daily 9am–4pm; $3.

One of the longest known underwater cave networks, this park is a worthwhile visit, especially for certified cave divers. Its six miles of caves, caverns and tunnels shelter bats *(visitor access restricted in Jun–Jul nesting season)*, and host an endemic species of blind crustaceans called Remipedia. You can also visit Burial Mound, where remains of Lucayan Indians have been found. Above ground, the 40-acre park sports an elevated boardwalk and nature trails culminating at the Gold Rock Creek and Beach, scenes in the first two *Pirates of the Caribbean* movies.

Fortune Beach★

East of Taino Beach, Grand Bahama.

If you like your beaches quiet, soft, secluded, and dazzling, head to Fortune Beach, where most of the noise you're likely to hear will come from Banana Bay restaurant. The beach is named for a shipwreck worth $2 million dollars found offshore.

Rand Nature Centre★

East Settler's Way. ✆ 242-352-5438. www.bnt.bs.
Open Mon–Fri 9am–4:30pm. $5.

The first sanctuary of its kind in the Bahamas, this center occupies 100 acres of prime real estate in downtown Freeport. Its nature trails take you through a pine forest, where you can glimpse a variety of birds and more than 130 native plants, including tropical orchids and bush medicine plants. Peak bird-watching season runs October to May, and there are bird-watching tours the first Saturday of each month year-round.

Port Lucaya Marketplace

Sea Horse Rd. ✆ 242-373-8446. www.portlucayamarketplace.com.
A visitor's one-stop-shop, Port Lucaya Marketplace offers a bit (actually, a lot) of everything in a tropical open-air setting. Among its 80 or so shops you'll find straw crafts, duty-free boutiques, souvenirs, designer fashion, and fine art. Most shops are open daily 10am–6pm. In addition, Port Lucaya offers watersports tours during the day and colorful shows nightly.

Smiling Pat's Adventures

Freeport. ✆ 242-533-2946, 242-559-2921. www.smilingpat.com.
$75 and up per person.

Smiling Pat says you haven't seen the Bahamas until you've seen her. After one of her tours, you might well be smiling too. Smiling Pat has created a few unique excursions in and around her native Grand Bahama, including tours to Gilligan's Island (also known as Sandy Cay) and Cat Island; a trip out to the island's historic West End (with a pit stop at Smiling Pat's grandmother's bakery); and a beach tour that includes Gold Creek.Andros, Berry and Bimini Islands

Travel Tip: It is possible to rent a car in Nassau using a US driver's license for up to 3 months. However, driving is on the left side of the road, and the roads can be confusing and chaotic, so you're better off relying on taxis or the public bus known as a jitney.

Andros, Berry and Bimini Islands

Three of the Bahamas' famed Out Islands, Andros, Berry, and Bimini are the country's northwestern-most islands. They share stunning natural environs, luring visitors who crave fishing, diving, hiking, beachcombing, bird-watching and swimming.

Andros

No place in the Bahamas lets you get away from it all quite like Andros. At 104mi long and 40mi wide, it's the largest but least populated island in the country, easily earning its local nicknames "The Big Yard" and "Sleeping Giant." Andros exudes an unspoiled majesty, with deserted beaches stretching for miles, a landscape punctuated with blue holes (sinkholes leading to underwater caves), dense forests and mangrove swamps harboring a variety of birds and wildlife, from wild boar to flamingos. Many people come to Andros to dive the third-largest **barrier reef** in the world, or wade across sandy flats that make it the world's premier bonefishing capital. The island is equally suited for the ecotourist and for the couple in search of a secluded romantic getaway or honeymoon. It might also be the perfect place to strike it rich, since Captain Morgan himself is rumored to have buried his treasure here.

Andros Barrier Reef★★★
Eastern coast of Andros.
The world's third-largest barrier reef lies roughly 1.5 miles off the eastern coast of Andros. Spanning an astounding 142 miles, the Andros Barrier Reef separates the island from the **Tongue of the Ocean,** a 6,000 foot drop of such a stark blue hue that it that can be seen from space. This area, home to a stunning variety of marine life, is an underwater treasure unparalleled in the Caribbean.

Berry Islands

Named for their thatch berry trees, the Berry Islands, are an enviable address to call home. This chain of 30 cays has a year-round population of about 700, and boasts more millionaires per square mile than most cities on earth; many of them live on the 6mi by 2.5mi Great Harbour Cay. Chub Cay is the billfish capital of The Bahamas, home to championship big-game fishing and bonefishing.

Bimini Islands

The Bimini islands are a place of legend and fish. Located just 50 miles off the coast of Florida, the 28-mile chain is the westernmost of the Bahamas. Pirates and rum runners are believed to have stored their loot in Bimini. Bimini Bay might just hold traces of the lost city of Atlantis. Ponce de Leon came here on his quest for the Fountain of Youth, and (the one legend that rings true) Ernest Hemingway endorsed it in his novel, *Islands in the Stream*. Its deep waters have earned a reputation as the big-game fishing capital of the world.

Travel Tip:
A passport is required when traveling to the Bahamas by sea or air. However, you can use the cheaper passport card if traveling on a cruise from Florida. It's similar to a traditonal passport, but is only good for travel by land or sea in the US, Mexico, Canada and the Caribbean.

Travel Tip: It's no coincidence that the Bahamas are known for shipwrecks. The coral reefs around the islands can be extremely dangerous to vessels. If you're not a very experienced sailor, go with a guide or charter a crewed boat.

Abacos

The Abacos have a unique story to tell: This island chain in the north was settled by British loyalists who fled the US after the American Revolution. They left such a deep imprint on the island that, centuries later, some residents even opposed Bahamian independence. Today, the pastel-colored colonial towns of the Abacos are better known for their world-class boating and sailing. Great Abaco and Little Abaco comprise their mainland.

Great Abaco

By Out Island standards, Great Abaco Island's **Marsh Harbour** is a bustling city; after all, it has the only working traffic light in the area. The economic center of the Abacos, Marsh Harbour has plenty of full-service marinas where you can charter a boat or hop on a ferry to explore the cays.

North of Marsh Harbour, **Treasure Cay** is a real estate development with a resort, golf course, marina, and a 3.5 mile beach that is consistently voted among the best in the world.

Boat Rentals
JIC Boat Rentals. Treasure Cay. ☎ 242-365-8582. www.jicboatrentals.com. $130 and up. Sea Horse Boat Rentals. Marsh Harbour. ☎ 242 366 0023. www.sea-horse.com. $165 and up daily, $105 and up weekly.

Hope Town, Man O'War and Great Guana Cay

The true charm of the Abacos might well lie in the cays on its eastern coast. Each has its own personality: chic **Hope Town** is known by the locals as Hollywood; **Man O'War**, the Abacos' boat-building headquarters, is a conservative town that prohibits the sale of liquor; **Great Guana Cay** has a marvelous 7 mile long beach. To get the most out of your trip, rent a golf cart and putter around at your leisure.

Hope Town Lighthouse★
Hope Town Harbour.
This famous red and white candy-striped lighthouse is a much-photographed icon in the Bahamas. The 120ft tall structure is beloved today, but was a source of controversy when it was being built in the 1860s. Hope Town residents knew the lighthouse would signal (pardon the pun) an end to their profitable trade in shipwrecking and salvaging. It's one of the only remaining lighthouses in the world to use kerosene-powered light.

CUISINE ...LIKE A LOCAL

Although you can find every type of cuisine on the islands—from hamburger joints to Chinese restaurants—Bahamian cuisine is gaining international recognition. Its flavors are Caribbean with heavy influence from British and even southern American cuisine. That blend of Caribbean and American is most evident in a dish known as peas and rice, usually made with pigeon peas, bacon and a tomato base. Bahamian johnny cakes are a sweet, dense type of bread. Curries, stews, chowders and fried foods are common, and seafood is almost always the star, with grouper and crayfish gracing most menus. Conch is another culinary staple, served every which way: raw, cracked, fried, stewed, salad... you get the picture. Wash it all down with a Kalik beer or Sky Juice (gin and coconut water with sweetened or condensed milk). End the meal with the Bahamian national dessert, guava duff—a type of steamed dough stuffed with guava and topped with a sweet sauce.

For a casual seafood meal, go to the **Fish Fry**, a strip of small, colorful restaurants on West Bay Street. Under the Paradise Island bridge is **Potters Cay Dock**, another local hangout with food vendors, farmers and fisherman selling their wares. Tucked in the corner of Dowdeswell and Armstrong streets is **Chea's Corner Bistro**, owned and operated by a Le Cordon Bleu-trained chef.

Even individual islands have their own specialties, like the soft, slightly sweet Bimini bread. Ask the locals where to find it and they'll tell you to go to "Charlie's house." Yes, it's actually the home of a man named Charlie who makes what is widely believed to be the best bread on the island. Charlie's Bread can be found on King's Highway in Bailey Town, two doors north of the Elks Pub.

Graycliff Restaurant, located in the luxury hotel of the same name has been serving upscale diners for decades, and continues to keep up with the times with a modern, fresh take on classic dishes. Its wine cellar and "cognateque" are internationally renowned, with more than 250,000 bottles, including a collection of some of the rarest, most expensive wines, ports and cognacs in the world.

Eleuthera and Harbour Islands

A nature-lover's playground, Eleuthera, Harbour Island and Spanish Wells form a remote and rustic oasis. This part of the Bahamas boasts pink sand beaches, a what-me-worry vibe, and upscale resorts catering to the rich and famous.

Eleuthera

In 1649, Puritans sailing from England in search of religious freedom shipwrecked on the shores of a long, narrow island. They named it Eleuthera (Greek for freedom), and formed the first English settlement in the Bahamas. Today, the island (110 mi long by 2mi wide) continues to be free—free of crowds, bustle, even cell phone service. It's a place of charming colonial fishing villages, picturesque beaches, pineapple plantations and verdant countryside. The Puritans weren't the only ones to run aground; reefs off Eleuthera have claimed more wrecks than any other Bahamian island, making this a favorite spot for divers.

Harbour Island and Spanish Wells

A community with a posh clientele that includes members of the British Royal Family, Harbour Island's **Dunmore Town★** was once the second largest settlement in the Bahamas. "Briland," as it's locally known, remains a meticulously preserved example of colonial tropical luxury. A big part of its allure is one-of-a-kind Pink Sands Beach. The 1.5 mile long **Spanish Wells Island**, discovered by Columbus and visited by Ponce de Leon, is a fishing village that has become the wealthiest community in the Bahamas, thanks to lobster fishing.

Pink Sands Beach★★★
Harbour Island, Atlantic side.
A perennial member of the Most Beautiful Beaches in the World club, this 3mi long beach is a natural consequence of surf, red conch shells, and white sand blended together to produce a captivating rose sheen. Hard packed and wide, it's got plenty of room to accommodate the crowds who come to rest and play.

Current Cut
Current, Eleuthera.
Current Cut is a narrow channel separating Current Island from North Eleuthera. It offers an exhilarating and fast-paced drift-diving experience wherein everything in the water with you (including sharks and rays) are pushed, carried and swept through the two-third mile long cut in the space of about 10 minutes. When the tide changes, you'll head in the opposite direction.

Exumas

A loose string of 365 cays that spans 100 miles, the Exumas and their variegated blue waters paint such a breathtaking landscape that half the fun is flying above them and gazing at the tropical canvas below. The other half lies in the myriad outdoor adventures these island jewels offer.

Great Exuma and Little Exuma

Home to 3,600 residents, the aptly named Great Exuma anchors the archipelago. Its tranquil capital, **George Town**, hugs the shore of small Lake Victoria. Here you'll find most of the area's hotels and restaurants. Skip across the demarcation line of the Tropic of Cancer and hop over the bridge to Little Exuma to visit splendid beaches and the remains of an 18C cotton plantation.

Exuma Cays★★

Discovering your favorite cay might be the most fun you'll have in the Exumas. From sandbars that vanish at high tide to the private islands of Hollywood superstars (which you can access if you have a boat, as all beaches in the Bahamas are public), you'll find magnificent beaches, hidden coves, ritzy yachts and fishing boats all along the island chain. You'll also enjoy the most dazzling azure, sapphire, and turquoise waters around. Particularly famous are the endangered iguanas at **Allan's Cay** and the swimming pigs (yes, swimming pigs) at **Major Cay**.

Thunderball Grotto★★

Northwest of Staniel Cay.

This magical place (actually a hollowed-out island) is named for its part in the James Bond movie *Thunderball*; it made a repeat appearance in Bond's *Never Say Never Again*, and was also featured in *Splash* and *Into the Blue*. Enjoy swimming, snorkeling or diving in its crystal-clear depths, made all the more magical by shafts of sunlight poking through the grotto's openings.

Exuma Cays Land and Sea Park★★

North Exuma Cays. ☎ 242-225-1791. www.exumapark.info.

The first park of its kind in the world, the 176sq mi park combines private cays and spectacular underwater marine gardens. It's the Caribbean's first marine fishery reserve, and a designated no-take zone, which means you can't remove anything from the park. Its native residents include the hutia—a large rodent and the only Bahamian land mammal—iguanas, sea birds, a stunning variety of fish and coral, and stromatolites—blue-green algae that are the oldest living evidence of life on earth.

Travel Tip: Like most of the Caribbean, hurricane season runs from June 1 through November 30. Rates can be much lower this time of year and there are fewer crowds, but purchase travel insurance to protect yourself in case of unforeseen circumstances.

Addresses

For price ranges, see the Legend on the cover flap.

WHERE TO STAY

$$ Club Peace and Plenty – *Queen's Highway, George Town, Great Exuma.* 242-336-2551, 800-525-2210. *www.peace andplenty.com. 32 rooms.* A former sponge warehouse is now Exuma's oldest hotel, with colorful, spacious rooms. A homey spot and a popular hangout, Club Peace hosts frequent cocktail parties and theme nights for its guests.

$$$ Abaco Beach Resort at Boat Harbour – *Bay St., Marsh Harbour, Great Abaco.* 242-367-2158, 242-367-2736. *www.abacoresort.com. 89 rooms.* A favorite with boaters thanks to its excellent marina, Abaco Beach Resort is the largest hotel in Marsh Harbour. The hotel offers easy access to many nearby cays, a private white beach, and upscale dining.

$$$ Atlantis Resort – *Paradise Island, Nassau.* 242-363-3000, 888-877-7525. *www.atlantis.com. 3,414 rooms.* The über-resort that put Paradise Island on the map, Atlantis is nothing if not big: the largest casino in the Caribbean, lagoons with 50,000 sea creatures, 40-odd restaurants, a famed water slide, a dolphin lagoon, and massive spa.

$$$ Compass Point – *West Bay St., Nassau.* 242-327-4500. *www.compasspoint beachresort.com. 18 rooms.*

Adorable huts, liberally splashed with tropical colors, offer a sense of privacy, comfort, and seclusion. Close to Cable Beach.

$$$ The Landing – *Harbour Island.* 242 333 2707. *www. harbourislandlanding.com. 12 rooms.* A 5min walk from Pink Sands Beach, this historic Colonial mansion is one of the hippest addresses in Dunmore Town. The Landing features graceful plantation-style rooms designed by India Hicks.

$$$ Old Bahama Bay Resort – *West End, Grand Bahama Island.* 242-350-6500, 888-800-8959. *www.oldbahamabay.com. 72 rooms.* This Colonial-style all-suite resort sits on the beach at the western edge of Grand Bahama Island. It boasts a ridiculously large 4,000sq ft swimming pool, outstanding diving and snorkeling facilities, and marina.

$$$$ Marley Resort & Spa – *West Bay St., Nassau.* 242-702-2800. *www.marleyresort.com. 16 rooms.* At this former vacation home of Bob Marley's family, you can feel the legend's presence. The chic and spacious resort is located on magnificent Cable Beach.

$$$$$ Tiamo Resorts – *South Andros Island.* 242-369-2330/1. *www.tiamoresorts.com. 10 cottages.* This eco-resort is accessible only by boat or seaplane. Its luxurious cottages, private beach and lack of phones, Internet and Wi-Fi make it pure sustainable heaven.

WHERE TO EAT

$ Chat 'N Chill – *Stocking Island, Exuma.* 242-336-2700. *http://chatnchill.com.* **Bahamian/American**. Fans of Chat 'N Chill will urge you to boat, kayak, swim or jet ski to this rustic shack where the frequent dances and bonfires are legendary, and the Sunday pig roast is hugely popular. The fries are the only fried food on the menu.

$ Goldies Conch House – *Arawak Cay, West Bay St., Nassau (opposite Fort Charlotte).* 242-325-4300. *www.goldies conchhousenaussau.com.* **Seafood**. Dining here is about as authentic a culinary experience you'll find in Nassau. Known as "The Fish Fry," it's home to a cluster of stalls that specialize in fried snapper, lobster salad and cracked conch. Many call Goldies the best of the bunch.

$$ Mangrove Cay Inn – *Mangrove Cay.* 242-369-0069. *www.mangrovecayinn.net.* **Bahamian/American**. A convivial spot with few frills but warm service, the Inn serves breakfast, lunch and dinner, along with fresh baked breads and desserts.

$$ Poop Deck West – *East Bay St., Nassau.* 242-393-8175. *www.thepoopdeckrestaurants. com.* **Bahamian/American**. One of two Poop Decks in Nassau, this popular duo is known for its never-frozen daily catches and seafood specialties like cracked conch.

$$ Sip Sip (Harbour Island) – *Court St., Harbour Island.* 242-333-3316. *Lunch only.* **International.** Travelers might bemoan the fact the Sip Sip (patois for gossip) closes for dinner, but take solace in their hearty lunches like conch curry and coconut cakes. Lively ambience.

$$ Tony Macaroni – *Taino Beach, Grand Bahama Island.* **Seafood**. A tried and true Bahamian beach shack, Tony's is known for roasted conch, Sunday Jazz jams and the "Rake and Scrapee on Da Beach" Wednesday nights.

$$$ Wally's Restaurant – *Bay St., Marsh Harbour, Great Abaco.* 242-367-2074. **Bahamian**. This two-story pink Colonial villa has long been a popular choice for gourmet Bahamian cuisine. Offering drinks like Wally's Special cocktail—a blend of fruit juices and rum— and a menu that ranges from conch cakes to steaks, the restaurant will do its best to make sure "nobody leaves here hungry."

$$$$ Dune – *One & Only Ocean Club, Paradise Island.* 242-363-2501. *www.oneandonlyresorts.com.* **French/Asian.** A sublime beachfront eatery from legendary chef Jean-Georges Vongerichten, Dune is housed in an annex overlooking the ocean. Come for the views, and stay for the innovative cuisine and attentive service.

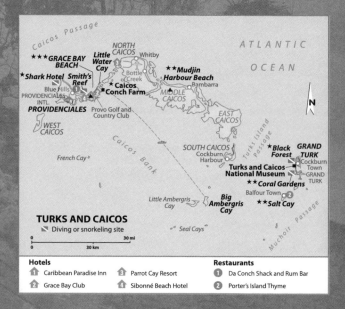

Hotels

1. Caribbean Paradise Inn
2. Grace Bay Club
3. Parrot Cay Resort
4. Sibonné Beach Hotel

Restaurants

1. Da Conch Shack and Rum Bar
2. Porter's Island Thyme

The Turks and Caicos consist of 40 islands and cays in the Atlantic Ocean (not the Caribbean Sea, contrary to popular belief), with vibrantly turquoise waters and 200 miles of sugar-white beaches that captivate all who step ashore. A British Overseas Territory located about 550 miles southeast of Miami, Florida, the inhabited islands are split up into the Turks (Grand Turk and Salt Cay) and the Caicos (West, North, Middle, East and South Caicos, and Providenciales). A third "set" of islands, Parrot Cay, Pine Cay and Ambergris Cay, are privately owned nuggets of land that attract the rich and famous seeking solitude and solace.

Once known primarily for its salt-raking industry, the Turks and Caicos have experienced rapid growth in tourism in recent years. Tourism centers on the island of Providenciales, known locally as "Provo," where the world-class Grace Bay Beach is widely consid-

PETER'S TOP PICKS

CULTURE

Experience local history and culture through the music of the Turks and Caicos. These islands are most well known for ripsaw music, which features instruments like goatskin drums, handsaws and hand accordians. (p **126**)

HISTORY

Located in a beautiful 19th century house, the Turks and Caicos National Museum on Grand Turk island has items dating back to the original Lucayan inhabitants, along with artifacts from the salt-raking days, the remains of the Molasses Reef Wreck, and an exhibit dedicated to astronaut John Glenn's landing just off Grand Turk in 1962. (p **130**)

STAY

On the north shore of Providenciales, Grace Bay Club sits on one of the loveliest beaches on the island, where the waters are calm and the sand is powdery and smooth. Look for a longtime local resident, JoJo, a wild and friendly dolphin who frequently comes to play. (p **133**)

PLAY

As one of the premier scuba-diving sites in the world, the Turks and Caicos Islands feature spectacular coral reefs teeming with brilliant tropical fish. Just off Grand Turk is Coral Gardens, where a 60-foot dive showcases the best of what the waters have to offer. (p **128**)

EAT

Conch World, the Caicos conch farm, takes you behind the scenes of a working hatchery, where they grow and harvest Queen conchs each year. You can taste and buy the freshest conchs here, and wash it down with the island's famous rum punch. (p **130**)

ered one of the most beautiful beaches in the Caribbean. A number of celebrities now call the Turks and Caicos home, including Bruce Willis, Donna Karan and most recently, Prince, who bought a multi-million-dollar home in Provo. The Turks and Caicos are only about a 90-minute flight from Miami, but are still relatively undiscovered by US travelers as compared to the nearby Bahamas chain. The coral reefs are a huge draw for scuba-diving enthusiasts, particularly in the Princess Alexandra National Park on Provo, where fishing is banned and rich marine life has flourished. However, as the stress of growing tourism as well as storms take their toll on the natural reefs, wetlands and lagoons, there has been an increased focus on conservation efforts to promote sustainable tourism.

4

Beaches

ASK PETER...

Q: What is the local island music like in the Turks and Caicos?
A: The Turks and Caicos Islands are most well known for ripsaw music, which has some similarities to Bahamian "rake and scrape" music, and even to southern American Cajun styles. Common instruments include goatskin drums, handsaws, acoustic guitars and hand accordians. You can also experience local music at Junkanoo, which is traditionally associated with the Bahamas, but is also celebrated here on Boxing Day and New Year's Day.

White-sand **beaches** edging turquoise blue waters with fabulous scuba **diving sites** are the twin attractions of the Turks and Caicos. Find your onshore haven among these strips of sand and stake your claim for a lazy afternoon.

Grace Bay Beach★★★
North shore of Providenciales, off Leeward Hwy., east of the airport.
Despite a backdrop of hotels, this beach is highly touted for its gorgeous pairing of sand and sea. Families tend to gravitate here for the calm waters and rockless shore. Take a leisurely stroll along the 12 miles of white, powdery sand to claim a private spot of your own. But keep your eyes peeled for JoJo, the local dolphin who lives in the wild and swims among snorkelers and swimmers in the bay.

Mudjin Harbour Beach★★
Middle Caicos, northwest of the airport.
It's no wonder this off-the-beaten-path beach has served as the background for many photo shoots of major magazines: the white sands of its crescent-shaped lagoon—sitting within the Atlantic Ocean—are picturesque and dramatic. Day- trippers love the unusual sandy expanse, especially its overhanging limestone cliffs and rocky outposts. Caves host stalagmites, stalactites, bats and a salt lake.

Salt Cay★★
6mi southwest of Grand Turk.
This most remote isle is small in size (2.5sq mi), but huge in stature. It serves as a time capsule of the days when Salt Cay was king of the Bermudian salt trade. Ruins here range from windmills to plantation houses, and relics from its heyday as a whaling port can still be found. The tiny cay is protected as a UNESCO World Heritage Site.

Big Ambergris Cay
South of South Caicos. Boats depart from Leeward Marina, Providenciales.
One of the joys of being in the Turks and Caicos is the ease of renting a boat (with captain) and exploring uninhabited cays. **Long Bay Beach** at Big Ambergris Cay is nothing less than stunning—and usually deserted. While away the hours sunning, swimming, snorkeling and fishing (if you brought your own pole).

WHEN TO GO

Temperatures average 85°F-90°F in the hottest months (Jun-Nov) in **hurricane season**. The drier months of Dec-May are **high season**, and generally cooler. On the beaches, trade winds bring cool air year-round. Expect crowds for the annual **Music and Cultural Festival** held Jul-Aug, and the November **Conch Festival** (www.conchfestival.com), celebrating the island's number one export.

GETTING AROUND

BY BUS – There is no official bus system in Providenciales or Grand Turk, but informal minivans known as **jitneys** operate between the main destinations.

BY TAXI – Taxis are available at the airport and port, and in all major towns; they are metered in Providenciales and Grand Turk. Always establish an estimated fare before entering a taxi. From Providenciales airport to Grace Bay costs about $25. Fares from the cruise ship terminal in Grand Turk to Cockburn town average about $7. Provo Taxi Association (Providenciales, &649-946-5314), Gardiner's Taxi (North Caicos, &649-946-7141).

BY CAR – Major rental-car companies and local firms have offices at the airport and cruise terminals. Rentals are pricey and start from about US$65-70 a day. Driving is on the left, following the British system. Gas prices are high compared to the US.

SCOOTERS can also be rented and are a safer option in Grand Turk, with its low traffic volume and low speed limit. The minimum rental age is 25 for cars and 18 for scooters.

BY FERRY – Daily between Providenciales and North Caicos: Caribbean Cruisin' (&649-946-5406; www.caribbean-cruisin.com; 25 min; $25 one way). A ferry runs between Salt Cay and Grand Turk Tues, Wed and Fri, departing 7am and returning 2:30pm (&649-241-1009, 1hr, $12).

BY AIR – Providenciales international airport: Air Turks and Caicos operates several daily flights from Providenciales to South Caicos ($120) and Grand Turk ($150 round-trip) (&649-946-4999, www.airturksandcaicos.com). Caicos Express Airways flies from Providenciales to Salt Cay ($170 round trip) Mon, Wed and Fri, with Sat flights in high season (&649-232-1982, www.caicosexpressairways.com).

VISITOR INFORMATION
Main tourism office:
Stubbs Diamond Plaza, The Bight, Providenciales. &649-946-4970. www.turksandcaicostourism.com
Important numbers
Police, Fire, Ambulance: 999
Medical Services:
Cheshire Hall Medical Centre, Providenciales, &649-941-2800
Cockburn Town Medical Centre, Grand Turk, &649-941-2900

MONEY/CURRENCY
Despite its UK connections, the official currency of the Turks and Caicos is the US dollar. Most credit cards are accepted at hotels and restaurants in main towns. Banks have ATMs for cash withdrawal by debit and credit cards. Traveler's checks are also accepted at many places.

Travel Tip: Eating local means seafood, since most meats have to be imported. Hit up Da Conch Shack on Provo for a perfect island day: right on the beach, conch is prepared every way imaginable—fritters, cracked, stir fried, or curried. Wash it down with the Shack's famous rum punch, and if you still have room, end with a decadent rum cake topped with rum-raisin ice cream.

Little Water Cay

East of Providenciales. ☎ 649-946-1723. Boats depart from Leeward Marina, Providenciales.

The only inhabitants you'll see here are animals. Protected by the islands' National Trust, Little Water Cay is known for its endangered rock **iguanas**. A boardwalk for day visitors provides added protection for these large lizards. You can take one of two trails through the native habitat, both interpreted by panels along the way. Don't forget your swim suit: the deserted beaches of Little Water Cay are great spots to surf and sunbathe.

Diving Sites

Scuba diving is the main draw in the Turks and Caicos. Depending upon the tides and currents, the waters offer optimum visibility for exploring a 7,000ft wall off Grand Turk and Providenciales. The archipelago is noted for spectacular corals, dramatic drop-offs and hundreds of nurse sharks that converge in French Cay two months of the year. Don't forget your underwater camera.

Coral Gardens★★

Off the west-central shore, Grand Turk. This popular 60ft-deep dive site offers lush and healthy coral beds (especially hard coral) populated by overly friendly fish like the yellowtail snapper and large Nassau grouper that follow divers around without mercy.

Black Forest★

Off the west-central shore, Grand Turk. Just a few fin kicks from the boat put you at the wall and the drop-off. The uniqueness here lies in the shadows, created by the wall's ledges, that harbor all sorts of creatures. Prize sightings include incredible sponges, octopus dens and three kinds of black coral.

Shark Hotel★

North West Point, Providenciales. Caution: for experienced divers only. Off Provo's north shore, a 17-mile barrier reef beckons seasoned divers. A short swim from the dive boat brings you to the edge of the wall, where you'll begin a popular deep dive. Be careful—the wall slopes steeply. Be ready for eye-candy that includes elkhorn and staghorn coral, stovepipe sponges, and the shark hotel itself: a composite of sand chutes that serves as bed chambers for dozing nurse sharks.

Smith's Reef
East of Turtle Cove, Providenciales.

Fan corals, parrot fish, sea anemones and turtles await snorkelers. Watch for underwater panels attached to orange floats that describe the marine life and the reef's ecology. Wade in where the floats begin, at the 5-foot water level (the reef's deepest point is 22 feet). Abundant ledges and clefts on the reef make the perfect habitat for spider crabs, moray eels and eagle rays. Bring your own snorkeling gear, or rent equipment and take classes, from Art Pickering's Provo Turtle Divers (*Turtle Cove Marina, ℘ 649-946-4232; www.provoturtledivers.com*).

Dive Shops
Local dive shops offer customized dive trips and diving instruction, certification and equipment rental. Here's a sampling:

Dive Provo – *℘ 649-946-5040; www.diveprovo.com.* This shop offers some 20 different dives to five areas within the Turks and Caicos.

Big Blue Unlimited – *℘ 649-946-5034; www.bigblue.tc.* Big Blue has been cited for its eco-tours.

Caicos Adventures – *℘ 649-941-3346; www.tcidiving.com.* This outfit has located 100 unchartered dive sites for its customers. Dives vary by week.

Salt Cay Divers – *℘ 649-946-6906; www.saltcaydivers.tc.* This Salt-Cay company specializes in dive sites around the island.

Other Diversions

Provo Golf Club
Grace Bay Rd., Providenciales. ℘ 649-946-5991, 877-218-9124. www.provogolfclub.com.

If you want to play golf in the Turks and Caicos, this 18-hole course is your best, and only, bet (for now). Tropical flowers and palm trees border greens and fairways that seem to end in turquoise waters and billowy white clouds. You can rent clubs (carts are required) in the pro shop. After your game, relax with a drink in the **Fairways Bar and Grill**.

Shambhala Spa at Parrot Cay
On Parrot Cay. US reservations: ℘ 904-288-0036, 866-388-0036. www.parrotcay.com. Parrot Cay is a private island. If you're not a guest at the resort, you will need advance reservations for the spa. The resort has its own ferry from Provo to Parrot Cay (35min).

A reigning sense of calm embraces all of Parrot Cay, but bodies and spirits get an extra dose of nurturing at Shambhala (trans-

Travel Tip: The Turks and Caicos Islands are home to some of the best bonefishing in the world, particularly around the south side of Providenciales, Pine Cay, North Caicos and Middle Caicos. Also known as "gray ghosts," bonefish are found in warm, tropical waters and are considered the crown jewel for anglers, due to their agility, speed and strength.

129

Travel Tip: The island of Providenciales is best explored by car, but it's possible to navigate Grand Turk island by bike or scooter. Explore Cockburn Town and see the historic Grand Turk Lighthouse on the north side of the island without having to get on a tour bus.

lation: center of peace), an Asian-inspired spa and healing retreat that entices the world's best known celebrities. Balinese therapists melt away stress with an extensive range of massages, wraps and body treatments based on ancient therapies from Japan, Indonesia, Thailand and China. Yoga is offered daily, and special healing weeks feature visiting instructors. After your treatment or yoga class, reserve a private mini-pavilion at the end of the boardwalk overlooking the sea and relax to the soothing lullaby of gentle waves.

Conch World★

Leeward Hwy., east of Leeward Marina, Providenciales.
649-232-5119. www.conchworld.com. Open year-round Mon–Sat 9am–4pm. $10, children $5.

Kids will be intrigued by these large mollusks, snug in their yellowy-white shells with pink interiors. At the farm's commercial hatcheries, conchs can mature safely, free from ocean predators, before they are sold around the world to the trendiest restaurants as a highly-prized gastronomic delicacy. Conch mariculture was first attempted in 1984 as a small start up. Today, conch is Turks and Caicos' main export and the farm is a major tourist attraction. The hatchery, nursery, and grow-out areas may look a little strange but they produce about a million conchs a year. Buy your own fresh conch here and cook it up island-style: diced raw into salads, served as crunchy crusted cracked conch, fried in fritters or stirred into a spicy chowder.

Turks and Caicos National Museum

Duke St., Cockburn Town, Grand Turk. 649-946-2160, www.tcmuseum.org. Open Tue–Sat 9am–1pm (Wed until 5pm). $7.

Want to see a real shipwreck? A magnet for treasure-seekers, the waters off the Turks and Caicos are said to hold what's left of many a ship that went aground. At this museum you can see the remains of a shipwreck dating back to 1513, the *Molasses Reef* wreck—probably the oldest in the Western Hemisphere. Also on hand are artifacts from early island inhabitants, including a 1,000-year-old paddle used by the Lucayan Indians. A marine exhibit and a space gallery round out the displays. Next door, aloe vera, sea grape, sea-island cotton and other native and imported plants fill the museum's arboretum.

A BIT OF HISTORY

Like many Caribbean islands, the Turks and Caicos have a long and complicated history of piracy, slavery and colonization, and the controversy continues today. The original inhabitants were the Lucayans, a branch of the Taíno, who also lived in the Bahamas in the same period. As in the Bahamas, the native people were wiped out within a few decades of Spanish arrival. As legend has it, Spanish explorer Juan Ponce de Leon landed on Grand Turk on his way to Florida and encountered only one aging native man still living on the island. The Turks and Caicos lay uninhabited for some time, until salt rakers from Bermuda arrived in the late 1600s and built the first permanent settlement.

After capture by both France and Spain, the Turks and Caicos went to the British after the French and Indian War. It became a refuge for loyalists to the British crown who fled the US after the American Revolution. It was during this period that slaves were brought over from Africa and from the US to work on cotton plantations. The islands also served as a convenient hideout for pirates who terrorized the Caribbean Sea, including two notorious female pirates, Ann Bonny and Mary Read, whose colorful tales became an integral part of pirate legends and lore.

The Turks and Caicos then became part of the Bahamas colony for some years, and were then annexed to the British Crown Colony of Jamaica. When Jamaica won independence, the Turks and Caicos became a separate crown colony. Today, the population consists of African descendants, often known as "belongers," as well as a sizable expatriate community from the UK, Canada, the US and the island of Hispaniola, but it remains a British Overseas Territory. There were attempts toward independence, and even a motion for the islands to be annexed by Canada. In 2009, the Turks and Caicos lost its elected government and most of its constitution was suspended by the British amid widespread allegations of corruption. Its interim government is currently run by a British governor while corruption investigations and fiscal overhaul continue.

OUT AND ABOUT
...LIKE A LOCAL

It's important to get out of the resort boundaries to get the really local experience. Most visitors stay on the north side of the island, but the quieter, more residential south side has its own personality that the locals appreciate. It's limited in terms of restaurants and amenities, but the south side receives a constant, light breeze, its water is shallower and warmer than the north side, and the coastline is rocky and dramatic. Come here just to watch the sun rise and it will be a moment you won't forget.

Then it's time to get off the island. Although Provo and Grand Turk are the stars of Turks and Caicos, the North and Middle Caicos and the various uninhabited islands and cays are ideal for snorkeling, kayaking and diving. A 30-minute ferry ride connects Provo with the North Caicos, where clear, shallow waters lap gently on the shores, protected by the barrier reef. On the northern coast lie the lovely, 7-mile long Whitby Beach and Three Marys Cays marine sanctuary, which has some of the best snorkeling on the islands. North Caicos is also home to the ruins of old plantations that were settled by loyalists to the British crown who fled the US after the American Revolution. The best-preserved of all the ruins is Wade's Green, established around 1789, which was one of the most extensive plantations of its time.

North Caicos is also a birder's paradise, and even boasts the largest flock of pink flamingos on the islands. North Caicos is best explored by car, and from there you can get on the causeway that connects to Middle Caicos. This is the largest of all the islands, but is sparsely populated with just three settlements: Conch Bar, Bambarra and Lorimers. Only 48 square miles, the island retains a natural beauty that is unspoiled and dramatic, with towering cliffs made of limestone, as well as lush mangrove swamps and low tidal flats that are ideal for kayaking and bird-watching. The Conch Bar Caves National Park comprises one of the largest cave systems in the Caribbean, where miles of limestone caves are teeming with stalagmites and stalactites. The island is free of developed hotel zones, but there are a handful of guest houses and vacation rentals to spend a night.

Addresses

For price ranges, see the Legend on the cover flap.

WHERE TO STAY

$$ Caribbean Paradise Inn – *Grace Bay, Providenciales.* ☎649-946-5020 or 866-946-5020. *www.caribbean-paradise-inn.com. 18 rooms.* This charming inn offers rooms in soft pastels with a refrigerator, ceiling fan and a balcony or a patio. The complimentary breakfast buffet is served on the cheerful, open-air terrace.

$$ Sibonné Beach Hotel – *Grace Bay, Providenciales.* ☎649-946-5547 or 800-528-1905. *www.sibonne.com. 28 rooms.* This low-rise complex picked the best location right on the white-sand beach. Wander among the shady palms in the resort's gardens as you head to the swimming pool or the restaurant. Each room has a ceiling fan, mini-refrigerator and courtyard patio. Good value for money.

$$$$$ Grace Bay Club – *Grace Bay, Providenciales.* ☎649-946-5050 or 800-946-5757. *www.gracebayclub.com. 89 rooms.* The well-heeled clientele come here to de-stress or exercise. Cycle, play tennis, kayak or simply laze about on the world-class beach. Guest quarters have a Spanish flair, Egyptian cotton linens and flat-screen TVs. Continental breakfast and afternoon tea are included in the rate.

$$$$$ Parrot Cay Resort – *Parrot Cay, off the western shore of North Caicos.* ☎649-946-7788. *www.parrotcay.com. 51 units.* Guests come to this private 1,000-acre island to unwind on the beach or improve their yoga postures at the Shambhala Spa. Rooms with verandas have four-poster beds draped with white muslin and sleek rattan or teak furniture. Enjoy Mediterranean cuisine at the resort's **Terrace ($$$$)** restaurant.

WHERE TO EAT

$$ Da Conch Shack and Rum Bar – *Blue Hills Rd., Providenciales.* ☎649-946-8877. *www.conchshack.tc.* **Caribbean**. Billed as one of the best beach bars in the Caribbean, this tiny shack is a great place to savor local conch raw, cracked, fried, curried or chowdered. Or try the jerk chicken, best enjoyed with an ice-cold Turks Head Lager in one hand and a vintage rum on the rocks in the other. Live music Thursdays.

$$$ Porter's Island Thyme – *North District, Salt Cay.* ☎649-946-697. *www.islandthyme.tc. Dinner reservations requested.* **International**. The friendly hosts take great care to provide diners with filling breakfasts. Local Caribbean favorites and Asian ingredients compose their fusion dinner dishes. Learn from the locals at the "zoo" bar, where Porter mixes mojitos. Happy hours and specialty nights.

Travel Tip: Although the Turks and Caicos are a British Crown Colony, the US dollar is the official currency on the islands. Most tourist places will accept credit cards, but at more local establishments, be sure to have some cash on hand and plan to tip about 15 percent.

DISCOVERING
CUBA★★★

Classic American cars and horse-drawn carriages transport you back to an island that seems to be frozen in time. Cuba is the largest and most populated island in the Caribbean, but it's the least known among Americans. The commercial, economic and financial embargo on Cuba was first imposed by the US in 1960, and strengthened in 1962, effectively closing off this Communist country to nearly all American travelers. In recent years, the US government has relaxed the rules that were tightened by the previous administration, allowing Americans to go with educational or religious programs and "people-to-people" exchanges.

The nation's population is as diverse as can be. Ever since Cuba was first colonized, immigrants from all over the world have mingled with the island's Taíno and other indigenous peoples. Most of the early Europeans who colonized Cuba were Spaniards. West Africans were shipped to the island as slave labor, and intermarriage between slaves and Hispanics saw the rise of the mestizo population. At the end of the 18th century, French immigrants arrived, fleeing the slave revolt on Haiti. Cuba's ties with the former Soviet Union led to a wave of Russian immigrants, along with European fortune-seekers.

The landscape in Cuba is as varied as its people, ranging from sparkling, white-sand beaches, vast farmland and mountainous skylines to decrepit urban buildings. The country is divided into five main areas: Varadero and the northern coast; the west, including Pinar del Río and the picturesque Viñales valley; the capital city of Havana; the center of the country, including Trinidad and Santa Clara; and the east, including Santiago de Cuba, the second-largest Cuban city.

For a map of Cuba, see inside front cover.

PETER'S TOP PICKS

CULTURE

Cuba boasts a vibrant art scene, and the Museo Nacional de Bellas Artes houses 50,000 works of art from all over Cuba and the world. You'll want to check out the Cuban collection in particular, featuring works by René Portocarrero and other Cuban artists. (p **138**)

HISTORY

For some of the oldest history in Havana, make sure you check out Plaza de Armas. The plaza contains the Museo de la Ciudad, which holds paintings, weapons, and other historical artifacts from different times in Cuban history. (p **136**)

STAY

Part of the Iberostar brand, Parque Central hotel has all the modern amenities, making it a welcome respite after you spend a day exploring this city lost in time. Order a mojito by the rooftop pool. (p **143**)

SHOP

A pedestrian street full of history and culture, the Prado (also known as Paseo de Martí) is a perfect place to people watch. On Saturday there is a local market where you can view and purchase Cuban works of art. (p **140**)

EAT

To get the true Cuban experience, dining in a *paladar*—a private, family-run restaurant—is a must. Restaurante La Casa is credited with pioneering modern Cuban cuisine featuring Creole and international flavors, not to mention its Thursday-night sushi menu. (p **143**)

ENTERTAINMENT

Once you've gawked at the grand structure of Gran Teatro de La Habana, step inside to see performances by Cuba's national ballet company, operas and concerts. (p **140**)

Havana★★★

ASK PETER...

Q: How can I get truly authentic Cuban food in Cuba?

A: Although it may be tempting to try some of the street food in Havana and other big cities, I can't wholeheartedly recommend it, as ice is not treated and there's no refrigeration for street vendors. My advice is tried and true in almost any country: peel it, boil it, cook it, or skip it. You don't have to be relegated to hotel dining or tourist restaurants. Cuba is known for its *paladares*, family-run restaurants in private homes. They are regularly inspected by the government and add local flavor without the risk of Montezuma's Revenge!

Facing the Straits of Florida, Cuba's 493-year-old city seems preserved in a time-warp, but this 2.2 million-strong metropolis is slowly modernizing. Eminently walkable, **Old Havana** (La Habana Vieja) is a World Heritage Site awash in Spanish Colonial architecture. **Centro Habana** and **Vedado** districts also hold attractions of interest to visitors, but require four-wheel transportation to access them.

La Habana Vieja★★★

Plaza de la Catedral

A true masterpiece of colonial design, this cobbled plaza is surrounded by lofty mansions built by Spanish nobles. Its centerpiece is the compelling **Catedral de San Cristóbal★★★** (*open Mon–Fri 11am–2:30pm, Sat 10:30am–1pm, Sun 9:30am–12:30pm; Mass Sun 10:30am; museum—open daily 9am–6:45pm*) with its undulating Cuban-Baroque façade. Opposite the cathedral, the **Palacio de los Condes de Casa Bayona★★**, now the **Museo de Arte Colonial★★** (*open daily 9am–6:45pm; 2CUC*) brims with Cuba's colonial era (16C-19C) artifacts.

Plaza de Armas★★★

Havana's oldest plaza (1582) is dominated by the **Palacio de los Capitanes Generales★★★**, which houses the **Museo de la Ciudad★★★** (*open Tue–Sun 9:30am–4:30pm*), a repository for paintings, documents, weapons, furniture and memorabilia that illustrate the main periods in Cuban history. Another significant building, the Classic-referenced **El Templete** (1827) marks the city's foundation in 1519.

Plaza de San Francisco de Asís★

Basilica Menor y Convento de San Francisco de Asís★★ (*open Sun–Mon 9:30am–12:30pm, Tue 9:30am–5pm, Wed & Sat 9am–7pm*) towers over the vast cobblestone square of the same name. The plaza's focal point, **Fuente de los Leones** (Lions' Fountain) is flanked by the imposing Lonja del Comercio (Commodity Exchange) on the north side and the Aduana (Customs House) on the east side. Today, classical and Cuban music concerts are held in the basilica.

Plaza Vieja★★★

Restored historic houses and mansions encircle one of the oldest squares (16C) in Havana. Highlights include the high-tech **Planetarium** (☏ 7-864-9165; *reservations in person or by phone*

WHEN TO GO

Havana is hot and humid year-round; temperatures average 22°C/72°F in winter and 27°C/81°F in summer. Thunderstorms are short but frequent during the **wet season** (May-Oct). Sept and Oct pose the greatest risks in **hurricane season** (Jun- Nov). Feb, March and Apr may be a good compromise for visitors who want to escape the crowds of **peak season** (Dec-Jan and Jul-Aug).

GETTING AROUND

BY BUS – Hop-on/hop-off **HabanaBusTour** runs daily 9am–9pm (3-5CUC).

BY TAXI – **Cubataxi** (✆7-855-5555). CUC fares must be negotiated as the meter is often "broken." In unmetered private taxis (*taxis particulares*), rides cost 10-20 CUP.

BICI-TAXI (bicycle carriages) fares are payable in CUC.

COCO-TAXI (three-wheel yellow vehicles) fares (in CUC) are usually higher than standard cab fares; you pay for the novelty.

GRAN CAR (✆7-881-0992), state-run, offers tours in vintage American cars. Fares from 25CUC/hr, including driver.

BY CAR – Reserve with national rental companies in advance: Cubacar Ave. 3ra and Paseo (Vedado), ✆7-833- 2164; Havanautos, Calles 23 and H (Vedado), ✆7-837-5901; REX, 5th Ave. 5ta and Calle 92 (Miramar), ✆7-209-2207.

VISITOR INFORMATION

Important numbers
Emergency (ambulance)**:** ✆7-838-1185

Police: ✆106
Fire: ✆105
Asistur
English-speaking staff available
✆7-866-4499
Infotur offices in Havana
524 Calle Obispo, between Calles Bernaza and Villegas (La Habana Vieja), ✆7-866-3333, www.infotur.cu.

MONEY/CURRENCY

The Cuban Convertible Peso (CUC) is used by foreigners and is pegged to the US dollar at 1 to 1 and to the British pound at 63 pence. The CUP national peso (*moneda nacional*) is valued at 23-25 to one CUC.

All major hotels have currency exchange desks. You can withdraw money using your credit/debit card (at exorbitant fees) or exchange cash or travelers' checks at most banks (note: travelers' checks and credit cards drawn on US banks are not honored in Cuba). Check with your credit-card issuer before departure to assure that your card will be accepted in Cuba.

You can withdraw convertible pesos from several ATM machines in Havana, including at some Cadeca (exchange) offices. Note: All exchanges between CUC and US dollars are subject to a 10 percent tax in addition to other exchange fees.

It is best to bring as much cash in sterling, euros or Canadian dollars to Cuba as you feel comfortable carrying.

Mon–Tue9:30am–3:30pmforshowsWed–Sun10am,11am,12:30pm and 3:30pm; Spanish guide only), and the **Casa del Conde de Jaruco** (1737), now housing La Casona art gallery and the Fondo Cubano de Bienes Culturales, which stages art exhibits and sells handicrafts.

Edificio Bacardí★★

Corner of Monserrate and San Juan de Dios.
Open during office hours.

This stylish 6-story building is an archetype Art Deco gem built in 1930 for Emilio Bacardí, a wealthy sugarcane plantation owner and founder of the famed brand of Bacardi rum.

The building's ochre-colored façade exhibits the linear symmetry and ceramic ornamentation associated with Art Deco; the roofline and central tower exhibit terracotta detailing. The figure of a bat at the top of the tower is the mascot that appears on the label of Bacardi products.

Museo Nacional de Bellas Artes★★

Arte Universal: Calle San Rafael between Zulueta and Monserrate.
𝒫 7-861-0241. Arte Cubano: Avenida de las Misiones and Trocadero. Open Tues–Sat 10am–6pm, Sun 10am–2pm.

Cuba's National Museum of Fine Arts has amassed nearly 50,000 works of art. The **international collections** are installed in the former Centro Asturiano (1927), which faces the Edificio Manzana de Gómez opposite Parque Central. The **Cuban collection** is housed in a 1950s building and features works by **Wifredo Lam** and **René Portocarrero**, among others.

Iglesia de Nuestra Señora de la Merced

Calle Cuba, at the corner of Calle Merced.

A three-nave church, begun in 1755, boasts a white façade with six pillars as well as late-Italian Baroque and early Neoclassical elements, but its rather unembellished exterior belies the glories within: the central cupola is decorated with stunning fantastical **frescoes** in glorious colors, as are other parts of the enormous church.

Centro Habana
Malecón★★

All year long hundreds of residents and tourists come here night and day to while away the hours sitting on this ocean-battered **seawall**. Here, youngsters scamper up the seawall, anglers watch their lines, vendors sell cheap cigars, lovers recline entwined, and men shout out compliments to female passersby, as vintage American cars and coco-taxis cruise Havana's busiest east-west boulevard.

The seawall extends about 8km/5mi on Havana's northern shore, from the Castillo de San Salvador de la Punta in La Habana Vieja west to the Almendares River, which separates Vedado from Miramar.

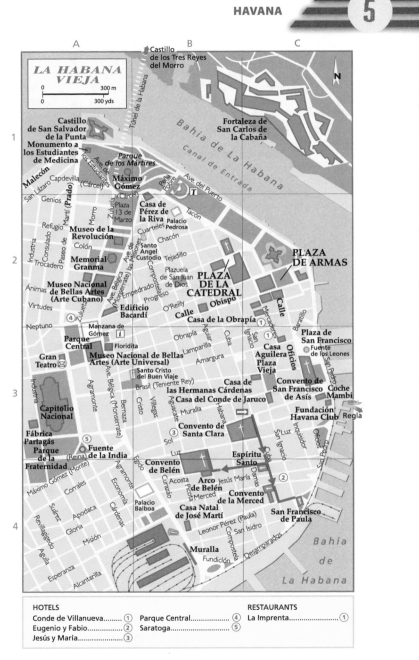

LA HABANA VIEJA

0   300 m
0   300 yds

Castillo de los Tres Reyes del Morro

Bahía de La Habana

Canal de Entrada

Fortaleza de San Carlos de la Cabaña

Castillo de San Salvador de la Punta
Monumento a los Estudiantes de Medicina

Parque de los Mártires

Máximo Gómez

Malecón

Capdevilla

Ave. de los Estudiantes (Cárcel)

San Lázaro

Genios

Paseo de Martí (Prado)

Refugio

Colón

Morro

(Cárcel)

Plaza 13 de Marzo

Casa de Pérez de la Riva

Palacio Pedrosa

Ave. del Puerto

Peña Pobre

Tacón

Cuarteles

Chacón

Museo de la Revolución

Industria

Consulado

Trocadero

Memorial Granma

Ánimas

Museo Nacional de Bellas Artes (Arte Cubano)

Virtudes

Neptuno

Santo Ángel Custodio

Ave. de las Misiones

Ave. Bélgica (Monserrate)

Compostela

Tejadillo

Plazuela de San Juan de Dios

PLAZA DE LA CATEDRAL

Obispo

Empedrado

Progreso

O'Reilly

Calle

Casa de la Obrapía

PLAZA DE ARMAS

Calle

Mercaderes

Edificio Bacardí

Manzana de Gómez

Parque Central

Floridita

Obrapía

Aguiar

Cuba

San Ignacio

Oficios

Plaza de San Francisco

Fuente de los Leones

Gran Teatro

Museo Nacional de Bellas Artes (Arte Universal)

Lamparilla

Casa Aguilera

Plaza Vieja

Baratillo

Amargura

Santo Cristo del Buen Viaje

Brasil (Teniente Rey)

Cristo

Casa de las Hermanas Cárdenas

Casa del Conde de Jaruco

Convento de San Francisco de Asís

Coche Mambí

Capitolio Nacional

Industria

Agramonte

Bernaza

Villegas

Aguacate

Habana

Muralla

Convento de Santa Clara

Fundación Havana Club

Regla

Fábrica Partagás

Fuente de la India

Sol

Luz

San Ignacio

Inquisidor

Oficios

San Pedro

Parque de la Fraternidad

Agramonte (Reina)

Egido

Luz

Espíritu Santo

Cuba

Máximo Gómez (Monte)

Corrales

Economía

Curazao

Convento de Belén

Acosta

Damas

Suárez

Apodaca

Cárdenas

Palacio Balboa

Arco de Belén

Jesús María

Merced

Convento de la Merced

San Francisco de Paula

Revillagigedo

Gloria

Misión

Casa Natal de José Martí

Picota

Leonor Pérez (Paula)

San Isidro

Compostela

Bahía de La Habana

Aguila

Esperanza

Alcantarilla

Muralla

Fundición

Desamparados

HOTELS		RESTAURANTS	
Conde de Villanueva......... ①	Parque Central.................. ④	La Imprenta..................... ①
Eugenio y Fabio................ ②	Saratoga........................... ⑤	
Jesús y María.................... ③		

Travel Tip: Be aware when trying to buy cigars in Cuba that black market illegal traders may approach you to sell you a box of cigars. Counterfeiters are excellent at making phoney cigar labels from banana leaves, substandard tobacco leaves, and imitation stamps mimicking the Cuban government official seal of approval. Make sure when you are buying cigars that you trust only reputable sources, like official government stores (these are always and only the official La Casa del Habano). Habanos, the official distributors, has issued new instructions for checking authenticity: www.habanos.com/ sellos?lang=en.

Prado★

This straight boulevard, with its broad, tree-lined pedestrianized thoroughfare (also named **Paseo de Martí**), divides Centro Habana from La Habana Vieja. Paved in marble and dotted with marble benches, the Prado was once the haunt of aristocracy. Today, locals ramble and children play, and on Saturdays, there's an artists' market.

Gran Teatro de La Habana★★

Between Calles San José and San Rafael.
Open Mon–Fri 9am–5pm. Guided tour available.
The Great Theater of Havana, once home to the Galicians' social club, sports an imposing Neo-Baroque façade designed with rounded ground-floor arches (*portales*), and embellished with balustrades, statues and balconies in white marble. Today the 1915 building is best known for its association with Cuba's national ballet and serves as the primary venue for Havana's International Ballet Festival. Operas and concerts are held in the evenings, as are performances of the Ballet Nacional de Cuba.

Capitolio Nacional★★

Closed for renovation.
This Neoclassical 200m/656ft-long replica of the US Capitol Building in Washington, DC, was home to Cuba's legislature for many years, and now houses a museum that is under restoration.

Fábrica de Tabacos Partagás★

No. 520 Calle Industria. Closed temporarily for renovation.
The Partagás, behind the Capitolio, is one of Cuba's oldest cigar factories and its most famous. When it's open, guided tours explore stages of the cigar-making process on the factory floor. There's a factory store on the premises where a selection of tobacco is for sale *(also closed temporarily).*

BASEBALL
...LIKE A LOCAL

The national game in Cuba may be dominoes—and you will see that the minute you step foot in Havana—but the most beloved national sport is baseball. You can attend, along with thousands of screaming Cuban fans, a baseball game at Havana's stadium, Estadio Latinoamericano, for the National Series team. The stadium is home to Cuidad Habana Industriales and is known to Cubans as "Colossus of Cerro."

Baseball season runs from November to April with each team playing 90 games during the regular season. The season finishes off with three playoff rounds to crown a champion team. There are two leagues consisting of amateur players (meaning they don't get paid) in Cuba: the East League and the West League. The players don't get traded to other teams like in the American leagues; they simply play for the provinces where they live.

Going to a game in Cuba is very straightforward. You cannot get tickets in advance unless you are on a group tour and the tickets are purchased through the tour, so it's best to just go to the stadium where the game is being played. Cubans play and watch for love of the game. There is no huge rivalry between the teams, and most Cubans cheer for both when either one does something good—or boo when an error is made.

Cubans' love of the game translates to one of the most affordable pastimes in the country. Tickets are literally pennies for locals. Even foreigners don't have to pay very much for a baseball game, with tickets usually costing about 3 CUC (Cuban convertible pesos).

Ask any local in Havana or other areas (there are baseball games all over) for the time of the game that day and they will be able to guide you. You can also plan in advance by checking out www.baseballdecuba.com for the complete schedule.

Travel Tip: Since 2004, American dollars have been subject to a conversion tax. Unlike euros, sterling or Canadian dollars that are simply converted to Cuban Convertible Pesos (CUC), American dollars have a lower exchange rate and also include an 10 percent tax. Credit cards affiliated with American banks (even Visa) are not accepted and do not work in Cuba.

Vedado★
La Rampa

Calle 23 runs more than 2km/1mi through Vedado from the Malecón southwest to the Columbus cemetery. Known as La Rampa along the stretch between the Hotel Nacional and Hotel Tryp Habana Libre, the thoroughfare is lined with travel agencies, airline offices and banks. Lively day and night, the street hums during business hours with commercial activity that gives way to the nightlife of bars and discotheques during off-hours. The landmark **Hotel Nacional★** rises at the base of La Rampa. Its handsome Art Deco silhouette has appealed to many since the 1930s, and a mojito on the terrace affords expansive views of Havana Bay.

Coppelia★
Calle 23 (La Rampa) at the intersection of Calle L.
Open Tue–Sun 10am–9:15pm.
This large glass and concrete circus pavilion houses the state-run Coppelia ice-cream parlor, a national institution. Designed by Mario Girona in 1966 in Modern style, it was immortalized in the award-winning Cuban movie *Fresa y Chocolate*.

Cementerio de Cristóbal Colón★★★
End of Calle 12. Open daily 7am–5pm. Guided tour available.
This vast monument to the dead lies on the border between the Vedado and Nuevo Vedado districts. Somber gray tombs stand next to richly ornate monuments and mausoleums where the remains of some of Cuba's most prominent political and cultural personalities are interred.

Outside Havana
Finca La Vigía★ (Hemingway's Home)
Calles Vigía and Steimbert, San Francisco de Paula, 13km/8mi southeast of Havana. ☎ 7-691-0809. Open Mon–Sat 10am–5pm, Sun 10am–1pm. Guided tours. Do not visit if it is raining: shutters will be closed.
American author **Ernest Hemingway** lived at Finca la Vigía from 1939-1960. It is now a museum where Hemingway's furniture, personal artifacts and memorabilia remain as they were when he lived here. Visitors may not enter the house, but can peer through the open windows from the outside. Also on the property are his small yacht, the Pilar, and the gravesites of his four dogs.

Addresses

For price ranges, see the Legend on the cover flap.

WHERE TO STAY

$ Eugenio y Fabio – *656 Calle San Ignacio, between Calles Jesús María and Merced. ℘7-862-9877. fabio.quintana@infomed.sld.cu. 3 rooms.* This colonial gem, with a rooftop terrace, overflows with period furniture and objets d'art.

$ Jesús y María – *518 Calle Aguacate, between Calles Sol and Muralla. ℘7-861-1378. jesusmaria2003@yahoo.com. 3 rooms.* This friendly family home offers a superb terrace, comfortable rooms, and pleasant covered patio.

$$$$ Conde de Villanueva – *202 Calle Mercaderes on the corner of Calle Lamparilla. ℘7-862-9293. www.habaguanex.cu. 9 rooms.* Designed for cigar aficionados, this old city Colonial mansion features a smoking lounge.

$$$$ Parque Central – *Calle Neptuno between Paseo del Prado and Zulueta. ℘7-860-6627. www.iberostar.com. 427 rooms.* Boasting two lovely rooftop pools and bars, this comfortable, modern hotel sits in an excellent location.

$$$$$ Hotel Saratoga – *Paseo del Prado 603 at the corner with Dragones. ℘7-868-1000. www.hotel-saratoga.com. 96 rooms.* The Saratoga is Old Havana's luxury address. Sip mojitos by the rooftop pool while admiring the capital's rooftops.

WHERE TO EAT

$$ Café Laurent – *257 Calle M, between Calles 19 and 21. ℘7-832-6890.* **International**. Penthouse paladar dining on a wonderful terrace with excellent service is available in this central Vedado mansion.

$$ La Imprenta – *Calle Mercaderes, between Calles Lamparilla and Amargura. ℘7-864-9851.* **Creole**. Typical Cuban platters are served in the alfresco patio of this attractive former printworks.

$$ Restaurante La Casa – *865 Calle 30, between Calles 26 and 41. ℘7-881-7000. http://restaurantelacasacuba.com.* **Creole/Japanese**. This *paladar* (family-run) serves up generous plates of fish, chicken and rabbit. A sushi menu is offered on Thursdays. The service here is friendly and attentive.

$$ San Cristóbal – *469 Calle San Rafael, between Calles Lealtad and Campanario. ℘05-292-1305.* **Creole**. A new, artfully decorated private house-turned-*paladar* offering well-prepared Cuban dishes.

$$$ La Guarida – *418 Calle Concordía, between Calles Gervasio and Escobar. ℘7-866-9047. www.laguarida.com.* **Creole**. A glorious film set-turned-*paladar*, this popular restaurant serves up tasty Cuban and international cuisine.

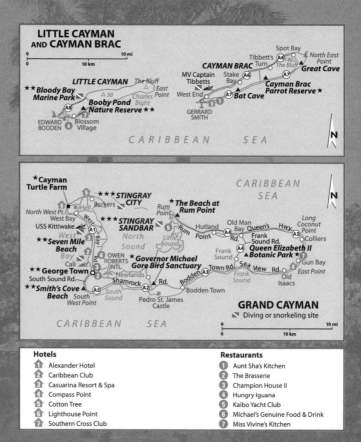

LITTLE CAYMAN AND CAYMAN BRAC

0 ——— 10 mi
0 ——— 10 km

Spot Bay
North East Point
Tibbett's △140 The Bluff
CAYMAN BRAC
MV Captain Tibbetts
Stake Bay A6 A7 **Great Cave**
LITTLE CAYMAN The Bluff
△ East Point
△50 Charles Bight
West End A7 **Cayman Brac Parrot Reserve ★**
★★Bloody Bay Marine Park **Booby Pond Nature Reserve ★★**
A8 Bat Cave
GERRARD SMITH
EDWARD BODDEN Blossom Village
C A R I B B E A N   S E A

N

★**Cayman Turtle Farm**

C A R I B B E A N S E A

N

★★★**STINGRAY CITY**
Barkers
Hell
North West Pt. West Bay
USS Kittiwake A1
★★★**STINGRAY SANDBAR**
★**The Beach at Rum Point**
Rum Point
North Sound
Little Sound
Rum Point
Hutland
Old Man Bay Queen's
A4 Hwy.
Frank Sound Rd.
A3
Long Coconut Point
Colliers
West Bay
★★**Seven Mile Beach**
Cali
OWEN ROBERTS INTL.
★**Governor Michael Gore Bird Sanctuary**
Frank Sound
Queen Elizabeth II Botanic Park ★
Gun Bay
East Point
★★**George Town**
South Sound Rd.
Newlands
Shamrock Rd.
Sea View Rd.
A4
Old Isaacs
★★**Smith's Cove Beach**
A5 South West Point
South Sound
Bodden A3
Town Rd.
Frank Sound
GRAND CAYMAN
Pedro St. James Castle
Bodden Town
◣ Diving or snorkeling site

C A R I B B E A N   S E A

0 ——— 10 mi
0 ——— 10 km

Hotels
1. Alexander Hotel
2. Caribbean Club
3. Casuarina Resort & Spa
4. Compass Point
5. Cotton Tree
6. Lighthouse Point
7. Southern Cross Club

Restaurants
1. Aunt Sha's Kitchen
2. The Brasserie
3. Champion House II
4. Hungry Iguana
5. Kaibo Yacht Club
6. Michael's Genuine Food & Drink
7. Miss Vivine's Kitchen

Just 480 miles south of Miami, the Cayman Islands are a British Overseas Territory where colonial influences and Caribbean culture come together. The three islands are geographically close, but each has its own unique personality and attributes. The largest of the three islands, Grand Cayman is about 22 miles long by 8 miles at its widest point. It's home to the majority of the Caymans' population, and is per-

PETER'S TOP PICKS

EAT

Cayman Brac is so small that it's impossible not to eat local. Aunt Sha's Kitchen on the southern side of the island specializes in island staples like fried conch and Cayman-style fish.
(p **153**)

SEE

Wander through an old-growth forest and catch sight of the brilliant Cayman Brac Parrots, the smallest of any Amazon Parrot. The 280-acre Cayman Brac Parrot Reserve is home to about 300 of these. (p **151**)

PLAY

The Cayman Islands have some of the most incredible natural dive sites in the world, but don't miss the very cool artificial reefs that include a Russian warship and a US submarine.
(p **151**)

haps best known for the hundreds of international banks and trust companies that make it a thriving offshore banking capital. It serves as the commercial, financial and administrative center of the territory, and is also a major tourist destination and busy cruise port city.

Iconic attractions include the quaint colonial capital in George Town, the magnificent Seven Mile Beach, and some of the best scuba-diving sites in the world. The western side up to George Town is the more developed part of the island, while East End offers a more untouched glimpse of what Cayman once looked like before it became populated with tourists.

Little Cayman is the smallest of the islands, located about 75 miles northeast of Grand Cayman and spanning a mere 10 miles, and only a mile in width. This island is so compact and sparsely populated that the airport, post office and fire station are all found in one modest white building. It's also an eco-lover's paradise, with pristine beaches, world-renowned dive sites, lush nature reserves and a healthy population of iguanas.

Cayman Brac is the easternmost island, measuring just 12 miles long and about 1 mile wide. The word "brac" is Gaelic for "bluff," namely for the limestone cliffs that dot the landscape through the middle of the island, ending in a dramatic 140-foot drop at the eastern end. This island offers ecotourism at its best, with ample hiking and biking trails, rock climbing, dive sites, and bird watching (or bat watching, if you prefer!).

Travel Tip: Little Cayman and Cayman Brac are small enough to explore by bicycle. In fact, many hotels and resorts offer complimentary bicycles, or you can rent one at a local shop on the islands.

Grand Cayman

Grand Cayman is divided into West Bay at its western end; Seven Mile Beach; George Town; Bodden Town; North Side; and East End. The western side up to George Town is the more developed part of the island, while East End offers a rather pristine glimpse of how Cayman once looked.

Stingray City★★★ and Stingray Sandbar★★★

North Sound, about 2mi east of Barkers. Captain Marvin's Watersports: ✆ *345-945-4590, 866-978-6364. www.captain marvins.com. Moby Dick Tours:* ✆ *345-925-5542. www.mobydicktours.com. Tours start at $35.*

Stingray City is a shallow sandy area in the 12ft-deep waters of North Sound. Since the 1950s (when Captain Marvin "founded" Stingray City), people have come to see scores of docile sting-rays that flock here looking for treats. The practice began with fishermen tossing their scraps overboard. As soon as your boat drops anchor, jump into the temperate water and let the rays brush past you at their leisure. Your guides will corral one for you to hold and even feed; the rays get a bit frisky, but they use their barbed, venomous tails only in self defense. If you aren't a swimmer, you can experience the same rush on **Stingray Sandbar**, where the water is waist-deep. After that, the tour continues to a snorkeling spot teeming with fish.

George Town★★

Rustic Bodden Town may be the first capital of the Cayman Islands, but George Town has long since taken its crown. It's the financial hub of the islands and its largest port. Take time to explore its scenic **waterfront** lined with historic buildings, duty-free shops and restaurants. From George Town you can go diving or snorkeling, take a pirate ship cruise, hop on a submarine, or enjoy a walking tour of its cultural monuments.

Atlantis Submarines★

30 S. Church St. ✆ *345-949-7700, 800-887-8571. www.caymanislandssubmarines.com. $79 and up. Two night dives scheduled daily between 7pm–8pm.*

If you've never scuba dived, this is about as close as you can get. The well-outfitted Atlantis will take you about 100 feet below the surface, close to the reef wall. The battery-operated sub, designed specifically for tours, offers unbeatable glimpses of sea life, including crabs, sponges, tarpon, lionfish, stingrays, and if you're lucky, turtles. Choose either a daytime or night dive.

ASK PETER...

Q: What are some natural sites beyond the beaches?
A: The Cayman Islands have a surprising amount of forest in addition to their beaches. The Botanic Park's Woodland Trail is less than a mile long, and traverses natural areas where you can get close to the local flora and fauna. The Mastic Reserve protects the old-growth forest with a 2-mile-long trail that takes you through various terrain within the interior of Grand Cayman.

WHEN TO GO

Temperatures range from 70°F–90°F, with an occasional Feb night dipping into the mid-60s. Mid-May–Oct is the summer, or "rainy" season. It's also the low tourist season, when you can find great deals. Mar–Apr are the driest months, although it can rain any time during the year; the western sections tend to experience higher rainfall. High tourist season is Nov–Apr.

GETTING AROUND

BY BUS – Licensed public buses (look for the blue number plates) run throughout Grand Cayman. Fares start at CI$2; both US and CI dollars are accepted. Buses have designated stops but can also be flagged down (*℘345-945-5100).

BY TAXI – Taxis can be flagged down and wait at resorts and the cruise-ship dock in George Town. **Ace Taxis** (*℘345-777-7777) and **Stingray Taxi Service** (*℘345-917-9820), **D&M Taxi Services** (*℘345-916-7226) on Cayman Brac; **McCoys** (*℘345-926-0104) on Little Cayman.

BY CAR – Major rental car companies have offices in Grand Cayman, at the resorts and the airport. Rates start at about $40 per day; minimum rental age is 21. All visitors are required to obtain a visitor's driving permit, which the agency will supply. Note: in Cayman, you drive on the left.

BY TWO-WHEEL – Scooters can be rented and cost around $40 a day. Most resorts offer complimentary bicycles to guests.

BY FERRY – There is no ferry service from Grand Cayman to Cayman Brac or Little Cayman, but you can charter a boat. However, the choppy seas make for a bumpy 4hr ride. **Cool Breeze Boat Charters** (www.coolbreezefishing.com, *℘345-924-2887) and **Cayman Luxury Charters** (http://caymanluxurycharters.com, *℘345-938-2525).

BY AIR – **Cayman Airways Express** (www.caymanairways.com, *℘345-949-2311) flies daily from Grand Cayman to Cayman Brac and Little Cayman. Paradise Cayman Vacations offers one-day package tours to Cayman Brac (www.paradisecayman.com, *℘345-947-7770, 800-742-3070).

VISITOR INFORMATION

Main tourism office:
Regatta Office Park Windward 3, Grand Cayman, *℘345-949-0623.
Important numbers
Emergency (24hrs): 911
Police: *℘345-949-4222
Crisis Hotline: *℘345-943-2422
Medical Services:
Ambulance Service: *℘345-244-2659
Cayman Islands Hospital, Grand Cayman: *℘345-949-8600
Faith Hospital, Cayman Brac: *℘345-948-2243

MONEY/CURRENCY

The official currency is the Caymanian dollar, which has an exchange rate of CI$1.00 to US$1.25. However, American dollars are accepted all over the islands. Major credit cards (except Discover Card), debit cards with Cirrus affiliation and internationally recognized traveler's checks are also accepted.

Travel Tip:
Merchandise in Grand Cayman ranges from local crafts and foods (including hot sauce and the famous rum cake) to duty-free luxury items like jewelry, leather goods and watches. Two main shopping destinations are Camana Bay, a pleasant open-air complex with high-end boutiques, restaurants, numerous public events and a 75-foot observation tower that offers 360-degree views of the island; and downtown George Town, where you can find art galleries and high-end boutiques.

Seven Mile Beach★★

1mi north of George Town.

No matter that Seven Mile Beach is actually only 5.5 miles long, it's still the most beautiful and expansive stretch of beach in Grand Cayman. Most of the island's resort hotels can be found perched on its white sands, but it also has plenty of public access (snorkelers will want to head to the Governor's Public Beach entrance). Because vendor-peddling along the beach is illegal, you won't be harassed while you're here.

USS Kittiwake★

Northern end of Seven Mile Beach. www.kittiwakecayman.com. Divetech: ☎ 345-946-5658. www.divetech.com. Red Sail Sports: ☎ 345-949-8745. www.redsailcayman.com.

On January 7, 2010, this decommissioned 251ft, 5-deck submarine rescue vessel was purposely sunk off Seven Mile Beach to serve as an artificial reef. It has quickly become a top diving and snorkeling attraction. Holes punched into the vessel allow divers to navigate inside the ship to check out the captain's quarters and the recompression chamber.

Cayman Turtle Farm★

786 Northwest Point Rd., West Bay. ☎ 345-949-3894. http://turtle.ky. Open Mon–Sat 8am–4:30pm, Sun 11am–4pm. $18 and up.

A one-of-a-kind attraction, the farm's star attractions are, of course, turtles (predominantly green sea turtles), which are raised at the farm and sorted into pools and ponds. The excellent staff will let you hold a turtle (although nobody can hold Sparky, the heaviest resident at around 550 pounds). The grounds also include an aviary, a predator tank where you can watch nurse sharks being fed, and a lagoon where you can swim with baby turtles and other marine life.

Queen Elizabeth II Botanic Park★

367 Botanic Rd., off Frank Sound Rd., North Side (on the east). ☎ 345-947-9462. www.botanic-park.ky. Open daily 9am–5:30pm. $8.

This 65-acre park, opened by the Queen, has a mile-long trail leading to a re-created traditional Cayman house and garden (note the bush medicine plants), another garden with flowers and plants grouped by color, a walk amid palms, and a boardwalk edged with orchids. The highlight is seeing free-roaming **blue iguanas**, among the most endangered iguanas in the world. For $30, take a well-worth-it tour of the **Blue Iguana Reserve★** for an up-close look at these reclusive lizards (the later you go, the bluer they are, as their bodies warm in the sun).

WHERE TO DIVE

With its incredible underwater visibility and dramatic marine life, Grand Cayman is also one of the premier diving destinations in the world. All types of diving are possible here, with plunging undersea walls, healthy coral reefs, and even a few artificial reefs created from sunken vessels. Options abound for absolute beginners to serious divers looking for the experience of a lifetime.

The west wall is accessible from **Seven Mile Beach** and known for its calm waters and great visibility that is ideal for beginners. On the northeast end of the island is the **Valley of the Dolls**, one of the prettiest dive sites in the region for its sponges and corals. A recent arrival is the sunken *USS Kittiwake*, a decommissioned Navy submarine rescue vessel, which formed an artificial reef just off Seven Mile Beach that is also accessible to beginners.

Little Cayman island is even more geographically diverse than its sisters, due to its proximity to the Cayman Trench, the deepest part of the Caribbean Sea. The northern edges of the **Cayman Trench** form the dramatic Cayman Ridge, which plunges more than 25,000 feet, the deepest point in the Caribbean Sea. Just off Little Cayman, **Bloody Bay** is a world-famous dive site, known for its sheer vertical walls that drop an astonishing 6,000 feet, with an abundance of colorful marine life in exceptionally clear waters.

Off Cayman Brac, the **Bluff Wall** is a deep dive that's reserved for experts only. And for a dive site with history, check out **Captain Keith Tibbetts Wreck**, a 330-foot-long Soviet warship that was taken from Cuba and sunk in 1996.

Of course, you don't have to be a diver at all to enjoy the underwater treasures. **Stingray City** is a can't-miss experience, where shallow reefs provide outstanding snorkeling. You can also snorkel at **Jackson Point**, which is part of **Bloody Bay Marine Park** and, for the most convenient location of all, just off Seven Mile Beach. **Eden Rock** and **Devil's Grotto** are both snorkeling sites within easy distance from the cruise ship port in George Town.

Travel Tip: A local legend is Bernard Passman, who pioneered the use of black coral to create exquisite jewelry and works of art. He was even commissioned by the Royal Family to create a gift for Prince Charles and Princess Diana's wedding. His work is on display and for sale at two galleries in George Town.

Pedro St. James Castle

Southeast of George Town at end of Pedro Castle Rd., Savannah. 345-947-3329, www.pedrostjames.ky. Open daily 9am–5pm. $8.

Pedro St. James is a castle by fabrication only, but it is the oldest standing structure in the Caymans. Built by William Eden in 1780, the three-story dwelling has withstood fires, abandonment, and the ravages of time. Meticulous restoration of the National Historic Site was completed in 1996. Explore the house and its period furnishings at your leisure, but begin the tour by watching the excellent multimedia presentation.

Little Cayman

More than anything, people come to Little Cayman to go diving: it has 50-plus dive sites. If you feel like exploring, some resorts offer complimentary bicycles to get around.

Bloody Bay Marine Park★★

Off the north shore, between Spot Bay and Jackson Point.

Of the more than 50 dive sites around Little Cayman, not one matches the fame and natural wonder of the two spectacular walls at Bloody Bay Marine Park: **Bloody Bay Wall** and Jackson's Wall. Starting at just 20 feet, Bloody Bay drops an astounding 12,000 feet into a deep blue abyss that's alive with sea turtles, groupers, snappers, sponges, stingrays, squid and other marine life. You might even spot a whale shark or manta ray. With visibility ranging from 100 to 150 feet, the marine park offers an unparalleled experience. If you don't dive, snorkeling here is quite rewarding, thanks to its shallow beginning. The legend himself, Jacques Cousteau, rated Bloody Bay Wall one of the most dramatic wall dives in the world.

Several dive companies operate here, including **Reef Divers** (*345-948-1033; www.littlecayman.com*) and **Pirate's Point Resort & Dive Center** (*345-948-1010; www.piratespointresort.com*).

Booby Pond Nature Reserve★★

67 A8, near Blossom Village. 345-749-1121. www.nationaltrust.org.ky.

Spread out over 334 unspoiled acres on a land-locked saltwater lagoon, Booby Pond is paradise for birders and a refuge for numerous species of wetland and shore birds. Leading the flock is the **red-footed booby**; roughly 5,000 breeding pairs of these birds make up the largest colony in the Western Hemisphere. The reserve is also home to the islands' only colony of breeding Magnificent Frigate birds.

At the traditional-style **visitor center**, check out the observation gallery equipped with telescopes for up-close viewing of the reserve's feathered residents.

Cayman Brac

Call it "getting Brac to basics," Cayman Brac is all about its natural environment.

Cayman Brac Parrot Reserve★

Take Ashton Reid Rd. to Major Donald Dr. ☏ 345-749-1121 www.nationaltrust.org.ky.

True to its name, the Cayman Brac Parrot is now found only on Brac, and this 280-acre reserve, located among the woodlands crowning Cayman Brac's bluff, is your best bet to spot one. You'll have to keep your eyes peeled: it's the smallest of any Amazon Parrot. The reserve houses about 300 of these rare birds, scattered amid an ancient dry forest (early morning and late afternoon are best sighting times). You might also see redlegged thrushes, white-crowned pigeons, and black-whiskered vireos, among the reserve's winged population. A mile-long nature trail loops through part of the grounds. One of the trail's distinctive features is the juxtaposition of hardwood trees and cacti, which are rarely found together in the same area.

MV Captain Tibbetts

Northeast end. Reef Divers: ☏ 345-948-1323 or 800-594-0843. www.bracreef.com. $65 and up.

Easily the most visited dive destination in Cayman Brac, this 330ft Russian warship was deliberately sunk off the coast in 1996. (She originally bore the catchy name of Russian Missile Frigate #356, but was rechristened after a Caymanian politician). The wreck has had a few years to develop into a reef, and today it supports an abundance of corals and sponges, tropical fish, garden and moray eels, and hawksbill turtles. Visibility often exceeds 100 feet, and positioned at 60 to 85 feet below the surface, it's a shallow wreck dive. Her cannons make for popular underwater photo ops.

Travel Tip: The Cayman Islands have an exceptionally low crime rate, despite a recent surge in gang-related incidents. Travelers should practice basic common sense to avoid petty crimes like pick-pocketing and purse-snatching, and avoid walking alone in deserted areas.

ASK PETER...
Q: How can I learn something about the history of the islands?
A: The Cayman Islands Natural History Museum covers both the natural and cultural histories of the three islands. From the Caymans' geological evolution to cultural and artistic treasures, this small building houses a surprisingly robust collection in the center of George Town.

Addresses

For price ranges, see the Legend on the cover flap.

WHERE TO STAY

$$ The Alexander Hotel – *Southern tip of Cayman Brac behind airport.* &345-948-8222, 800-381-5094. *www. alexanderhotelcayman.com. 32 rooms.* Brac's most elegant boutique hotel, The Alexander was opened in 2009 by island native Cleveland Dilbert. The ocean-view rooms are inviting and spacious, and come with full kitchens.

$$ Compass Point – *Austin Connolly Dr., Grand Cayman.* &345-947-7500, 800-348-6096. *www.compasspoint.ky. 28 rooms.* This oceanfront hotel and dive shop prides itself on a "green shorts service" that takes care of guests' scuba gear. The 1-, 2-, and 3-bedroom units have kitchens and additional Murphy beds. The hotel also has the deepest pool on the island for scuba training.

$$$ Lighthouse Point – *571 Northwest Point Rd., Grand Cayman.* &345-946-5658. *http://lighthouse-point-cayman. com. 9 rooms.* The ultimate in eco-friendliness, Lighthouse Point uses solar and wind power and recycled materials without sacrificing comfort. The 2-bedroom units sleep up to six. Divetech (*see USS Kittiwake above*) operates here, fronting one of the best shore dives on Grand Cayman.

$$$ Southern Cross Club – *South Hole Sound, Little Cayman.* &345-948-1099, 800-899-2582.

www.southerncrossclub.com. 12 rooms, 1 cottage. Little Cayman's oldest hotel, founded when the island had a population of 12, boasts a "barefoot elegance" philosophy, top-ranked diving and fishing operation, and pleasant beachfront bungalows.

$$$$ Caribbean Club – *871 West Bay Rd., Grand Cayman.* &345-623-4500, 800-941-1126. *www.caribclub.com. 37 rooms.* Luxury apartment living meets elite hotel service at the Caribbean Club's luxurious 3-bedroom residences. Amenities include daily housekeeping, concierge service, an expansive pool, and Seven Mile beachfront access.

$$$$ Casuarina Resort & Spa – *Seven Mile Beach, Grand Cayman.* &345-945-3800, 800-937-8461. *http://westincasuarina. com. 343 rooms.* This Westin resort faces 700 feet of pristine white sand and features numerous restaurants, a spa, and a dive shop. It is in the midst of major renovations, with the pool area already updated and room renovations taking place in late 2012.

$$$$$ Cotton Tree – *375 Conch Point Rd., Grand Cayman.* &345-943-0700. *www.caymancottontree.com. 4 cottages.* Tucked into the northernmost point of West Bay, Cotton Tree's intimate 2-bedroom cottages include kitchens, a personal chef upon request, and perks like Apple TV and Nintendo Wii video games. Guests can also enjoy a small gym, pool and spa.

WHERE TO EAT

$ Aunt Sha's Kitchen – *South Side, Cayman Brac. ℘345-948-1581*. **Caymanian**. A secluded spot on the southern side of the island, always popular Aunt Sha's specializes in down-home local staples like conch fritters and fried or grilled catch of the day.

$ Champion House II – *43 Eastern Ave., George Town, Grand Cayman. ℘345-949-7882. www.championhouse.ky*. **Caribbean**. The extensive menu at Champion House, an affordable, few-frills local favorite in George Town, focuses on island recipes like turtle steak and conch stew.

$ Miss Vivine's Kitchen – *Gun Bay, East End, just past Wreck of the 10 Sails, Grand Cayman. ℘345-947-7435*. **Caymanian**. Many locals call Miss Vivine's the best Caymanian food on Grand Cayman Island; she cooks in her house, and you can sit indoors or on the porch facing the water as you feast on specialties like turtle stew, goat curry and fried grouper.

$$ Hungry Iguana – *Paradise Villas, Little Cayman. ℘345-948-0007. http://hungryiguana.com*. **American/Caribbean**. The only à la carte restaurant on Little Cayman also offers a set menu along with daily specials, depending on what is available (supplies are brought in once a week). There's sure to be something that suits your tastebuds.

$$ Kaibo Yacht Club – *585 Water Cay Rd., Cayman Kai, Grand Cayman. ℘345-947-9975. www.kaibo.ky*. **Caribbean**. Kaibo offers a laid back thatch-roof bar on the beach that serves gourmet sandwiches and a mean coconut curried grouper. An elegant upstairs dining room opens in high season.

$$$ The Brasserie – *171 Elgin Ave., Cricket Square, George Town, Grand Cayman. ℘345-945-1814. http://brasseriecayman.com*. **Continental**. Not only does The Brasserie have an ample organic garden, it's the only restaurant on Grand Cayman with two fishing boats securing daily fresh catches just for it. The casual-style gourmet gem lies off the tourist path in George Town's banking district.

$$$ Michael's Genuine Food & Drink – *47 Forum Lane, Canella Court, Camana Bay, Grand Cayman. ℘345-640-6433. www.michaelsgenuine.com*. **American**. This inventive import from Miami's chef Michael Schwartz combines his signature dishes with locally inspired recipes like breadfruit salad and lionfish *escabeche*.

DISCOVERING

JAMAICA★★

The poster child for the Caribbean, Jamaica is its third-largest island, tucked 90 miles south of Cuba's eastern end. It's a 2-hour flight from Orlando and 4 hours from New York, as well as a popular cruise ship port stop. Along with mining and agriculture, tourism is a primary industry, mostly centered on a few well-developed communities. Geographically, Jamaica is divided into 14 parishes. The capital, Kingston, is surrounded by St. Andrew. St. Ann is the famed "garden parish," and the birthplace of Jamaican icons Marcus Garvey and Bob Marley, with the cruise ship town of Ocho Rios its tourism center. Montego Bay, the island's tourism hub, has a mix of large, all-inclusive resorts, boutique hotels, budget dives and upscale villas. At Jamaica's western tip, Westmoreland is home to Jamaica's quintessential beach town, Negril.

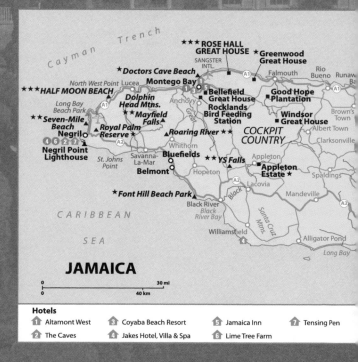

JAMAICA

Hotels			
1 Altamont West	3 Coyaba Beach Resort	5 Jamaica Inn	7 Tensing Pen
2 The Caves	4 Jakes Hotel, Villa & Spa	6 Lime Tree Farm	

PETER'S TOP PICKS

SEE

Half Moon Beach near Negril, a quieter alternative to Seven Mile Beach. (p **166**)

DO

Play golf on one of the most scenic courses in the world: the White Witch Golf Course at the Ritz-Carlton Golf & Resort Spa. (p **161**)

LEARN

Get a taste of Jamaican history at Greenwood Great House, a former sugar estate mansion with an impressive collection of antiques and rare books. (p **164**)

EAT

Go where the locals like to eat. The original Scotchies in Montego Bay serves Jamaican jerk that's slow cooked for hours over an open grill. Order extra hot sauce at your own risk. (p **169**)

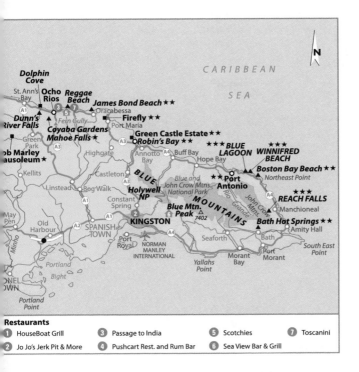

Restaurants

1. HouseBoat Grill
2. Jo Jo's Jerk Pit & More
3. Passage to India
4. Pushcart Rest. and Rum Bar
5. Scotchies
6. Sea View Bar & Grill
7. Toscanini

Kingston and Area

The country's sprawling capital is its historical center and cultural heart. New Kingston is the main corporate district and Half Way Tree is the capital's teeming commercial center. With myriad recording studios, bumping street life and a throbbing club scene, Kingston is a must for visitors who want to experience the sights and sounds of Jamaica's cultural hotbed. Yet the city has crime-ridden areas that must be avoided. Stick to main streets and business areas rather than wandering into unfamiliar neighborhoods or streets.

Sights

The National Gallery★

12 Ocean Blvd. ☏876-922-1561. www.natgalja.org.jm. Open Tue–Fri 10am–4:30pm (Fri until 4pm) Sat 10am–3pm. US$5.
Jamaica's most extensive gallery is an essential stop for any art lover. Contemporary Jamaican art falls into two distinct schools, Intuitive and Mainstream; the gallery adeptly covers both. The permanent collection is especially rich in paintings and sculptures by Jamaican Intuitive master Mallica "Kapo" Reynolds, considered a major artist of the 20C; works on paper and paintings by Milton George; and works on paper by Omari Ra.

Devon House★

26 Hope Rd. ☏876-929-6602. www.devonhousejamaica.com. Tours Mon–Fri 9:30am–4pm.
This National Historic Site is located at the heart of Uptown Kingston. Built by **George Steibel,** Jamaica's first black millionaire, the stately mansion was designed in Jamaican-Georgian (English 1714-1811) style. Now a government-owned museum, the former residence contains late-19C period furnishings and paintings as well as exhibits about Steibel's travels. The complex holds shops and restaurants as well. Lines for Devon House I-Scream are especially long Sunday afternoons. Things Jamaican, Wassi Art, and Starfish Oils and Molasses are worth a browse.

Bob Marley Museum★★

56 Hope Rd. ☏876-927-9152. www.bobmarley-foundation.com. Tours Mon–Sat 9:30am–4:30pm. US$20.
This museum is easily Kingston's top tourist draw, welcoming busloads of visitors flocking to pay tribute to Jamaica's beloved son, the King of Reggae. Be sure to take the concise and informative tour, which is not to be confused with the tour at Nine Mile, Bob Marley's birthplace in the countryside of St. Ann.

WHEN TO GO

Day temperatures of 72°F to 88°F dip to near freezing in the high mountains, and frequently rise to over 100°F in the hottest months of Jun-Aug. Rainfall increases Apr-May, and Jul-Oct when the occasional hurricane hits. **Low tourist season** is mid-Apr–mid-Nov; prices are lower.

GETTING AROUND

BY BUS – Mass transit is a mishmash of buses from state run operators like the **Jamaica Urban Transit Company** (www.jutc.com) in Kingston and privately operated **Coaster buses**, which crisscross the island from major urban areas. Jamaica Union of Travelers Association (JUTA) offers inexpensive transport for tourists and runs regular service between Negril and Montego Bay (www.jutatoursnegrilltd.com). The most comfortable coach between Kingston, Ocho Rios and Montego Bay is **Knutsford Express** (www.knutsfordxpress.com).

BY TAXI – For shorter distances, **route taxis**, privately operated and licensed, run between neighboring towns cramming passengers in. Dispatch taxi services in Kingston and Montego Bay are the most inexpensive option, with timely service, at rush hour and when it's raining. Kingston's better services include El-Shaddai (☎876-969-7633) and On Time (☎876-926-3866). Off-duty route taxis offer "charter" service, but typically gouge passsengers.

BY CAR – Driving is on the left. Rentals cost US$80/day up after insurance; fuel is not cheap. Island Car Rentals and Budget offer pick-up service at both major international airports.

BY TWO-WHEEL – Mopeds and motorbikes can be rented on Norman Manley Boulevard in Negril. It's not advisable for riders unfamiliar with Jamaican roads to rent bikes elsewhere.

BY AIR – Jamaica Air Shuttle flies three times daily between Kingston and Montego Bay; Skylan Airways (www.skylanjamaica.com) flies the route Mon, Wed and Fri. Aerodromes in downtown Kingston, Port Antonio, Negril and Treasure Beach are used for small private and charter aircraft.

VISITOR INFORMATION

Main tourism offices: Jamaica **Tourist Board** (www.visitjamaica.com) in Kingston (64 Knutsford Blvd.; ☎876-929-9200) and Montego Bay (18 Queens Dr.; ☎876-952-4425).

Important numbers
Police Emergency (24hrs): 119
Ambulance/Fire Emergency: 110
In an emergency, notify the police but take action if personal safety is at risk: response times are typically slow.

Medical Services:
Kingston: Andrews Memorial Hospital (27 Hope Rd.; ☎876-926-7401; www.amhosp.org)
Montego Bay: Mobay Hope Medical Center (☎876-953-3649; www.mobayhope.org).

MONEY/CURRENCY

The official currency is the Jamaican dollar, which has an exchange rate of about J$84 to US$1. American dollars are accepted all over the islands. The best exchange rate can be obtained at exchange houses, or *cambios*, as they are known locally. Scotia DBG and FX Trader are two good options.

Hope Botanical Gardens

Hope Rd. ☎ *876-970-3505. Open daily 6 am–6:30pm.* This 200acre oasis is a great place to seek quiet in the shade amid some of the island's exotic plants like mango trees, bougainvillea and hibiscus.

Night Spots

Kingston's has two main nightlife hubs: New Kingston Knutsford Boulevard and Market Place in Half Way Tree. **Club Riddim** (Knutsford Blvd.; 876-754-7823; Ladies Night Tue and Swagga Thu) recently opened and claims to be the official club of dance-hall music. It replaced what was The Building, which in turn had replaced a long-time dance-hall institution, Asylum. **Privilege** (14-16 Trinidad Terrace; 876-622-653; www.clubprivilege.com), another newcomer, sits above a gaming lounge next door to Quad. It attracts a young, uptown crowd, especially on Fridays. **Quad** (20-22 Trinidad Terrace; 876-754-7823), located around the corner from Privilege, is the longest-running night club in town, three floors high. **Fiction Lounge** (Market Place, 67 Constant Spring Rd., in Half Way Tree; 876-631-8038. www.fictionloungeja.com) is the most popular club among Kingston moneyed hipsters. Opened in 2011, **Rev** (shop 25 Portmore Plaza, Bridgeport; 876-998-6888; Thu-Sat) took over the former Cactus night spot in Portmore, St. Catherine, a bedroom community west of Downtown across the toll causeway.

Blue Mountains and the East

Jamaica's most significant mountain ranges, the misty Blue and John Crow Mountains, cover parts of St. Andrew, St. Mary, Portland and St. Thomas parishes. It's here that the famous **Jamaica Blue Mountain Coffee** is cultivated, and the country's biodiversity is at its fullest. Two main troughs cut into the hills with passable roads, one running between the cooperage and Buff Bay, often interrupted by landslides in Portland, the other running to Gordon Town, Mavis Bank and across the Yallahs River and up to Whitfield Hall, where hikers begin the ascent to **Blue Mountain Peak** (2,256m/7,401ft), the island's highest point. **Holywell** is a national park with hiking trails and spectacular views at Hardwar Gap. With a backdrop of the Blue Mountains stretching to the sea, **Port Antonio**★★ has gorgeous, uncrowded beaches, and a few decent restaurants; opt to stay at a staffed villa, where delicious local food is prepared.

Hire a taxi or take an organized tour of the Blue Mountains area, rather than try to find your own way around. Barrett Adventures can arrange tours: 876-382-6384; www.barrettadventures.com.

Beaches

Winnifred Beach★★★ – Northeast of Port Antonio, off A-4 This public beach (donations accepted at the gate) is enjoyed by lo-

JAMAICA
...LIKE A LOCAL

To experience Jamaica like a local, all you have to do is get out of the resort boundaries and onto the lesser-known beaches, jungles and mountains. The island's south coast is far less developed than communities like Montego Bay and Ocho Rios. Here, tropical foliage, old fishing villages and absence of overt commercialism make it an appealing destination for those looking to escape the crowds. Bordered roughly by Bluefields Beach to the north and Treasure Beach to the south, a day here is less about zip-lines and beach bars, and more about sunbathing on your own swatch of sand, driving up the misty mountains, and exploring the roadside seafood stands.

Locals mix with tourists on Lost Beach and Treasure Beach, and accommodations include guest houses, private villas, and funky boutique hotels like Jake's Treasure Beach Hotel. Sandals Whitehouse is a rare all-inclusive, adults-only property in this part of the island that also happens to be located inside a 500-acre nature reserve.

High up in the mountains is the charming town of Mandeville. It's 2,000 feet above sea level so the climate is much cooler and mistier than down below. Reminiscent of an English village, there are village greens, golf courses, and even a British-style pub inside the Mandeville Hotel (4 Hotel Street, Mandeville). To reach Mandeville, you'll drive under a canopy of bamboo shoots that arch over the road, known locally as Bamboo Alley.

There are some organized experiences on the south coast, namely the Appleton Rum Estate in St. Elizabeth and the High Mountain Coffee Factory (Jamaica's "other" well-known coffee) in Williamsfield. Take a side trip to the cascading YS Falls, where you can take a dip in the natural freshwater pool below, and to the nearby wetlands of the Black River Great Morass to spot tropical birds and alligators.

Getting there is half the fun—unless you're prone to motion sickness. The roads from Ocho Rios and Negril are relatively wide and well-paved, but the mountainous road as you get closer to the south coast is riddled with stomach-churning curves and bone-jarring potholes.

Travel Tip: Getting around on your own in Jamaica is for the most part safe, but there are certainly inner city areas of Kingston and Montego Bay, especially, where it's best not venture unaccompanied by a local resident. If in doubt, err on the safe side. People who hustle in Jamaica's tourist trade can be quite pushy and intimidating, but rarely resort to violent confrontation or muggings unless instigated. When out late at night in Negril, Montego Bay, Ocho Rios or Kingston, stick to lit areas where there are plenty of people around. If you keep your guard up and your wits about you, the likelihood of being taken advantage of is greatly reduced. To be on the safe side, avoid Spanish Town altogether.

cals and a sparse trickle of tourists. Don't be turned off by th bumpy road down from the main road. A hearty seafood lunc costs about $10US at Cynthia's, and Dorraine can often be foun making conch soup (US$2) on the far end of the beach.

Boston Bay Beach★★ – *7mi southeast of Port Antonio, off A* James Bond actor Roger Moore once owned this beach. Afte he donated it to the government, the public beach becam known for its jerk shacks. After a swim, wash down a snack o zesty chicken or pork with a cold Red Stripe beer.

Natural Sites

Blue Lagoon★★★ – *7mi east of Port Antonio, at end of San Sc District.* A natural spring pumps fresh water from depths o more than 46m/150ft into a lagoon in a deep cove surrounde by lush vegetation. The mix of fresh and sea water makes th water look blurry, while the difference in temperature betwee the spring and the sea makes for an exhilarating dip.

Reach Falls★★★ – *About 7mi east of Manchioneel. ☎876-83 6740. Open Wed–Sun 8:30am–4:30pm. $10US.* A favorite amon active hikers, this series of short falls cascades into a large cer tral pool. The natural attraction is managed by the Urban Deve opment Corp., and local guides take adventure seekers to clim the falls to their heart's content.

Bath Hot Springs★★ – *About 50mi east of Port Antonio, nec Bath Fountain Hotel & Spa in Bath.* Turkish bath house mee Rastafarian bush doctor at this naturally hot sulfur spring in th heart of St. Thomas. A windy, narrow road leads to the hotel an spa from the Botanical Garden in Bath, where guests can rent modern hot tub or tiled tank by the hour. Masseurs solicit bus ness outside the parking lot gate and lead willing visitors to th source of the hot water: a spring 100m/328ft upstream wher massage techniques include flogging with a hot towel.

Ocho Rios and the North Coast

The largest population center in **St. Ann** parish, Ocho Rio is a cruise-ship port in the middle of the North Coast. Och as locals call it, comes from the name given to the are by the Spanish, chorreras, which means waterfalls. Th Spaniards built their first capital at New Seville, a 15mi drive west along the coast. Farther west, Runaway Bay is small community with two large resorts and a smatterin

WHERE TO GOLF

Golf enthusiasts have long appreciated Jamaica's challenging courses, but even the most casual golfer will be enchanted by the incredible scenery from the greens. The turquoise Caribbean Sea and the Jamaican Mountains are the backdrop as palms sway in the ocean breezes. At **Cinnamon Hill Ocean Course** (N. Coast Hwy., Montego Bay), part of the Wyndham Rose Hall Resort in Montego Bay, the view is so spectacular you might get distracted from the game! It's laid out on the site of a sugar plantation, interspersed with stone walls, an aqueduct and other ruins. Hole 5, known as Majestic Blue, nudges up against the sparkling blue waters, but watch out for the strong trade wind coming off the shores!

You'll need a good caddy to tackle the 18-hole championship course at **Half Moon Golf Club** at Rose Hall. Sitting at the foot of Montego Bay's lush, green hills, the course has more than 7,000 yards of difficult driving areas. It was designed by star architect Robert Trent Jones, Sr., and renovated by Roger Rulewich, and is perfectly integrated into the natural landscape. Prepare to be challenged: half of the holes face into the trade winds, making this course as tough as it is beautiful.

White Witch Golf Course at the Ritz-Carlton Golf & Resort Spa (1 Ritz Carlton Dr., St. James) is another exceptionally scenic place to play, winding through the 600 acres of the lush Rose Hall Plantation. Of course, it's that very topography that has caused more than one frustrating game, contending with ravines, gorges and jungle foliage. But to make up for it, 16 holes overlook the breathtaking Caribbean and offer mountain views.

Home to the Johnnie Walker World Championship, among other tournaments, **Tryall Golf, Tennis and Beach Club** (N. Coast Hwy., Sandy Bay) endures as one of the best courses in all of the Caribbean. You'll understand why when you reach the 7th tee, shot through the pillars of a historic aqueduct. Nine holes border the sea, so keep your eyes open—not just for the next shot, but for sightings of dolphins and tropical sea birds off in the distance.

of luxury villas. Discovery Bay, farther west still, is a luxury villa hot spot along with popular Puerto Seco Beach. Bordering St. Ann to the east, **St. Mary** is a quiet parish where agriculture and fishing are still important to the economy. Ian Fleming made his home in Oracabessa at Goldeneye, where he penned several 007 novels. Noël Coward established his home Firefly in nearby Galina. East of parish capital Port Maria, Robin's Bay is home to Green Castle Estate and Strawberry Fields, both low key ecotourism attractions with on-site accommodations.

Chukka Caribbean Adventures can arrange tours to this area:
℘ 888-224-8552; www.chukkacaribbean.com.

West of Ocho Rios
Coyaba Gardens and Mahoe Falls★★

Take the A3 towards Kingston, turn opposite St. John's Anglican Church on Millford Rd. Follow signs half a mile. ℘ 876-974-6235. www.coyabagardens.com. Open daily 8am–5pm. US$10.

St. Ann is known as the "garden parish," and there's no better kept floral sanctuary. The attraction is owned by a family who traces its roots to one of Jamaica's foremost visionaries of the colonial era, John Pringle, a proponent of stewardship. It's in this spirit that visitors are welcomed to the well-maintained park featuring waterfalls and fish ponds and native flowers.

Bob Marley Mausoleum★

South of Runaway Bay in village of Nine Mile, which is east of Alexandria. ℘ 876-843-0498, US$20. Caution: Expect very persistent hustlers.

The Reggae legend's birthplace and place of final rest are one and the same. His survivors built a restaurant, bar and gift shop to entertain visitors who are led on a tour up a series of steps to see Bob's humble one-room board house with its single bed. He was buried in the mausoleum with his guitar.

East of Ocho Rios
James Bond Beach★

In Oracabessa, 9km/15mi east of Ocho Rios, off A3. www.chukkacaribbean.com.

Stingray City, where visitors can swim with large fish, and decent swimming waters make this beach an entertaining stop. The beach park comes alive several times a year for massive parties with live music, particularly Beach J'ouvert, during Jamaica's Carnival season, when patrons splatter others with paint while bouncing to Soca. Other annual events held here include the Follow Di Arrow and Pepsi Teen Splash celebrations.

Firefly★★★

Port Maria, east of Ocho Rios. 📞 *876-975-3677.*
Open Mon–Sat 9am–5pm. US$10.

English playwright **Noël Coward** (1899-1973) who penned *Blithe Spirit* and *Private Lives*, built his second home in Jamaica on this hillside property that is now preserved as a museum. A statue in Coward's likeness sits on a bench in the yard, immortalizing his love affair with the property and its stunning **view★★★** of the coastline from Galina and Port Maria northeast to Portland.

Robin's Bay★★

East of Port Maria.

Green Castle Estate (*Robin's Bay Rd.;* 📞 *876-881-6279, www.gc jamaica.com*) is a massive land holding covering much of Robin's Bay. Slated for ecological residential tourism development, the estate raises cattle and produces orchids within commercial greenhouses. Endless trails crisscross the hills, a haven for birders and nature lovers.

Montego Bay and Area

With its cruise-ship terminal, Jamaica's "vibes city" thrives on tourism. "Hip Strip" winds along **Gloucestershire Avenue**, better known as Bottom Road, lined with bars, restaurants, gaming lounges—and best of all, beaches that make **Montego Bay** (Mobay, as locals call it) a bona fide beach town; tourists are often seen shirtless along the road. Downtown, around Sam Sharpe Square, it's a different world: here local commerce carries on somewhat removed from beach life. East of Sangster International Airport, Ironshore is a residential neighborhood neighbored by Rose Hall, perhaps Jamaica's most auspicious address. Today, Rose Hall Estate is home to a string of reputable hotels, and on the other side of the highway, Spring Farm houses some of the country's most luxurious villas. The town of Falmouth, about 30 miles east of the airport, is rich in Georgian architecture.

Chukka Caribbean Adventures can arrange tours to this area: 📞 *876-953-6699; www.chukkacaribbean.com.*

Beaches

Doctors Cave Beach★, **Cornwall Beach** and Aquasol Beach Park stretch along Gloustershire Road, making Montego Bay unique as being a relatively large city with crystal-clear waters and white sand beaches within easy walking distance. At the

Travel Tip: Coffee fiends covet Jamaica's mild but flavorful Blue Mountain coffee, which is harvested by just a handful of farmers below a certain elevation in the Blue Mountains. But beware of imposters. True Blue Mountain Coffee has a specially designed seal to signify that it's been licensed by the Jamaican Coffee Board to safeguard the authenticity of this pricey treat. Top brands include Langford Brothers, Jablum, Wallenford Blue, Salada and Jamaica Standard.

ASK PETER...

Q: Where can I go hiking that's safe and not too strenuous?
A: The Holywell Recreational Park in the Blue Mountain and John Crow Mountains National Park is ideal for a short morning or afternoon hike. It's about a 90-minute drive from Kingston, sitting 3,500 feet above sea level. The Oatley Trail is a steep, but manageable walk with several viewing areas where you can soak in the panorama from the mist-covered forest. If you feel up for a longer hike, there are some 2 to 4-hour treks that show off the park's beautiful waterfalls and rivers, but you're best off tackling those with a guide.

end of the airport runway, **Dead End Beach** is the free public alternative, where young Montegonians park along the sea wall in the evenings and blast music from car stereos.

Great Houses

Bellefield Great House – *Fairfield district, east of Catherine Hall in Montego Bay. ☎ 876-952-2382. www.bellefieldgreathouse.com. Culinary tours are available for groups of 10 or more (☎ 876-446-7289).* Offering a visit to the grounds' fruit, herb and vegetable gardens and jerk pit as well as a peek into the rooms of the colonial manor, the tour culminates with buffet lunch.

Rose Hall Great House★★★ – *10mi east of Montego Bay, off A1. ☎ 876-953-2323. Open daily 9am–6pm. US$20.* Slave master Annie Mae Palmer ruled the sugar plantation of this old estate house (1780) with an iron fist until she was killed in 1831 in a slave uprising known as the Christmas Rebellion. Rumored to have killed her three husbands, she was immortalized in Herbert de Lisser's *The White Witch of Rose Hall*, a title that refers to suspicions that Palmer practiced black magic. The restored colonial-era mansion can be toured.

Greenwood Great House★ – *15mi east of Montego Bay, off A1 (and 5mi east of Rose Hall). ☎ 876-953-1077. Open daily 9am–6pm, US$20.* This former sugar estate mansion perches on a hill overlooking the sea. It was built in 1790 by the family of English poet Elizabeth Barrett Browning. Born in the area, Elizabeth's father was a large landowner; the Barrett family was instrumental in establishing nearby Falmouth. The current owners offer tours of the house, which retains the Barrett family's books.

Good Hope Country House – *About 20mi inland from Falmouth. www.goodhopejamaica.com. ☎ 876-469-3444.* Orange groves and misty hills dominate the 2,000 acres of Good Hope estate, which sits in Cockpit Country. Available for comfortable one-of-a-kind accommodations, several refurbished colonial-era buildings dot the property reserved for family retreats. The restored Georgian-style Great House, built in 1755, alone has 10 bedrooms. Chukka Caribbean arranges well-conceived activities here from zip-lining and horse-drawn carriage rides to culinary offerings.

Cockpit Country

About 15mi southeast of Montego Bay. Managed by Windsor Research Centre in Trelawny: ☎ 876-997-3832. www.cockpitcountry.com. Untamed and rather inaccessible, this vast tropical forest of limestone hills, mottled with underground rivers and caves,

occupies Jamaica's northwest interior. It is known for its biodiversity and Maroons, former slaves who engaged the British in two wars in the early 18C. Their descendants still inhabit the area, but none remain In Maroon Town. The area's name was coined by British troops for the limestone sinkholes that reminded them of the cockpits of their warships, where seamen wounded in battle were placed.

Though many animals here are nocturnal and therefore difficult to spot, the refuge harbors a variety of reptiles and birds (including the Jamaican owl and potoo) as well as insects, butterflies and bats. **Windsor Great House**, originally constructed in 1795, is the site of Windsor Research Centre's talks and a four-course meal, usually once a week.

Negril and the West

Beach bums flock to Jamaica's westernmost region where Negril is the island's foremost beach town. Until 40 years ago, Negril was little more than a fishermen's outpost. Tourism development began in the 1970s, starting out with humble cottages perched on the cliffs that make the West End so unique, and facing the water on Jamaica's longest strip of continuous sand, Seven-Mile Beach. Beyond core activities like jumping from cliffs into crystal clear waters and lazing at Bloody Bay or more remote Half Moon Beach, worthwhile attractions include Kool Runnings Waterpark, Brighton Blue Hole, Mayfield Falls and Blue Hole Garden at the source of Roaring River.

Heading east from Negril, Little Bay and Brighton are neighboring communities where the latter's Blue Hole has developed into one of the best new attractions in the parish: swimmers jump into a spring-fed cavern's crystal waters 20ft below; a volleyball court, pool, jerk pit and bar add to the fun. **Coral Cove** is a boutique destination resort in Little Bay that's popular for weddings in a quiet seaside community where Bob Marley had a beloved getaway.

Southeast of Negril, adjacent communities **Bluefields** and **Belmont** embody peaceful country life; **Bluefields Beach** is popular with locals. High-end villas in Bluefields complement a few humbler lodgings in Belmont. On the Westmoreland-St. Elizabeth border, you'll find Scott's Cove.

Closer to Montego Bay in Hanover parish, Round Hill and Tryall Club are enclaves of luxury tourism, while the **Dolphin Head Mountains** afford enterprising travelers the opportunity to hike in Jamaica's second-highest range and a biodiversity hotspot.

Travel Tip: Look for some unexpected ways to get around the island. Hooves Jamaica (61 Windsor Road) offers horseback rides through the forest and wetland, followed by a casual saunter along the beach. Your horse will walk on the sands and then head into the ocean, leg-deep in the waves. Or try the Bush Doctor Mountain ride, a glorious saunter through the lush mountainside. The Rain forest ride takes you trotting amid bamboo trees and other tropical flora of the forest. When you book these rides through your hotel, you'll be picked up and driven to the stables. Or, for an even more unusual way to get around: by dog sled! Chukka Caribbean can set you up with a real Jamaican musher and his 15 dogs for the ride of a lifetime— expect to get muddy! Be sure to wear clothes that you don't care about wearing ever again.

Beaches

Seven-Mile Beach★★ – *Along Norman Manley Blvd., Negril. Signs designate sections where nudity is allowed.* Fine white sand and a gradual slope into warm Caribbean waters make this Jamaica's most popular beach, though lined with resort hotels. Its crystal-clear waters are good for swimming and snorkeling. During Spring Break in mid-March and Independence Emancipation festivities, the beach is invaded by throngs of partygoers.

Half Moon Beach★★★ – *North of Negril, near Green Island.* This quiet cove is isolated enough to insure that only a few people will be found wading in its calm waters. A restaurant/bar and modest cabins make it a one-stop-shop for those looking to stay a bit longer.

Natural Sites

Royal Palm Reserve★ – *About 3mi east Negril, in Sheffield.* ☏876-364-7407. *US$15.* Endemic palm trees, waterfowl and fish are among the life forms that make this conservation area a rewarding half-day excursion. There's a boardwalk through a swamp and an on-site museum. Red-billed streamertails, Jamaica's national bird, might be seen. Nearby **Bongo's Farm** (☏876-880-7500) offers guided hikes and natural foods.

Roaring River★★ – *About 40mi east of Negril near Savanna-la-Mar.* This gushing river has carved out caves where tours (US$10) are provided by local guides who can be a bit aggressive when it comes to soliciting business. Located near the source of the river, **Blue Hole Garden** (US$10) is a spring-fed sink hole that's a secluded and peaceful destination. A few cabins are available for rent to travelers who choose to stay overnight.

Mayfield Falls★★ – *About 45mi east Negril and north of Savanna-la-Mar, in Glenbrook.* ☏876-610-8612. *www.mayfieldfalls.com. US$15.* This river park encourages visitors to walk up the middle of the river with the help of a guide. The current can be quite strong, and the river bed is pebbly, so strength and waterproof footwear are needed. Fern-lined banks edge natural pools and several waterfalls.

The South

Jamaica's most off-the-beaten-tourism path covers some of the country's most productive agricultural lands. St. Elizabeth parish has earned the moniker of Jamaica's bread bas-

ket due to the large amount of fruit and vegetables it produces. The main draws are the slow pace of rural life, lack of crowds and some of the island's best seafood. Swimmers should use caution at Treasure Beach because of strong currents and undertow.

Font Hill Beach Park★

Between Westmoreland-St. Elizabeth border, southeast of Negril. US$5.

Ringed with coral and surrounded by a wildlife preserve, this small, fine-sand beach is seldom visited by tourists. Its location in the countryside ensures that there won't be crowds, while grills and picnic tables make it ideal for a barbecue on the beach.

YS Falls★★

In Black River, off A2. ☏ 876-997-6360. www.ysfalls.com. Open Tue–Sun 9:30am–3:30pm. US$15.

The most popular waterfalls on the South Coast are a hub for tubing, zip-lining and a rope swing (*each costs extra*). The Black River spills over in seven cascades that create deep pools ideal for swimming. It slows down along its course through farm lands where racing horses and cattle graze in lush green fields dotted with massive gungo trees.

Appleton Estate★

Northeast of YS Falls, off B6. ☏ 876-963-9215. www.appletonrum.com. US$22.

The top rum brand in Jamaica is produced at this sprawling sugar estate in the back bush of St. Elizabeth parish. An entertaining tour covers the history, processing and consumption of the country's most exquisite of spirits. The admission price includes a bottle for you to carry home.

Travel Tip: US dollars are widely accepted in the tourist zones of Jamaica. However, the smaller mom-and-pop shops, roadside stands and B&Bs are less likely to accept American currency, so always have a stash of Jamaican dollars with you. Withdraw cash from an ATM, or get it changed at a local bank or *cambio*.

A BIT OF HISTORY

Jamaica's strategic position in the middle of the Caribbean and its lucrative agricultural industries made it a hotly contested region for centuries. It was originally inhabited by Taíno natives when Columbus first landed on his second voyage to the New World in 1494. Spanish settlers quickly enslaved and wiped out the native population, and brought over West African slaves to work on sugarcane and coffee plantations. In 1655, British soldiers captured the island from the Spanish and took control for more than 300 years. Jamaica established its independence in 1962, and today it still reflects strong elements of its multicultural heritage.

Addresses

For price ranges, see the Legend on the cover flap.

WHERE TO STAY

$ Altamont West – *Gloucester Ave., Montego Bay. 876-952-9087. www.altamontwesthotel.com 31 units.* This boutique hotel with cozy rooms smack in the middle of Mobay's Hip Strip offers practicality and comfort. Robin's Prime Steakhouse is located on property. A pool and deck area creates a little oasis out back. A/C and TV come standard.

$$ Jakes Hotel, Villas and Spa – *Calabash Bay, St. Elizabeth. 876-956-7050 or 800-972-2159. www.jakeshotel.com. 49 units.* Quaint cottages and luxurious villas dot the coastline of Treasure Beach. Rooms come with a garden or sea view, mini-fridge or kitchen. Villas have one-of-a-kind decor and lots of art. Comfortable cottages are individually furnished as well. A pool and two on-site restaurants, plus a farm-to-table dinner series once a month.

$$$ Coyaba Beach Resort – *Ironshore, Montego Bay. 876-953-9150. www.coyabaresort jamaica.com. 50 units.* Excellent food delivered to your room or served tableside in the on-site restaurant, coupled with prime oceanfront acreage make this weekend getaway one of Mobay's top boutique properties. The hotel boasts a private beach, pool and tennis courts.

$$$ Lime Tree Farm – *Tower Hill, St. Andrew. 876-881-8788. www.limetreefarm.com. 4 units.* Offering the best views of the Blue Mountains, this homey hilltop farm has all-inclusive accommodations for hikers seeking a bit of real country life without sacrificing comfortable linens and hot showers.

$$$ Tensing Pen – *West End Rd., Negril. 876-957-0387 or 1-800-972-2159. www.tensingpen.com. 22 units.* Tasteful elegance marks these picturesque cabanas perched on pillars above crystalline waters lapping limestone cliffs. Bamboo furniture, a pool carved into the rock, spa treatments and fine dining contribute to this boutique hotel's romantic allure. Ledges along the cliffs and an iconic bridge invite a jump into the sea.

$$$$ Jamaica Inn – *Main St., Ocho Rios, 876-974-2514 or 800-837-4608. www.roundhilljamaica. com. 63 units.* Regal service from check-in to check-out, a respect for rest and leisure, and impeccably appointed chambers makes this a top-rated hotel again and again, the same way its guests keep going back.

You won't find TVs in the rooms, and Wi-Fi is confined to the library to ensure priorities are kept in order during your stay. The menu features the finest in Caribbean fusion.

$$$$$ The Caves – *West End Rd.,Negril. 876-957-0270 or 800-OUTPOST. www.islandoutpost.com. 12 units.* Record mogul Chris Blackwell teamed up with

Negril-based entrepreneurs to design a lodging fit for James Bond. Carved out of limestone cliffs overlooking the sea, the all-inclusive resort has 24/7 self-serve bars stocked with top-shelf liquor, and food. Relax in a Jacuzzi in candlelit caves hewn from the sea-facing rock.

WHERE TO EAT

$ Jo Jo's Jerk Pit & More – *12 Waterlook Rd., Kingston.* ℘*876-906-1509.* **Jamaican**. In the heart of Half Way Tree, this open-air eatery features Jamaica's time-honored tradition of jerking meats, whether pork, chicken, conch or lamb. A popular bar and regular music performances and DJs on weekends attract a strong contingent of regulars.

$ Scotchies – *Carol Gardens, Montego Bay.* ℘*876-953-3301.* **Jamaican**. Jamaica's most popular jerk chain was launched at this location before establishing satellites in Ocho Rios, Kingston and Port Maria. Whether you favor pork, chicken, or roasted fish, the aroma of seasoned meats on the grill is hard to resist.

$ Sea View Bar & Grill – *West End Rd., Negril.* **Jamaican**. Don't mind the raucous locals playing billiards and drinking. Tony Montana mans the grill and serves the best roasted conch in Jamaica, traditionally accompanied by water crackers. Other specialties eaten at a few picnic tables by the roadside with music blaring in the background include pan chicken, and steam fish.

$$ Passage to India – *Sonis Plaza, 50 Main St., Ocho Rios.* ℘*876-795-3182. www.hibiscus jamaica.com.* **Indian**. This popular rooftop restaurant attracts locals and visitors alike. Here northern dishes prevail, including *palak paneer*, vindaloo chicken and sides like *aloo parotha* and nan.

$$ Pushcart Restaurant and Rum Bar – *West End Rd., Negril.* ℘*876-957-4373. www.rockhousehotel.com.* **Jamaican**. Jamaican street food like pepper shrimp, seafood fritters, jerked meats and traditional staple dishes like oxtail and curried goat are served in a panoramic clifftop setting overlooking the sea.

$$$ The HouseBoat Grill – *Southern Cross Blvd., Freeport Montego Bay.* ℘*876-979-8845.* **International**. For *the* place to pop the question, this one-of-a-kind floating restaurant on Mobay's Bogue Lagoon marine sanctuary may be your best bet. The menu features lobster selected live from a tank in the hull.

$$$$ Toscanini – *Harmony Hall, Tower Isle, St. Mary.* ℘*876-975-4785.* **Italian**. Located on the ground floor of an old plantation house, Toscanini brings diners in with its picturesque setting and inviting patio that complement excellent dishes from the old world.

DISCOVERING
DOMINICAN REPUBLIC★

Hotels

1 Casa de Campo
2 Casa Colonial Beach and Spa
3 Hostal Nicolas de Ovando
4 Villa Taina

Restaurants

1 El Conuco
2 Meson de Bari
3 Pat'e Palo European Brasserie
4 Sam's Bar and Grill

The Dominican Republic shares two-thirds of an island with Haiti, known collectively as Hispaniola. It's the second-largest island in the Caribbean, after Cuba. This is the place where Christopher Columbus landed during his first voyage to the New World in 1492, and it was immediately claimed for Spain, hence the original name, La Española. Its ancient Taíno heritage and its pivotal role in Spanish colonization and the African slave trade is still evident today in its language, culture and food. For a time, the nation was unified under Haitian rule, until an underground resistance group, La Trinitaria, led by Juan Pablo Duarte, mobilized and launched attacks on the Haitian army. The country gained independence in 1844, and was officially named República Dominicana (Dominican Republic).

PETER'S TOP PICKS

CULTURE

Immerse yourself in the real local flavor through the art of *merengue*. Santo Domingo's annual Merengue Festival is one of the year's premier events. (p **175**)

HISTORY

Santo Domingo's Zona Colonial is an introduction to the nation's complicated history, featuring some of the first structures in the New World, including the oldest cathedral in the Americas. (p **172**)

STAY

One of the most luxurious resorts in the country is Casa de Campo in the southern village of La Romana. This sprawling, 7,000-acre resort sits on a former sugar-mill site, and attracts everyone from A-list celebrities to politicians and golf enthusiasts eager to play the championship course designed by Golf Hall of Fame member Pete Dye. (p **175**)

EAT

Dine at El Conuco, where national staples like Dominican-style *mofongo* and *sancocho caribeño* (meat and vegetable stew) are served in tandem with colorful dance shows. (p **175**)

PLAY

From mid-January to mid-March, Samaná Peninsula attracts thousands of humpback whales migrating along the coast to the balmy waters to mate and calve. (p **174**)

Today, the country's primary industries are mining, manufacturing and tourism. The variety of experiences available here has made it a prime destination for vacationers of all types. Its white-sand beaches offer much more than just sunbathing—they're an outdoor adventurer's paradise, with some of the best conditions in the world for windsurfing and water sports. World-class golf courses abound, attracting avid golfers to resorts like Casa de Campo in the old sugar town La Romana and the highly touted Tom Fazio-designed Corales Course at Puntacana Resort & Club.

Locally, the Dominican Republic is home to a variety of joyous festivals all year long, where you can catch a glimpse into its cultural heritage with folk dancing and music, colorful costumes and street parades. The most anticipated event of the year is Carnival in Santo Domingo, where locals don elaborate masks and intricate costumes and take to the streets in February.

Santo Domingo★★★

The conquest of the New World by Spanish conquistadors began in what is now the country's capital. The best preserved colonial city in the Western Hemisphere and a UNESCO World Heritage Site anchors Dominican Republic's south coast. East of the touristy resort of Puerto Plata on the northern coast lies the bustling strip of hotels, beach bars and surf shops of Cabarete. The stunning scenery of the Samaná Peninsula in the northeast is reason enough to explore its towns and beaches.

Zona Colonial, Santo Domingo★★★

Slip on comfortable shoes and take to the cobbled streets of **Calle de Las Damas** to see the impressive fortifications of the **Torre del Homenaje**. Follow in the footsteps of Christopher Columbus and English privateers like Sir Francis Drake, as you explore the city's medieval churches and historic plazas along the banks of the Río Ozama.

Top sights include the oldest cathedral (1540) in the Americas, **Catedral Santa Maria de la Encarnacion** *(open daily 8am–6pm)*, and **Parque Colon**, where you can contemplate the statue of Columbus as you sip a coffee at one of the many cafes. More than a historic theme park, the Zona Colonial is a vibrant center of classy boutiques, chic eateries and bustling bars that should be explored at leisure.

Museo del Hombre Dominicano

Plaza de la Cultura Juan Pablo Duarte, Calle Pedro Henríquez Ureña, Santo Domingo. Open Tue–Sun 10am–6pm. RD$50. ℰ 809-687-3622. www.museodelhombredominicano.org.do.

The history of the country is traced through 10,000 objects, beginning with the indigenous Taíno and a fascinating collection of their ceramics, weapons and healing practices, to the arrival of Columbus and the Spanish, the impact of slavery on the island and the modern traditions of Carnival. On the same square is the **Museo de Arte Moderno** *(open Tue–Sun; RD$50)*.

Other Sights

Cabarete

On the northern coast, Cabarete is lined with surf shops, hotels and bars. During the day, strong winds on Playa Cabarete and nearby Kite Beach create a windsurfing and kiteboarding

WHEN TO GO

Average temperatures range from 84°F in the Dec-Apr **dry season** to a high of 88°F in the rainy season months of May-Nov. The **hurricane season** in Aug-Oct can bring heavier rainfall and stronger winds, although showers are generally short and followed by clear skies. This year-round sun and sea destination has two peak seasons for tourism, coinciding with the US and European winter and the summer school holidays. Expect crowds in La Vega and Santo Domingo during the annual Carnival celebrations in February.

GETTING AROUND

BY BUS – Private bus companies in Santo Domingo cover long-distance destinations and are inexpensive, with a 3.5 hour trip to Puerto Plata on an air-conditioned bus about US$8. Try Caribe Tours (www.caribetours.com.do) or Metro (www.metroserviciosturisticos. com). Private buses known as *guaguas*, are minivans playing loud music that ply all routes between most destinations and can be flagged down anywhere along the route. Guaguas charge about RD$10-RD$20 per journey and you pay the driver's assistant, known as the *cobrador*.

BY TAXI – Taxis are available from the airport, port, all major towns and are unmetered. Establish the fare before boarding, use taxi ranks or hotel taxis. Avoid unmarked taxis in the street. A taxi from the airport to Santo Domingo costs about US$15. **Tecni-Taxi** (☎809-567-2010).

BY CAR - Major rental car companies have offices at all the main airports. Rentals start from about US$50 per day. SUVs will be considerably more. Rental age is 25 to 80. Erratic driving by locals and poor road conditions can make things difficult, especially at night.

VISITOR INFORMATION

Main tourism office: Calle Cayetano Germosen, Ave Gregorio Luperon, Santo Domingo. ☎809-221-4660. www.godominicanrepublic.com.
Important numbers
Police, Fire, Ambulance: 911
Medical Services:
Centro Medico Semma: Calle Jose Joaquín Perez, Josefa Perdomo Gazcue. ☎809-686-1705.

MONEY/CURRENCY

The official currency is the Dominican peso (RD$). At the time of publication the official exchange rate at banks was $1 US = RD$38. Check a currency conversion site (www.xe.com) before travel. US dollars can be exchanged at banks and *casas de cambio*, where you will get the best rates. Keep receipts so you can change back unwanted pesos at the airport. Major hotels and restaurants in Santo Domingo and other main cities will also exchange dollars but at a poorer rate. You can usually pay in dollars at all-inclusive resorts but will need local currency if you venture out. All major credit cards and most debit cards are widely accepted but it is harder to cash traveler's checks. ATMs operate 24hrs in main towns and dispense cash in local currency.

paradise for beginners and experts. At night, the fun continues along the strip as the music cranks up and surfers start to party. Rent a board for US$300 a week or take classes at one of the many windsurfing centers like Carib BIC Center (809-571-0640. www.caribwind.com) or Villa Taina hotel (*see WHERE TO STAY*).

BEACH LIFE

The well-developed beaches are on the north and east coasts of the island, where most tourists convene at the multiple resorts, shops and thrumming night spots. The northeast beaches of **Punta Cana** and **Bávaro** are brimming with activities, from boating and kayaking to diving and snorkeling.

Only 20 minutes from **Puerto Plata**, on the Atlantic-facing north coast, is the town of **Cabarete**, a world-renowned spot for windsurfing and kiteboarding. Although much the country has good locations for these sports, the eastern trade winds blowing across Cabarete are among the most powerful and consistent throughout the year, with conditions becoming only a little less reliable between October and December. The strong winds and the location of an offshore reef that keeps the waters relatively calm combine to create an ideal spot whether you're a beginner or an advanced athlete. Since its unique windsurfing and kite-surfing conditions were discovered in the 1980s, this once-sleepy little beach village has grown into a thriving tourist hub, and has hosted a number of international competitions.

The country's south coast beaches are less developed than the north and east sides, but a handful of resorts and amenities make these spectacular beaches accessible. The village of **Bayahibe** is an excellent jumping-off point for scuba diving and for hopping aboard a catamaran to the paradise that is **Saona Island**. This tiny island is part of the **Parque Nacional del Este**, and its protected status means miles of beautifully kept white-sand beaches and a thriving ecosystem for rich marine life.

Samaná Peninsula

Tours: Kim Beddal. ✆ *809-538-2494. www.whalesamana.com.*
The stunning scenery of the Samaná Peninsula in the northeast is reason enough to explore its towns and beaches, but from mid-January to mid-March visitors who flock here come for one reason: the chance to see thousands of humpback whales migrating here to breed and nurse their young. Off the coast, along the Silver Bank reef and inshore in Samaná Bay, more than 12,000 whales arrive each year, creating a magnificent spectacle and an opportunity to get up close to these amazing mammals and witness their tender courtship rituals. Veteran whale watcher and conservationist Kim Beddal, a Canadian by birth, has been leading boat tours to see the whales for more than 25 years.

Addresses

For price ranges, see the Legend on the cover flap.

WHERE TO STAY

$ Villa Taina – *Calle Principal, Cabarete.* ☎809-571-0722. *www.villataina.com. 57 rooms.* Popular with sportsmen and families who come to learn windsurfing, this condo-style hotel on Cabarete is at the heart of the action. Beach bar, small pool and in-room Wi-Fi.

$$ Hostal Nicolas de Ovando – *Calle de Las Damas, Santo Domingo.* ☎809-685-9955. *www.mgallery.com. 104 rooms.* This 1502 mansion blends a modern minimalist aesthetic with authentic features. Part of the M chain of boutique hotels, it has a cool swimming pool and a restaurant serving French cuisine, **La Residence ($$)**.

$$$ Casa de Campo – *Playa Minitas, La Romana.* ☎809-523-8396. *www.casadecampo.com.do. 267 rooms.* A mammoth resort that attracts A-listers, this casa has 14 swimming pools, gyms, a shooting range and a Pete Dye golf course. Private villas come with butler, chef and maid.

$$$ Casa Colonial Beach and Spa – *Playa Dorada, Puerto Plata.* ☎809-320-3232. *www.casa colonialhotel.com. 50 rooms.* This luxury boutique has a grand house and lush gardens. Jacuzzis and an infinity pool with sea views grace the rooftop terrace and the **Lucia** restaurant (**$$$**), serving Asian fusion food, is minimal and chic.

WHERE TO EAT

$ Sam's Bar and Grill – *In the Castilla Hotel, Calle José del Carmen Ariza 34, Puerto Plata.* ☎809-586-7267. **Dominican**. A popular haunt for expats in the 1970s, this unassuming corner bar lures visitors with a reasonably priced steak-and-eggs menu and vintage decor. Come here for morning pancakes, fish and chips at night, or just to surf the internet while nursing a beer.

$$ El Conuco – *Casímiro de Mora 152, Gazcue, Santo Domingo.* ☎809-686-0129. *www.elconuco. com.do.* **Dominican**. This touristy haunt offers merengue dance shows alongside traditional food. Try the *mangu* (mashed plantains), *mofongo* (mashed plantains with pork rinds), and *asopao de camarones* (shrimp stew).

$$ Meson de Bari – *Calle Hostos 302, Santo Domingo.* ☎809-687-4091. **Dominican**. This classy spot in a restored colonial house serves *empanadas lambi* (filled with conch) and grilled crabs. Live Latin music in the downstairs bar on weekends.

$$$ Pat'e Palo European Brasserie – *Calle Atarazana 25, Santo Domingo.* ☎809-687-8089. *www.patepalo.com.* **French**. This upscale French-style brasserie in the colonial city serves rabbit and Chablis sausages, and a risotto with calamari ink and shrimp *brunoise*. A break from *mofongo*.

Travel Tip: Music and dance are an integral part of the Dominican Republic's cultural heritage. The nation is most closely associated with merengue, which has deep African roots and is tied to a Haitian version of the art form. Merengue *típico* can be heard throughout the country in its nightclubs and beaches, and the popular Santo Domingo Merengue Festival on El Malecón boardwalk.

9 DISCOVERING
PUERTO RICO★★★

The 110-mile-long island, 40 miles at its widest, lies east of Hispaniola. Puerto Rico was ceded to the US in 1898 at the end of the Spanish-American War, but Spain's legacy endures in the language, architecture and culture. Appointed governor in 1508, Juan Ponce de Léon named the island Puerto Rico, Spanish for "rich port." Though the gold the Spanish mined is long gone, the island is not bereft of treasure: its capital city includes the 500-year-old walled town of Old San Juan—a UNESCO World Heritage Site—as well as New San Juan, with its flashy hotels, casinos and nightlife, stretching eastward along the northern shore. Most of Puerto Rico's 3.8 million residents live in or near the capital of San Juan, a busy port of call. Eastern Puerto Rico claims the large rain forest of El Yunque. Laid-back Vieques and Culebra islands boast powdery white beaches. On the south coast the second-largest city, Ponce, preserves an impeccably maintained colonial zone.

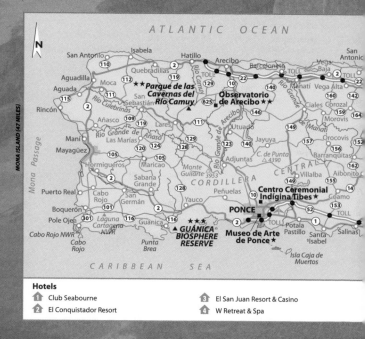

Hotels

1. Club Seabourne
2. El Conquistador Resort
3. El San Juan Resort & Casino
4. W Retreat & Spa

PETER'S TOP PICKS

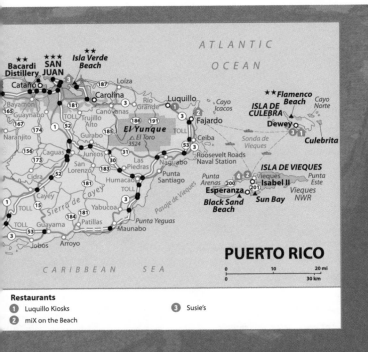

CULTURE

Walk the blue cobblestone streets of old San Juan to explore the Colonial architecture and lively social scene of this charming, 7-block area. (p **178**)

HISTORY

El Morro is truly a majestic sight, perched on a promontory overlooking the sea. But don't just go for the fortress alone. On Sundays, the area comes alive with locals flying colorful kites. (p **178**)

EAT

Dining at the food kiosks around Luquillo Beach has become a favorite memory for many a traveler. Dozens of ramshackle buildings serve everything from empanadas to ice-cold beers. (p **187**)

SEE

Get out of the city and into paradise with a short trip to Vieques and Culebra, both protected from over-development. (p **182**, p**184**)

PUERTO RICO

Restaurants

1. Luquillo Kiosks
2. miX on the Beach
3. Susie's

177

San Juan★★★

Home to the majority of the island's almost 4 million residents, Puerto Rico's capital is the largest city in the Caribbean and the island's cultural, artistic and commercial center. Located along the northeast coast of Puerto Rico, San Juan is a major port, boasting one of deepest natural harbors in the region. Founded in 1521, the city offers something for every visitor, from historic **Old San Juan** to **New San Juan's** glitzy beaches, hip resort district, casino hotels, roaring nightlife, the Caribbean's most sophisticated convention center, and numerous cultural institutions.

Old San Juan★★★

Bounded mainly by Calle Norzagaray and Paseo de la Princesa.
The Colonial architecture, pastel-colored façades, blue-tinged cobblestone streets, evocative sculptures and graceful monuments of *la ciudad murallada* (walled city) make it the most enchanting destination in Puerto Rico. Stretching only seven square blocks, Old San Juan occupies the western end of a peninsula fronting San Juan Bay. The former military stronghold is now a shopping, dining, and cultural hub; small wonder that the entire historic area has been named a UNESCO World Heritage Site.

Castillo San Felipe del Morro★★★

501 Calle Norzagaray. ☎ 787-729-6960. www.nps.gov/saju. Open daily 9am–5pm. $3.
Begun in 1539, the fortress known as El Morro ("The Promontory") was a formidable guardian of Puerto Rico for centuries, repelling attacks by the French, Dutch, and in 1595, England's Sir Francis Drake. El Morro fell only once—to the Earl of Cumberland in 1598, who conquered it by land. El Morro comprises six levels, housing dungeons, barracks, passageways, storerooms, and a distinctive lighthouse. Interspersed along its ramparts are iconic *garitas* (sentry boxes), a quintessential feature of military architecture of the era.

La Fortaleza★★

Calle Recinto Oeste off Calle Fortaleza. ☎ 787-721-7000. www.fortaleza.gobierno.pr. Open Mon–Fri 9am–4pm.
The oldest governor's mansion in the western hemisphere, La Fortaleza ("The Stronghold") is officially known as El Palacio de Santa Catalina. Completed in 1540 as one of the island's earliest fortifications, the structure was renovated several times un-

ASK PETER...

Q: How can I avoid the crowds at El Yunque rain forest?
A: Although El Yunque is spread over 28,000 acres, the scenic beauty of this misty, subtropical rain forest makes it a huge attraction for visitors and locals alike. The biggest crowds arrive on weekends, so the old adage of traveling midweek holds true. El Yunque closes at 6pm, but it opens early—so your best bet to get in there at the crack of dawn is to stay at one of the hotels next to the rain forest or in the foothills. Then spend the afternoon at Luquillo Beach and grab lunch at one of the beachside kiosks.

WHEN TO GO

Temperatures year-round range from 71°F to 89°F degrees. It can rain anytime, but the driest months are January to April. Forecasts for Vieques and Culebra Islands can differ significantly from San Juan. Peak tourist season is December to April, but you can find bargains May to November.

GETTING AROUND

BY BUS – The public bus system (locals call buses *guaguas*) has two routes—A5 and B21—covering the tourist areas. ☎866-797-1262. The **Metrobus** covers the greater metro area. 37 Ave. Diego, Río Piedras, San Juan. ☎787-294-0500. www.dtop.gov.pr

BY TRAIN – San Juan's **Tren Urbano** (Urban Train), the Caribbean's first rapid transit system, serves the metropolitan area but not Old San Juan or the tourist zones of Condado and Isla Verde. ☎787-763-4141. www.dtop.gov.pr.

BY TAXI – The official **Tourist Taxi** can be found at designated taxi stands; it charges fixed rates by zone. ☎787-969-3260. www.cabspr.com. You can also call independent taxi companies like **Metro Taxi**, ☎787-725-2870.

BY PÚBLICO: Independently owned passenger vans travel all over the island (and Vieques and Culebra). Look for their yellow license plates ending in "P" or "PD." **Chóferes Unidos de Ponce**, ☎787-764-0540, **Terminal de Transportación Pública**, ☎787-860-1820.

BY FERRY: From San Juan to Hato Rey and Cataño, ☎787-729-8714, from Fajardo to Culebra and Vieques, ☎787-860-2005. www.dtop.gov.pr.

BY TROLLEY – A free trolley putters around Old San Juan. You can wait for it at clearly designated stops or flag it down.

VISITOR INFORMATION

Main tourism office: La Casita, Plaza de la Dársena, Old San Juan, ☎787-722-1709 or 800-866-7827 (toll-free).

Important numbers
Emergency (24hrs): 911
Police: ☎787-726-7020
Fire Department: ☎787-725-3444
Medical Services:
Ashford Presbyterian Community Hospital, Condado, San Juan ☎787-721-2160, www.presbypr.com

Medical emergencies: ☎787-754-2550.

MONEY/CURRENCY

The US dollar is Puerto Rico's currency. Locals call dollars *pesos*.

---

til it was finally converted in 1846 to the official residence of Puerto Rico's governors. Tours take you to the dungeons and a few official rooms, and the lovely gardens. Note in particular the mahogany clock in one of the corridors: before he left, the last governor of Spain struck its face with his sword, stopping time at the very last second of Spanish rule in the New World.

Castillo San Cristóbal★★

Off Calle Norzagaray. ☎787-729-6960. www.nps.gov/saju. Open daily 9am–5pm. $3.
The 27-acre Fort San Cristóbal is the largest fort constructed by the Spanish in the New World. The massive citadel rises almost 150 feet above sea level and was begun in 1634 to guard against

Travel Tip: Getting around Puerto Rico by taxi or rental car is preferred by most visitors, as it only takes about 3 hours to go from one end of the island to the other. However, if you're planning to stick to San Juan, the bus is an exceptionally affordable (if slow) way to go. Get around Old San Juan via a free trolley service.

a land assault from the east. Like El Morro, its design follows a layered "defense-in-depth" model. It was from here that the first shot of the Spanish-American War was fired by the Spanish. Check out its tunnels, dungeons, batteries, cannons and *garitas*, as well as the incongruous World War II bunkers installed by the US Army in 1942.

Catedral de San Juan

151-153 Calle del Cristo. ✆ *787-722-0861. www.catedralsanjuan.com. Open Mon–Sun 8am–5pm (Sun until 2pm).*

This stately cathedral, Puerto Rico's most important religious institution, has suffered multiple hurricanes and lootings. Rebuilt and restored through the centuries, it now holds the remains of Ponce de León in a marble tomb, and a wax-covered, glass-encased mummy of St. Pio, a Roman martyr. Apart from its beautiful stained-glass windows, most of its opulence has vanished over time.

SAN JUAN

Hotels		Restaurants					
🏨 1	La Concha	● 1	Budatai	● 3	La Casita Blanca	● 5	Pikayo
🏨 2	El Conquistador Resort	● 2	Dragonfly	● 4	La Fonda del Jibarito		

PORT CITY – SAN JUAN

Founded in 1521 by Ponce de León, San Juan is the oldest city on US territory. The city is broken up into several neighborhoods, though tourists tend to cluster in just a handful: **Old San Juan**, with its cobblestone streets and fortress walls, is a UNESCO World Heritage Site as well as a popular cruise-ship port; the bustling **Condado** neighborhood is brimming with beach resorts, boutique shops, restaurants and nightspots; and elegant, upscale **Miramar**, where cruise ships also dock in the Pan-American Pier.

But San Juan isn't just known for its urban offerings. It's also home to the 16th century **El Castillo de San Felipe del Morro** (aka El Morro), an imposing Spanish citadel on a rocky promontory. Together with **Castillo de San Cristóbal**, the fortress makes up part of the San Juan National Historic Site, overseen by the National Park Service. Explore tunnels and dungeons, and take a walk along the city walls between the two fortresses, overlooking the San Juan Bay below. Go on a Sunday and you'll be greeted with a colorful spectacle as families gather on the sprawling, open space to fly kites by the sea.

On the south side of Old San Juan is **El Paseo de la Princesa**, a lovely promenade where you can take a stroll alongside the city walls to soak up ocean views and catch sight of La Fortaleza, the governor's grandiose palace.

The beauty of San Juan is that visitors party right alongside the locals. Spend the day at the beach lazing on white sand and snacking at the nearby food vendors selling kebabs, empanadas and flavored ice. In the evening, head to the famed **Nuyorican Café** (*312 Calle San Francisco*), where art lovers gather for an eclectic mix of salsa, spoken word and poetry. Then do as the locals do and go across the street to **Cafe Celeste**, a tiny joint that's got a jukebox full of Latin rhythms playing into the night.

Travel Tip: San Juan is considered to be a safe city, but common sense always prevails. Avoid roaming around areas like La Perla, next to El Morro in Old San Juan, even in daylight. The neighborhood of Santurce, near Condado, is quite lively with local restaurants, theaters and museums (including the Puerto Rican Museum of Art), but after hours the streets empty out and it's not advisable to walk around late at night.

ENJOYING THE LOCAL CUISINE

The national dish of Puerto Rico is mainly *arroz con gandules* with *tostones* and *lechón Asao* (rice with pigeon peas, plantain chips and roasted pork). Another signature dish in Puerto Rico is the famous *mofongo*, which is mashed plantain with pungent garlic that's fried and stuffed with your favorite meat, seafood stew or even fried pork. A variant of this, *mofongo relleno*, is stuffed and topped with stewed meat. Don't worry, it's well-worth the calories.

Bacardi Rum Distillery★★

Rte. 165 at KM 6.2, Cataño. ℘ 787-788-8400. http://casabacardi.org. Open Mon–Sat 8:30am–5:30pm, Sun 10am–5pm.

In the municipality of Cataño, facing San Juan across San Juan Bay, the Bacardi family has offered free tours of Casa Bacardi since 1962. The largest rum distillery in the world, Casa Bacardi earns its nickname "the Cathedral of Rum." Hop aboard a trolley and learn about 150 years of rum production, with interactive exhibits, historic re-creations, and two free samples of a Bacardi cocktail at tour's end.

Isla Verde Beach

Isla Verde, Carolina, southeast of San Juan.

Along with **Condado Beach** to its west, Isla Verde Beach lies at the feet of many of Puerto Rico's most desirable hotels. Ringed by palm trees, the wide, deep crescent of golden sand faces the Atlantic Ocean. Its calm waters attract swimmers, sunbathers and watersports enthusiasts.

Travel Tip: Although Puerto Rico is a warm-weather Caribbean destination, not all of its attractions are as sun-soaked as its beaches. El Yunque rain forest has its own unique ecosystem shrouded by a constant mist or soaked by rainfall. The underground cave network is also cool. Throw some additional layers into your suitcase along with the swimsuit and shorts.

Vieques

Located just seven miles off Puerto Rico's east coast, Vieques is a 21mi long by 4mi wide island with only two small towns: Isabel II and Esperanza. Two-thirds of the island was occupied by the US navy for decades, leaving the vast majority of Vieques undeveloped. But it's the wonderful variety of beaches, from the powder-soft Sun Bay to the volcanic Black Sand Beach, that draw devoted visitors each year—that, and a glow-in-the-dark natural wonder. The island also offers excellent opportunities for snorkeling, scuba diving and kayaking.

VIEQUES AND CULEBRA
...LIKE A LOCAL

For decades, tiny Vieques—which extends 21 miles long by 4 miles wide—was managed by the US Navy, meaning it was off-limits to tourists and developers. And for one controversial reason: Vieques was bombed early, often, and constantly as part of Navy target practice and weapons testing. Finally, local conservation groups persuaded the Navy to order a permanent cease fire in 2001. That's when a massive cleanup effort started. In 2003, the Navy turned the land over to the US Fish and Wildlife Service, and it continues to be a rugged wildlife refuge under strict management.

Just 7 miles away from Puerto Rico's east coast, Vieques has everything you want from a Caribbean island. It's home to secluded, white-sand beaches with little development and, best of all, no crowds. **Media Luna Beach** is one of the more family-friendly beaches, with shady areas and shallow waters curving against the half-moon shaped sands. Other beaches that were formerly restricted by naval forces are now among the most sought-after, including **Blue Beach** (Playa de la Chiva), which is ideal for sunbathing and snorkeling.

Also in Vieques, the famous bioluminescent waters of **Mosquito Bay** are a magical natural wonder, where tiny, glowing organisms are thought to be the brightest in the world. Kayak along the mangroves at night and prepared to be awed.

Vieques' even smaller sister, **Culebra**, is largely undeveloped, with only one town, **Dewey**. In 1909 President Teddy Roosevelt designated about a third of the island as a National Wildlife Refuge, making it one of the oldest in the entire system. This is a birder's paradise, where tens of thousands of sea birds breed each year; its beaches are also a haven for nesting sea turtles.

Flamenco Beach (Playa Flamenco) is among the prettiest on the island, a 1.5-mile stretch of land in a protected cove with tranquil waters. Don't miss what some consider a jarring sight on this peaceful crescent of land: a partially submerged US military tank. Because it's one of the few beaches with ample amenities like restrooms and food, it can get busy (relatively speaking), so go early or mid-week.

There are two ways to get to Vieques and Culebra, by plane or by ferry. Flying is a quick and easy jaunt from San Juan International Airport; ferries leave from the town of Fajardo, about 40 miles east of San Juan.

Travel Tip:
Puerto Rico is a
self-governing
commonwealth but
debates continue
over whether it
should retain its
current status,
become a state, or
become its own
independent nation.
As it stands, US
citizens don't need
a passport to enter
Puerto Rico, and the
currency is the US
dollar, making it an
attractive destination
for Caribbean-bound
Americans.

Vieques Biobay★★★

*Abe's Snorkeling & Biobay Tours. ☎ 787-741-2134, 787-436-2686.
www.abessnorkeling.com. Island Adventures. ☎ 787-741-0720,
787-741-2544. www.biobay.com. $30 and up.*

Technically called Mosquito Bay, Vieques Biobay—as it is known
locally—is one of the most brilliant bioluminescent bays in the
world, the result of a unique ecosystem that's a breeding ground
for microscopic organisms that glow in the dark when agitated.
When you swim in these waters at night, you glow neon green.
It's a spectacular phenomenon well worth the guided tour to
the bay, which you can take by kayak with **Abe's** or on an electric pontoon boat with **Island Adventures**.

Culebra

**If you think Vieques is rustic, wait until you land on Culebra.
A mere 7mi by 4mi, the island of Culebra is located 17 miles
east of mainland Puerto Rico and 9 miles north of Vieques.
Its lone town, Dewey, has but one gas station, a cluster of
small hotels, and the most beautiful beach in Puerto Rico,
Flamenco Beach★★. Culebra also has its own tiny islands,
of which Culebrita is a dazzling slice of beachfront practically untouched by man. Humans aren't Culebra's only
visitors; from April to June, the island is a favorite nesting
ground for leatherback turtles.**

Flamenco Beach★★

End of Carretera 251.

A deep horseshoe of white sand fronting azure waters and
ringed by verdant hills, Flamenco Beach is postcard-perfect. It
has the most facilities of any beach in Culebra, including showers, campgrounds, lifeguards, and kiosks selling food, clothing,

---

UNDERGROUND TREASURE

A great underground adventure awaits you at 268-acre Parque
de las Cavernas del Río Camuy on the northwest side of the
island. Leave the sunshine and descend 200 feet underground
where you'll explore subterranean caverns carved out by the
Camuy River over a million years ago. It's one of the largest
cave systems in the Western Hemisphere. A guide will take you
through caves as tall as 150 feet, teeming with 1,000-year-old
stalagmites and stalactites.

and beach accessories. Mired in the sands of the beach are two brightly painted but rusted tanks.

Ponce and the South Coast

Ponce

Known as the "Pearl of the South," Ponce is a cultural gem in the south of the island and the second-largest city in Puerto Rico. Its elegant architecture and rich heritage give it a quaint, dignified personality. Ponce's **Carnival** is Puerto Rico's largest and most popular event, and its outstanding cultural institutions include the world-class **Museo de Arte de Ponce★** (Ponce Museum of Art); **Castillo Serrallés**, a museum and former home of the family behind Don Q Rums; and the ancient indigenous **Tibes Ceremonial Center★**.

Guánica Biosphere Reserve★★★

25mi west of Ponce by Rte. 2 west and Rte. 116 south.
Any visit to Ponce should include a trip to this reserve, which has been designated a World Biosphere Reserve by the United Nations. Come here to hike through the 1,600-acre Guánica Dry Forest, home to 48 species of rare trees and 135 species of birds. The reserve also includes a pleasant beach and the ruins of an abandoned sugar mill.

Western Puerto Rico

Observatorio de Arecibo★★

Rte. 129, Arecibo. Take Rte. 22 west of San Juan, then Rte. 129 and follow signs. ☎ 787-878-2612. www.naic.edu. Open daily 9am–4pm. Closed holidays. $10.
The National Astronomy and Ionosphere Center houses the world's largest radio telescope. It boasts a satellite dish that's bigger than 12 football fields. Come to see the excellent science exhibits that explain the workings of the telescope as well as the cosmos.

Rincon Beach★★

On the island's westernmost point, 92mi west of San Juan.
Rincon is the island's best beach, with pale golden sands, gin-clear waters and a backdrop of emerald hills. It's a favorite of the surfer set, since it has some of the best surfing waves. In January and February, you might even spot humpback whales from the beach.

Addresses

For price ranges, see the Legend on the cover flap.

WHERE TO STAY

$$ Club Seabourne –
Calle Fulladoza, KM 1.5, Culebra Island. ☎787-742-3169. www.club seabourne.com. 13 rooms. Following a recent renovation, Culebra's most beautiful hotel has only gotten better. Guest rooms are located in cozy plantation-style cottages nestled in tropical landscaped grounds. The hotel's restaurant offers the best gourmet food on the island.

$$ El Conquistador Resort
– 1000 Conquistador Ave., Fajardo. ☎787-863-1000, 877-999-3223. www.elconresort.com. 750 rooms. A destination unto itself, this sprawling Waldorf Astoria property lies on the eastern end of Puerto Rico, overlooking the Caribbean and Atlantic. The resort boasts its own private island, waterpark, six pools, golf course, casino, a great spa and spacious, inviting rooms with separate seating areas and roomy bathrooms.

$$ El San Juan Resort & Casino
– 6063 Isla Verde Ave., Isla Verde, Carolina. ☎787-791-1000, 888-579-2632. www.elsan juanhotel.com. 390 rooms. An icon of the golden age of Puerto Rican tourism, this resort hosted the original Rat Pack back in the 1960s; its retro-cool vibe lives on in its magnificent lobby lounge and casino. The hotel has top-class dining options, and the renovated guest rooms are minimalist chic.

Travel Tip: Familiarize yourself with the rules before you pick up a bottle or two of that famous Puerto Rican rum. Airlines won't allow the bottles in your carry-on bag, and some cruise lines will temporarily confiscate purchased liquor until the end of the trip.

$$$ La Concha –
1077 Ashford Ave., Condado, San Juan. ☎787-721-7500. www.laconcha resort.com. 483 rooms. In the fashionable Condado district of San Juan, this chic member of the Renaissance group has quickly become the darling of the neighborhood, thanks to its see-and-be-seen lobby bar, spectacular clam-shell themed **La Perla** restaurant, and guest rooms that offer the latest amenities in a contemporary urban style.

$$$ Hotel El Convento –
100 Cristo St., Old San Juan. ☎787-723-9020 or 800-468-2779. www.elconvento.com. 58 rooms. Few places capture Old San Juan's romantic charm quite like El Convento, a 16C convent transformed into a luxury boutique hotel. The elegant furnishings, arched windows, and antiques throughout the hotel transport guests to another era without sacrificing modern creature comforts.

$$$$ W Retreat & Spa –
State Road 200, KM 3.2, Vieques Island. ☎787-741-4100. www.wvieques.com. 156 Rooms. Anchoring a pristine stretch of beachfront, the luxurious W has been designed to be in harmony with its lush natural setting. Enjoy the infinity pool, minimalist-style guest rooms, well-appointed Away Spa and superb fine-dining restaurant in Alain Ducasse's **miX on the Beach**.

WHERE TO EAT

La Casita Blanca – *351 Tapia St., Santurce, San Juan.* ☏*787-726-5501. www.casitablancapr.com.* **Puerto Rican**. One of the most beloved eateries in San Juan, La Casita Blanca is tucked away in a residential neighborhood, but everyone from tourists to senators will happily make the trip for the rich, flavorful cuisine. The menu is scribbled daily on a chalkboard.

La Fonda del Jibarito – *280 Sol St., Old San Juan.* ☏*787-725-8375. www.eljibaritopr.com.* **Puerto Rican**. A local institution for 36 years, El Jibarito is perhaps your best bet for cheap, authentic Puerto Rican cuisine in Old San Juan. "Jibarito" is a Puerto Rican term for the island's rural mountainfolk.

Luquillo Kiosks – *Along Rte. 3, Luquillo.* **Medley**. Travel along Route 3 heading east from San Juan, and you'll eventually arrive at the famed Luquillo Kiosks: 60 rustic stalls, independently named and managed, that offer everything from crispy local snacks to gourmet burgers to surprisingly upscale cuisine.

$ Dragonfly – *364 Fortaleza St., Old San Juan.* ☏*787-977-3886. www.oofrestaurants.com.* **Asian-Caribbean Fusion**. The southern end of Fortaleza Street, or "SoFo," is Old San Juan's famed restaurant row, and Dragonfly is one of its stars. Come for the tropics-inspired sushi, duck-flavored nachos, and other fusion specialties.

$$ Susie's – *Downtown Dewey across the bridge, Culebra.* ☏*787-742-0574. www.susiesculebra.com.* **Puerto Rican**. Susie calls her cuisine "Puerto Rican cooking kicked up a notch." It's an apt description for the gourmet dishes you'll find in this funky, casual eatery in downtown Dewey.

$$$ Budatai – *1056 Ashford Ave., Condado, San Juan.* ☏*787-725-6919. www.budatai.com.* **Puerto Rican-Asian Fusion.** Serving a creative and delicious blend of Asian and Puerto Rican flavors, this restaurant is among the most popular eateries in San Juan. Budatai is the brainchild of star chef Roberto Treviño.

$$$ miX on the Beach – *W Retreat & Spa, State Road 200, KM 3.2, Vieques Island.* ☏*787-741-4100. www.wvieques.com.* **Caribbean Fusion**. Famed chef Alain Ducasse brings his signature flair and his mushrooms duxelles to the W Retreat in Vieques. It's easily the most refined and creative cuisine on the island.

$$$ Pikayo – *Conrad Condado Plaza, 999 Ashford Ave., San Juan.* ☏*787-721-6194. www.pikayo.com* **Puerto Rican**. For nouveau Rican cuisine, look no farther than Pikayo. One of Puerto Rico's top chefs, Wilo Benet, produces outstanding, inventive cuisine with deep island roots and sophisticated flavor combinations.

Travel Tip: Need to store your luggage before heading to the airport? Barrachina Restaurant in Old San Juan will hold it for you at no charge, with the understanding that you'll at least sit and have a drink. It does, after all, claim to be the birthplace of the pina colada.

US VIRGIN
ISLANDS★★

A lively cruise port, historic Danish architecture and national parkland await those who venture here. Located 13 miles east of Puerto Rico, the US Virgin Islands (USVI) are an official territory of the United States. Tourism is centered on the three largest islands: St. Thomas, St. John and St. Croix. Most lodgings are clustered on **St. Thomas**, the primary hub for families and couples. The capital city of Charlotte Amalie offers duty-free shopping along the cruise-ship harbor and on Main Street. **St. Croix** is the largest of the three islands and the farthest south, 36 miles from St. Thomas. It combines Danish buildings and historic plantations with splendid beaches and rain forest. **St. John** is the smallest of the three islands. Nearly two-thirds of the island is devoted to Virgin Islands National Park. Nature lovers come here to lie on the white-sand beaches, hike through the dense wilderness and plantations, and get out on the water for world-class snorkeling, diving and boating.

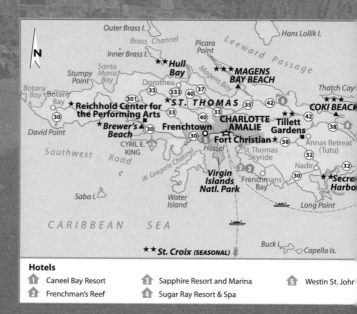

Hotels
1 Caneel Bay Resort
2 Frenchman's Reef
3 Sapphire Resort and Marina
4 Sugar Ray Resort & Spa
5 Westin St. John

PETER'S TOP PICKS

🍴 EAT

Oceana is upscale dining at its best on St. Thomas in the Frenchtown area. Located in a former great house on the waterfront, the open-air restaurant serves seafood, seafood, and more seafood, with unbeatable ocean views. (p **199**)

✈ PLAY

When cruise ships arrive at St. Croix, **Strand Street** in Frederiksted becomes an outdoor party, with mocko jumbie stilt dancers, live music and street vendors. (p **195**)

🍸 DRINK

Escape the crowds for classic French cuisine and wine at **Epernay Bistro** in Frenchtown. (p **190**)

✈ DO

Trunk Bay on St. John has an unusual "snorkeling trail" that stretches 675 feet underwater with signs identifying the corals and fish. The bay is gentle and clear enough that first-timers and old hacks alike can enjoy it. (p **194**)

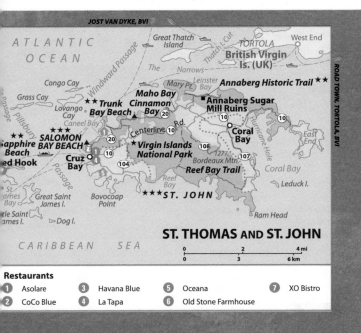

ST. THOMAS AND ST. JOHN

Restaurants

1. Asolare
2. CoCo Blue
3. Havana Blue
4. La Tapa
5. Oceana
6. Old Stone Farmhouse
7. XO Bistro

St. Thomas★

ASK PETER...

Q: What is St. Thomas' bar scene like?

A: Nightlife ranges from rowdy dance clubs and crowded beach bars to quieter, more upscale venues. Even locals linger around boisterous **Iggies Beach Bar & Grill** at the Bolongo Bay Beach Club (Rte. 30), with karaoke, live music , dancing in the sand, even night volleyball. **Duffy's Love Shack** is a lively hotspot in Cruz Bay where you'll drink and dance under a thatched roof. Potent drinks named Jaws or Baracuda Bomber go with your Jamaican jerk nachos. **Greenhouse Bar and Restaurant** (Waterfront Hwy., Charlotte Amalie) is a casual eatery with burgers and fish tacos; by night, it's a dance club with live reggae. For a more intimate experience—and classic French cuisine, **Epernay Bistro** (24-A Honduras, Frenchtown) has wine by the glass, with caviar or brie with crostini, and calypso music.

Also known as "Rock City" for its hills and high mountain St. Thomas measures only 13 miles long and almost half a wide. With just over 50,000 residents, it hosts 48 percer of the archipelago's population. The cosmopolitan capit of USVI and duty-free port of **Charlotte Amalie** (ah-MA ya) occupies the south-central portion of the island, whe it is served by countless ferries, and to the west, the Cy E. King Airport. It's the most visited of the islands, brin ming with fast-food chains and cruise-ship day trippe The downtown's historic government buildings, plac of worship and waterfront restaurants are worth a loo Come nightfall, the lively scene moves to Frenchtown an the East End, aka Red Hook, where nightclubs and ba abound.

Charlotte Amalie and Area

Referred to locally as "downtown," the city sees high cruise-sh traffic, thanks in large part to its deep-water harbor, guarde since 1672 by Danish-built **Fort Christian★** (℘ 340-774-834. Nearly every day, hundreds of passengers disembark to brow the 300 or so jewelry stores crowding the main street a blo north of the harbor. Check especially **Havensight Shoppin Place** (Southside 00802, ℘ 340-777-5313) for good deals on a cohol, china, crystal, perfumes and cameras as well as jewelr Don't miss a **view** of the busy harbor from the 5min **Skyrid** (℘ 340-774-9809; www.sttparadisepoint.com) or a climb downtown's **99 Steps**, constructed in the mid-1700s of bri brought from Denmark as ship ballast.

In the evening, **Frenchtown**, just west, is the place to go f classy food and drinks. But for a night of bar-hopping, you car beat **Red Hook**, lying 12 miles southeast of the capital. Dubbe the "East End" by locals, this yachting hub boasts more bars ar restaurants than elsewhere on the island. It is also the departu point for ferries to St. John.

Beaches
Magens Bay★★★

Rte. 35, on the island's nortside, due north of Charlotte Amalie. Open daily 8am–5pm. $4 entrance fee.

Besides being known as a shoppers' paradise, St. Thomas most famous for this heart-shaped bay with its mile of powde white sand, serviced by a water-sports rental station, one bar, grill and a small gift shop.

HEN TO GO

e Virgin Islands' coolest months are
c–Jan; with an average temperature
78°F/25°C. Temperatures the rest of
e year hover around 83°F/28°C with
gh humidity. While it can rain at any
e, **rainy season** in the Virgin Islands
Aug–Nov. **Hurricane season** happens
thin those months too. **High season** is
nsidered mid-Dec–Apr. The best time to
it is Nov–early Dec or May.

ETTING AROUND

N FOOT – The only part of St. Thomas
at can be explored on foot is Charlotte
nalie. All other parts of the island require
otored transportation.

TAXI – Open-air cabs known as
faris only cost one dollar; they encircle
e island stopping on the main road
addy Friday's Road) at each drop-off
cation every 5-10 minutes. Compact-size
ns (VI Taxi Association, ☎340-774-7457)
rvice the more high-traffic areas; they
arge by distance and the number of
ople traveling, from $5 up with tips
pected.

BY CAR – Car rental agencies are located
at the airport, and within main hotels.

BY FERRY – Ferries depart Red Hook and
downtown every hour on the hour for
St. John and St. Croix a couple of times
weekly, depending on passenger volume.
(Varlack Ventures ☎340-776-6282; $6
each way).

BY TWO WHEEL – Renting a scooter
(Rent-a-Motion, ☎340-774-5840, about
$32/ day)

VISITOR INFORMATION

Main tourism office: ☎1-800-372-USVI
Important numbers
Emergency (24hrs): 911
Medical Services: Roy Lester Schneider
Hospital, 9048 Sugar Estate, St. Thomas,
☎340-776-8311

MONEY/CURRENCY

The official currency is the US dollar,
since these islands are a U.S territory.
Major credit cards, most debit cards, and
traveler's checks are widely accepted.
Fees apply if you use your ATM card to
withdraw cash.

ull Bay★★

est of Magens Bay.
ull, the bay next to Magens Bay, faces the Atlantic Ocean; in
nter it is the island's only **surfing** bay.

ewer's Beach★

e. 30, northwest of the airport.
is small, tamarind-lined beach near the island's university is
pecially rewarding at sunset, even though the airport's land-
g strip lies on the other side of the bay.

apphire Beach★★

e. 38, east end of the island, just north of Red Hook.
is wide expanse of snow-white sand and its clear, coral-filled
aters lure sunbathers and windsurfers. Open to the public,
arby Sapphire Beach Resort rents snorkeling, windsurfing
d other equipment.

Travel Tip:
US citizens need no passport to fly into the US Virgin Islands or to island hop between St. Thomas, St. John and St. Croix, and even to Puerto Rico. That said, it's a good idea to bring it anyway in case you want to explore nearby Tortola, which is part of the British Virgin Islands.

Coki Beach★★★
Rte. 388, northwest of Sapphire Beach.
With its calm, shallow water, Coki Beach is a great place for ki to learn to snorkel. In water only 3 to 4 feet deep, you can fe fish with dog treats sold for that purpose onshore, but ther no food service here for humans other than a smoothie stan

Secret Harbour★★
Rte. 32, just west of Red Hook.
This private resort in the area of Nazareth allows visitors to u its beach. A beach cafe called Blue Moon offers free soda ref and a Bloody Mary spiced with Caribbean seasonings.

St. John★★★

Lying a mere three miles east of bustling St. Thomas, : John is laid-back in comparison. That's because two-thir of the land was donated in 1956 by Laurance Rockefel for a national park. The result is an unspoiled get-aw with tranquil beaches, sleepy lagoons, underwater co gardens, scenic roads, well-maintained walking trails a intriguing plantation ruins. St. Johnians are friendly, qui to lend a hand and most in love with their island. Two co munities, **Cruz Bay** and **Coral Bay**, sit at opposite ends the island. At Cruz Bay, ferries unload passengers and v hicles from St. Thomas.

Virgin Islands National Park★
1300 Cruz Bay Creek. ℘*340-776-6201. www.nps.gov/viis.*
Cruz Bay Visitor Center open daily 8am–4:30pm; closed Dec 25.
Thank Laurance Rockefeller for placing three-fifths of St. Joh 20 square miles of emerald-green hills, white sandy beach and plantation-era ruins into the protective custody of the N tional Park Service. Explore this vast park on 22 easy-to-diffict hiking trails, or take a guided hike with a national park rang Sign up for guided hikes at the **visitor center**, which han out free descriptions of trails, as well as schedules of lectures park rangers at Annaberg Sugar Mill ruins.

GETTING AROUND ST. JOHN
By Taxi – VI Taxi Association and VI Taxicab Division, $7-$25.
By Car – L&L Jeep Rental. ℘340-776-1120, Cruz Bay.

MUSIC ...LIKE A LOCAL

Beyond the duty-free shops and beach bars lies the cultural side of the USVI. The authentic rhythms of the Virgin Islands date back to the days of the African slave trade. Slaves were forbidden by colonists to perform their own dances or music. But the self-taught musicians, who made instruments from animal skins and discarded materials, learned to camouflage their bamboula rhythms and cariso melodies within traditional European jigs and military tunes. The resulting musical style, known as **Quelbe**, became an integral part of their work, worship and celebration. In 1969 the local St. Croix band "Stanley and the Ten Sleepless Knights" resurrected Quelbe.

Today you can hear its lively beat in festivals throughout the islands. To spark your island spirit, seek out St. Croix-based **Caribbean Dance Company**, founded in 1977 to preserve the rich heritage of West Indian folk dance. The company is based in St. Croix, but they often perform at the Reichhold Center for the Performing Arts in St. Thomas. They have received international acclaim for their performances in the Americas and throughout the Caribbean.

Lively beats, haunting music and colorful costumes make for a dazzling performance you'll never forget. Performances often feature stilt-dancing **mocko jumbies**, an integral part of island culture that originated in ancient West Africa. The towering 10- to 20-foot high stilts traditionally worn by a mocko jumbie gave him power to see approaching enemies or evil spirits in time to warn fellow villagers. A goat-skin mask decorated in cowrie shells kept his identity secret and inspired fear in the villagers, especially children.

When West African slaves landed in the Virgin Islands, colonists prohibited this ancient African art form. In the 1940s John Farrell and Fritz Sealy reintroduced the mocko jumbies to the isles. In 1959, Alli Paul began a lifelong fascination with the practice. He introduced acrobatics to his stilt dance and toured the world, the first mocko jumbie to do so. Today men, women and children of all nationalities dress up and dance on stilts as mocko jumbies.

Annaberg Historic Trail★★

This marked trail leads to the **Annaberg Sugar Mill ruins**; c.1733 remnants of the mill, slave quarters and sugar factory— and stunning views of the azure sea and British Virgin Islands. At times artisans demonstrate island crafts or play music on old-time instruments.

Reef Bay Trail★

The 2.5mi path begins on Centerline Road, descends through a shady forest and passes several sugar plantations. Watch for ancient rock carvings made by Taíno Indians. The trail ends at Reef Bay sugar mill near Genti Bay.

Beaches
Trunk Bay★★

Rte. 20, northeast of Cruz Bay in Virgin Islands National Park. $4.
This often-crowded beach is well known for its talcum-powder sand and 650ft **underwater trail** marked by sea-bottom-placed plaques that describe coral formations and fish found in these waters. Rent snorkeling gear from the water-sports center and keep a look out for sea turtles. The beach has showers, restrooms, a food concession and a gift shop.

Cinnamon Bay

Rte. 20, just east of Trunk Bay.
Extending a mile, this beach is one of the longest in Virgins Island National Park. It's a great place for snorkeling, swimming and kayaking. Snorkeling is best on the right side of the beach; a nature trail begins across from the campground. Campgrounds have restrooms, showers, a food concession and water-sports rentals.

Maho Bay

Rte. 20, just east of Cinnamon Bay.
The shallow, protected waters here are ideal for children. You'll probably see many boaters snorkeling, but be careful: you might step on a stingray while submerged.

St. Croix★★

St. Croix's history spans the rule of seven nations, primarily Denmark and Britain, each influencing island customs, character, language and architecture. The small island blends the urban vibe of St. Thomas and St. John's natural setting with its own culture and Old World charm. St. Croix is accessible by cruise ship, commercial flights from the mainland and from St. John via ferry or seaplane. Its beaches are individual: some with quiet coves and others, like **Cane Bay**, world renown as a dive site. Snorkeling is popular, given the abundant sea life and coral reefs close to shore. The Caribbean Sea's high salt content provides more buoyancy, so snorkeling here is easy. Two towns monopolize island life: **Christiansted**, along the northcentral coast, and Frederiksted, anchoring the island's west end.

Historic Sites

Christiansted
Northcentral coast.
Founded in 1734, Christiansted was once the capital of the Danish West Indies. Today a National Historic Site, it offers a feast of architectural delights left by the Danish. Most of the faded yellow buildings of this capital city are listed on the US National Registry of Historic Places. Narrow streets were wide enough for the mule carts of the 1800s. Once filled with the elegant houses and mercantile shops of wealthy Danes, the area now forms the main shopping and restaurant district. Plans are underway for the restoration of historic buildings on the outskirts of town.

Frederiksted
West end of island.
Victorian structure with gingerbread trim, wide streets and a picturesque waterfront the full length of town make this town one of the most appealing in the Caribbean. Known as Freedom City, it owns a rich history. Smugglers and pirates of the mid-1700s necessitated the construction of Fort Frederik in 1752. The city was destroyed by fire in 1758, and rebuilt in the Victorian style of the era. Time seems to have passed the city by, but the open-air mart comes alive when cruise ships arrive at the new pier. On those evenings, Harbour Night turns **Strand Street** into a festival, with **mocko jumbie** stilt dancers, steel-pan bands, and street vendors selling local foods and drink. Navy ships and subs from US and foreign fleets dock here often and frequently give tours of the vessels.

ASK PETER...
Q: I've heard the shopping in the USVI is excellent. Where should I go?
A: Shopping is practically the lifeblood of St. Thomas, especially when the cruise ships come into port. One block north of St. Thomas Harbor, shop 'til you drop in the swank stores and duty-free shops that line Main Street and Back Street. But it's not all jewelry and perfume shops on the island. S.O.S. Antiques (5132 Dronningens Gade 1) is owned by a commercial diver and charter boat captain who collects and sells a dizzying array of nautical antiques and shipwreck finds. Farther out, Tillett Gardens (4126 Anna's Retreat, St. Thomas) has shops that sell raku pottery and other local crafts, and there's an art gallery showcasing water colors and oil paintings by local artists.

GETTING AROUND ST. CROIX
By Taxi – St. Croix Taxi Association, ☎340-778-1088.
By Car – Car rental agencies are located at the airport.

Whim Plantation★★★

Rte. 70, Estate Whim, southeast of Frederiksted. ☎ *340-772-0598.*
www.stcroixlandmarks.com. Open Mon, Wed, Fri & Sat.
10am–3pm. $6.
One of the best-preserved plantation estates in the whole Caribbean, Whim Plantation showcases a mid-18C manor, a cookhouse, a windmill and other buildings, ruins of a sugar factory and gardens where sugar cane is still grown. You can watch the cane being processed and listen as guides interpret life on an 18C sugar plantation.

St. George Village Botanical Gardens★★

127 Estate St. George (off Centerline Rd.). ☎ *340-692-2874.*
www.sgvbg.org. Open daily 9am–5pm. $6.
Some 1,500 varieties of exotic and native plants—including palm trees, orchids, bromeliads and cactus—grace 16 acres of this former 19C sugar plantation. Walk through the rain forest among heliconias and butterfly ginger. Some of the acreage overlaps the site of what was once an indigenous settlement some 2,000 years ago.

St. Croix Heritage Trail★★

St. Croix Landmarks Society, 52 Whim Estate, Frederiksted.
☎ *340-772-0598. http://heritagetrails.stcroixlandmarks.org.*
The best way to become intimate with St. Croix is to rent a car and drive this 72mi-long self-guided driving tour. It circles the island, linking the historic seaport of Frederiksted with Point Udall, the easternmost point of the US in the Western Hemisphere. One of 50 Millennium Legacy Trails, the trail showcases the island's architecture, culture, history and natural sites. If you're fortunate, you may have an opportunity to meet the locals and learn about their oral traditions, food and music. Trail brochures and maps are available from the St. Croix Landmarks Society *(contact information above).*

Cruzan Rum Distillery

#3 Estate Diamond, Frederiksted. ☎ *340-692-2280.*
www.cruzanrum.com.
At this historic distillery, located in the heart of the island, visitors witness the rum-making process and the traditions of this

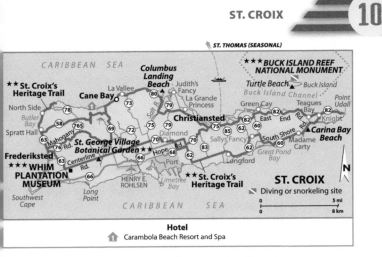

ancient craft. Watch coopers fabricate barrels as they have for centuries and see the old windmills used for power before electricity was available.

Beaches

Carina Bay Beach
East side of island.
Beach-goers enjoy sophisticated seclusion at this beach, which lies along an isolated stretch dotted by palms and swaying hammocks, just steps from the lively Carina Bay Casino (the only casino in the Virgin Islands).

Columbus Landing Beach
Rte. 80, Salt River Bay. 📞 *340-776-6201 ext. 238 www.nps.gov/sari*
Christopher Columbus and his crew are known to have disembarked at this Salt River site in 1493. It is also known that fighting broke out between his men and the area's Carib islanders.

Turtle Beach
Buck Island. www.nps.gov/buis.
Considered one of the most beautiful beaches in the Caribbean, Turtle Beach sits on Buck Island, which has been declared a national monument. It is accessible by charter boats that visit the island each day. Its underwater **snorkeling trail** is worth a venture.

Cane Bay Beach
Rte. 80, northwest coast.
This spectacular stretch of white sand and crystal clear waters is deemed the Caribbean's best snorkeling beach. It's also a divers'

haunt because of its "wall," or underwater drop-off, that teems with coral formations. With a dive center, beach bars, kayak rentals and horseback riding tours, this beach is most active on the weekends when locals enjoy the beach, bars/restaurants and warm ocean waters as well as the tourists.

Addresses

For price ranges, see the Legend on the cover flap.

WHERE TO STAY

$$ Sapphire Beach Condominium Resort –

6720 Estate Smith Bay, St. Thomas. ☎800-524-2090. www.antilles resorts.com. 171 units. This large resort, sitting on its own beach a mile north of Red Hook, offers spacious suites in condos with sea or marina views and full kitchens. Activities include snorkeling, windsurfing, tennis, volleyball, and swimming in the on-site pool.

$$$ Carambola Beach Resort and Spa –

Estate Davis Bay, St. Croix. ☎340-778-3800. www. marriott.com. 150 rooms. This Marriott property welcomes guests to its own beach, spa, pool, fitness trail and golf course at nearby Carambola Golf Club. Spacious rooms are done up Island style and offer views of the Caribbean or the resort's gardens. Enjoy breakfast on the terrace of Saman Restaurant and the Friday night pirate buffet with evening entertainment.

$$$ Frenchman's Reef –

5 Estate Bakkeroe, St. Thomas. ☎340-776-8500. www.marriott. com. All-inclusive plan available. 450 rooms. The largest resort in the US Virgin Islands, this high-rise Marriott property lies six miles from the airport and overlooks Charlotte Amalie harbor. Guests enjoy a private beach, on-site pools, restaurant, spa and tennis courts. Frenchman's Reef shares restaurant and beach facilities with the adjacent beachside Morning Star Resort.

$$$ Sugar Bay Resort & Spa –

6500 Estate Smith Bay, St. Thomas. ☎800-927-7100. www.sugarbay resortandspa.com. All-inclusive plan available. 294 rooms. Located within easy distance of the airport, this resort offers amenities like lit tennis courts, mini golf course, and jet skis and catamarans for its private beach. Relax in the spa and dine in one of several restaurants.

$$$ Westin St. John –

3008 Chocolate Hole, Cruz Bay, St. John. ☎340-693-8000. www. westinresortsst.john.com. 175 rooms. Overlooking Cruz Bay, this resort has a host of water sports as well as tennis courts, a kids' club and a spa. Several restaurants on the premises serve by the pool or private beach. Mango Deli delights guests, and locals too.

$$$$ Caneel Bay Resort –

Salomon Bay Road, St. John. ☎340-776-6111. www.caneelbay. com. 166 rooms. Rimming seven white-sand beaches, this dreamy 170-acre vacation retreat lies within St. John's untrammeled national park. Each room is an island-style sanctuary decked

out in wood and stone and furnished with rattan and wicker. Guests can choose among several on-site restaurants and relax with a massage in an outdoor cabana. Tennis and art lessons are available as well.

WHERE TO EAT

$$ Cultured Pelican – *5000 Estate Coakley Bay, East End, St. Croix. 340-773-3333. www. culturedpelican.com. Dinner only & Sunday brunch.* **Italian-American**. In an airy, casual setting with wood floors and ceiling fans, diners choose from seafood and pasta dishes based on old family recipes. Try the pizza or the *roti*, a kind of meat or vegetable wrap. The popular Sunday brunch is accompanied by live music.

$$$ Blue Moon – *Strand St., Frederiksted, St. Croix. 340-772-2222. Dinner & Sunday brunch only.* **Cajun-Caribbean**. Blue Moon orders up a good dose of conviviality at its historic waterfront location, where traditional Cajun dishes are enhanced with Caribbean ingredients. Live jazz Wed, Fri and Sunday brunch.

$$$ Coco Blue – *American Yacht Harbor, Red Hook, St. Thomas. 340-774-7253. www.cocobluerestaurant.com.* **Caribbean**. This waterfront restaurant counts its strong point as ultra-fresh fish, right off the boat. Snapper, sea bass and Caribbean lobster are among the seafood standouts. Sushi is a menu staple.

$$$ Oceana – *8 Honduras, Frenchtown, St. Thomas. 340-774-4262. www.oceanavi.com. Dinner only. Closed Mon.* **Seafood**.

Ensconced in a "great house" once used as a Russian consulate, Oceana perches above the water. Try the grilled Asian-rubbed Ahi tuna or bouillabaisse with clams and mussels, prepared by the female chefs.

$$$ La Tapa – *Cruz Bay, St.John. 340-693-7755. www.latapastjohn.com. Dinner only. Off-season closed Tue.* **Mediterranean**. This two-story hipped-roof house has outdoor seating. and a rustic decor indoors. The casual eatery serves up everything from gazpacho to escargot and foie gras to oysters. The menu changes daily. Live jazz pulls patrons in on Mondays.

$$$$ Asolare – *Estate Lindholm Hotel, Cruz Bay, St. John. 340-779-4747. Dinner only.* **French-Asian**. Set on a hilltop amid the national park, Asolare offers splendid views of Cruz Bay. The kitchen emphasizes fine-dining dishes made with fresh local ingredients. Seafood, meat and fowl are given a decidedly Asian-French take. End with a selection from the restaurant's delicious desserts.

$$$$ Old Stone Farmhouse – *Mahogany Run Golf Course, St. Thomas. 340-777-6277. www.oldstonefarmouse.com. Closed Mon.* **International**. Housed in what was once an 18C plantation outbuilding, this popular island staple crafts a sophisticated menu of entrées ranging from surf and turf and osso bucco to a Thai hot pot. Golfers love the steak. For dessert, slip down a house-made passion fruit sorbet. Reservations are a must.

BRITISH VIRGIN ISLANDS★★★

Together with its US counterparts, BVI, as commonly known, make up the Virgin Islands archipelago bordering the Atlantic and the Caribbean. This British Overseas Territory comprises four major islands: Tortola, Virgin Gorda, Anegada and Jost Van Dyke, along with 50-plus smaller islands. Tortola's constant trade winds have made it a top sailing destination. Virgin Gorda is a popular spot for sailors to hobnob in its quiet coves. Anegada island is made entirely of coral. Jost Van Dyke is the smallest of the four islands, boasting a busy port, beach bars and restaurants. Getting here is as easy as a short-hop flight from San Juan, or a ferry ride from St. Thomas (don't forget your passport).

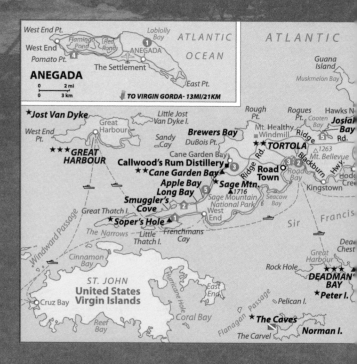

PETER'S TOP PICKS

CULTURE

The islands may be small, but they pack in a lot of history. Learn about the early history of Tortola at the Virgin Islands Folk Museum, and peek inside Old Government House and Museum, the island's governor's residence until 1997. (p **202**)

SEE

Gorda Peak National Park is a 265-acre park that has the highest peak on Virgin Gorda, standing 1,359 feet tall. This is a protected site that is home to several endangered plants and animals, including the tiny Virgin Gorda gecko. (p **203**)

STAY

On the island of Tortola, Tamarind Club is a quiet little hideout tucked in the hills. It's not fancy, but it's friendly and affordable with its own swim-up bar and lively dining scene. (p **206**)

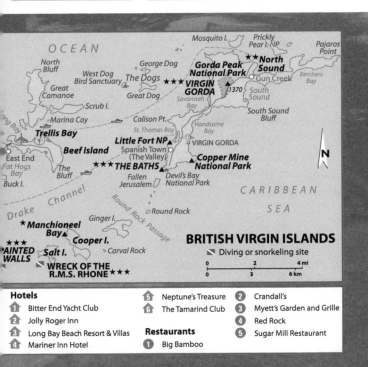

Hotels

1. Bitter End Yacht Club
2. Jolly Roger Inn
3. Long Bay Beach Resort & Villas
4. Mariner Inn Hotel
5. Neptune's Treasure
6. The Tamarind Club

Restaurants

1. Big Bamboo
2. Crandall's
3. Myett's Garden and Grille
4. Red Rock
5. Sugar Mill Restaurant

Tortola★★

Often referred to as "the sailing capital of the world," Tortola is a sailor's paradise, with good harbors, easy anchorage, lots of yacht charters and plenty of surrounding islands. Need we mention beach bars, restaurants and great shops to get provisions? Toss in spectacular scenery, lush mountains, beaches galore, and cerulean-colored waters, and it's no wonder people come back year after year. If you don't plan to captain your own boat, book at least one day-sail; excursions usually include lunch, visits to smaller islands and diving or snorkeling.

Road Town

The capital of the islands is small, but holds a few worthwhile sights. Close to the waterfront, the center of town has lots of shops, banks, marinas and restaurants (don't be surprised if chickens weave between tables as you eat). For an overview of Tortola's history, visit the **Virgin Islands Folk Museum** (℘ 284-494-3701; open Mon–Fri 8:30-4:30pm) located in a charming section of Main Street. For other peeks into island history, a short walk south of the ferry dock along Waterfront Drive leads to **Old Government House and Museum** (℘ 284-494-4091; open Mon–Fri 9am–3pm; $3), the former governor's residence built in the early 1920s, and remnants of Dutch-built **Fort Burt's** 17C stone foundations and artillery magazine.

The 3-acre **J.R. O'Neal Botanic Gardens**, in the center of town, is chock-o-block full of indigenous plants, an aviary and orchid house (℘ 284-494-3904; open Mon–Fri 8:30am–4:30pm; $3).

Island Routes

Two main routes with offshoots span the length of the island. **Ridge Road** runs smack through the middle, skirting mountain tops. While not for the faint of heart, due to steep inclines and hairpin turns, this road permits sensational **views** of mountainous terrain, lush vegetation and the sea. You'll pass **Sage Mountain National Park★** which is always open, and is the island's highest point (elevation 1,710ft). Take one of its three trails to admire bullet wood, elephant ear vines, old fig trees, and maybe a Bo-Peep tree frog. From Ridge Road, access **Brewer's Bay**, along the northcentral coast, and the island's best place to snorkel companioned by tropical fish. South of Sage Mountain lies **Cane Garden Bay★★**, a coconut palm, beach bar-lined harbor. Nearby, **Callwood's Rum Distillery**, a family operation since the late 1800s, produces rum in a traditional way. If you continue south, you'll pass favorite surfer waters at **Apple Bay**.

For a little privacy, continue to Long Bay (the longest beach on the island) and stroll south on the beach to the left. About 1 mile farther south, **Smuggler's Cove** was the film location for the 1990 movie version of Hemingway's *The Old Man and the Sea*. Carry on up, over and down the hills through Belmont Estates, detouring farther south to **Soper's Hole★**, a yacht-filled anchorage popular for rum drinks at **Pusser's Landing**. From here (the West End) the road is flat and follows the coast into Road Town. En route, drop by **Nanny Cay** for island-style food, entertainment, clothing and gifts. At the other end of the island **Trellis Bay** on Beef Island (accessible by bridge and close to the airport), is famous for not only its anchorage but also artisans' collective and full-moon parties.

Virgin Gorda★★★

Approaching Virgin Gorda (Spanish for "fat virgin") eastward from Tortola, it's easy to see how the island got its name. From the island's center, Gorda Peak National Park (*North South Rd.*) **sticks up over the horizon 1,370ft looking like a plump damsel on her back. The 265-acre park is home to rare and endangered species like the billbush (shrub), Christmas orchid, and Virgin Gorda gecko—the smallest lizard in the world. But do not touch the flora or fauna: the park is protected as a U.K. Darwin Initiative Site for preservation.**

At the island's southwest extremity, **The Baths★★★** gets most of the oohs and ahhs from visitors. Imagine a white satin beach sporting house-size boulders surrounding turquoise pools of water, mysterious caves and cathedral-style grottoes. Two gorgeous beaches flank its sides—**Devil's Bay** and **Spring Bay**, linked by trails. Part of BVI National Parks Trust, the site is always open, but go early morning or late afternoon to avoid crowds.

Aside from beaches with a wow factor of 10 out of 10, Virgin Gorda is known for its upscale resorts.

Yet there's also simplicity and stories to discover in small spaces. **Copper Mine National Park** (called Coppermine Point by locals), located east of The Baths, occupies a scraggly hill above Spanish Town (the main business and shopping district, close to the ferry terminal) and contains the remains of a mine active in the mid 1800's.

Ruins of a 19C sugar plantation scatter the grounds of **Nail Bay Resort**, centrally located on the island's south side. **Little Fort National Park** (south of Yacht Harbor) is a 36-acre wildlife sanctuary with remains of a Spanish fort.

WHERE TO SAIL

Steady winds, easy line-of-sight navigation, and good anchorages are just a few reasons that the British Virgin Islands are considered one of the best sailing destinations on the globe. This region is a water-lover's paradise, so you can sail into hidden coves, go scuba diving or snorkeling, or simply splash around the calm, balmy waters. You can charter a bareboat, captained or fully crewed, vessel throughout the island. There are charter companies all over Tortola that can arrange all the details for you, whether you're looking for a romantic catamaran cruise or a multi-day, island-hopping yachting adventure. If you're planning to sail into the BVI or exit the territory on your journey, you'll be required to go through customs.

In addition to boat charters, **The Moorings** (*Wickhams Cay II, Road Town, Tortola;* ℘ *888-952-8420, www.moorings.com*) can hook you up with the Offshore Sailing School to learn all the basics of operating a monohull or catamaran. Within a week, you'll be able to charter your own bareboat vessel and explore the Caribbean waters. **Horizon Yacht Charters** (*Nanny Cay Marina, Road Town, Tortola;* ℘ *877-494-8787, www. horizonyachtcharters.com*) has a fleet that ranges from a 2-cabin Bavaria 31 cruiser to a 50-foot Voyage catamaran that sleeps up to 10 people. **Virgin Traders Motor Yacht Charters** (*Nanny Cay Marina, Road Town, Tortola;* ℘ *888-684-6486, www.virgintraders.com*) has high-speed options in its fleet of more than 20 motor yachts.

On the upper east end of the island, **North Sound★★** is a sailor's playground. This high-spirited hub of marine activity is a paradise for **water sports**: you can kayak, windsurf, parasail, paddleboard and kiteboard. It's mere minutes from islands with names like Mosquito, Prickly Pear, Necker, Eustasia and Saba Rock. Although there are no roads past the Sound's village of Gun Creek, you can explore these islands by boat: **Biras Creek, Bitter End**, and several restaurants on the North Sound islands provide free ferry service.

Other Islands

Jost Van Dyke★
Lying about 4 miles northwest of Tortola, this small, sparsely populated island is known worldwide for its beach bars. South-

WHEN TO GO

The best time to visit is early Nov–May when temperatures hover between 77º-82ºF/25º-28ºC; evening temperatures drop 5 degrees. The hottest time is Jun–Aug when temperatures increase to by 4-5 degrees. Though cooler, Sept and Oct see rainfall and increased humidity. **Peak tourist season** is mid-Dec–mid-Apr.

GETTING AROUND

BY AIR – Island-hopping by chartered flights: Air Sunshine (*&*284-495-8900), Caribbean Wings (*&*284-495-6000) or Fly BVI (*&*284-495-1747).

BY CAR – Averaging $75/day, car rentals are available at ferry terminals on each island. In Tortola, rent in Road Town, West End, East End and at the airport. Rent a jeep if you plan to drive off main roads. Dede's Car Rentals (*&*284-495-2041; www.dedebvi.com), Dollar Rent a Car (*&*284-494-7837; www.dollar.com), or National Car Rental (*&*284-494-4085; www.nationalcar.com).

BY FERRY – Ferries run (not always as advertised) between Tortola (Road Town and West End), Virgin Gorda, Anegada, Jost Van Dyke, and smaller islands as well as to St. Thomas (USVI). For fares and schedules: www.bviwelcome.com/ferries.php.

BY WATER TAXI – Custom day trips and inter-island transportation can be arranged with Dohm's Water Taxi (*&*340-775-6501) or Speedy's (*&*284-495-5240)

BY TAXI – Taxi fares run $10 for 10 min tours to $30 for 30min. Many taxi drivers are for hire for longer periods of time and enjoy giving private tours. www.britishvirginislands.com/ga.htm.

VISITOR INFORMATION

Main tourism office: BVI Tourist Board, AKARA Building, 2nd Floor, Road Town, Tortola *&*284-494-3134 or 800-835-8530; www.bvitourism.com.

Accommodations: For a selection of lodgings, see Where to Stay at the end of this chapter.

Important numbers
Emergency and Ambulance service: 999 or 911
Emergency at sea: 767 or Marine Channel 16
Royal Virgin Islands Police Force: *&*284 494-3822
Medical Services:
Peebles Hospital, Road Town, Tortola: *&*284-494-3497
Eureka Medical clinic, Geneva Place, Road Town, Tortola: *&*284-494-2346.

MONEY/CURRENCY

All transactions are in US currency; American dollars are accepted everywhere on the islands. Major credit cards, most debit cards, and internationally recognized traveler's checks are widely accepted. ATM machines are located in all towns, major hotels, and marinas; fees apply.

DEPARTURE TAXES

BY AIR – $15 per person and Security Tax $5 per person.
BY SEA – $5 per person ($7 for cruise ship passengers).

central **Great Harbour★★★**, where the ferry docks, hugs a half-moon beach and is a popular watering hole. It's also famous for New Year's Eve parties at Foxy's. Another fun spot is the Soggy Dollar Bar (named after a patron swam ashore) located in White Bay, west of Great Harbor. Most action on Jost Van Dyke centers on bar culture and starts late in the afternoon.

Anegada

BVI's only coral atoll is a snorkeler's paradise located about 13 miles northeast of Tortola. Come to this flat, sand-rimmed island to see roseate **flamingos** holed up in salt ponds around the island, rare indigenous iguanas nurtured in a small nursery in the village, and an astonishing variety of tropical fish.

Southern Islands

Southwest of Tortola in the Sir Frances Drake Channel, a cluster of island gems include **Norman Island** ("the caves" and good snorkeling), **Peter Island** (famed private resort and romantic beach of **Deadman's Bay★★★**), **Salt Island** (marine park with dive site **Wreck of the R.M.S. Rhone★★★**) and **Cooper Island** (**Manchioneel Bay★**, beach club, conch fritters—and goats). All islands are accessible by ferry or water taxi.

Addresses

For price ranges, see the Legend on the cover flap.

WHERE TO STAY

$ Jolly Roger Inn –
Near West End ferry, Soper's Hole, Tortola. ☎*284-495-4559. www.jollyrogerbvi.com. 5 rooms.* Situated just steps from the ferry in West End and close to Soper's Hole, this no-frills inn is bright and cheery and sits right on the water. Cozy rooms come with private or shared bath, and there's a bar and restaurant on the premises.

$$ Neptune's Treasure –
Anegada. ☎*284-495-9439. www.neptunestreasure.com. 9 rooms, 2 cottage units.* This three-generation family-run beachfront property embodies the carefree Caribbean style. Rooms are smallish but nicely decorated. Known for the freshest fish on the island, the on-site restaurant serves up three meals a day.

$$ Tamarind Club – *Josiah's Bay, East End, Tortola.* ☎*284-495-2477. www.tamarindclub. com. 8 rooms.* This intimate hideout tucked into the hills sits only minutes from the airport and is a 10-minute walk to the beach. Rooms are basic but comfortable. A large pool with a swim-up bar, restaurant and free continental breakfast are added amenities.

$$$ Mariner Inn Hotel –
Waterfront Dr., Wickham's Cay 2, Road Town, Tortola. ☎*284-494-2332. www.bvimarinerinnhotel. com. 40 rooms.* This two-story inn is centrally located on a huge marina. Large, modern rooms are handsomely furnished (with refrigerator). Bonuses include an on-site spa, pool, and waterfront restaurant serving *rotis* (West Indian wraps).

$$$$ Long Bay Beach Resort & Villas – *Long Bay, Tortola.* ☎*954-481-8787. www.longbay.com. 123 units.* This 52-acre hillside-

beach resort is dotted with airy waterside cabanas, family villas and estate homes, all decorated with colorful bedding and curtains. Guests have access to a mile-long beach, on-site spa, fitness center, tennis courts and two dining areas.

$$$$$ Bitter End Yacht Club – *North Sound, Virgin Gorda. Accessible only by boat or ferry.* ℰ*284-494-2746. www.beyc.com. 85 units.* This luxury waterfront resort bills itself as a "rollicking nautical village," offering sailing lessons, regattas, extraordinary brunches and after-dinner movies under the stars. Guests stay in secluded bungalows with private decks or beachside villas with hammock-equipped wraparound porches.

WHERE TO EAT

$ Crandall's – *Waterfront Dr., Road Town, Tortola.* ℰ*284-494-5156.* **West Indian**. This small cafeteria is known island-wide for traditional food. Specialties include conch patties as well as pig's feet soup and coconut bread. Eat-in or take-out dining available.

$$ Big Bamboo – *Loblolly Bay, Anegada.* ℰ*284-495-8129. www.bvitourism.com/activity/big-bamboo-restaurant.* **Seafood/ West Indian**. Fun and friendly, this cavernous open-air beach bar/restaurant rises next to miles of coral beach great for snorkeling. Bamboo's grilled lobster is legendary, but grilled chicken comes in a close second.

$$ Red Rock – *Penn's Marina, Fat Hog Bay, East End, Tortola.* ℰ*284-495-1646. www.redrock bvi.net.* **International**. Newly renovated, the Red Rock really rocks. Meals can be as speedy or as laid-back as you please. Pastas and seafood rule here, so try the crispy seared mango prawns, and enjoy great value for your money in the process.

$$$ Myett's Garden and Grille – *Cane Garden Bay, Tortola.* ℰ*284-495-9649. www.myettent.com.* **Caribbean**. Myett's is a casual, open-air dining spot overlooking the beach. Patrons watch as lobster, shrimp, steaks and fish are prepared on an open grill. Vegetarian dishes are available, and key lime pie is a tempting top-off to a meal.

$$$$ Sugar Mill Restaurant – *Apple Bay, Tortola.* ℰ*284-495-4355. www.sugarmillhotel.com.* **International**. This 370-year-old stone mill, formerly a rum distillery, now embraces diners within old brick walls at candle-lit tables with cane-back chairs. The appetizers alone are intoxicating: try the oyster gratin with smoked bacon and Guinness hollandaise before moving on to the eggplant Creole with Caribbean coconut rice. The building may be old, but the menu is decidedly modern.

THE LESSER ANTILLES★★

The Lesser Antilles aren't just one cluster of islands: the term refers to the long swath of islands stretching all the way from the US Virgin Islands in the north down to the islands of Trinidad and Tobago. That group is further broken down into the Windward Islands (in the north), the Leeward Islands (in the south) and the Leeward Antilles just off the Venezuelan coast.

Don't expect the islands to be interchangeable simply because they're grouped together. Of the southerly Leeward Islands, each one has its own geographical, social and cultural makeup. Anguilla is small, yet boasts at least 33 of the quintessential white-sand Caribbean beaches and is surrounded by rich coral reefs. Just a 20-minute ferry ride south is the island shared by Saint-Martin

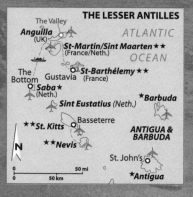

(French) and Sint Maarten (Dutch), which is bustling with resorts, casinos, and so many restaurants that it's been dubbed the Gastronomic Capital of the Caribbean. Glitzy St-Barthélemy, widely known as St. Barths, is the playground for the champagne and caviar set, with luxury resorts, duty-free boutiques, and French-speaking locals.

St. Kitts and Nevis are separated by only a 2-mile channel. They are somewhat hidden gems of the Caribbean where you can still experience the typical West Indian lifestyle, culture and cuisine without a lot of the tourist trappings. Antigua is a seafarer's delight with a lively yachting culture, and Barbuda stands out for its secluded beaches, glowing pink with crushed coral.

In the Leeward Antilles, tiny, secluded Saba has only one dark-sand beach, but is an ecotourist's dream of misty mountains and lush hiking trails, while the island of Sint Eustatius, known locally as Statia, has one fairy-tale village and miles of tropical rain forest and hilly terrain.

PETER'S TOP PICKS

CULTURE

Antigua has a small, but history-packed place just southeast of St. John's called Betty's Hope. It was once a mid-17th century sugar plantation with an old windmill—apparently the only working one in all the Caribbean. (p **226**)

GREEN SPACES

For some of the best green spaces in the Lesser Antilles you need to visit Saba. Not known for its beaches, Saba is a mecca of moutains and lush landscapes. If you are looking for an adventure in the hills, check out the many hiking trails. (p **216**)

HISTORY

Old House and Rhum Museum is quite an experience. Step back in time to an 18th century Creole-style house once inhabited by a sugar plantation owner. You can see some of Saint-Martin's oldest culture. (p **216**)

STAY

Although a little pricey, Hôtel Guanahani is a St. Barths icon. It is located on its own peninsula on the island and blends French and Creole style. (p **228**).

SHOP

In Anguilla, shop for souvenirs made from natural resources, like limestone or shells. Cheddie's Carving Studio has some awesome sculptures. (p **211**)

EAT

Abracadabra in Antigua is more than just a cool name; it also has some of the best Italian food on the island, which is hard to come by on Caribbean islands. (p **229**)

Anguilla

ASK PETER...

Q: How can I find the local hangouts instead of the tourist spots?

A: If you really want to hang with the locals, first know the lingo. Liming (or limin') is translated loosely as "chilling out," whether it's over evening cocktails or on the beach until early morning. The good news is that anyone can join the party. Don't ask the concierge where you should go, or he'll point you exactly to the busiest tourist spots. Instead, talk to the bellhop, the housekeeping staff, the waiters, and ask where they go in their off time.

Shaped like an eel (*anguille* in French), this coral island (19 miles long and 3 miles at its widest) is famous for beaches, crystalline waters and undersea world. With 45 white-sand beaches lining its quiet bays and inlets, Anguilla may well be the beautiful-beach capital of the Caribbean. Along the West Shore, **Rendezvous Bay★★★** is the island's quintessential white-sand beach, an away-from-it-all stretch intertwined with salt marshes. To the southwest lies **Maunday's Bay★**, a half-moon cove with clear waters and sparkling sand. Farther north, gentle waves caress the beach at **Meads Bay★**. The north shore boasts **Shoal Bay East★★**, renowned for its fine-grained quartz sand and turquoise waters; day-trippers, live music and beer joints can give this picturesque bay a rowdy feel. For perhaps additional rowdiness in the evenings, try the haunts below.

Night Spots

Dune Preserve

Rendezvous Bay. Beach front, just west of the CuisinArt Golf Resort & Spa. ℘264-729-4215. www.bankiebanx.net/restaurant.html.

Put together with pieces of old boats and driftwood by famed musician Bankie Banx, this beach bar appeals to lovers of music and the scene. Sundays it's a good bet you'll hear live music, maybe even Banx himself. "Moonsplash"—three days of partying to live music under the full moon—is an annual March event.

Sandy Ground Village

Located between North Hill and South Hill, Sandy Ground is the island's hotspot for local nightlife. **Johnno's Beach Shop** (℘264-497-2728) is considered the best "jumpup" on the island (a Caribbean tradition where you just jump up and dance). You'll find yourself jivin' in the sand or on the piers jutting out over the water. **The Pumphouse** (℘264-497-5154, www.pumphouse-anguilla.com) rocks nightly after the restaurant shuts down at 10pm, but on Saturdays, when live local bands play, the roof nearly blows off! Try their authentic rum punch.

Mayoumba Folkloric Theatre

Keeping Anguilla's pre-20C music, dance, storytelling and costumes alive, this troupe stages elaborate productions year-round. They have a **weekly** gig at Anacaona Hotel in Meads Bay (*Thu 8:30pm; ℘264-497-6827; www.anacaonahotel.com*).

WHEN TO GO

Aguilla is known for its idyllic weather. Year-round temperatures average 80°F. It is a relatively dry island. A normal year sees most rain in Sept and Oct, also hurricane season. Peak tourist season is from December to March.

GETTING AROUND

The island is 16mi long and has one main road running end to end. **Taxis** are widely available and rates are fixed. **Bike** rentals start at $10US daily; try Premier Mountain Bike Rentals ✆264-235-8931.

VISITOR INFORMATION

Main tourism office: ✆1-800-553-4939 (toll-free) www.ivisitaguilla.com.

Important numbers
Emergency (24hrs): 911
Fire and Rescue: ✆264-497-2333
Medical Services:
Princess Alexandra Hospital, The Valley:
✆264-497-2551

MONEY/CURRENCY

The official currency is the Eastern Caribbean dollar, fixed at a 2.7 exchange with the US dollar, which is also generally accepted. For credit, debit, and ATM cards, fees apply. Internationally recognized traveler's checks in US dollars are another option.

Shops
Anguilla Arts and Crafts Center

Upstairs Brooks & Sons Complex. ✆264-497-2200.
Open Mon–Fri 9am–4pm. Closed weekends.
This is *the* place to find locally made souvenirs such as hot sauces, jams, ceramics, cloth dolls, needlework and gifts crafted from shells. Check out the unusual homemade flower wines.

Cheddie's Carving Studio

West End Rd., The Cove. ✆264-497-6027.
Open Mon–Sat 10am–6pm.
Anguilla-born Cheddie Richardson scours local beaches for limestone and other natural materials. He then carves them into sculptures of birds and other island wildlife.

Saint-Martin★★/Sint Maarten★★

One island, two personalities: French and Dutch. Lying 5 miles south of Anguilla, this 35-square-mile island is the world's smallest island divided into two sovereign states. Here the French and the Dutch coexist so peacefully that there is no border crossing. The French zone, with its capital in **Marigot**, occupies the northern part of the island. Sint **Maarten**, with its capital based in **Philipsburg**, forms the

Travel Tip: Keep your wallet handy at the airport. The only island in the Lesser Antilles that does not require a departure fee is St. Barths. Saint-Martin/ Sint Maarten, Saba and Sint Eustasia all charge a fee of $30 to depart. Antigua and Barbuda charge $14 to get off the island. Anguilla charges $20. Finally, St. Kitts-Nevis will cost you $22 to get home. Make sure you keep this cash aside so you don't run into any problems at the airport.

**ST-MARTIN/
SINT MAARTEN**

ANGUILLA · ST-BARTHÉLEMY

SABA

0 1 2 mi
0 2 km

Pointe des
Froussards

★ **Anse
Marcel**

Eastern Point

Baie de
Grande Case
Grand-Case

Îlet
Pinel

★★ **ST-MARTIN** (France)

L'ESPÉRANCE

N 7

★ **Baie
Orientale**

Caye
Vert

Rambaud

★ **Pic du
Paradis** ▲1492

**Butterfly
Farm**

★ **Baie
Rouge**

★ **Fort St. Louis**

Baie aux
Prunes

Terres Basses

D 208

Baie Nettlé

**Loterie
Farm**

■ **The Old House
and Rhum Museum**

MARIGOT

**Marigot
Museum** ★

Quartier d'Orleans

Étang
aux
Poissons

Baie
Longue

Grande Etang de Simpsonbaai

Cupecoy Bay

Mullet Bay

Sentry Hill
△ 1116

N 7

❶

Oyster
Pond

PRINCESS
JULIANA

Maho Bay

Simpson
Bay

Salt Pond

Guana Bay

N

Guana Bay
Point

★★ **SINT MAARTEN**
(Netherlands)

Great
Bay

PHILIPSBURG

Fort
Amsterdam

CARIBBEAN   SEA

SABA

Point Blanche

Hotels		**Restaurants**	
🏠	Mary's Boon Beach Plantation	❶	Captain Oliver's
🏠	Privilege Resort and Spa	❷	The Lolos

WHEN TO GO

Average annual temperatures stay around 80°F. In the dry season, which is also **peak tourist season** (Dec-Apr), temperatures drop at night, but rarely below 70°F.

GETTING AROUND

Taxis are readily available and charge a fixed fee; some accept only dollars. **Cars, motorcycles** and **scooters** can be **rented. Mini buses** pick up at bus stops.

VISITOR INFORMATION

Main tourism office: Office de Tourisme de Saint Martin, Route de Sandy Ground – Marigot. ℘590-87-57-21. www.stmartinisland.org

Important numbers
Emergency (24hrs): 911 or 542-2111
Police: 911 or 542-2111
Medical Services:
Louis Constant Fleming Hospital, Corcordia: ℘590-522-525
Sint Maarten Medical Center, Cay Hill, Sint Maarten ℘242-502-1400

MONEY/CURRENCY

The Netherlands Antilles Guilder is the currency in Sint Maarten. In Saint-Martin, it is the euro. Dollars are generally accepted, along with major credit and debit cards and traveler's checks. Fees apply.

southern part. In the last 30 years, the island has become a top destination for international travelers in search of duty-free shops, Las Vegas-style casinos, authentic French restaurants and white-sand beaches. English is widely spoken in both parts of the island.

Beaches

Anse Marcel★

Northwest Grande Terre, Saint-Martin. After passing L'Esperance Airport, take the road on your left; drive 1 mi and turn left.

Marcel Cove is a lovely cove with golden sand that was wilderness only 10 years ago. Today its beach hosts a marina and a vast hotel complex, Le Méridien. The beach lies within the hotel perimeter, but you can access the sands here even if you're not staying at the hotel (*see the warden at the estate entrance*). The gentle waves are ideal for youngsters.

Baie Orientale★

Northeast Grande Terre, Saint-Martin, about a half mile before the Quartier d'Orléans.

Orient Bay is probably the best-known beach on the island. The mile-long stretch of fine sand attracts a lot of tourists; beach chairs and umbrellas can be rented. The seashore is lined with hotels, restaurants, bars, fashion boutiques and watersports pavilions (windsurfing, surfing, diving, jet-skiing, waterskiing). Swimsuits are optional at nearby Club Orient Naturist Resort—the island's only such resort, and perhaps the single beach where full nudity means no legal woes.

Baie Rouge★

Grande Terre, Saint-Martin. Just west of Baie Nettlé, make an abrupt turn and take the dirt road.

Powerful waves sometimes batter the "reddish" sands of vast **Red Bay Beach**—one of the island's most popular beaches. There's no shade here, but beach umbrellas can be rented at the east end. If it's a calm day and you are a strong swimmer, stroke out through the mini rock arch to a secluded, cliff-hugging beach.

Sights

Fort Saint-Louis★

North of Marigot village, Saint-Martin.

Climb to the summit of the hill to visit the ruins of this fort, the largest historical landmark in Saint-Martin. Built by the French in 1767 to ward off invaders and protect Marigot's warehouses, it was abandoned by them twice. During the French Revolution, it was briefly occupied by the Dutch. Today the fort offers unparal-

Travel Tip: In Saint-Martin, it is customary to tip at least 15 percent at restaurants. Check the bill to see whether a gratuity has already been included, and ask if you're not sure. When it comes to your hotel, leave a tip for the maid after your first night—not at the end of your stay. It will get you much better service overall.

leled views of Marigot Bay and Anguilla, Simpson Bay, and Baie Nettlé. Bilingual panels at the site describe its cultural history.

Marigot Museum★

Between Rue Fichot and Rue Pérrinon, Marigot, Saint-Martin. ✆ 590-29-48-36. www.museesaintmartin.com. Open Mon–Fri 9am–5pm; Sat 9am–1pm. 5 euros.

Some 5,000 years of Saint-Martin's history are displayed here. Dedicated to pre-Columbian times, one room features ceramics and costumes found during excavations at the island's Hope Estate plateau, where archaeologists uncovered a settlement. The first people to bring pottery and horticulture to the plateau arrived in canoes from neighboring islands. The display includes exquisite pottery. Another museum room is dedicated to the arrival and legacy of the Europeans from the 15C on. Additionally, a series of old photographs and displays of local flora and fauna shed new light on the island.

WHERE TO ENJOY THE NIGHTLIFE

The dual island of Saint-Martin/Sint Maarten might be best known for its sparkling waters and beautiful beaches, but its nightlife is also a main attraction.

The island's casino culture is clustered on the Dutch side, with mainstays like the ancient-mariner-themed **Atlantis World** (*Cupecoy Beach, Rhine Rd.; ✆ 599-545-4601; www.atlantisworld.com*), which is open 24/7. Casino Royale at the **Sonesta Maho Beach Resort & Casino** (*Maho Bay, Sint Maarten; ✆ 599-545-2115; www.mahobeach.com*) has something for everyone—with hundreds of slot machines, craps, baccarat, blackjack, and some of the highest-stakes private gaming tables on the island. A pulsating nightclub and a free show every Friday and Saturday night brings in the crowds all night long.

Want to dance? Sint Maarten has a collection of clubs catering to every style, from throbbing crowds dancing the night away in the open-air venue at **Bliss** (*Caravanserai Beach Resort, 2, Beacon Hill Rd., Sint Maarten; www.bliss-sxm.com*) to the family-friendly **Cheri's Cafe** (*45 Cinnamon Grove Shopping Centre, Maho District, Sint Maarten; ✆ 305-677-3586 US; www.cheriscafe.com*), which has a nightly live show and music.

WHERE TO SHOP

Saint Martin/Sint Maarten is rapidly becoming a shopping mecca; visitors are allowed to bring back up to $600 worth of duty-free items. Instead of spending money on chintzy jewelry or flowery sarongs, picking up a quality piece of art is a great way to commemorate your travels—especially if you can zero in on small art galleries that highlight the works of local islanders. But then the catch is how to you schlep home that new piece of art? If it's a small painting or portable, no problem. Ask the gallery to pack it up for you to be transported in your suitcase. They've got the right materials to protect the item from being scratched or dented, but add an extra layer of protection by wrapping it up in soft clothing or towels.

If you're purchasing a larger item that doesn't fit in your suitcase, ask the gallery to handle the packing, shipping and insuring. That way, if something goes wrong, they're liable, not you. For a larger framed picture, say 15x20, ask if they can pack it in a light wooden crate. If the gallery doesn't handle shipping, ask your hotel. Larger properties like the Westin St. Maarten Dawn Beach Resort & Spa will handle filling out the customs forms for you.

While on Saint-Martin/Sint Maarten, be sure to visit some of the top local artists on the island. At **Roland Richardson's Gallery** on Saint-Martin (*6 Rue de la République, Marigot, Saint-Martin; ☏ 590-590-87-32-24; in the US 443-982-0683; www.rolandrichardson.com*), the artist himself may be putting the finishing touches on a still life in his studio at the back. His colorful canvases capture the beauty of Saint-Martin's meadows, flowers and dwellings.

Le St Geran Gallery (*117 Front St., Philipsburg; ☏ 721-542-1023*) features local works and artists from neighboring Caribbean islands.

Les Exotiques (*76 Rue de la Fibuste, Oyster Pond; ☏ 590-590-29-53-76, www.ceramexotic.com*) showcases the work of Marie Moine who specializes in hand-painted ceramics and watercolors.

Art Box (*Bobby's Marina, Philipsburg; ☏ 721-588-5999*) features handcrafted West Indies jewelry from local artist Zdenka Kiric.

Antoine Chapon Art Gallery (*Marina Port Royale, Marigot; ☏ 590-590-52-93-75*) specializes in watercolors of the ocean and seascapes. You can meet with the artist by appointment only.

Loterie Farm

Rte. de Pic du Paradis, Saint-Martin; ☏ 590-87-86-16. www.loterie-farm.com. Open Tue–Sun 9am–4pm. Activities from 5-35 euros.
Located at the base of 1,492-foot **Pic du Paradis★** (Paradise Peak), this farm was converted to a 150-acre nature preserve by

Travel Tip: Stop by the **Guavaberry Shop** to check out the headquarters of the Guavaberry Company (*8-10 Front St., Sint Maarten; ℘599-542-2965; www.guavaberry.com*). This colorful Creole house was once the governor's residence. The Guavaberry Company makes its namesake Guavaberry Rum Liqueur from rum, sugar and guavaberries on the premises. Bring home a jar of banana jam or mango chutney for some real variety.

an ex-Californian. A hike along its forested trails or a zip-line ride over them reveals mango, guavaberry and mammy (apricot, trees, as well as waterfalls and birds. The renovated main house dates to 1721.

Butterfly Farm

Le Galion Beach Rd., Quartier d'Orléans, Saint-Martin. ℘590-87-31-21. www.thebutterflyfarm.com. Open daily 9am–3:30pm. $14 US, children half price, under 3 free. Pay once and receive a free return pass valid for the length of your stay.

Watch caterpillars transform into butterflies at this living museum. Then wander through tropical gardens and waterfalls (covered by large mesh enclosures) populated with colorful, exotic butterflies from many parts of the globe. Morning visits ensure lively *papillons* (butterflies in French), while afternoons are better for photography because the butterflies slow down. Bright attire and citrusy perfume attract these fluttering creatures.

Old House and Rhum Museum

On the road between Orléans and Orient Bay, Saint-Martin; ℘590-87-32-67; Open daily 9am–4pm. 5 euros.

This 18C Creole-style house was once home to an overseer of a sugar plantation owned by Beauperthuy family. Their descendents have opened it to the public to showcase original antiques and other reminders of Saint-Martin's heyday. Next door the **Rhum Museum** displays old bottles, labels and a recipe for rum made in bygone years. The "gold book" was signed by Holland's Queen Juliana and other notables.

Saba★

This **5sq-mi extinct volcano, the smallest island of the Netherlands Antilles, does not claim idyllic beaches or posh hotels. Instead, Saba [SAY-bah] offers mountainous landscapes, challenging hiking trails and some 1,500 welcoming residents. The official language is Dutch, but everyone speaks English.**

Travel Tip: Saba isn't just about outdoor recreation. It's also home to coveted Saba lace, painstakingly handcrafted by local women. Check out the Saba Lace Boutique in Hell's Gate for a large selection of lacework, including dresses, tablecloths and pillowcases.

Scenic Drive

Hire a taxi to take you up **The Road**, with its 15 hairpin curves, on a Sunday afternoon when you can watch or play croquet. It's best to wear white, the attire of choice for this island fixture (and post-game Mimosas). In **Hell's Gate** village, you'll see stone or picket fences, country gardens and typical Saban cottages. Stop

in **Windwardside** at the former home of a sea captain to see antiques and furniture at the **Henry L. Johnson Museum**. Continue to the hillside village of **St. John's**. Before beginning your descent, look down from the road's edge to see what is believed to be the main crater of Saba's volcano. Continue to **The Bottom**, the tiny, sleepy capital, whose official buildings are nestled in a valley. Turn south on the road that runs through a gorge. The 800ft descent leads to **Fort Bay**, the base of dive operations for **Saba Marine Park**, which encircles the island.

Hike

Saba's many marked trails (Boiling House, Booby Hill, Mary's Point and Mt. Scenery, to name a few) vary in difficulty. Pick up a brochure and find a guide (*all-day hike $50*), at the Saba Conservation Foundation's **Trail Shop** (*599-416-3295*), located behind the tourist office in Windwardside.

Sint Eustatius

Like Saba, Sint Eustatius is a small, volcanic island in the Netherlands Antilles. Only about 12sq mi in size, the island lies 33 miles south of Sint Maarten. The official language of "Statia" (its nickname) is Dutch, but everyone speaks English. In the capital of Oranjestad, the island's only town, planters travel on donkeys and houses show off gingerbread trim.

Sights
Sint Eustatius Center for Archaeological Research
599-318-0066. www.secar.org. $500 US for one week including tuition and housing.
Take part in an ongoing **dig** organized by this center, where aspiring archaeologists with no excavation experience can work at island sites like a prehistoric one or Pleasure Estate, a sugar plantation active from 1742 to 1977.

Statia Marine Park
West side of the island, near Lowertown.
Divers might discover a piece of an antique plate or a clay pipe below the waters of this national park, where, two centuries ago, some 200 ships sank. A number of the shipwrecks are popular dive sites. Don your gear to see the barracuda, spotted moray eels, eagle rays, black-tip sharks and schools of snapper that scour the decks now. These dive companies are authorized to

operate within Statia Marine Park waters: **Dive Statia** (☎ 599-318-2435); **Golden Rock Dive Center** (☎ 599-318-2964; www.goldenrockdive.com); **Scubaqua** (☎ 599-318-5450 or ☎ 599-318-5452; www.scubaqua.com).

Quill National Park

Park office on coastal road in Gallow's Bay, just south of Oranjestad. Buy a $3 permit at the office and get a trail map. Rosemary Lane leads to Quill Trail. ☎ 599-318-2884. *www.statiapark.org.*

The most popular trail on the island is a 2,000ft climb to this **dormant volcano** known as **The Quill** ("pit" in Dutch). Stop for a breather and then hike down 900 feet into the crater (the last eruption was about 400AD), where a lush rain forest shelters rare orchids, bromeliads, raspberry bushes, giant elephant-ear plants and other flora. You might see a purple-throated Carib, a red-necked pigeon or a killy killy (the American kestrel), which is a commonly sighted bird of prey on the island.

Sint Eustatius Historical Foundation Museum

Upper Town, Oranjestad. ☎ 599-318-2288. *www.steustatiushistory.org.*

In 1780 Sint Eustatius was a bustling port; it was common for 200 ships to be waiting in the harbor to unload legal—or smuggled—cargo. Statia smuggled arms and supplies to the Americans during the Revolutionary War. The museum showcases blue-glass beads used as trading money and other artifacts from the island's heyday.

Saint-Barthélemy★★

Tiny, hilly 8sq-mi **St. Barths**, in contemporary lingo (also **St. Barts**), sits 19 miles southwest of Sint Maarten. This **Paris of the Caribbean** oozes sophistication, savoir faire— and hefty prices. The capital of Swedish-named **Gustavia** lies on the west coast. **Saint-Jean**, on the north shore, is a shopper's mecca. Carefree beaches and duty-free boutiques are major draws. It's polite to say "bonjour" to shopkeepers as you enter stores.

Beaches

Anse du Grand Cul-de-Sac★★

Northeast shore, Rte. D 209.

Translated as Grand Cul-de-Sac Cove, this beach is breathtaking. A sand bar encloses the bay, creating a separate body of

Travel Tip: Since St. Barths is a French island, the standard currency is euros, but US dollars are also accepted at many shops and restaurants. In fact, some of the more touristy locations will even list the prices in both currencies. Rather than exchanging US dollars for euros at the airport or in a bank, use your ATM card to withdraw the cash you need.

WHEN TO GO

This island rarely dips below 80°F in its cooler season called *carême* (Dec-May), and can reach 90°F in late summer during *hivernage* (Jun-Nov), St. Barths' other season. Sept and Oct are high **hurricane season**.

GETTING AROUND

Your best bet is to rent a **car** or **scooter**. You can do so on arrival at the airport.

VISITOR INFORMATION

Main tourism office: Saint Barth Tourism Committee, Gustavia, ☎590-27-87-27. www.saintbarth-tourisme.com.

Important numbers
Emergency (24hrs): 18
Police: ☎590-590-27-60-12

Medical Services:
Hospital De Bruyn, Gustavia: ☎590-590-27-60-35 and ☎242-322-2861

LANGUAGE

French is the island's official language. English is widely spoken, especially by those in the tourism industry.

MONEY/CURRENCY

The euro is official currency, but the US dollar is also widely used. Major credit, debit and ATM cards, as well as traveler's checks, are generally accepted, but you ought to ask ahead before relying on one. Fees do apply.

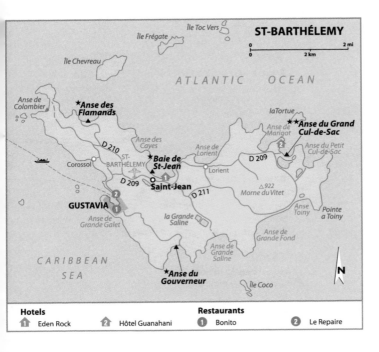

MADE IN ST. BARTS

Live among the luxury set with Ligne St Barth, a line of skin-care products made exclusively on the island. All the cosmetics are made from plants, fruits and flowers found on the island. For many years, the company didn't actually export them, so you could get them only on the island or in a limited number of hotels. Select stores in the US now sell the line, but it is still easiest to get items from their online store. The production facility, located at the base of a mountain and constructed as a log cabin in keeping with the natural elements used in the line, is a retail outlet too (*Rte. de Saline, L'Orient; ☎ 590-27-82-63; www.lignestbarth.com*)..

water. Waves break gently on coral reefs offshore, making the calm waters suitable for children.

Anse des Flamands★

Northwest shore, Rte. D 210.

Coconut-lined **Flemish Cove** is ideal for sunbathing. If you're an inexperienced swimmer, be careful: the waves can be strong at times. Around the point separating Anse des Flamands and Petite Anse, the seabed is worth exploring, so take diving gear along.

Anse du Gouverneur★

South-central coast. Accessible through a dead-end road south of Gustavia, beyond the Carl Gustav hotel.

White sand, red latan palms, and views of Saba and Sint Eustatius compete with topless (but not nude—that's against the law) sunbathers on this lovely stretch of sand called **Governor's Cove**.

Baie de Saint-Jean★

Saint-Jean, Rte. D 209.

White sand along a half-moon curve of shoreline and a wind-surfing club overrule close proximity to the island's airstrip at **Saint John Bay**, the most famous of St. Barths' beaches.

Shops
Boutique Paradoxe

Rue du General de Gaulle, Gustavia and Villa Creole, St-Jean. ☎ 590-27-84-98.

This chic boutique promises a selection of high fashion with matching price tags.

Héna
Villa Creole, St-Jean. ℘*590-29-84-05.*
This alluring boutique is filled with soft, revealing French lingerie, along with head-turning French swimwear. Don't bypass the selection of French perfumes.

Ligne de St Barth
Rte. de Saline, L'Orient. ℘*590-27-82-63.* *www.lignestbarth.com.*
Made from flora found on St. Barths, this coveted line of natural cosmetics is used in the world's best spas. Fresh papaya is whipped into a fragrant moisturizer and seeds of the native *rou-rou* (a fruit tree bearing red pods) are pulverized into sunscreen lotion. Products can be purchased at the production facility on Route de Saline in L'Orient. *See sidebar opposite.*

Lolita Jaca
Le Carré d'Or, Gustavia. ℘*590-27-59-98.* *www.lolitajaca.com.*
A feast of colorful fabrics and the heavenly scent of incense await shoppers in this tiny boutique of hand-designed, classy women's clothing with a traditional flair.

St. Kitts★★ and Nevis★★

Part of the British Commonwealth, these islands make up an independent federation ruled by a governor general appointed by the Queen. British influence can be seen in the Nevisian passion for cricket, and in Basseterre—St. Kitts' capital—a traffic roundabout patterned on London's Piccadilly Circus. Called the Maui of the Caribbean, Nevis [NEE-vis] is nurtured by lush rain forests that hug the velvety-green slopes of Nevis Peak; the island's liveliest hub is Charlestown, the capital. St. Kitts is a little busier (but not much), with more shops, and a casino at the base of Mount Liamuiga [Lee-a-MWEE-gah], a dormant volcano.

St. Kitts★★
SOUTH END
Sand Bank Bay Beach★★
Southeast peninsula.
This secluded, half-moon-shaped beach is touted as the island's best place to take a walk or a swim. Even though the beach lies on the Atlantic side, its shallow coves make it ideal for families.

Sugar Train★★

Departs from Needsmust Station at the airport. ☎ 869-465-7263. www.stkittsscenicrailway.com. Contact the railway because schedules vary, with more frequent tours Nov-Apr. $89US, children ages 3-11 $44.50US.

The 30-mile **St. Kitts Scenic Railway** chugs down tracks buil in 1912 to carry sugarcane from the plantations to the mill ir Basseterre. Hop aboard the double-decker coach cars for a 4 hour scenic ride along the coast to see such sights as Brimstone Hill, Thomas Jefferson's great grandfather's grave and the rair forest of Mount Liamuiga.

Dr. Kennedy Simmonds Highway★★

Leave Basseterre, by Pond Rd., heading south to Frigate Bay, where the highway begins.

Rent a car to experience this scenic drive along St. Kitts' penin sula—the narrow strip of land at the island's southern end. The wide paved road runs six miles from Frigate Bay to Majors Bay through the wildest landscape on the island. You'll be treated

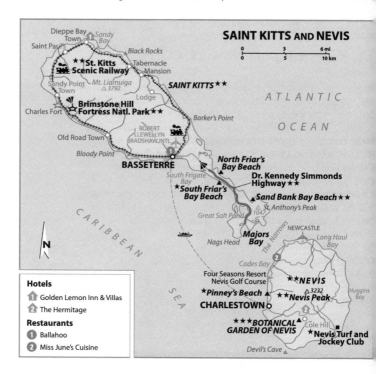

WHEN TO GO

These tropical marine islands enjoy mild temperatures of 75–80°F and low humidity pretty much year-round. Rainfall is low, increasing slightly May-Oct. **Hurricanes** can, and have, hit the islands Aug-Nov.

GETTING AROUND

Taxis and **mini buses** are widely available at fixed rates. **Rent a jeep**, **scooter**, or a **bike**. Four **ferry companies** make runs daily.

VISITOR INFORMATION

Main tourism office: St. Kitts Tourism Authority, Pelican Mall, Basseterre. ℘869-465-4040. www.stkittstourism.kn. Nevis

Tourism Authority, Main St, Charlestown. ℘869-469-7550. www.nevisisland.com.

Important numbers
Emergency (24hrs): 911
Police: 869-469-5391
Medical Services:
Joseph N. France General Hospital,
St. Kitts: ℘869-465-2551
Alexandra Hospital, Nevis: ℘869-469-5473

MONEY/CURRENCY

The official currency is the East Caribbean dollar, which has a $2.75 US dollar exchange. Major credit, debit and ATM cards, as well as international traveler's checks in dollars, are accepted, but fees apply for cards.

to vistas of hills covered with dry grass anchored by brackish ponds, and virgin beaches nestled in picturesque bays, dominated by the pyramidal mass of Nevis Peak. Stop at the small parking area on Sir Timothy's Hill for a stunning view of the peninsula and its beaches. Below, in the foreground, you'll notice the stagnant waters of the Salt Ponds (*return to the crossroads and turn left*). The road ends at the low point of **Majors Bay**, a cove with a creek.

NORTH END

Brimstone Hill Fortress National Park★★

10mi northwest of Basseterre. Turn right before Charles Fort. ℘869-465-2609. www.brimstonehillfortress.org. *Open daily 9:30am–5:30pm. Closed Good Friday & Dec 25. $8US.*

In a grown-up version of the childhood game "capture the flag," this military construction went from British to French to British hands in just two years. Completed by the English in the 18C, the fort was captured by the French in 1782. A year later, the Treaty of Versailles returned it to the British crown. Today the fortress and the national park are a UNESCO World Heritage Site.

Watch a video on fort history in the welcome center. Then dawdle among the buildings, which include the bastion, the hospital and the ammunition warehouses. The main structure, **Fort George Citadel**, houses a museum (*$5US*), several rooms of which are dedicated to the British and the short-lived French occupations. Perched on **Brimstone Hill**, the site makes a van-

tage point for views of the sugarcane fields and the island of S Eustatius offshore; if visibility is good, you can see the outline of Saba and St. Barthélemy.

Nevis★★
Botanical Garden of Nevis★★★
Cole Hill, south of Charlestown. From the main road, turn right toward Montpelier Plantation Inn and follow the signs. ☎869-469-3509. www.botanicalgardennevis.com. Open Mon–Sat 9am–4:30pm. Closed Christmas, and New Year's Day. $13US.

The sound of flowing water makes a pleasant background for leisurely stroll through these eight acres, planted with bamboo cacti, ficus and fruit trees. Paths are framed by orchid terrace water-lily-filled ponds are graced by bronze sculptures of do phins and mermaids, and a collection of palms has been assem bled from all parts of the globe. The Maya-themed **Rain Fores Conservatory** showcases Caribbean ecosystems. Lunch an afternoon tea are served on the veranda of the **Tea House**.

Nevis Peak★★
Center of the island.

This mountain has the feel of sacred ground—a silent, deif presence that pervades the whole island. An ascent up this dra matic 3,232ft peak is a challenging hike that lands you at th crater of a dormant volcano. There are easier hikes through th mountain's rain forests, with guides. **Sunrise Tours** (☎869-469 2758) can provide local guides with encyclopedic knowledge.

Nevis Turf and Jockey Club★
Indian Castle Race Track, Gingerland. One Sunday a month, usually on a holiday, at 2pm. For more information, contact The Hermitage Plantation Inn: ☎869-469-3477.

Horse racing is second only to cricket in popularity here, so a rive early and place your $2 bet on a minimum of five race Then cheer for your pick of the island's thoroughbreds as the race this sandy oceanside track, where a goat or donkey oc casionally slips into the pack. After the races, stay on at the clu for the traditional barbecue, cold Caribbean beer and late-nigh dancing.

Pinney's Beach★
1mi north of Charlestown, Nevis.

Perhaps Nevis' most famous beach, Pinney's is the occasiona haunt of movie stars and other celebrities. Order a tropical drin from Sunshine's Beach Bar & Grill (☎869-469-5817) and loung beneath a palm-topped hut.

Antigua★ and Barbuda★

Antigua's protected harbors and clear waters draw plea-sure-seeking yachties, while nature lovers head to sparsely populated Barbuda. Due east of Nevis 43 miles, Antigua [an-TEE-gah] is known for pretty beaches, cricket games and historic sites. Barbuda, 26 miles north, boasts pink-sand beaches, shipwrecks and **Codrington Lagoon**, a ha-ven for frigatebirds.

Antigua★
Nelson's Dockyard★★
English Harbour, south coast. ☎ 268-481-5041.
Open Mon–Sat 9am–5pm. $8US.
This historic dockyard is protected inside the deep bay of **English Harbour** and was once commanded by England's most famous naval officer, Admiral **Horatio Nelson**. Built in 1743, the naval base served as headquarters of the British navy for the West India Islands. Explore restored Georgian buildings then enjoy dinner and browse the gift shops.

Half Moon Bay Beach★
Southeastern shore, 1.5 mi from Freetown.
Considered the best beach on Antigua, this long curve of shel-tered shore enjoys trade winds and agitated Atlantic waters that lure windsurfers looking for a challenge. The rough sea is not great for swimming.

WHEN TO GO
Most visitors come from Nov-Mar to enjoy 80°F days and 70°F nights. The trade winds are a constant cooling presence year round. Late July and early August host an influx of visitors to Carnival. Sept through Nov—the hurricane season—are the wettest months.

GETTING AROUND
Rent a car or hire a **taxi** that comes complete with a driver/tour guide.

VISITOR INFORMATION
Main tourism office: Antigua & Barbuda Tourism Authority, ACB Financial Centre, High Street, St. John's, Antigua, ☎268-562-7600, www.antigua-barbuda.org.
Important numbers
Emergency (24hrs): 999 or 911
Police: (268) 462-0125/999
Medical Services:
Mount St. John's Medical Center, St. John's: ☎268-484-2700
Spring View Hospital, Barbuda: ☎268-460-0409

MONEY/CURRENCY
The Eastern Caribbean Dollar is official, but the US dollar is generally accepted. Additional fees are applied to the use of credit, debit, and ATM cards.

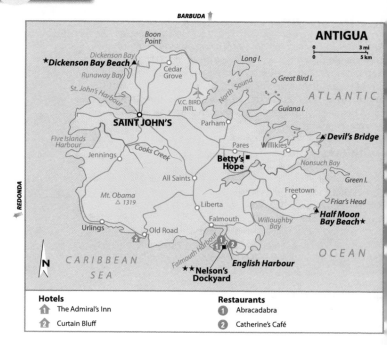

ANTIGUA

BARBUDA

Boon Point

Dickenson Bay
★Dickenson Bay Beach▲

Runaway Bay

St. John's Harbour

Cedar Grove

Long I.

Great Bird I.

ATLANTIC

V.C. BIRD INTL.

North Sound

Guiana I.

SAINT JOHN'S

Parham

Pares

Willikies

▲▲Devil's Bridge

Five Islands Harbour

Jennings

Cooks Creek

Betty's Hope

Nonsuch Bay

Green I.

All Saints

Mt. Obama
△ 1319

Liberta

Freetown

Friar's Head

Half Moon Bay Beach★

Urlings

Old Road

Falmouth

Willoughby Bay

REDONDA

N

CARIBBEAN
SEA

Falmouth Harbour

★★**Nelson's Dockyard**

English Harbour

OCEAN

Hotels		**Restaurants**	
🏠	The Admiral's Inn	①	Abracadabra
🏠	Curtain Bluff	②	Catherine's Café

Betty's Hope

Southeast of St. John's, near village of Pares. 📞 *268-462-1469. Open Mon–Sat 9am–4pm. $2US.*

Begun in the mid-17C, this former sugar plantation features a restored windmill—reputedly the only one in the Caribbean that still works—and a museum that includes heart-wrenching histories of slavery.

Barbuda★
Southern Beach★★

South end of island, between Martello Tower and Coco Point.

This 5mile-long beach shimmers with pink sand. Its protected waters are ideal for swimming and snorkeling. Remember that topless and nude sunbathing are illegal on Antigua's public beaches.

Bird Sanctuary★

North end of Codrington Lagoon. Arrange a boat tour in advance with your hotel or at the pier with a local fisherman in the settlement of Codrington. 50EC.

Codrington Lagoon hosts the largest colony of frigate birds

GREATER AND LESSER

The islands known as the **Greater Antilles** occupy the Western Caribbean (Cuba, Cayman Islands, Jamaica, Dominican Republic, Puerto Rico
and the Virgin Islands). The **Lesser Antilles** make up the Eastern Caribbean, and consist of the French Antilles (Guadeloupe, Martinique, Saint-
Barthélemy, Saint-Martin); the Netherlands Antilles (Aruba, Bonaire, Curaçao, Saba, Sint Eustatius, Sint Maarten); the United Kingdom's Anguilla
and Montserrat; and the independent countries of Antigua and Barbuda, Barbados, the Federation of St. Kitts and Nevis, Dominica, Grenada,
St. Lucia, St. Vincent and the Grenadines, Trinidad and Tobago.

With administrative ties to France, the Netherlands and the United Kingdom, the insular little worlds of the Lesser Antilles offer a wide range
of landscapes, nuances of climate and diverse cultures. Ancient volcanoes, rugged coasts, arid deserts and white-sand beaches backdrop an
equally diverse mix of West African, Dutch, French, Creole and British
architecture, cuisine, and traditions. Strung out like a strand of pearls,
this arc of more than 35 large and small islands stretches 750 miles from
the Anegada Passage in the north to the waters off Venezuela, bordered
by the Atlantic Ocean on the east and the Caribbean Sea on the west.
In the Middle Ages, the term "Antila" was used to describe a legendary
island in the middle of the Atlantic Ocean. After Columbus' voyages, the
Spanish preferred "Indies" for their newly discovered continent of America. The Lesser Antilles themselves were sometimes called "The Cannibal
Islands" due to mispronunciation of the word "Caribbean." During the
17C and 18C, the term "Antilles" was still seldom used; the archipelago
was normally described as the "West Indies" or "American Isles." It was
not until the French Revolution in 1789 that the term Antilles came into
common use in France.

In 1780 **Sint Eustatius** was a bustling port; it was common for 200 ships
to be waiting in the harbor to unload legal—or smuggled—cargo. In
fact Statia smuggled arms and supplies to the Americans during the
Revolutionary War. According to folklore, instead of fighting to establish the border on the island of **Saint-Martin/Sint Maarten**, the early
Dutch and French settlers each sent one of their own citizens to walk the
perimeter of the island. The point where their paths crossed would be
the border. Armed with a flask of gin; the Dutch representative headed
south; carrying a carafe of wine, the French designee headed north. The
Frenchman walked faster, gaining 21 square miles to the Dutchman's 16
square miles. Some say the gin got the better of the Dutchman.

in the West Indies. These fork-tailed seabirds, with wingspans of more than 6 feet, have made huge nests in the mangrove swamps here. The tour boat stops only a few yards from the nests.

Addresses

For price ranges, see the Legend on the cover flap.

WHERE TO STAY

$$ Admiral's Inn – *English Harbour, St. John's, Antigua.* ℘*268-460-1027. www.admirals antigua.com. 14 rooms.* Built in 1788, this three-story brick building was a former warehouse in Nelson's Dockyard. The ceilings in upstairs rooms retain original timbers; some rooms have canopied four-poster beds. An apartment called the Joiner's Loft overlooks the harbor.

$$$ Mary's Boon Beach Plantation – *117 Simpson Bay Rd., Sint Maarten.* ℘*599-545-7000. www.marysboon.com. 32 units.* In business here 40 years, this favored lodging sits on Simpson Bay Beach. Returning guests like its convenient location, atmosphere and charming rooms, each with a terrace.

$$$$ Golden Lemon Inn & Villas – *Dieppe Bay, St. Kitts.* ℘*800-633-7411. www.golden lemon.com. 26 units.* Expansive grounds with tropical flora set the stage for the handsome two-story 17C Great House, painted a pale yellow with a wraparound veranda. A black-sand beach lies steps away.

$$$$$ Curtain Bluff – *Old Road Village, Antigua.* ℘*268-462-8400 or 888-289-9898. www.curtainbluff.com. 72 rooms.* A haven for bon vivants, this clubby resort caters to families with children. Rooms are graced with fresh flowers and balconies that overlook Morris Bay and Grace Bay. Rates include three meals a day and afternoon tea.

$$$$$ Eden Rock Hotel – *Baie St. Jean, St-Barthélemy.* ℘*590-29-79-99. www.edenrock hotel.com. 16 units.* On a rocky promontory above St. Jean Bay, this hotel is a St. Barts' legend. Topless sunbathing on its two picturesque beaches is de rigeur. The sophisticated decor is laced with Caribbean charm.

$$$$$ Hôtel Guanahani – *Grand Cul de Sac, St-Barthélemy.* ℘*590-27-66-60. www.leguana hani.com. 69 units.* This St. Barts' icon, sitting on its own 16-acre peninsula, is a perfect blend of French joie de vivre and West Indian- Creole architecture. Each intimate cottage offers laid-back, high-styled comfort in rare island wood. Private patios have lovely sea views.

$$$$$ Privilege Resort and Spa – *Anse Marcel, Saint-Martin.* ℘*590-87-38-38 or 800-874-8541. www.privilege-spa.com. 22 units.* Backed by lush green hills, the resort hugs a sheltered bay with a yacht-filled marina. Rooms come with marble bathrooms, and a terrace or balcony.

$$$$$ The Hermitage – *St. John's Parish, Nevis.* ✆*800-682 -4025. www.hermitagenevis.com. 15 cottages.* This relaxed yet elegant plantation inn, perched 800ft above sea level, edges a rain forest. Around sunrise, expect sightings of the elusive green-velvet monkey. The breeze-cooled cottages, decked out with canopy beds and antiques, dot acres of cashew and mango trees.

WHERE TO EAT

$$ Abracadabra – *Dockyard Dr., English Harbour, Antigua. Closed Jul–Sept.* ✆*268-460-2701. www. theabracadabra.com.* **Italian**. Expect a lively atmosphere while you dine. This crowded trattoria becomes a popular night spot that fills with a youthful crowd on the dance floor. For the extraordinary, try the *porceddu*.

$$ Ballahoo – *The Circus, Basseterre, St. Kitts. Closed Sun.* ✆*869-465-4197. www.ballahoo. com.* **Caribbean**. Ballahoo's dining room is large and pleasant, with a view of the town's clock tower. It's great for a quick breakfast or lunch, or a leisurely dinner.

$$ Captain Oliver's – *Oyster Pond, Saint-Martin.* ✆*590-87-40-26. www.captainolivers.com.* **Seafood**. Popular with boaters, this open-air restaurant, situated above a lagoon, overlooks a yacht-filled marina. Oliver's chef emphasizes fresh seafood; select your own lobster from the tank.

$$ Catherine's Café – *English Harbour's wharf, Antiguan Slipway, Antigua. Lunch only Mon. Closed Tue & Sept.* ✆*268-460-4050.* **French**. Overlooking the harbor, Catherine's offers French classics such as *salade niçoise*, crêpes, quiches and seafood dishes. A great wine selection, delicious coffee.

$$ Hevéa – *In Hevéa hotel, 163 Blvd. de Grand-Case, Saint-Martin. Closed Mon in summer.* ✆*590-87-56-85.* **Creole/French**. This small, formal restaurant is favored locally for its Creole and French cuisine. Dinners focus on traditional entrées like scallop cassoulet, or escalopes of veal with Calvados and cream. Lobster is a menu staple.

$$ Le Repaire – *Quai de la République, Gustavia, St-Barthélemy.* ✆*590-27-27-48.* **French-Creole**. Locals arrive early for authentic French breakfasts at this open-air brasserie. Lunch and dinner are just as popular, especially the seafood and French pastries.

$$$ Bonito – *Rue Courbet, Gustavia, St-Barthélemy. Dinner only.* ✆*590-27-96-96.* **French**. Watch the harbor from the sophisticated dining room while savoring South American-inspired French cuisine. Try the roasted rib eye with *aligot purée*. The extensive ceviche bar is a bonus.

$$$$ Miss June's Cuisine– *Jones Bay, Nevis.* ✆*869-469-5330. Reservations required.* **International**. One night a week, this Trinidad native welcomes guests into her West Indies home for global dishes. The set price covers cocktails, hors d'oeuvres, soup and two courses, as well as wine with dinner.

GUADELOUPE

◥ Diving or snorkeling site

```
0        5        10 mi
0       10       20 km
```

Pointe de la Grande Vigie

Anse-Bertrand

ATLANTIC

Nord de la Grande-Terre

OCEAN

Port-Louis

Îlet à Fajou

Vieux-Bourg

le Moule

Ste-Rose

Grand Cul-de-Sac Marin

Morne-à-l'Eau

N5

Deshaies

Baie-Mahault

N5

Pointe des Châteaux

Lamentin

POL'E CARAÏBES

les Grandes Fonds

N4

POINTE-À-PITRE ★

St-François

Pointe Noire

Grande Plaine

Versailles

Gosier

Ste-Anne

LA DÉSIRADE

Îlets de Pigeon

Mahaut

Îlet du Gosier

Réserve Naturelle de Bouillante

Petit-Bourg

ATLANTIC

Bouillante

Parc National de la Guadeloupe

GUADELOUPE★★★

OCEAN

★★ **La Grivelière Plantation**

Vieux-Habitants

St-Claude

★★★ **LA SOUFRIÈRE**

Capesterre-Belle-Eau

Grosse-Pointe

MARIE-GALANTE

BASSE-TERRE

St-Sauveur

les Bas

St-Louis

les Hauts

N9

Trois-Rivières

Vieux-Fort

★ **Plage de Pompierre**

Grand-Bourg

D201

CARIBBEAN

Fort Joséphine

Capesterre

★★★ **LE CHAMEAU**

TERRE-DE-HAUT★★★

D203

Pointe des Basses

SEA

Terre-de-Bas

TRACE DES CRÊTES★★★

★★★ **LES SAINTES**

DOMINICA, MARTINIQUE

Hotels

1 Gîtes de Lucette Promeneur
2 Habitation Massieux
3 Hôtel Village Soleil
4 L'Auberge de la Vieille Tour

Restaurants

1 La Case aux Epices
2 L'Oiseau du Paradis
3 Le Plaisancier
4 Total Végétal

Nowhere is French influence more visible than on Guadeloupe and Martinique. Both islands are an overseas region of France, and members of the European Union. The currency is the euro, and French the official language, but Antillian Creole, a pidginized version of French, is also spoken. Within the Lesser Antilles group, these French territories and nearby islands of Marie-Galante and

PETER'S TOP PICKS

🛩 CULTURE

Check out the Darse District of Guadeloupe, where you can visit Place de la Victoire, a square with palm trees symbolizing the liberty of the island after the victory over Britain in the French Revolution. (p **232**)

🛩 GREEN SPACES

Martinique's volcanic origins are unmistakable, especially when you set eyes on Presqu'île de la Caravelle. Jutting into the Atlantic Ocean, this volcanic peninsula is a geological wonder with varied terrain, a portion of which is a protected nature reserve. (p **241**)

🛩 HISTORY

The imposing Saint-Louis Cathedral in Fort-de-France is actually the seventh structure on this site, as its predecessors were destroyed by natural disasters and fire. The current building, which dates back to 1978, was designed to withstand destructive forces. Step inside to really appreciate the craftmanship and history. (p **240**)

🛩 STAY

Located right by the sea, L'Auberge de la Vieille Tour, in Guadeloupe, is a tranquil hotel built in a tropical garden, with direct beach access. (p **237**)

🛩 SHOP

Guadeloupe's largest city, Pointe-à-Pitre, is the first stop for most cruise-ship passengers, with busy markets that are packed with locals and tourists alike. (p **232**)

🛩 EAT

In the village of Les Trois-Îlets on Martinique, Fleur de Sel, situated inside an unassuming Colonial brick house, is known for its creative French cuisine using local ingredients. (p **243**)

Les Saintes, along with Saint-Barthélemy and Saint-Martin, make up the French Antilles, otherwise known as the French West Indies. Guadeloupe's economic hub is Pointe-à-Pitre, while Martinique's administrative capital and main port, Fort-de-France, is the first stop for most visitors.

Guadeloupe★★★

Sitting 38 miles south of Antigua, Guadeloupe's two islands of Basse-Terre and Grande-Terre, each resembling a butterfly's wing, are connected by a bridge. Basse-Terre is home to the administrative capital as well as la Soufrière, an active volcano that towers at an elevation of 4,815 feet. Grande Terre's economic hub is Pointe-à-Pitre, an active port and shopping mecca. Sidekick island Marie-Galante lies 16 miles southeast, peaceful and largely undeveloped. About 6 miles off Guadeloupe's southwest shore, two islands (Terre-de-Bas and Terre-de-Haut) and seven islets make up the volcanic archipelago of Îles des Saintes, a nature-lover's paradise.

Pointe-à-Pitre★

Avoid the city at night when many streets are deserted.

Sitting on the southwest side of Grande-Terre, Point-à-Pitre is the economic capital of Guadeloupe and the country's "front door." Yet the city (pop.17,500) doesn't merit more than a half day's visit, since it has few tourist sights and no particularly exceptional lodging. Most of its charm is found by walking the streets lined with old houses. Be sure to visit the markets where vendors sell spices and punch from colorful stalls.

Darse District

Avoid the crime-prone Carénage and Zamia court district to the southeast.

Start at **Place de la Victoire**. Victor Hugues, a colonial administrator, had palm trees planted in this square as symbols of liberty. It is named in remembrance of the victory over the British in the French Revolution. In the center is a 1930s bandshell.

North of the square, the **Old Parsonage** (soon to house the tourism board's new office) stands as a grand example of traditional island architecture. To the southeast the yellow façade of the **Sous-prefecture**, a 19C barracks, dominates the square. South of the square, the bustling **Darse Market** (*open Mon–Sat*) borders the sea. Vegetable sellers in brightly colored dress teach visitors how to make a Creole potage. Next to the market fishermen unload their catch for the day: wahoo to mahi-mahi.

Old Pointe-à-Pitre

The city's busiest street, **Rue Frébault** begins at the wharf and winds through this old section. At almost every step, stalls offer practically everything, except food. The best place to buy food

WHEN TO GO

Temperatures hover around 27ºC/81ºF. The best period to visit is Dec-May during the **dry season**. The other months have much more rain.

GETTING AROUND

BY BIKE – Guadeloupeans love biking. Renting a bike is a good way to meet the locals.

Dom Location, Rue Ste-Aude-Ferly, St-François; ☎590-88-84-81. 10 euros half day/15 euros full day. **Tropico Vélo**, Galerie Marchande Sea-Side, Terre-de-Haut; ☎590-99-88-78. Mountain bikes and children's bikes are available. 4 euros/hour, 9 euros/day.

BY BUS – Bus systems exist in larger towns, but schedules are not precise. Generally, buses leave when full. Service ends at dusk and is limited on Sundays. If you are outside town, you won't find many bus stops. If you wave down a bus, it will stop for you.

BY CAR – The best way to see Guadeloupe is to reserve a car ahead of time. Larger, international companies are more dependable and are found at Pointe-à-Pitre airport and larger hotels.

Avis – Pointe-à-Pitre International Airport; ☎590-21-13-54. **Voitures des îles** – Pointe-à-Pitre International Airport; ☎590-89-22-10.

BY FERRY – Contact companies in advance, since schedules vary greatly per season and school year. Ferries between Guadeloupe, la Desirade, Les Saintes and Marie-Galante, as well as to Martinique,

Dominica and St. Lucia, leave often.

Caribbean Spirit, Pointe-à-Pitre; ☎590-57-45-74. **L'Express des îles**, Pointe-à-Pitre; ☎825-35-90-00. **Brudey Frères**, Trois-Rivières; ☎590-90-04-48. **CTM Deher**, Basse-Terre; ☎590-99-50-68.

BY SCOOTER – Scooters are commonplace in the Saintes, Desirade and Marie-Galante. Elsewhere in Guadeloupe, traffic and long distances make scooter use dangerous. Inclines on most of Guadeloupe are steep, especially in the Saintes. Helmets and a driver's license are musts.

VISITOR INFORMATION

Main tourism office: Comité du tourisme des îles de Guadeloupe, Pointe-à-Pitre, 5 sq. de la Banque; ☎590-82-09-30. www.lesilesdeguadeloupe.com.

Important numbers
Emergency: Fire 18; Ambulance 15; Poison ☎590-91-39-39
Police: 17
Medical Services: Centre hospitalier régional universitaire (University Hospital Center). ☎590-89-10-10

MONEY/CURRENCY

Guadeloupe and Martinique's official currency is the **euro**. ATMs are plentiful, except on the islands of Desirade and the Saintes. On weekends and during festivities, ATMs are often out of cash by the afternoon. Credit and debit cards are accepted in most hotels and most stores, but smaller restaurants, hotels and artisans often accept only cash. Smaller merchants tend to refuse large denominations.

---

is **St-Antoine Market**★ *(Rue Saint-John Perse and Rue Schoelcher)*. Starting at 6am, madras-attired vendors sell their spices, punch and other local fare, at times aggressively. Check out these streets for their handsome 19C houses: **Nozières, Jean-Jaurès, Peynier and Achille-René-Boisneuf.**

Musée Saint-John Perse★

9 rue de Nozières. ℘590-90-01-92. Open Mon–Fri 9am–5pm, Sat 8:30am–12:30pm. 2.5 euros.

Housed in a striking colonial building, this museum has assembled personal items from its namesake Nobel Prize-winning author. Mannequins portray the life of a bourgeoise Creole family in the 19C. Changing displays showcase Perse's life and work.

La Soufrière★★★

The "Old Lady" of Basse-Terre Island is one of Guadeloupe's defining features. Named for its sulfuric fumaroles, La Soufrière lets you know it's an active volcano. Other surrounding turbulent volcanoes, such as l'Échelle, la Citerne, and Carmichaël, make this part of Basse-Terre a "must-see." La Soufrière acts as an immense water reservoir: its slopes receive up to 14m/46ft of precipitation each year.

Hiking to La Soufrière's Summit

12km/7.5mi round-trip. Moderate to high intensity. Allow 3hrs. Contact National Park of Guadeloupe in advance about conditions. Obey all access restrictions. Danger of landslides and deadly gases. Depart from Bains-Jaunes parking lot. Do not venture past la Savane-à-Mulets where sulfur emissions are highest.

The best marked trail is **Le Chemin des Dames** that begins at the old Savane-à-Mulets parking lot. This rocky path rises past the **Eboulement Faujas** (Faujas fissure), which appeared in 1798, and then to the **Grande Faille (Great Fault)**, where the path rises higher, to the crater. Follow signs and watch out for acid fumes that can irritate the respiratory tracts. Return via the same route.

La Grivelière Plantation★★ – Maison du Café

Northwest of Basse-Terre. Past the coffee museum and before Grande-Rivière, turn right on D27 for about 8 km/5mi. ℘590-98-63-06. http://habitationlagriveliere.com. Open daily 10am–5pm. Guided tours hourly until 4pm. Closed Sept–first week of Oct. 5.80 euros (7.50 euros includes coffee or fruit juice tasting; 24 euros for tasting and fixed meal).

In Vieux-Habitants, one of the first European colonies, the aroma of coffee and vanilla pervades the southwestern area of Basse-Terre, harking back to an older Guadeloupe. Sitting within a lush valley, this old coffee plantation is classified as a historic monument. It represents the best restored assembly of buildings from the 18C on the island. A visit here provides a look into the self-sufficient operation of a coffee plantation. Coffee as well as bananas, cacao and vanilla are still grown on the premises.

St-Pierre

The May, 8 1902 eruption of Mont Pelée decimated the Martinique town of St-Pierre. Although the volcano was showing signs of eruption for several months, officials assured citizens that there was no cause for concern—even blocking their exit because a government election was nearing. The cataclysmic explosion killed its 29,000 residents. St-Pierre had to be rebuilt from the ground up, never quite restoring its former glory as an idyllic Caribbean village.

Terre-de-Haut★★★

South of Basse-Terre, the small Saintes archipelago offers the best things about Guadeloupe: pristine beaches, gorgeous landscapes and breathtaking ocean fauna. Two islands make up **Les Saintes★★★**: Terre-de-Haut and Terre-de-Bas. Populated by descendants of fishermen from Brittany, Terre-de-Haut thrives on tourism. Many vacationers come for the day, but a stay of several days affords an appreciation of its tranquility and beauty.

Tour of the Island★★★

Caution: If you rent a scooter, be forewarned that the inclines of the roads can be dangerous.

Shops and cabins line the streets of **Terre-de-Haut**. Begin your tour at city hall. Nearby a church, badly damaged in a 2004 earthquake, is made of volcanic rock. Head out of town towards the wharf that faces Cabrit islet. The remains of **Fort Joséphine** can be found on this islet. This infamous penitentiary served as an antechamber to the Cayenne penal colony until 1902.

Travel Tip: Although Martinique's south side is teeming with high-end resorts and hotels, another option is to stay in a *Relais Créole*, a family-run guesthouse that offers a more local, immersive experience.

A DAY IN GUADELOUPE

Although most visitors to Guadeloupe remain on beachy Grand-Terre, **Basse-Terre** was tailor-made for nature lovers, with forested mountains, snaking rivers and abundant hot springs. One of the must-sees of Guadeloupe is **Chutes du Carbet** (Carbet Waterfalls), where three waterfalls cascade in the dense jungle foliage. You can see the first two falls from the parking lot, and a hiking path leads to the bottom of the second waterfall. This is the most easily accessible of the three, although it's a challenging hike. Swimming is allowed, so bring a bathing suit and douse yourself in the cool, refreshing waters.

Move even farther away from civilization by getting off the island and onto the nearby archipelago of **Îles des Saintes** by plane or ferry. Among this cluster of tiny islands and rocks is **Terre-de-Haut**.

In the morning, see the fishermen hauling in their catch for the day. Spend an afternoon browsing the small shops and French bakeries in the single village on the island. **Fort Napoléon** is a former French fort and current-day local-history museum and garden. End the day with a leisurely Creole dinner overlooking the Saintes' Bay at the outdoor restaurant of **Hotel Auberge Les Petite Saints aux Anacardiers** (*La Savane, Terre-de-Haut; ☎ 590-590-99-50-99, www.petitssaints. com*). This is Caribbean living as you imagined it, so take the time to pause, reflect and enjoy

FLIPPER FUN

Jacques Cousteau's Underwater Reserve is a 990-acre marine sanctuary just off the west shore of Guadeloupe's Basse-Terre. Also known as the **Bouillante Nature Reserve**, the subterranean refuge protects waters around Malendure and the Pigeon Islets. Within this area, the Îlets de Pigeon Dive Site has more than 12 sites for experienced divers, including wrecks. The sites are manageable even for beginner divers, but other options include snorkeling or exploring the reserve on a glass-bottomed boat. Get your flippers ready.

Travel Tip: Don't miss Cimetière du Morne-à-l'Eau (Cemetery of Morne-á-l'Eau) in Grande-Terre. This unusual cemetery consists of above-ground tombs and funerary chapels covered with black and white checked ceramic tiles. Nowhere else in Guadeloupe or Martinique does anything like this exist. The graveyard is a veritable "city" of the dead. It's off Rte. N5, Morne-à-l'Eau, north central Grande-Terre.

As you continue to **Anse Mire** beach, notice the bizarre house made of boats. From the beach, climb to **Fort Napoléon★★★** (*℘690-61-01-51; open daily 9am–12:30pm; 4 euros*), built from 1845 to 1867 to counter English attack, to enjoy an extraordinary **view** of the archipelago. Descend by taking the road towards **Pompierre** beach, the most beautiful on the island.

La Trace des Crêtes★★★ (Hilltop Trail) juts off the eastern end of Pompierre beach and leads to **Grande-Anse**, another gorgeous stretch of sand. Grande-Anse is not developed and swimming is not permitted. Follow the trail toward the calm **Anse Rodrigue** beach. **Snorkelers** delight in the abundant sea life found off the left side. Head toward the city by taking the trail in the direction of **Anse du Figuier**, where you will pass Fond du Curé wharf.

Pain du Sucre Trail★★★ (*allow 20min*) starts at the wharf and passes beneath basalt rock formations. A stony trail leads to a small beach shaded by coconut palms, where the snorkeling is rewarding, but do not swim around the boulder: recreational boats pass very close to it. Continue to **Morne du Bois Joli** at island's end. Below lies the gray-sand beach of **Anse Crawen**, a longtime nudist beach, but not as much of late.

For an excellent **panorama** of the archipelago, take the tarmac road that inclines sharply from Pain du Sucre Trail to **Chameau★★★**, the highest point of the Saintes islands.

Addresses

For price ranges, see the Legend on the cover flap.

WHERE TO STAY

$ Gites de Lucette Promeneur – *Baie du Moule, north Grande-Terre.* ☎590-23-60-12. *5 rooms with cooking facilities.*
This convivial establishment sits in a large garden. While rooms are not very spacious, each has its own terrace. Musical *gwoka* evenings are organized by the hostess.

$$ Habitation Massieux – *Bouillante, west Basse-Terre.* ☎590-98-89-80. *www.habitation-massieux.com. 4 cabins.*, This former 17C sugar plantation was redesigned by two Bohemian aristocrats enamored with the place. Canopy beds, exposed beams, a large terrace and big breakfasts tempt guests to prolong their stay. A fixed-price dinner (*26 euros*) is served.

$$ Hotel Village Soleil – *Marina de Bas-du-Fort, Pointe-à-Pitre.* ☎590-90-85-76. *www.hotel-village-soleil.com. 67 studios.*
In a lush, tranquil location, this hotel has functional rooms with decor inspired by the marina just below. Rooms with a balcony are available, and all rooms have kitchenettes. Free boat shuttle to Gosier Beach 3km/1.8mi away.

$$$ L'Auberge de la Vieille Tour – *Montauban, Gosier, 7km 4mi southeast of Pointe-à-Pitre.* ☎590-84-23-23. *www.auberge-de-la-vieille-tour-guadeloupe.com. 103 rooms.* This luxurious hotel was built near an 18C mill in a tropical garden overlooking the sea. It boasts several bars and restaurants (*open Fri–Wed for dinner only*), and beach access.

WHERE TO EAT

$ Total Végétal – *Rue Général-Delacroix, south Basse-Terre.* ☎590-92-05-81. **Light Fare**.
Don't expect fast service, but the wait is worth it, since tasty pizzas and sandwiches are made with organic ingredients. Good bakery bread and pastries as well.

$$ L'Oiseau du Paradis – *Morne Hoël, Rte. de la Soufrière, Basse-Terre.* ☎590-99-59-88. **Fusion**. Creole, French and Indian cuisine infused with other interesting ingredients come together in dishes like chutney of mango-veal-*ouassou* or queen conch stew.

$$ Le Plaisancier – *Marina du Bas-du-Fort, Pointe-à-Pitre.* ☎590-90-71-53. **Creole**. This restaurant probably has the best food for the money in the area. The fixed-price menu starts around 17 euros for appetizer, entrée and dessert.

$$$ La Case aux Epices – *Plage de la Colline, Fond Curé in Terre-de-Haut.* ☎590-98-07-88. **Creole/European**. This airy restaurant has a terrace overlooking a secluded beach. Creole as well as modern French dishes are served. The menu is short, but all the options are fresh. Crayfish specialties start at 25 euros.

Travel Tip: A fun word that once meant "to go out and party," *zouk* now refers to Martinique's hottest dance music with Creole lyrics and a seductive beat that you'll hear spilling from the bars and clubs in Fort-de-France.

Martinique★★★

An 81-mile jump over Dominica from Guadeloupe leads to the island of Martinique, where nature competes with the skyscrapers of its capital, Fort-de-France, but 4,577ft Montagne Pelée towers over all. Francophiles have long considered the 425sq mi island the Paris of the Lesser Antilles. Most tourists cluster around the well-developed south side of the island, where beaches feature the quintessential white sand lined with waving palm trees and shallow waters. The more rugged north coast is a world away, with charcoal and jet-black beaches, a testament to the island's volcanic origins.

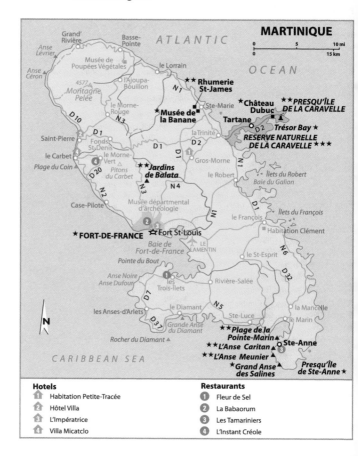

Hotels		Restaurants	
1	Habitation Petite-Tracée	1	Fleur de Sel
2	Hôtel Villa	2	La Babaorum
3	L'Impératrice	3	Les Tamariniers
4	Villa Micatclo	4	L'Instant Créole

WHEN TO GO

Daytime temperatures hover around 28ºC/82ºF all year, with a small drop at night. **High season** is Dec–Apr. The best time to go to Martinique is during the **dry season** (Jan–Apr), but it is also the time when costs are the highest (especially around New Year's and Carnival in Feb or Mar). Mid-Jan is a good compromise in terms of nice weather and affordable airfares.

GETTING AROUND

BY BUS – Bus service is mainly available in Fort-de-France and outlying suburbs. The transit system is called Mozaïk. Stops are designated by small glass shelters. There are no line numbers, just the final destination on the front of the bus. Tickets: 1.10 euros at newsstands; 1.30 euros on the bus.

BY CAR – During high season, reserve a car several weeks in advance, preferably from an international company like Avis, Budget or Hertz. Rental companies are located at Fort-de-France airport. Expect to pay about 250 euros/week in low season and 350 euros in high season.

BY FERRY – Ferries depart Fort-de-France frequently for Pointe-du-Bout, L'anse Mitan, L'anse à l'Âne and the small town of Trois-Îlets. Tickets can be bought onboard. Check schedules ahead as they vary per season and school year. **Madinina** (✆596-63-06-46) ferries leave hourly from Quai Ouest Mon–Fri 6am–6:30pm and less frequently Sat–Sun; 4 euros one-way/6.5 euros round-trip.

BY TAXI – Taxi companies are regulated. Rates range from .76 to 2.12 euros per kilometer according to the time of day and number of passengers. Baggage costs extra. For longer trips, set a price with the driver. Expect to pay 40 euros from Fort-de-France to Saint Pierre and 60 euros to Sainte-Anne. **Madinina Taxi**: ✆596-70-40-10. **Martinique Taxis**: ✆596-63-63-62; 24 hour service. **Radio Taxi Service**: ✆596-63-10-10; 24 hour service. **Airport taxis**: ✆596-42-16-66.

BY TWO WHEEL – It is best to rent **bikes** for short trips, since Martinique is very hilly and hot. Most roads in the south are open to mountain bikes. Many companies offer mountain bike trips (including rental). Reserve in advance in high season. Expect to pay 20 to 40 euros for a 3hr group tour. **Scooter** rental is scarce on the island. Narrow roads and inclines make riding dangerous. **Locabike**, 12 rue Pierre-et-Marie-Curie, Terres-Sainvilles, Fort-de-France; ✆596-63-33-05; 36 euros/day.

VISITOR INFORMATION

Main tourism office: Le Comité Martiniquais du Tourisme, "Le Beaupré" Building, Pointe de Jaham Schoelcher. ✆596-61-61-77.
Important numbers
Emergency: 15 or ✆596-75-15-75; Poison ✆590-75-15-75
Police: 17
Medical Services
Centre Hospitalier General Louis Domergue de Trinite ✆596-66-46-00; Hopital du Saint Esprit ✆596-77-31-11; Centre Hospitalier du Lamentin ✆596-57-11-11.

MONEY/CURRENCY

See Guadeloupe Practical Information.

ASK PETER...

Q: What is Carnival like in Martinique?
A: Simply put, the four-day Carnival festival is a joy. Locals in brilliantly colorful costumes and elaborate floats make their way down the streets as throngs of onlookers cheer them on from sidewalks and balconies. The events start as early as Epiphany Sunday and run all the way through Ash Wednesday, when the king of Carnival, Vaval, is burned in effigy. But wait, it's not over yet. The festivities return about 3 weeks later for mid-Lent, known as Mi-Carême.

Fort-de-France★

Martinique's capital moves to the rhythm of water: the Alma River to the north, the Petit-Paradis River to the west, the Jambette to the east, and the Bay of Flanders at its southern doorstep. Across the bay stretch the beaches of **Anse Dufour★** and **Anse Noirea**. If you follow the narrow streets that crisscross downtown for any distance, you'll find yourself atop foothills where the temperature drops several degrees; natives, called "Foyalais," have lived here for years. Back in the heart of town, stop by the bustling **Grande Marché**, the large produce market (*Blenac at Isambert St.*), to sample *cannelle de coco*, a candy made from coconut. Two blocks east, you'll reach Martinique's monumental cathedral.

Saint-Louis Cathedral

Rue Victor-Schoelcher. ℘596-73-59-78. Open daily 6:30am–11:30am, 2:30pm–5:30pm.

This eye-catching cathedral is the seventh on this site; fire, an earthquake and a hurricane destroyed its predecessors. Rebuilt in 1978 based on Parisian architect **Henri Picq's** design, the structure typifies 19C metal-frame construction: concrete walls are reinforced by a skeletal cast-iron frame to minimize fire damage. The bell tower, whose spire reaches 58m/190ft, sports 3,000 bronze-colored aluminum (which is fire-resistant) scales. Inside the spacious interior, stained glass (*behind the choir*) charts the life of Saint Louis himself. Little but the pulpit, pews, and marble altar has survived nature's destructive forces.

Schoelcher Library★★

Rue de la Liberté at Rue Victor-Sévère. ℘596-70-26-67.
Open Mon 1pm–5:30pm, Tue–Fri 8:30am–5:30pm (Fri 5pm),
Sun 8:30am–noon.

This remarkable building was constructed in Paris in 1887 by Henri Picq, then shipped to Fort-de-France piece by piece and reassembled here. Housing 300,000 works, the structure draws on an astonishing variety of styles, from the metal structures of Eiffel's workshops to Greek pilasters with Corinthian columns, Byzantine mosaics and inside, Art Nouveau detailing.

Fort Saint Louis

Chevalier-de-Sainte-Marthe Blvd. Closed to the public. To best see the fort, take a ferry from la Pointe-du-Bout or Les Trois-Îlets.

On the peninsula jutting into the bay, this fort was constructed under Louis XIV after the 1674 Rum Victory, in which a French garrison repulsed Dutch attempts to take the harbor. Still an active military site, the citadel retains its original artillery battery.

Jardin De Balata★★

10km/6mi north of Fort-de-France via the N3. ✆ 596-64-48-73. www.jardindebalata.fr. Open daily 9am–5pm (last entrance 4pm). 12.50 euros.

A visit here recalls the origin of Martinique's name, *Madinina*, "island of flowers." Gardening remains a favorite island pastime. Famous for their colors and robustness, the flowers of Martinique have been exported to the world since the mid-19C. Horticulturist Jean-Philippe Thoze took 20-plus years to assemble 3,000 plants on his ancestral property. Today heliconia, Porcelain Roses, hibiscus and begonias intertwine with orchids and lotus flowers, bamboo and palm groves. From some places, you can see Salomon Cape and the peaks of Carbet, and from an elevated pathway, you'll get a bird's-eye view of the garden. At the entrance, a traditional Creole dwelling houses an art exhibit, and a botanical store sells flower bulbs.

Presqu'île de la Caravelle★★

Among the most remarkable sites in Martinique, this heavily indented peninsula off the northeast coast is made of volcanic rock that rose out of the Atlantic Ocean 50 million years ago. Attracting geologists, mineralogists and scientists every year, the rocky, wind-blown strip holds incredibly rich fauna and varied landscapes. The welcoming fishing village of **Tartane** sits on the northern coast. Nearby, less hospitable barrier reefs, nicknamed "the wolves," hide just below the water's surface. Many shipwrecks line the bottom of **Trésor Bay★**.

Reserve Naturelle de la Caravelle★★★

D2 roadway ends at the reserve's entrance. Cars may continue to the intersection of the roads to Chateau Dubuc and the weather station. A sign indicates the trails. Picnicking is not permitted.

Dominating the headlands, this virginal expanse is ideal for exploring on foot. Two marked trails, one that is easy and one moderately difficult, cut through the vegetation.

The **short trail** (*1hr 30min; yellow-white markings*) loops through dry forests and mangroves. En route **Château Dubuc★** (*✆ 596-58-09-00; open daily 8:30am–5pm; 3 euros*) is the ruins of an old sugar plantation with an adjoining museum.

The **long trail** (*3hrs 20min, blue-white markings*) begins with a 20min ascent through dry savanna before arriving at a **lighthouse★★**, which affords a magnificent **view** of the rugged coasts. The trail leads to the weather station and around Trésor Bay.

As you exit the peninsula, drive north to Ste-Marie to visit the **St. James Rum Distillery★★**, and the **Banana Museum★**.

Travel Tip: Not widely known, Martinique is one of the best places in the world to buy rum. In fact, the rum produced in Martinique has been awarded the French label "appellation d'origine controlee" or AOC, usually reserved only for French wines: it is the French system for controlling the geography and quality of alcohol and food.

A DAY IN MARTINIQUE

Although the busy crowded port can be a turnoff for many an incoming passenger, Martinique is so spread out that there are plenty of options, even for the most discerning traveler. The main port in Martinique is just a hop and a skip away from the city center of Fort-de-France. A proliferation of cafes, shops and outdoor markets means you could spend the day simply browsing and people-watching. By night, Martinique is a party, with friendly locals and live music. Cotton Club, on the beach at **Anse Mitan** (Trois Îlets) features nighly live jazz and zouk, while **Casino de la Batelier Plaza** (Rue des Alizes, north of Fort-de-France) is the most popular casino on the island; but most people head to **Casino Trois-Îlets** (Kalenda Resort, Pointe du Bout) for dancing as much as gambling.

Or you can opt to get out of the city. After all, two-thirds of Martinique is protected national land. The northern side of the island is a natural paradise, with ancient forests, tumbling waterfalls and vast plantations that still produce sugarcane and bananas. The south side of the island has a truly unusual feature: the **Savane des Pétrifications**, a savanna of petrified trees. The landscape is dominated by 4,500-foot **Mount Pelée**, the volcano that famously erupted in 1902, where you can set out on a day-long hike to explore its unique flora and soak up some of the most majestic views on the island.

Travel Tip: Don't be surprised if you see octopus on Martinique. Frequently you'll see fishermen on shore with their catch of octopus. These 8-armed mollusks come in 50 varieties, but the most common in the Caribbean is octopus *briareus*, a chewy (if eaten raw) and much-appreciated delicacy offered in restaurants throughout the island.

Presqu'île de Sainte-Anne★
This southern peninsula holds the island's loveliest beaches.

Sainte-Anne★
Sitting on the west side of the peninsula, this small fishing village is surrounded by tropical flowers and greenery. Sainte-Anne is known for its beaches, many accessible by the scenic 28km/13mi **Trace des Caps** biking and walking trail.

Presqu'île's Beaches★★
These beaches have white sand and superb coves. Among them **Plage de la Pointe-Marin** (*3.50 euro vehicle entrance fee*) offers plenty of shade and calm waters north of Sainte-Anne; **L'anse Caritan** lies south of Sainte-Anne; **L'anse Meunier** (*accessible only by foot*) is connected to Trace des Caps, but quite a distance away; and **Grande Anse des Salines★** (*off the D9 roadway*), Martinique's most famous beach, is crowded at times.

Addresses

For price ranges, see the Legend on the cover flap.

WHERE TO STAY

$ Villa Micatclo – *Morne Savane, Carbet.* ☏*596-78-09-92. www.micatclo.com. 6 rooms.* Housed in a lovely Creole villa, this bed and breakfast inn is located on the heights of Carbet. Its simple and well-kept rooms are offered at reasonable prices. A pleasant lounge and large communal terrace permit views of Carbet peaks.

$$ Habitation Petite-Tracée – *Rue de la Paix in the Petite-Tracée quarter, Gros-Marne.* ☏*596-67-90-02. 10 bungalows (2-4 people).* This small estate is hidden within a large tropical garden in the countryside. Yet it is still close to the beach and water activities. Bare feet or flip flops is the trend here. Bungalows are well furnished and inviting.

$$ Hotel Villa – *Rue Bouille at Rue du Petit-Versailles, Saint-Pierre.* ☏*596-78-68-45. 9 rooms.* Quite modern, this is the only hotel downtown. Rooms are designed with discreet luxury, several of which have ocean views. Guests are made comfortable by the excellent staff. The hotel restaurant (*closed on Mon; reservations required*) offers French cuisine with Creole accents.

$$ L'Impératrice – *Place de la Savane, 15 Rue de la Liberté, Fort-de-France.* ☏*596-63-06-82. 24 rooms.* Facing Place de la Savane in the heart of the city, this hotel resembles an ocean liner. It's a good option if you wish to enjoy downtown's attractions. The

hotel restaurant *Le Joséphine* has a solid reputation (fixed-price menu starts at 20 euros).

WHERE TO EAT

$$ Le Babaorum – *Villa Roseraie, 42 Rte. Châteaubœuf, Fort-de-France.* ☏*596-75-03-32.* **Creole**. This restaurant has built a reputation on its modern spin on Creole food. The menu changes weekly. Meals are served on the terrace of an old colonial home, where cell phones are prohibited. Concerts certain nights.

$$ L'Instant Creole – *Place de la Chapelle, Morne-Vert.* ☏*596-55-55-64.* **Creole**. Tasty home cooking is prepared before your eyes here. The ventilated terrace offers an ocean view. The service is attentive and the portions are generous.

$$ Les Tamariniers – *Place de l'Eglise, Sainte-Anne.* ☏*596-76-75-62.* **Creole/Mediterranean**. The main room is tastefully decorated. Les Tamariniers' menu features Mediterranean, Creole and modern French dishes. Good value for quality of food.

$$$ Fleur de Sel – *27 Ave. de l'Impératrice-Joséphine, Le bourg de Trois-Îlets.* ☏*596-68-42-11.* **French/Caribbean**. In the oldest house in the village, this gourmet restaurant is one of the best on the island, serving "bourgeois cuisine revisited." Try the bouillabaisse soufflé, cream of sea urchin soup, and porcini mushroom bread. Pleasant covered patio.

DISCOVERING

DOMINICA★

DOMINICA

Guadeloupe Channel

Capucin Cape · Carib Point

Cabrits National Park
Fort Shirley
Portsmouth
Prince Rupert Bay

Waitukubuli Natl. Trail
Morne aux Diables
Hampstead

Crompton Point

ATLANTIC

Indian River

Dublanc

NORTHERN
Morne Diablotin
4748
FOREST
RESERVE

MELVILLE HALL
Kalinago Territory

Pagua Bay
Bataka
Salybia
Sineku

Marigot

Syndicate Nature Trail

Salisbury

Saint Joseph

Layou

Waitukubuli Natl. Trail
Castle Bruce
Emerald Pool
Belle Fille

OCEAN

CANEFIELD
Laudat

★★ MORNE TROIS PITONS
Rain Forest Aerial Tram

Trafalgar Falls

ROSEAU

Boiling Lake ★
NATIONAL

Délices

PARK

Sari Sari Falls

Victoria Falls

CARIBBEAN

SEA

Soufrière

Soufrière Scotts Head Marine Reserve
Scotts Head

Berekua

Waitukubuli Natl. Trail

Martinique Channel

N

POINTE-À-PITRE, GUADELOUPE

FORT-DE-FRANCE, MARTINIQUE

0   3   6 mi
0   5   10 km

Hotels

1. Beau Rive
2. Crescent Moon Cabins
3. Jungle Bay Resort
4. Papillote Wilderness Retreat
5. Rosalie Bay Resort
6. Secret Bay
7. Zandoli Inn

Restaurants

1. Citrus Creek Riverside Café
2. The Fish Pot
3. Four Seasons Restaurant
4. Iguana Café & Restaurant
5. Islet View
6. Le Bistro
7. Talipot Gallery

Nature as it was intended—the Old Caribbean, undeveloped and unspoiled—that's the Commonwealth of Dominica. Rightfully calling itself "The Nature Island," this sparsely populated island nation is a lush, mountainous zone blanketed in tropical forest. Less than 290 square miles in size, Dominica emerges from the ocean between Martinique and Guadeloupe, the most mountainous island

PETER'S TOP PICKS

HISTORY

The Kalinago Barana Aute is a living history museum that illustrates the old lifestyles, heritage and skills of the island's native Carib population. See the ancient arts of basket weaving, canoe building and bread making that sustained the natives long before Europeans set eyes on the island. (p **226**)

EAT

A local couple serves up the freshest catch any way you want it at The Fish Pot. The experience here is so interactive that you get to pick your seafood, and then explain how you'd like it cooked and with what sides. (p **126**)

SEE

Dominica's volcanic origin is evident in its bubbling sulphur springs and boiling lakes that claim to have healing properties. The spa village of Wotten Waven has several natural springs and mud pots for soaking. (p **246**)

of the Lesser Antilles. Early navigators could see its 3,000-foot peaks from a long way off. Formed by geothermal volcanic activity, the island is continuously evolving. It has only a few beaches of gray sand, but offers a world of experiences in ecotourism and total immersion for nature lovers. Trails thread the mountainous sections, and hundreds of rivers snake through the region, passing cascading waterfalls and lush forests. Hot springs that dot the landscape and the aptly named Boiling Lake are reminders of the island's volcanic heritage.

Dominica was named by Columbus for the day of the week he spotted it, Sunday. (It was originally called Waitukubuli by the indigenous Carib tribe.) European forces drove away the Carib inhabitants, and battles continued over who maintained official control. France handed over the tiny island to the United Kingdom in 1763. It achieved indepedence in 1978, and is populated by a mix of English, French, African and Carib descendants, with England and Creole as the primary languages (even English is tinged with a French lilt).

ASK PETER...

Q: What outdoor activities can I do even if I'm not in great shape?
A: Dominica's landscape is so vast and lush that there are adventures for all fitness levels. There are plenty of manageable trails, like the short, easy trail to Trafalgar Falls. Just west of the village of Laudat, the path takes only 10 minutes, starting 1 mile beyond the outskirts of Trafalgar. You'll reach a vantage point where you can enjoy a spectacular view of the falls, which are 197 feet high. Hope you've brought your swimsuit—one of the pools makes a good swimming hole. And if you don't feel like hiking at all, you can still get a beautiful view of the island's natural wonders on the Rainforest Aerial Tram, which departs near Laudat for a 90-minute, round-trip canopy ride in an 8-seat gondola with an onboard guide.

Roseau

Dominica's capital is home to the **Bay Front** with ferry and cruise-ship jetties, a fruit and vegetable market, the **barracoon building** where newly-arrived slaves were once held, and **Fort Young**, the island's most historic hotel. King George V Street runs through the historic **French Quarter**, site of the **Old Market Square** with its craft and souvenir stalls. Several buildings sport traditional wooden verandas and *jalousie* windows. **Roseau Cathedral** rises atop a hill. At the end of King George V Street, the **Botanical Gardens★** *(open daily dawn–dusk)* oversee cricket matches, tropical trees and two parrots found only in Dominica, the sisserou and the jaco.

The South

Roseau Valley's spa village of Wotten Waven has several natural hot springs. Most notable among them is **Screw's Sulphur Spa★** *(𝒫 767-440-4478; open Tue–Sun)*, but **Tia's** *(𝒫 767-448-1998; open daily)* and **Ti Kwen Glo Cho** *(𝒫 767-440-3162; open daily)* are also inviting. The twin **Trafalgar Falls** at the head of the valley are spectacular waterfalls and a much-visited attraction. Gardening buffs should head for the colorful **Papillote Gardens** *(𝒫 767-448-2287; www.papillote.dm; open Nov–Apr daily; guided tours available)*.

The East

Descendants of the island's original people inhabit the semi-autonomous **Kalinago Territory**. At **Barana Auté** *(𝒫 767-445-7979; www.kalinagobaranaaute.com; guided tours)* in Crayfish River and **Touna Auté** *(𝒫 767-285-1830, 767-316-7655; guided tours)* in Concord, their heritage and native skills can be observed in traditional thatched shelters, as well as demonstrations of basketmaking and canoe building. Near the villages of Delices and La Plaine, in the southeast, **Victoria Falls** and **Sari Sari Falls** are two of the island's tallest waterfalls.

The North

Take a boat trip along the mystical **Indian River**, a *Pirates of the Caribbean* film location. The nearby **Cabrits National Park** has forest walks to battlement ruins, cannons and the restored **Fort Shirley Garrison**. For hikers it also marks the finish line of the 115 mile **Waitukubuli National Trail** *(www.waitukubulitrail.dm)*.

WHEN TO GO

Dominica's peak tourism season is Nov–May, when the majority of cruise ships arrive. The Jan–Jun **dry season** is a good time to hike and explore the island. Temperatures usually hover around 85°F/29°C.

GETTING AROUND

BY BUS – Public buses (minibuses) serve most of the island and are inexpensive. Their registration number always begins with the letter H. Rather than numbers, buses have the driver's name or motto on the windscreen.

BY CAR – Major rental companies have an office at the airport. Expect to pay about US$50 per day. You must also purchase a visitor license ($12US) from the car rental company. Driving is on the left, following the British system.

BY TAXI – Private taxis offer island tours. **Ken's Hinterland Adventure Tours** ☎767-448-1660, toll free ☎866-880-0508; www.khattstours.com. **Eddison Tours** ☎767-225-3626; www.eddisontours.dm.

Bumpiing Tours ☎767-315-0493; www.bumpiingtours.com.

BY FERRY – From Bay Front, **L'Express Des Iles** high-speed ferries serve Guadeloupe, Martinique and St. Lucia: Purchase tickets online at www.express-des-iles.com or call ☎825-35-9000. Dominica agents: Whitchurch Travel ☎767-448-2181.

VISITOR INFORMATION

Main tourism office:
Discover Dominica Authority,
1st Floor Financial Center, Roseau;
☎767-448-2045; www.dominica.dm.

Important numbers
Emergency (police and fire services): 999 and 911
Medical Services: Princess Margaret Hospital ☎767-448-2231.

MONEY/CURRENCY

The island's currency is the **Eastern Caribbean Dollar**, but the US dollar is accepted everywhere. The Eastern Caribbean dollar is fixed to the US dollar at a rate of EC$2.7 = US$1.

The Center

Morne Trois Pitons National Park is a UNESCO World Heritage Site with hiking trails, rain-forest-covered mountains, hundreds of rivers, waterfalls and **Boiling Lake★**, second-largest of its kind in the world. Swimming is possible in nearby **TiTou Gorge**, which also has a waterfall.

The West

Dominica's endemic parrots can be observed on the **Syndicate Nature Trail** near the village of Dublanc. For scuba divers, the coral reefs and pinnacles of the **Soufrière Scotts Head Marine Reserve** are a treat. Boat trips are available to watch

Travel Tip:

Dominica is one of the top places in the Caribbean for whale watching. Its sheltered bay is a warm-water haven for sperm whales all year long. The males migrate to the balmy waters in winter for breeding, while females and calves remain near the island year-round. These giants are friendly and sociable, but getting too close isn't recommended (not to mention, they have teeth!). Go with a reputable operator who encourages the look-don't-touch philosophy.

whales and dolphins that swim off the west coast year-round. For scuba diving trips and whale watching tours, contact **Dive Dominica** ✆767-448-2188, www.divedominica.com; **Anchorage Dive Centre** ✆767-448-2638, www.anchoragehotel.dm or **ALDive +** ✆767-440-3483, www.aldive.com.

Addresses

For price ranges, see the Legend on the cover flap.

WHERE TO STAY

$$ Beau Rive – *Castle Bruce.* ✆*767-445-8992. www.beaurive. com. 8 rooms.* This elegant yet casual hotel has a traditional feel. It's located close to the Kalinago Territory in a peaceful setting, and carries an excellent reputation.

$$ Crescent Moon Cabins – *Riviere La Croix.* ✆*767-449-3449. www.crescentmooncabins.com. 4 units.* These cabins make an idyllic forest retreat. It has welcoming owners, organic gardens and a farm. It's a good choice for eco-kids.

$$ Papillote Wilderness Retreat – *Trafalgar.* ✆*767-448-2287. www.papillote.dm. 6 rooms.* This is a long established eco inn set in lush tropical gardens with natural hot pools. It is an ideal retreat for nature lovers.

$$ Zandoli Inn – *Stowe.* ✆*767-446-3161. www.zandoli.com. 5 rooms.* Zandoli is a comfortable inn perched above Grand Bay. It boasts fabulous coastal views, expansive forest gardens, and high quality dining.

$$$ Jungle Bay Resort – *Delices.* ✆*767-446-1789. www. junglebaydominica.com. 35 cottages.* This award-winning

resort is located in the south east and has romantic hardwood cottages in a forest and beach setting with restaurant, pool and spa.

$$$ Rosalie Bay Resort – *Rosalie.* ✆*767-446-1010. www. rosaliebay.com. 28 rooms.* This indulgent beach and riverside eco resort has tropical gardens, restaurant, pool, spa and more. The resort also has a large wind turbine and turtle nesting sites.

$$$$ Secret Bay – *Petite Baie, Portsmouth.* ✆*767-445-4444. www.secretbay.dm. 4 units.* These unique eco-luxury villas and bungalows are sited above Secret Bay, a secluded cove with a white sand beach. Ideal for couples and honeymooners.

WHERE TO EAT

$ The Fish Pot – *Pointe Michel;* ✆*767-316-1821. Dinner only.* **Caribbean**. Select your own freshly caught fish and tell the cooks how you'd like it at this rustic waterside eatery. Popular with locals and visitors, it is an unforgettable experience.

$ Iguana Café & Restaurant – *Glanvillea, Portsmouth.* ✆*767-277-2535.* **Caribbean**. Authentic and wholesome Dominica food is served up by a friendly Rasta couple. Seafood is their specialty.

$ Islet View – *Castle Bruce.* ✆*767-446-0370.* **Caribbean**. With more rum fusions than you

A DAY IN THE LIFE OF PETER GREENBERG

The landscape here is so quintessentially wild and untouched it should come as no surprise that it was used as the backdrop for the Pirates of the Caribbean movies. The film crew made its base on the southern end of Dominica, but shot scenes on some of the more notable sites on the island.

One of the most intriguing is Ti Tou Gorge, which is Creole for "Little Throat Hole." Definitely enlist the help of a tour guide to swim in the cool waters, winding your way though the narrow opening between two rock walls until you reach the base of tumbling waterfalls. Nearby, a hot spring outside the gorge makes an inviting place where you can warm up after exploring the falls.

The scene in which Captain Jack Sparrow narrowly escapes capture from a village of cannibals was shot in High Meadows on the southwest coast, overlooking the Soufrière Bay. Another film location was Hampstead on the northeast coast of the island, just outside the village of Calibishie. This secluded bay features a sparkling, black-sand beach surrounded by verdant foliage, making it the perfect backdrop for a legendary pirate island.

---

thought possible, the rustic Islet View is popular with locals and visitors. Traditional food with awesome scenery.

$$ Citrus Creek Riverside Café – *Taberi, La Plaine.* ☎*767-446-1234. Lunch only.* **Creole**. Escape to the countryside and dine on whatever is fresh that day. Afterwards cool off with a soak in a river pool nearby.

$$ Four Seasons Restaurant – *Sunset Bay, Coulibistrie.* ☎*767-446-6522.* **Caribbean/ International**. Noted for its lobster and crayfish dishes, this waterside restaurant offers casual dining against the backdrop of a gorgeous Caribbean sunset.

$$ Le Bistro – *Castle St., Roseau.* ☎*767-440-8117. Reservations preferred. Dinner only.* **Creole**. Chef Vincent Binet serves haute cuisine in this very popular Old French Quarter restaurant.

$$ Talipot Gallery – *Victoria St., Roseau;* ☎*767-276-3747. Reservations preferred.* **Creole/ International**. Fine art meets fine dining in Talipot's traditional Caribbean setting on the veranda of the historic Palm Cottage.

Travel Tip: Several cruise ships make Dominica a port stop, but the capital city of Roseau is also easily accessible by ferry from Martinique, Guadeloupe and St. Lucia aboard a high-speed catamaran. (www.express-des-iles.com)

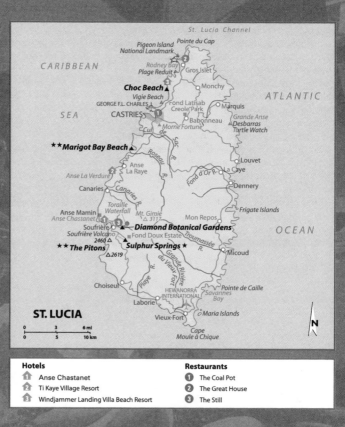

St. Lucia Channel

CARIBBEAN

Pigeon Island
National Landmark
Pointe du Cap

Rodney Bay
Plage Reduit
Gros Islet

SEA

Choc Beach ▲
Vigie Beach
GEORGE F.L. CHARLES ✈
CASTRIES

ATLANTIC

Monchy

Fond Latisab
Creole Park
Babonneau
Marquis

Morne Fortune
Cul

Grande Anse
Desbarras
Turtle Watch

★★ Marigot Bay Beach ▲

Anse
La Raye

Anse La Verdure

Canaries
Canaries R.

Louvet
La Caye
Fond d'Or R.

Dennery

Anse Mamin
Anse Chastanet
Soufrière
Soufrière Volcano
2460 △
★★ The Pitons
△ 2619

Toraille
Waterfall
Mt. Gimie
△ 311?

Diamond Botanical Gardens
Fond Doux Estate
Sulphur Springs ★

Mon Repos

Frigate Islands

OCEAN

Micoud

Choiseul

Laborie

du Vieux Fort
HEWANORRA
INTERNATIONAL
Pointe de Caille
Savannes
Bay

ST. LUCIA

Vieux-Fort

Maria Islands

Cape
Moule à Chique

N

0   3   6 mi
0   5   10 km

Hotels
1. Anse Chastanet
2. Ti Kaye Village Resort
3. Windjammer Landing Villa Beach Resort

Restaurants
1. The Coal Pot
2. The Great House
3. The Still

A land of volcanic mountains blanketed in tropical rain forests, with natural harbors sheltering uncrowded beaches, St. Lucia is perhaps most recognizable by its signature twin peaks of the Pitons that dominate the landscape. It's known for a "drive-in" volcano in the little town of Soufrière. About 240sq mi in size, St. Lucia sits north of St. Vincent and the Grenadines in the Atlantic Ocean and Caribbean Sea: vacationers get a different beach ex-

PETER'S TOP PICKS

CULTURE

While it's tempting to spend long, lazy days on the beach, it's worth getting out of the resort and into the community. Heritage Tours take visitors into working farms and plantations, and into off-the-beaten-path natural environments to see what really makes the island tick. (p **254**)

SEE

St. Lucia's "drive-in" volcano is an absolute must, whether you're a first timer or a veteran visitor. Bask in the steaming, bubbling waters of Sulphur Springs in the semi-active volcanic area in Soufrière. Just be prepared for the powerful sulfuric smell emanating from the land. (p **252**)

STAY

Despite St. Lucia's reputation as a honeymooner's paradise, it's also an exceptional family-friendly destination. Windjammer Landing Villa Beach Resort in Castries has villa-style accommodations and activities specifically geared toward children and teens. (p **254**)

EAT

The Coal Pot, named for a traditional island dish, is an upscale dining experience overlooking the marina, with inventive French-Creole cuisine. (p **254**)

PLAY

Most hikers will tackle the ascent of Gros Piton, which is a tough but safe trail that's best ascended early in the day. Petit Piton is smaller, but extremely challenging with no marked trails, so make sure you're in good condition and are prepared for the climb. (p **252**)

perience depending on which side they visit. The nation is an independent democracy in the British Commonwealth, but England and France alternately owned the island over 150 years. Cars are driven on the left, villages have French names and the official language is English, but locals also speak French patois. Most residents are of African and Caribbean descent.

Q: Where are some of the best spas on the island?

A: The landscape of St. Lucia allows spa-goers to receive treatments from indigenous ingredients, sourced from the island's rainforests and volcanic soils.

Jalousie Plantation (*Val des Pitons, Forbidden Beach, La Baie de Silence; ℘ 758-456-8000; www.jalousie plantation.com*), uniquely positioned between the Pitons, is renowned for its use of indigenous plants and sulfur mud.

Kai Belté Spa at Anse Chastanet Resort (*Soufrière; ℘ 758-459-7000; www.ansechastanet. com*) is beautifully situated on a 600-acre private estate. A honeymooners' haven, it has treatments geared toward couples, like an in-room massage and a couple's mini-massage course.

Beaches

Besides its famous peaks and alluring mineral baths, St. Lucia oversees some luscious beaches that tempt travelers to this friendly paradise.

Marigot Bay Beach★★

Central west coast, near Anse La Raye.

This bewitching bay was used as the setting for the 1967 film *Doctor Dolittle*. Steep forested hills sweep down to majestic coconut palms, soft sand and clear waters to create a miniature Garden of Eden, where swimming is pleasant.

Choc Beach

Northwest coast, north of Castries.

You'll find easy access from the coastal road to this agreeable stretch of sand and palms. Calm waters make the beach ideal for families with little children.

The Pitons★★

Anse des Pitons, southwest part of the island.

The island's most popular hike is the ascent of **Gros Piton** (2,619ft) on a steep but safe trail best taken early. For more daring hikers, a scramble up **Petit Piton** (2,460 feet) requires rock climbing. To hike either peak, you must get permission from the Forest and Lands Department (*℘ 758-450-2231*). To arrange a trip call the Gros Piton Guides Association (*℘ 758-459-9748*) or SunLink Tours (*℘ 758-456-9100; www.sunlinktours.com*).

Soaking Springs

Southwest section of the island. Take the road on the right about 2mi before Soufrière. ℘ 758-459-7565. Open year-round Mon–Sat 10am–5pm, Sun & holidays 10am–3pm (Dec 25 til 2pm). $15.

Soufrière Sulphur Springs★ is an active volcanic area with sulphur fumes and steaming brooks that you can bask in if you bring your swimsuit. Keep to the paths and consider taking a

WHEN TO GO

Peak tourist season is during the driest months (mid-Dec–mid-Apr). The **rainy season** (Jun–Nov) has higher temperatures and coincides with the hurricane season. Average temperatures range from 75°F in Jan to 82°F in Jun, with more humidity in jungle areas and cool breezes on beaches.

GETTING AROUND

BY BUS – Minibuses link most destinations but do not have fixed timetables and stop by 10 pm (Gros Islet buses operate later Fri for street parties). Fares start at $1US; from Castries to Soufrière costs about $5US. There are fixed stops but you can get on and off wherever you want.

BY CAR – The best way to explore the island is by rental car. Driving is on the left. Major rental car companies have offices in Castries, Soufrière and at the airport. From $45US/day to $300US/week. Non-islanders must purchase a temporary St. Lucian driving license ($20US).

BY TAXI – Taxis are available from the airport, port, the capital of Castries and other towns and can be flagged down. They are unmetered but journeys have fixed rates. Always establish the fare before boarding and if in doubt ask at a tourist booth. A taxi from Castries to Rodney Bay costs about US$15. Courtesy Taxis (☎758-452-1733/3555), Vigie Airport Taxi Service (☎758-452-1599).

VISITOR INFORMATION

Main tourism office: Sureline Bldg., Vide Bouteille, Castries. ☎758-452-4094/5968. www.stlucianow.com.

Important numbers
Emergency (24hrs): 911
Police: ☎758-052-2854
Medical Services:
Victoria Hospital, Castries: ☎758-452-2421/7059
St. Jude's, Vieux Fort: ☎758-454-6041
Soufrière Hospital: ☎758-459-7258/5001

MONEY/CURRENCY

The official currency on St. Lucia is the Eastern Caribbean Dollar. The official exchange rate at banks is $1 US = $2.70 EC, although lower rates are sometimes given by hotels and taxis. US dollars are accepted in most places. All major credit cards, most debit cards, and traveler's checks in dollar denominations are widely accepted. You can also use your ATM card to withdraw cash.

guide from the entrance: some mud pools boil at an impressive 300°F.

You can also soak in the mineral baths at **Diamond Botanical Gardens** (*drive 1.2mi on Soufrière River Rd. and turn right;* ☎*758-459-7155; http://diamondstlucia.com; $5*). The baths were built in 1785 at the request of French king Louis XVI and used by Napoleon's queen Josephine.

Travel Tip:
Community tourism in St. Lucia gets you out of the resort boundaries and in the midst of the rich culture.
Heritage Tours (☎ 758-451-6058; www.heritagetours-stlucia.com) arranges local experiences throughout the island. Spend a night in Grande Anse to track the indigenous leatherback turtle populations. See the operations of a working cocoa plantation at Fond Doux Estate, and take a tour of a local farm adjacent to a tropical forest and bird sanctuary.

Addresses

For price ranges, see the Legend on the cover flap.

WHERE TO STAY

$$$ Ti Kaye Village Resort – *Anse Cochon, Vieux Fort, north of Soufrière.* ☎*758-456-8101. www.tikaye.com. 33 cottages.* Ti Kaye is St. Lucian patois for "small house," which perfectly describes the gingerbread-trimmed guest cottages clustered above the cliffs. Perks include a private outdoor shower, and a porch with a hammock. Some 166 steps lead down to a wide, sandy beach in a protected cove.

$$$$ Windjammer Landing Villa Beach Resort – *Labrelotte Bay, Castries.* ☎*758-456-9000 or 800-958-7376. www.windjammer-landing.com. 237 units.* White-stucco Mediterranean-style villas with red-tile roofs occupy tropical gardens above the bay. The 55-acre resort is popular with newlyweds; parents love the kids' club and there's a program for teens. Spacious guest quarters have a kitchen and terrace. Four restaurants and four swimming pools, a fitness center and tennis courts can be found on-site.

$$$$$ Anse Chastanet – *Anse Chastanet Beach, Soufrière, on the southwest coast.* ☎*758-459-7000 or 800-223-1108. www.ansechastanet.com. 49 units.* Surrounded by 600 acres of jungle, the resort cascades down a hill to a beach with fine views of the Pitons. Walls have largely been eliminated from elegantly furnished cottages so you feel you're living in a tree house, with no phones or TV. Diversion include diving, snorkeling, tenni and biking.

WHERE TO EAT

$$ The Still – *Bay St., Soufrière.* ☎*758-459-7232/7261. www.the stillplantation.com.* **Creole**. This eatery, popular with cruise-ship passengers, sits on a working cocoa plantation on a hillside. The resort's two large dining rooms can seat several hundred diners. You'll feast on fish, beef or pork courses, accompanied b local vegetables and fruits.

$$$ The Coal Pot – *Vigie Marina, Castries. No lunch Sat. Closed Sun.* ☎*758-452-5566. www.coalpotrestaurant.com.* **French**. Overlooking the marina this French-Creole restaurant extends a big welcome to diners Expect imaginative sauces (mushroom, ginger or garlic butter) to enhance the chef's lamb or broiled fish entrées. Chicken, beef and duck are also on the menu.

$$$ The Great House – *Cap Estate, Gros Islet. Dinner only. Closed Mon.* ☎*758-450-0450.* **French-Creole**. Sitting on the site of a once-magnificent plantation manor, this restaurant has a reputation for romantic dining. Served by a staff in island dress, local crab, shrimp and chicken dishes are often topped with a spicy sauce.

GASTRONOMIC DELIGHTS

The island's fertile volcanic soil and diverse cultural influences have made St. Lucia a culinary standout in the Caribbean. A bounty of tropical fruits, cultivated root vegetables, and locally caught seafood are just a few staples that inspire island-born and international chefs who come here for the abundance of fresh ingredients.

Many of its signature dishes are Creole in nature, like *callaloo* soup and coquilles St. Jacques. Saltfish and green figs (actually green bananas) are another local favorite, with salted cod and spicy hot sauce. Traditional island bread is made from cassava flour baked on a banana leaf or a griddle. Tasty and filling, this is a perfectly portable food for hiking and day trips. Meanwhile, several other ethnic influences have crept into the mainstream. There are even East Indian influences from a period in the mid-19th and early 20th centuries when immigrants came from India as indentured servants. The remaining Indian population means you can find a variety of curries and roti—flatbread rolled and stuffed with potatoes, meats and vegetables, which you can find in restaurants and road stands around the island.

Another rustic St. Lucian favorite is the coal pot, a Carib dish that uses the cooking vessel to create deep, rich stews that vary depending on who's making them. Watch out for the heavy use of fiery Scotch bonnet peppers! The island is known for its weekly street festivals where you can sample these local dishes, from coal pot to barbecue to the can't-miss "fish fry" in communities like Anse La Raye and Dennery. Vendors cook up fried fish and whole lobsters, while Caribbean tunes and live bands get the crowds going. Of course, rum punch is a popular island drink, and rum can be purchased in specialty shops called *cabawes*. Piton beer is another local favorite, brewed and bottled on the island.

ST. VINCENT★ and
THE GRENADINES★★

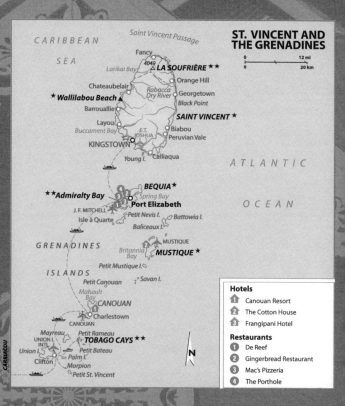

**ST. VINCENT AND
THE GRENADINES**

CARIBBEAN

SEA

Saint Vincent Passage

Fancy

Larikai Bay   △ **LA SOUFRIÈRE ★★**
4049

Chateaubelair   ○ Orange Hill
                Rabacca   ○ Georgetown
                Dry River ○ Black Point
★ **Wallilabou Beach ▲**

Barrouallie   **SAINT VINCENT ★**

Layou ○   ○ Biabou
Buccament Bay (E.T. JOSHUA) ○ Peruvian Vale
        ○ **KINGSTOWN**
            Young I. ○ Calliaqua   **ATLANTIC**

                                        OCEAN

★★**Admiralty Bay**   ○ **BEQUIA ★**
                Spring Bay
            Port Elizabeth
J. F. MITCHELL ○   *Petit Nevis I.* ○ *Battowia I.*
    Isle à Quarte   ○ *Baliceaux I.*

GRENADINES   ○ MUSTIQUE
                Britannia **MUSTIQUE ★**
                Bay
            Petit Mustique I. ○

ISLANDS

        Petit Canouan ○ ° *Savan I.*
        Mahault
        Bay
            ① **CANOUAN**
                ○ Charlestown
            CANOUAN

Mayreau ○ *Petit Rameau*
UNION I. ✦ **TOBAGO CAYS ★★**
INTL.   ○ *Petit Bateau*
Union I. ○ ○ *Palm I.*
    Clifton   ○ *Morpion*
            ° *Petit St. Vincent*   **N**

0 ——————— 12 mi
0 ——————— 20 km

Hotels
🏠 1 Canouan Resort
🏠 2 The Cotton House
🏠 3 Frangipani Hotel

Restaurants
① De Reef
② Gingerbread Restaurant
③ Mac's Pizzeria
④ The Porthole

One of the best-kept secrets in the Caribbean, St. Vincent and the
Grenadines are an idyllic collection of islands and cays in the Windward Islands, 26 miles south of St. Lucia. Much of this 40-mile-long
chain of islands has only been discovered by a privileged few, like
avid sailors and celebrity residents. A total of 33 islands, all begging to be hopped, they arc the waters of the Caribbean Sea and

PETER'S TOP PICKS

🛬 SEE

Mustique Island is known as the playground for the (very) rich and (very) famous. Spot the A-list crowd without paying exorbitant prices at Basil's Bar. (p **258**)

🛬 DO

Although St. Vincent's white and black-sand beaches are tempting, spend a morning hiking up the active volcano of La Soufrière, simply for the astonishing views. (p **258**)

🛬 EAT

Go island casual at The Porthole on Bequia, where home-style cooking combines local seafood and produce with Creole and West Indian influences. (p **260**)

the Atlantic Ocean. The largest island, St. Vincent, spans a mere 18 miles long by 11 miles wide, and is home to the port city of Kingstown. You can easily escape the busy port to nearby black-sand beaches, a blanket of rain forest, and the mighty La Soufrière volcano. St. Vincent serves as the gateway to the Grenadines, which is comprised of elusive islands like Bequia and Mustique. These islands traverse south toward the jaw-droppingly beautiful Tobago Cays, an archipelago of uninhabited islands.

Although it's easy simply to lay about and soak up the laid-back island atmosphere, activities abound on these islands. Barefoot Yacht Charters (📞 784-456-9526; www.barefootyachts.com) is one of the best live-aboard sailing schools in the Caribbean, whether you're a first-timer or an advanced sailor seeking bareboat certification.

On the exclusive island of Mustique, where the rich and famous come to hide, act like a local by getting out on the trails with Mustique Equestrian Center (📞 784-458-4316) for a horseback ride ending with a gallop on the beach.

Admiralty Bay on Bequia Island is one of the most striking bays in the region, where sailboats and cruise ships gather at the mooring. Friendly locals and cheerful, wooden houses shaded by almond trees are a welcoming sight. Take a stroll on the walkway along the piers and the hotels close to the shore.

Sail on a catamaran from Union Island to the lovely and remote Tobago Cays—from the private resort of Palm Island to the waters between Petit Rameau and Petit Bateau.

ASK PETER...

Q: Can a tourist drive on St. Vincent?
A: Yes, you can rent a car on the island without requiring any special permit. There are a couple of spectacular drives on the island, namely the Leeward Highway, which travels along the stunning Caribbean coast, and the Windward Highway, which follows the Atlantic coast. Remember, driving is on the left side of the road, so allot some time to adjust. The roads can be tricky, with rugged terrain and steep inclines, not to mention limited signage. Don't be afraid to stop and ask for directions.

St. Vincent★

St. Vincent island holds the capital city of Kingstown. While there, don't miss the oldest botanical garden in the Caribbean or the walk up to Fort Charlotte on Berkshire Hill for the views. North of Kingstown lie the volcanic island's black-sand beaches, the best of which is Wallilabou★.

Hire a guide (*HazEco Tours* ✆ *784-457-8634*) for a four-hour, round-trip hike to the active volcano of **La Soufrière★★**, rising 4,000ft on the northwest end of St. Vincent. Despite the smell of sulfur, it's the spectacular waterfalls, tropical forest and panoramic views you'll want to inhale.

The Grenadines★★

Bequia, Mustique and Tobago Cays aside, other Grenadines are worth exploring. Sun on Mahault Bay's secluded beach, or hike the white-cedar forests of Mount Royal on Canouan (CAN-oh-wan) island. Stroll to Salt Whistle Bay on the northern tip of Mayreau★ island. On the private island of Petit St. Vincent, resort cottages have no phones, TV or AC.

Bequia★
Access by 1hr ferry from Kingstown, St. Vincent.
Bequia attracts an arty crowd and yachting folks: witness picturesque **Admiralty Bay★★** filled with sailboats and giant cruise ships. Explore **Port Elizabeth** before heading to **Friendship Bay** for swimming and snorkeling.

Mustique★
Ferry from St. Vincent or flight from St. Vincent or Bequia (Mustique Airways ✆ 784-458-4380; www.mustique.com).
A paradise for billionaires and royals, this small island has few shops or restaurants. Rub shoulders with the A-list at **Basil's Bar** (*Britannia Bay;* ✆ *784-458-4621*), an affordable blues joint favored by celebrities in the music industry.

WHEN TO GO

Average temperatures of 79°F- 82°F drop to around 75°F at night, but beaches are cooler due to trade winds. **Peak tourism season** coincides with the dry season (mid-Dec mid-Apr). Short tropical downpours occur in May. **Hurricane season** peaks Oct-Nov. Expect crowds in Bequia for the **Easter Regatta**, and in St. Vincent for **Vincy Mas** (Jun-Jul).

GETTING AROUND

BY BUS – Minibuses ("dollar vans") are inexpensive and can be flagged down. Fares start at EC$1 for short trips on St. Vincent, so carry change.

BY TAXI – Taxis are available on main islands at the airport, port, major towns. They are unmetered so always establish the fare (and the currency) before boarding. Fare from Kingstown to airport is about EC$25. Sam Taxi and Tours (☎784-458 3686), Kingstown Taxi (☎784-457-2560).

BY CAR – Avis and local rental companies operate on St. Vincent. Cars, open-sided mini-mokes, scooters and jeeps can also be rented in Bequia and Mustique. Rentals start from US$50/day-US$300/week. If you have no international driving licence, you must purchase a temporary driving permit (US$20). Drive on the left.

BY FERRY – Bequia Express (☎784-457-3539, www.bequiaexpress.com) operates regular passenger and car ferries between St. Vincent and Bequia (1hr, EC$20 one way). Jaden Sun (☎784-451-2192, www.jadeninc.com) is a fast ferry service from St. Vincent to Bequia, Canouan and Union Island (Mon–Fri, 30min, EC$30-$55). The M/V *Endeavour* (☎784-457-1531) connects St. Vincent to Mustique (2hrs, EC$25).

VISITOR INFORMATION

Main tourism office: SVG Tourism Authority, 2nd Floor, NIS Building, Upper Bay Street, Kingstown. ☎784-456-6222. www.discoversvg.com

Important numbers

Police, Fire, Ambulance: 911, 999

Medical Services: General Hospital, Kingstown ☎784-456-1185

MONEY/CURRENCY

The official Eastern Caribbean Dollar (EC$) is pegged to the US dollar at about EC$2.7. US dollars are accepted in most places but change given in EC$. All major credit cards, most debit cards, and US traveler's checks are widely accepted in St. Vincent, Bequia and Mustique. Cash is available from ATMs in main towns on St. Vincent, Bequia, Canouan and Union islands.

Tobago Cays★★

Captain Yannis Day Charter catamaran cruises depart from Union Island year-round. ☎784-458-8513. www.yannissail.com. $75.
Board a 60ft catamaran for a voyage around the four islets called the Tobago Cays (Tah-BAY-go KEYS). First stop is 100-acre Palm Island, a private resort, for a swim in the warm waters. Then the anchor is dropped between Petit Rameau and Petit Bateau for a buffet lunch and snorkeling a coral reef.

Travel Tip: An island taxi is one of the best ways to get around Bequia. These famous, open-backed vehicles offer good views of the landscape. Or pick up a water taxi at Frangipani or Gingerbread dock. You'll spot them by their fun names like "No 'fraid Dat" or "Why Worry," and they crisscross the harbor for easy barhopping and shopping.

Addresses

For price ranges, see the Legend on the cover flap.

WHERE TO STAY

$$ Frangipani Hotel – *Belmont Walkway, Port Elizabeth, Bequia.* ☎*784-458-3255. www.frangipanibequia.com. 15 rooms.* Built by a local sea captain, this century-old, shingle-sided house offers modest rooms with a shared or private bath. The beach bar serves up creative cocktails and opportunities to ogle yachts; the outdoor restaurant is known for barbecues and steel-pan jump-ups.

$$$$$ Canouan Resort – *Canouan Island.* ☎*784-458-8000. www.canouan.com/resort.asp. 156 units.* This high-end, 300-acre resort includes an extra-long pool and spa treatment rooms. Seven restaurants serve culinary feasts. Play poker at the Trump Club Privée casino, or golf at the Trump International Golf Club, an 18-hole course that excites even jaded golfers.

$$$$$ The Cotton House – *West Coast of Mustique.* ☎*784-456-4777. www.cottonhouse.net. 17 rooms.* Hobnob with the rich and famous at this refined plantation-style inn. The rooms, suites and cottages of the hilltop estate have plush furnishings, and beds draped in mosquito netting. There's a great on-site spa.

WHERE TO EAT

$ De Reef – *Lower Bay, Bequia.* ☎*784-458-3484. Dinner reservations essential.* **Caribbean.** This popular bayside lunch option also serves up breakfast, dinner, and live music Sunday afternoons. Fresh seafood dishes spotlight conch, shrimp and lobster.

$ Mac's Pizzeria – *Belmont Walkway, Admiralty Bay, Bequia.* ☎*784-458-3474.* **Creole.** Savor world-famous lobster pizza on the bayfront porch. Other house specialties include conch nuggets and homemade key lime pie. To find this favored eatery, follow the smell of fresh-baked banana bread.

$$ Gingerbread Restaurant – *In Gingerbread Hotel, Admiralty Bay, Port Elizabeth, Bequia.* ☎*784-458-3800. www.gingerbreadhotel.com.* **Caribbean.** Delicious home cooking keeps patrons coming back to the veranda of this bayside cafe for freshly squeezed juices, Bequian cakes and sweet-potato pudding. Dinner brings seafood, steaks and spicy curries. Accommodation is offered in nine rooms.

$$ The Porthole – *Front St., Port Elizabeth, Bequia. Closed Sun.* ☎*784-458-3458.* **Caribbean.** This airy eatery on Admiralty Bay pulls in islanders for hearty home-cooked food. Specialties include conch, grilled fish Creole-style, and curried ginger chicken. For a quick snack, opt for a spicy *roti*.

WHERE TO HIKE

Hiking to the summit of **La Soufrière volcano** is a must when visiting St. Vincent. But for a less-intensive, but still rewarding outdoor experience, there are a number of other attractions that are worth exploring.

The **St. Vincent Botanical Gardens** just outside of Kingstown (*www.bgci.org*) were established in 1785, making them one of the oldest in the region. This quiet, tranquil setting is ideal for strolling through the well-maintained grounds, inhaling the fragrance of its exotic blossoms.

The **Nicholas Wildlife Aviary Complex** is home to a captive breeding program to help conserve the dwindling population of the St. Vincent Parrot.

The **Montreal Estate Gardens** (*www.montrealestgdns.f9.co.uk*) is a 7.5-acre plot of land that's rich with tropical foliage, surrounded by thick jungle and sprawling farms. Spend a quiet moment in the stone gazebo or look out onto the majestic Grand Bonhomme mountain. Although you can easily spend a morning wandering the grounds yourself, you'll get more out of the experience with a local guide who can point out native and tropical plants and take you through nearby rain forest and banana plantations.

The **Vermont Nature Trail** traverses two miles of a vast rain forest. Besides feeling like you've stepped back into prehistoric times, the biggest appeal of this jungle wonderland is the small colony of St. Vincent Parrots living in their natural environment.

17 DISCOVERING
GRENADA★

Hotels
1. Green Roof Inn
2. Petite Anse
3. Spice Island Beach Resort
4. True Blue Bay Resort
5. Villa Sankofa

Restaurants
1. The Aquarium
2. Bogles Round House
3. Laluna
4. Slipway
5. Vastra Blanken

UNION ISLAND
Gun Point
Anse La Roche
Bogles
High North
National Park
Windward
Petit Martinique
Sandy Island
Paradise Beach
Hillsborough
771 Top Hill
LAURISTON
Tyrell Bay
CARRIACOU
Manchineel Bay
Mushroom I.
Saline I.
Frigate I.
Large I.

CARIBBEAN SEA
Petite Anse
Sauters Bay
Sugar Loaf
Green I.
Sandy I.
Duquesne Bay
Sauteurs
Duquesne
Morne Fendue
River Sallee
Victoria
Union
★Belmont Estate
Antoine
River Antoine Rum Distillery
Tivoli
La Poterie
Gouyave
2757△ Mt. St. Catherine
Pearls
Dougaldston Spice Estate
Concord
Grenville
ATLANTIC
Halifax Harbour
Grand Etang
Grand Etang Lake
St. Margaret's Falls
Marquis I.
National Park
OCEAN
ST. GEORGE'S
GRENADA★
Grande Anse Beach
Point Salines
MAURICE BISHOP INTERNATIONAL
Calivigny I.
GRENADA

N

0   3   6 mi
0   5   10 km

Though it spans a mere 133 square miles, Grenada distinguishes itself in a big way. Often called the Spice Island for its predominant nutmeg crop, Grenada was the largest exporter of nutmeg and mace in the world until its industry was devastated by Hurricane Ivan in 2004, from which it's slowly recovering. This precious crop might be the reason that this now-Commonwealth nation has spent most of its history being fought over by imperial powers. Grenada is located in the eastern Caribbean, 100 miles north

PETER'S TOP PICKS

SEE

The Antoine Rum Distillery is the oldest functioning water-propelled distillery in the Caribbean. Tour the factory to see its traditional methods and sample the powerful wares. (p **267**)

STAY

Next to the secluded Petit Anse Beach at the northern end of the island, the Petite Anse Hotel offers views of the neighboring islands of the Grenadines. It also has a great view of leatherback turtle hatchings between April and July. (p **265**)

EAT

Bogles Round House is a collection of small cottages in a quiet Carriacou village, but its restaurant has been making a name for itself internationally. With a celebrated chef at its helm, the restaurant specializes in seasonal and local Caribbean cuisine. Don't miss the coconut-crusted mahi mahi and the homemade ice cream made in house. (p **266**)

of Venezuela. Though geographically part of the Grenadines, nearby Carriacou and Petit Martinique are politically joined with Grenada. The island was named by the Spanish, who thought its green hills looked like those of Granada, but it was the French and English who spent centuries fighting over the island's ownership. After Grenada became a sovereign state in 1974, a revolutionary period followed, ending with the controversial intervention of American and Caribbean military forces.

The invasion restored democracy to Grenada, and locals commemorate the invasion of the island with a Thanksgiving holiday in October. Just don't expect turkey. Grenadians celebrate with their national dish—oil down, a single-pot concoction of dumplings, breadfruit, callaloo, Irish potatoes, plantains, carrots, assorted meats, and a soup of coconut milk and spices.

Travel Tip: You can buy some of the spices that Grenada is famous for at market square in St. George's. Usually nutmeg, clove, ginger, cinnamon tumeric and other island spices are for sale from the local vendors there.

Grenada★

St. George's

Overlooking the sea from a hillside, Grenada's capital is blessed with a historic harbor, the **Carenage**, and a modern sailboat anchorage, the **Lagoon**. **Market Square** shows off the many spices the island produces.

Just south of St. George's, secluded bays and beaches stretch two miles along Grand Anse Bay. Powder-white **Grand Anse Beach** is fringed by fine hotels and resorts. In the bay south of Grand Anse, sheltered **Morne Rouge Beach** is ideal for kids.

Grand Étang National Park

8mi northeast of St. George's. Follow the signs.
Open daily dawn–dusk.

This park covers much of the island's central interior. Hike to **Seven Sisters Waterfalls** (*southeast of the park visitor center; $5 EC*) and look out for native **mona monkeys**. Take a refreshing dip in the **Concord Falls** (*look for signs on West Coast Hwy., north of St. George's; $5 EC*), or just enjoy the views of forest-covered mountains, such as **Mount Qua Qua**, and serene **Grand Étang Lake** (*both accessed via the park visitor center; $5 EC*).

Carriacou

Carriacou Beaches

While away the hours on **Anse La Roche** (*north of Hillsborough*) or **Paradise Beach** (*south of Hillsborough*), both pristine stretches of white sand on the island of Carriacou (CAR-ee-ah-coo), and often completely deserted. From Paradise Beach, a water taxi runs to **Sandy Island** or **Mabouya Island** in Hillsborough Bay (*water taxis operate from the beach and the Hardwood Bar; fares negotiable*).

High North National Park

Carriacou has easy walking trails that incorporate beaches, historic sites and the woodlands of this park, which cover the northern tip of the island.

Northeast of Hillsborough, look for windmill ruins and a teak and mahogany forest at **Belair Estate**, a former sugar plantation. From Belair and nearby **Mount Royal**, just south, views of the Atlantic and Caribbean coasts are grand.

WHEN TO GO

Grenada's **peak tourism season** is Nov-May. Temperatures hover in the mid-80s°F/29°C. The **dry season** begins in Jan, when sailing regattas and Spice Island Billfish Tournament are held.

GETTING AROUND

BY BUS – Inexpensive public buses operate from the terminus on Melville Street in St. George's. All routes are numbered

BY CAR – Major rental companies have offices at the airport. Expect to pay about US$60/day. You must purchase a visitor license (US$12) from the rental company. Drive on the left.

BY TAXI – Private taxis offer island tours. **Caribbean Horizons** ✆473-444-1555, www.caribbeanhorizons.com. **Henry's Safari Tours** ✆473-444-5313, www.henrysafari.com. **Mandoo Tours** ✆473-440-1428, www.grenadatours.com. **Sunsation Tours** ✆473-444-1594, www.grenadasunsation.com.

BY FERRY – A high-speed ferry runs from St. George's to Hillsborough on Carriacou: **Osprey Ferry** (✆473-440-8126; www.ospreylines.com).

BY AIR – From Grenada's **Maurice Bishop International Airport** to Carriacou's **Lauriston Airport** is a short flight with SVG Air (✆473-444-3549; www.svgair.com).

VISITOR INFORMATION

Main tourism office: Grenada Board of Tourism, www.grenadagrenadines.com. Grenada office: Wharf Rd., Carenage, St George's; ✆473-440-2279. Carriacou office: Main St., Hillsborough; ✆473-443-7948.

Important numbers
Emergencies (police, fire, ambulance) 911
Medical Services: St. George's General Hospital ✆443-440-2051

Money/Currency

The currency is the **Eastern Caribbean Dollar** but the US dollar is welcome everywhere. The Eastern Caribbean Dollar is fixed to the US dollar at a rate of EC$2.7 = US$1.

Addresses

For price ranges, see the Legend on the cover flap.

WHERE TO STAY

$$ Green Roof Inn – *Beauséjour, Hillsborough, Carriacou.* ✆473 443 6399. www.greenroofinn.com. *5 rooms.* This charming inn lies minutes from Hillsborough. Rooms have a sea or garden view, veranda and ensuite bath. The self-catering cottage sits in tropical gardens. Noted for its fine dining, the on-site restaurant serves breakfast, lunch and dinner.

$$ Petite Anse Hotel – *Sauteurs, Grenada.* ✆473-442-5252. www.petiteanse.com. *11 rooms.* This charming hotel graces idyllic Petite Anse Beach in the island's north. Fishing boat rides and delicious food in the on-site restaurant help make for a memorable stay.

$$$ True Blue Bay Resort – *True Blue, Grenada. ✆473-443-8783. www.truebluebay.com. 38 units.* True Blue offers comfortable rooms, suites and villas. Amenities include the Dodgy Dock restaurant, swimming pools, dive center, and small private beach.

$$$$ Villa Sankofa – *Craigston, Carriacou. ✆310-472-2343. www.sankofainternational.com. 1 villa, 3 rooms.* This stylish two-story villa sports a contemporary tropical design and includes a fully equipped kitchen and large veranda. With fabulous sea views, it is perfect for a romantic interlude.

$$$$$ Spice Island Beach Resort – *Grand Anse, Grenada. ✆473-444-4258. www.spiceislandbeachresort.com. 67 rooms.* One of Grenada's most lauded luxury hotels, Spice Island has all the creature comforts you will ever need; it is located on Grand Anse Beach.

WHERE TO EAT

$$ The Aquarium – *Maca Bana Villas, Magazine Beach, Grenada. ✆473-444-1410. www.aquarium-grenada.com. Reservations advised. Closed Mon.* **Caribbean/International**. This artistically decorated restaurant is sought out for its fresh catch of the day. Try the ginger-glazed lobster or the coconut shrimp. Don't miss Sunday afternoon BBQ and live music on the deck.

$$ Bogles Round House – *Bogles, Carriacou. ✆473-443-7841. Dinner by reservation. Closed Wed.* **Caribbean/International**. Carriacou's most famous restaurant has charm and quality dining based on what is fresh and seasonal. Try the coconut-crusted mahai mahi and Bogles' famous homemade ice cream for dessert.

$$ Slipway – *Tyrell Bay, Carriacou. ✆473-443-6500. Reservations preferred. Closed Sun & Mon.* **Caribbean/International**. An imaginatively designed restaurant with a distinctly nautical feel, Slipway offers delicious fare focused on fresh local produce and the catch of the day.

$$ Vastra Banken – *Le Phare Bleu, Petite Calivigny, Grenada. ✆473-444-2400. www.lepharebleu.com. Reservations required. Dinner only. Closed Sun-Tue.* **Caribbean/International**. Enjoy contemporary fine dining aboard a restored Swedish lightship. Try the homemade fettuccine with lobster, shrimp and *lambie* (queen conch), or the pan-fried grouper fillet.

$$$ Laluna – *Morne Rouge, Grenada. ✆473-439-001. www.laluna.com. Reservations required.* **Caribbean/Italian**. A delicious fusion of Italian and Caribbean cuisine is served in a Balinese-style setting beside secluded Portici Beach. Try the sea-crab linguini or *pappardelle Laluna* with nutmeg cream sauce.

SPICE TRADE

There's a good reason that Grenada is called the **Spice Island.** The spicy, floral scents of nutmeg, mace, cinnamon, cloves and other spices hit you the moment you step onto the island. Although Grenada's primary export, nutmeg, took an enormous hit after Hurricane Ivan in 2004, farmers are regaining their foothold. And nutmeg is everywhere on the island.

Nutmeg trees grow wild and locals even grow it in their front lawns. You'll find it flavoring rum punches, sauces and pastries, ice cream, and even in the colors of the island nation's flag. The fruit looks like a small peach, and makes excellent jellies and jams. Nutmeg spice is made from the seed kernel inside the fruit. The red, waxy exterior of the kernel is dried in the sun and made into mace.

The nuts have long been given special properties, often used to treat ailments from diarrhea to indigestion, and during the Middle Ages, nutmeg was used to ward off the plague. Nutmegs were often made into amulets to protect against illness and danger. In Grenada, you can purchase a little bit of your own luck by buying a nutmeg necklace while on the island, or picking up small bags in the market at St. George's.

The spice processing plant at the **Gouyave Nutmeg Pool** (*Central Depradine St., Gouyave;* ✆ *473-444-8337*) has scaled back its operations since the hurricane, but still offers tours to show how nutmeg is made. **Dougaldston Spice Estate** (Gouyave) is a ramshackle, former spice factory turned museum that showcases the island's long love affair with nutmeg.

Need a break from the spice immersion? **Belmont Estate** (*Belmont, St. Patrick;* ✆ *473-442-9524; www.belmontestate net*) is a long-running, organic cocoa plantation. Its crops were heavily damaged by the hurricane, but it continues to function as a living history plantation. **Antoine Rum Distillery** (*River Antoine Estate, St. Patrick's;* ✆ *473-442-7109*) has been operating nonstop since 1785, and it's the oldest functioning water-propelled distillery in the Caribbean. You'll have an opportunity to sample the over-proof rum: with an alcohol content of 75 percent, it might just bowl you over.

BARBADOS★

BARBADOS

North Point   Animal Flower Cave

St. Nicholas Abbey

Nesfield   CherryTree Hill

Farley Hill National Park ▲   ▲ **Barbados Wildlife Reserve**

Speightstown

★ **Mullins Beach** ▲   Belleplaine

Mount Hillaby △ 1116   Bathsheba

ATLANTIC

OCEAN

Holetown

★ **Sandy Lane Bay Beach**   ★ **Harrison's Cave**

★ **Paynes Bay Beach** ▲   Gun Hill Signal Station

Tyrol Cot Heritage Village   Ellerton   **Sunbury Plantation Home**   ▲ **Bottom Bay Beach** ★

BRIDGETOWN   Six Cross Roads   ▲ **Crane Beach** ★★

St-George Valley

Carlisle Bay

Barbados Museum ■   GRANTLEY ADAMS INTERNATIONAL

Oistins

CARIBBEAN SEA   South Point   ▲ **Silver Sands Beach** ★

Ragged Point

Hotels
🏠 The Crane
🏠 Sandy Lane Hotel and Golf Club
🏠 Tamarind Cove Hotel

Restaurants
1 David's Place
2 Mullins Beach Bar & Restaurant
3 Pisces
4 Waterfront Cafe

Geographically, the island of Barbados stands apart from the rest of the eastern Caribbean nations. While the other islands curve from Puerto Rico to Venezuela, Barbados is an outlier too far to the east. Location is not the only place where Barbados stands apart.

The island is not one, but two landmasses that gradually merged together over time. The 166-square-mile island boasts magnificent golden beaches, as well as colonial architecture and stately plantation houses that tell the story of its complicated past.

Portuguese travelers en route to Brazil were the first Europeans to encounter Barbados. The Portuguese never stopped to lay down roots, but they did pause to name the island Los Barbados, or "the

PETER'S TOP PICKS

CULTURE

Experience a bit of American history in the Caribbean by visiting the Bush Hill House. The residence is the only place that Founding Father George Washington ever visited outside the continental US. (p **270**)

HISTORY

Escaping from persecution in Brazil, Jewish immigrants built up Barbados' rum trade. You can visit the island's Jewish past at the Nidhe Israel Museum and Bridgetown Jewish Synagogue. (p **273**)

STAY

Dating back to 1887, the Crane is the oldest resort in the Caribbean. The resort retains many of its original four-poster beds and wooden balconies, but you can enjoy modern comforts too like a kitchen or Jacuzzi. (p **272**)

EAT

Head over to David's Place for a seafood lunch straight from the fisherman's net. You can also try out Bajan dishes like cou-cou, bread made of cornmeal and okra. (p **272**)

---

bearded ones," after the hairy, bearded fig trees on the island. It was the British who colonized the island, and put the deepest mark on the country. Their influence is most prominent in the island's capital and only city, Bridgetown. One of the oldest settlements in all of the Caribbean, Bridgetown is connected from the north to the south by two bridges constructed over the Careenage River by the British. The British also constructed Gothic Revival-style Parliamentary Buildings that you can visit when parliament is in session. Even typical British traditions like high tea and cricket are commonplace activities among locals.

Barbados' easterly location and lucrative sugarcane industry made it one of the largest West African slave traders in the Caribbean, and today, the majority of its population are descendants of slaves. To get a real feel for how the people of Barbados, known as the Bajans, live, head to the southeast of the island, where tourism never took a strong hold. It's worth making the trek to Bottom Bay, a sugary beach that is a favorite of the locals.

ASK PETER...

Q: What's with all the monkeys on the island?

A: Though they tend to be shy, you'll probably come across green monkeys around the island and at the Barbados Wildlife Reserve. Brought by slave traders as pets, these furry intruders became prolific, and there are an estimated 5,000 monkeys roaming Barbados. Their tendency to eat crops hasn't made them popular, so for centuries there have been bounties on them. Today, local conservationists offer a larger incentive to bring in the monkeys alive.

Beaches

For child-friendly calm seas head for the west coast beaches of **Paynes Bay★**, **Sandy Lane Bay★** and **Mullins Bay★** near Holetown. For surfing, head east to rugged Bathsheba and its rough waves.

The constant winds at **Silver Sands Beach★,** east of Oistins Fish Fry at the island's southernmost tip, have made the spot a world-class windsurfing destination. Farther east, **Crane Beach★★** has a bank of reefs offshore protecting the two strips of pinkish-white sand that make this one of the most beautiful beaches on the Atlantic coast.

Harrison's Cave★

Rte. 2, south of town of Welchman Hall, parish of St. Thomas. ℘ 246-417-3709. www.harrisonscave.com . Open year-round daily 8:45am–3:45pm. $30.

Situated in the heart of Barbados, this cave is part of a network of caverns carved into the limestone by subterranean rivers. Tours begin with a video on island geology. Then visitors don hard hats for a mile-long train ride through this mammoth cave with its dazzling stalactites and stalagmites.

Barbados Wildlife Reserve

Opposite Farley Hill National Park, parish of St. Andrew. ℘ 246-422-8826. Open daily 10am–5pm. Closed Jan 1 & Dec 25. $12.

The animals at this sanctuary are free to roam, apart from the reptiles (read pythons!) and the birds. Mantled in a mahogany forest, the reserve is home to species native to Barbados, other Caribbean isles and elsewhere. Watch for green monkeys, parrots, turtles, iguanas, flamingos, agouti (which look like large rabbits), and other creatures as well as plants like flowering cactus.

WASHINGTON WAS HERE

Barbados shares a bit of American history in that it was the only place outside the continental US that George Washington ever visited. Washington lived on the island for two months as a teenager with his ailing brother Lawrence, who was suffering from tuberculosis. The plantation home in which he lived, known as **Bush Hill House** (*Garrison St., Bridgetown; ℘ 246-228-5461*), is restored and open to the public. Visitors to Bush Hill House can get a look at what life was like 250 years ago when Washington inhabited the house.

WHEN TO GO

Average temperatures range 80°F-85°F/26°C-29°C dropping 5-10°F at night. **Peak tourist season** is mid-Dec–mid-Apr when weather is cooler and drier. **Rainfall** is likely Jun–Nov during hurricane season.

GETTING AROUND

BY BUS – Inexpensive and frequent, public buses are blue with yellow stripes, private minibuses are yellow with blue stripes; white minivans also operate. Fares start at US 75 cents, so carry small change. Destinations are shown on the front of buses.

BY TAXI – Available at the airport, port and all major towns, taxis can be flagged down. They are unmetered, with rates fixed by the government, but always establish the fare (and the currency) before boarding. A taxi from Grantley Adams Airport to Bridgetown costs about $20, as will most hour-long rides. Ambassador Taxi and Tours (246-424-9653), Johnson's Tours (246-434-8430).

BY CAR – Major rental car companies operate here, with offices at the airport and Bridgetown. Rentals run from about US$35/day at local rental firms to US$240/week.Open-sided automatic mini-mokes rent for less than 4-wheel drive jeeps. Scooters can be rented. Non-islanders must purchase a temporary driving permit (US$5). Driving is on the left.

VISITOR INFORMATION

Main tourism office: Harbour Rd, Bridgetown. 246-427-2623. www.visitbarbados.org

Important numbers
Police: 211
Fire: 311
Ambulance: 511
Medical Services: Queen Elizabeth Hospital, Lower Collymore Rock, St. Michael: 246-436-6450
Bay View Hospital: St Paul's Ave, Bayville, St. Michael. 246-436-5446

MONEY/CURRENCY

The official currency is the Barbadian dollar. The official exchange rate at banks is $1 US = $2 BBD, although lower rates are sometimes given by hotels and taxis. US dollars are accepted in most places. All major credit cards, most debit cards, and US traveler's checks are widely accepted. ATMs operate 24hrs in main towns and dispense cash in local currency.

Travel Tip: The island's golden-sand beaches are the great equalizer. According to Barbados law, all of its beaches are public and most are accessible by road. Even if a beach appears to be private because it can only be reached through a resort property, it's still open to the public.

Addresses

For price ranges, see the Legend on the cover flap.

WHERE TO STAY

$$$ The Crane – *Crane Bay, St. Philip.* ☎*246-423-6220. www.thecrane.com. 230 units.* The oldest resort in the Caribbean, The Crane dates to 1887. Renovated and updated with modern amenities, it has retained the four-poster beds and wooden balconies, but some units have kitchens or Jacuzzis. The swimming pool is perched above the beach.

$$$$$ Sandy Lane Hotel – *Hwy. 1, Sandy Lane Bay, St. James.* ☎*246-444-2000. www.sandylane.com. 112 units.* Royalty and celebrities favor this stylish luxury resort. Suites come with sea views and verandas. Spacious rooms are equipped with plasma TVs, DVD players and other high-tech gadgets. Four restaurants, 3 golf courses, tennis courts, a spa and a beach lie outside your doorstep.

$$$$$ Tamarind Cove Hotel – *Paynes Bay, St James.* ☎*246-432-1332 or 800-326-6898. www.eleganthotels.com. 104 rooms.* Mediterranean-style rooms have beds with mosquito netting. Diversions include four swimming pools, 3 restaurants, tennis courts and a fitness room. The Caribbean cousin of its London counterpart, chic Italian restaurant **Daphne's** (☎*246-432-2731; www.daphnesbarbados.com)* serves delights like mahi mahi with *peperonata* and olive mash.

WHERE TO EAT

$$ Mullins Beach Bar & Restaurant – *West coast, north of Holetown.* ☎*246-422-2204. www.mullinsbarbados.com.* **Seafood.** Opening onto the beach, this bar/restaurant offers salads, burgers and tuna-melts for lunch and curried shrimp and rack of lamb for dinner. Catch of the day can be red snapper or barracuda.

$$ Pisces – *Near St. Lawrence church, St. Lawrence Gap, Christ Church.* ☎*246-435-6564. www.piscesbarbados.com. Dinner only. Reservations recommended.* **Seafood.** Spiny lobster, flying fish and Atlantic salmon vie with jerk pork and Caribbean curries at this smart seafront spot.

$$ Waterfront Cafe – *Careenage (Marina), Bridgetown. Closed Sun.* ☎*246-427-0093. www.waterfrontcafe.com.* **Caribbean.** Enjoy a seafood lunch here. Try a flying-fish sandwich or local Bajan specialties like ***cou-cou*** (cornmeal and ocra). Live jazz enlivens the summer months.

$$$ David's Place – *St. Lawrence Main Rd., Christ Church Parish. Dinner only. Closed Mon.* ☎*246-435-9755. www.davidsplacebarbados.com.* **Caribbean.** Candles, soft music and sea views greet diners as they prepare to savor fish broth followed by barracuda, mackerel or red snapper. Lamb rack, curry chicken and rabbit are also on the menu.

ISLAND JEWS

The Caribbean is known for its diverse culture due to early colonization, and Barbados is no exception. One popular site, the Jewish Synagogue in Bridgetown, is evidence of the island's unique **early settlers**. In the mid-17th century, a small population of Jewish people left a colony located in present-day Brazil, after it was passed to the Dutch from England. The Dutch-persecuted Jews settled in Barbados making it the first British territory in which a Jewish population was granted full political rights. In 1654, the Jewish community in Bridgetown erected a synagogue, K. K. Nidhei Israel, meaning "The Dispersed Ones of Israel," a now-famous landmark.

The Jewish settlers were skilled in the **sugar trade** and quickly introduced Barbados landowners to crop cultivation and production. The influence the Jewish population had on sugar production in Barbados was remarkable; almost 95 percent of the island's export was sugarcane. The Jews helped Barbados become a leading colony in the Caribbean sugar trade.

By 1679, the Jewish population had grown to nearly 300 people, expanding their community to nearby Speighstown, 10 miles north of Bridgetown. While the British government considered the Jews good businessmen and industrious, they accused them of illegal dealings and were suspicious of their trade with the Dutch. The Jews acquired great wealth during their tenure of trade until 1668, at which time all Jewish merchants were prohibited from foreign and local trade. After the **trade restrictions** were enacted, the once wealthy, successful community of Barbados was forced to live in a Jewish ghetto.

Today, the Jewish population has dwindled to about 40 residents. The Bridgetown **Jewish Synagogue** (Synagogue Lane, Bridgetown), which is still active today, was destroyed by a hurricane in 1831. It was rebuilt but eventually fell into disrepair, and was sold in 1929. The temple was bought back and renovated by the community in 1983. It can be seen in its beautifully restored condition in the heart of Bridgetown. The nationally protected synagogue is the oldest in North America and sits adjacent to the Nidhe Israel Museum, another point of interest that exhibits the island's rich Jewish history.

19 DISCOVERING
TRINIDAD★ and TOBAGO★★

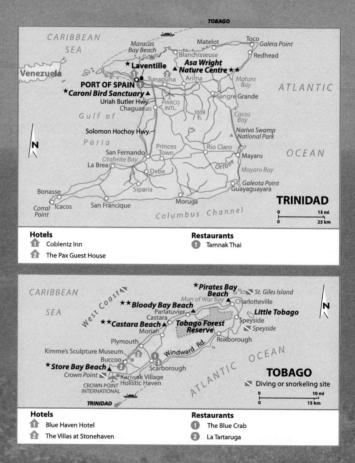

Hotels

1. Coblentz Inn
2. The Pax Guest House

Restaurants

1. Tamnak Thai

Hotels

1. Blue Haven Hotel
2. The Villas at Stonehaven

Restaurants

1. The Blue Crab
2. La Tartaruga

Here's how you can tell Trinidad and Tobago apart: Locals like to say Trinidad is the place you go for Carnival and to party, and Tobago is where you go to sleep it off. In fact, Carnival in Trinidad is often more fun than its counterpart in Rio de Janeiro---it's local,

PETER'S TOP PICKS

GREEN SPACES

It doesn't get greener than a rain forest. The Tobago Forest Reserve has miles of hiking trails. (p **280**)

CULTURE

Panyard bands, which use steel drums (or pans) as percussion, are a uniquely Trinidad experience. Desperados Panyard in Laventille is the spot to hear steel pan bands and have a few local drinks. (p **280**)

STAY

If you can't get to a deserted island, why not stay where Robinson Crusoe was thought to be stranded? The Blue Haven Hotel in Tobago has more than a few local amenities with exceptional food, villa-style accommodations and live music. (p **281**)

EAT

Marcia's Diner in Bon Accord has curried conch as well as all different kinds of stews and curries. Don't forget to leave room for cassava pudding for dessert. (p **279**)

it's hot, and you're definitely part of the party. Living like a local in Trinidad and Tobago means drawing from many different cultures. The islands have passed through Dutch, French, Spanish and British hands before declaring independence from Great Britain in 1962. Today's population is a mix of descendants from the indigenous Arawak and Carib tribes, as well as a European, West African, and strong South Asian population. Trinidad has an estimated 1.25 million people and Tobago has another 54,000.

Unlike other Caribbean islands, Trinidad is an active industrial hub, and the economy is not solely driven by tourism. In fact, Trinidad and Tobago have the Caribbean's strongest economy, one fueled by manufacturing as well as heavy industry from the energy sector; oil, natural gas and petrochemicals make up 70 percent of the country's exports.

Located in the southeast region of the Caribbean, Trinidad is just 7 miles from Venezuela and about 86 miles from Grenada. Tobago is 22 miles northeast of Trinidad. Industry centers on Trinidad's capital, Port of Spain, which is full of traffic, fast food and all the trappings of a modern city. But outside the city there is an abundance of tropical rain forests and island wildlife. Tobago is even more rural and devoid of development. Its rain forests and coasts are so epic that it is thought to be the location of Daniel Defoe's *Robinson Crusoe* as well as home of Robert Louis Stevenson's *Treasure Island*.

Beaches

ASK PETER...

Q: Should I hire a guide to go to the Tobago Forest Reserve?

A: While technically the park is open to everyone, locals strongly recommend you hire a guide. Just going to the park will let you experience nature, but if you go with a guide, you're sure to learn something about the park's wildlife and history.

Bloody Bay Beach★★

Northwest coast of Tobago (last beach access before heading into the rain forest).

Named after a 1666 naval battle in which the British defeated combined Dutch and French fleets, this beach is a glorious place to swim or sunbathe. Save for a fisherman or two, you'll probably be the only one on these golden sands.

Castara Beach★★

West central coast, Tobago.

With two golden-sand beaches, Castara is a great place for families. Relax on the Big Bay side near Castara village or pitch in and help the fishermen "pull seine" (pull in their nets). Sunset is best enjoyed from the Cascreole Restaurant (*Castara Beach Rd., Castara; ☎ 868-639-5291*).

Pirates Bay Beach★

20min walk northwest of Charlotteville, Tobago. Access via an old cocoa plantation and 170 steps down.

Named for the swashbuckling privateers who hid out here over three centuries ago, this picture-postcard beach was the backdrop to the 1952 movie *Robinson Crusoe*. Friendly vendors sell fruit and coconut water.

Travel Tip:

How about an island getaway inside another island getaway? If you head to Nariva Swamp, the island's largest wetlands, you can kayak out to Bush Bush island, which is home to 57 different mammals, 171 species of birds, 8 species of edible fish, 12 kinds of crustaceans, and 7 amphibians. There are also 37 different kind of reptiles, including the anaconda—the world's largest snake.

Store Bay Beach★

South of Pigeon Point, southwest coast, Tobago.

The favorite public beach on the island has changing rooms, lifeguards, and plenty of options for food and lodging.

Best of all, vendors sell crab-n-dumplings, the signature Tobagan dish. Because of its popularity, the beach gets crowded

ISLAND GOATS

You'll find more than your fair share of goats in Trinidad. You'd expect to see goats on a farm. The Goat Dairy Orange Hill Nature Ranch above Scarborough invites visitors in for a cheese-making workshop. Another surprise comes on Easter Monday and Tuesday, when you'll see goats racing through Buccoo and Mount Pleasant. It's a tradition dating back to the 1920s. Today jockeys run barefoot alongside the goats urging them to the finish line. If goat racing wasn't bizarre enough, you can also catch a crab race during the same Easter festivities.

WHEN TO GO

The weather is best in the Jan–Apr **peak season**, when temperatures average 87°F/29°C, cooling to 75°F at night. From May, dry season temperatures rise until the start of the **rainy season** in June, when short tropical downpours bring cooler temperatures. September has its own month-long dry spell, known as the *petit carem*. Hotels have to be booked well in advance for February's Trinidad Carnival.

GETTING AROUND

BY BUS – Inexpensive buses serve Trinidad and Tobago, but reaching remote spots can be a slow process. Destinations are shown on the front of the bus. The main City Gate terminal in Port of Spain serves most of Trinidad. In Tobago, the main terminal is in Scarborough.

BY TAXI – Taxis are unmetered and work on fixed rates from the main airports. Always agree on a price before getting in. Rates range from about US$25 for a trip from Piarco Airport to Port of Spain, and about US$11 from Crown Point to Scarborough. Higher rates apply after 10pm. Piarco Airport Taxi Co-op Society (868-669-1689) Tobago Taxi Services (868-660-4616).

BY CAR – Renters must be over 25 and have had a driving license for 2 years. Hertz and Thrifty operate on both islands, but local firms offer lower rates, starting at US$35-US$70/day. Gas stations are rare in remote areas so fill up before you set out and watch for potholes. Drive on the left.

BY FERRY: Inter-island ferries run from the jetty in Port of Spain to the cruise ship harbor in Scarborough twice a day. The ferry takes 2.5 hours and costs 50TT dollars one way and 100TT dollars round-trip. (www.patnt.com).

VISITOR INFORMATION

Main tourism offices: Trinidad: Maritime Centre, 10th Ave., Barataria. 868-638-7962.
Tobago: N.I.B. Mall, Wilson St., Scarborough. 868-639-2125. www.gotrinidadandtobago.com.
Important numbers
Police: 999
Fire Brigade and Ambulance: 990
Medical Services:
Port of Spain General Hospital, 160 Charlotte St., Port of Spain, Trinidad. 868-623-2951
Scarborough Regional Hospital, Scarborough, Tobago. 868-639-2551

MONEY/CURRENCY

The official currency is the Trinidad and Tobago dollar (TT$) at an exchange rate of $1 US = 6.35 TT$. You can change dollars and traveler's checks at local banks at the airport, Port of Spain and Scarborough, and in most large hotels. You can pay at many establishments in the two main cities with international credit cards, and withdraw cash from ATMs. You will need cash to pay taxis, buses and food and bar bills at the beach.

(by Tobago standards). If you need a break, hotels, motels, restaurants and shops line the sand.

Birding Sites

Asa Wright Nature Centre★★

Off Blanchisseuse Rd., north-central Trinidad. 868-667-4655.
www.asawright.org. Open daily 9am–5pm. $10.

Travel Tip: You might hear "mesi," "sa'w fe" and "pli ta" which are patois phrases that mean "thank you" "how are you" and "see you later." These phrases, along with a handful of others, have worked their way into day to day island speech. Originally used by slaves to communicate with each other, Trinidad's patois is also closely aligned with Martinique's Creole. Many native speakers have died, but you can hear the language in the hillside village of Paramin.

THE GRANDDADDY OF THEM ALL

Carnival is celebrated all throughout the Caribbean, but Trinidad has the largest (and many say the best) celebration. Festivities start in December and run until Ash Wednesday. The island tradition began in the 1700s when French Catholic settlers held masquerades before Lent. The official Carnival events begin two days before lent with "J'overt," the opening ceremony in which participants parade through the streets of Port of Spain covered in mud, oil and paint. The next two days include masquerade (mas bands), steel pan, calypso, soca, fetes (parties) and competitions. Locals caution that Carnival isn't for the faint of heart or fair of skin—wear lots of sunblock and good shoes to prepare for non-stop partying and dancing. Earplugs are also a good idea since the music trucks in the streets generate about 110-120 decibels, equivalent to standing 200 feet from a jumbo jet at take off.

This former cocoa and coffee plantation in Arima Valley is now a privately run reserve. It is aimed at serious birders and casual nature lovers, including those who overnight in the center's 24-room lodge. At the 250-acre estate, guests and non-guests can take guided hikes (*reservations advised*) to see rare oilbirds, or just sit on the lodge's veranda and marvel at the toucans, hummingbirds, agoutis, armadillos and other wildlife that might pass by (*best viewing Jan–May & Oct*).

Caroni Bird Sanctuary★

Off Uriah Butler Hwy., 7 mi south of Port of Spain, Trinidad.
☏ 868-645-1305. Reserve tours with Winston Nanan,
☏ 868-645-1305. $10).
View the mangrove trees at dusk for the best sightings of their resident scarlet ibis (the national bird), stunning in their rich red plumage. Clearly, seeing these birds is the highlight of a 3-hour tour of the swamps, home to caimans and tree snakes. The 337-acre wetlands, part of the Caroni Swamp National Park, attract some 130 species of birds, from pelicans to roseate spoonbills and the rare red-capped cardinals. Long sleeves and insect repellent are a must at sunset, when the ibis return to their nests to roost.

Tobago Forest Reserve

From Speyside, head south on Windward Rd. to Roxborough.
Take Roxborough-Parlatuvier Rd.
Hire a guide to hike just over a mile (*2.5hrs*) through the lush

EAT ...LIKE A LOCAL

It's one thing to talk about the islands' culinary diversity, but you have to taste it to really understand the complexity. You'll finds elements of Indian, African, European, Chinese and Latin American flavors in local dishes. Case in point, look at curry. There are curries on the menu on both islands, but it's not just one curry. In fact, depending on the spot and the town's culture, you could be dining on Chinese, Indian, West African or African curries.

Curry even comes into play for breakfast on the islands. Take Trinidad doubles, for example. This street food snack is made with two *barra* (deep-fried flatbreads) with *chana* (curried chickpeas) in between, and it's a staple all across the islands. It is served with a variety of chutneys as well as hot sauce made from fiery *congo* (a Trinidadian habanero-style pepper) or Scotch bonnets. If you're not in the mood to start your day with spice, then say "no pepper"; if you're a little bolder, order yours "slight pepper."

Today, 40 percent of the island is of East Asian descent, and pungent curry spices —cumin, turmeric, coriander—are prevalent. In Trinidad, you'll find *roti* on every street corner. A national dish, *roti* uses Indian flatbread to sandwich meats and vegetables. Goat curry *roti* is a must.

Tobago is also famous for its curry crabs and dumplings. The dish mixes seasonal green curry sauce with boiled dumplings, local blue crabs and traditional Caribbean sides like sweet potato, eddoes, *dahseen* and green fig. **Marcia's Diner** in Bon Accord is my pick for the dumplings. Her other curries are equally delicious, and you must order her cassava pudding for dessert.

Yes, curry is prominent. But like all Caribbean islands, Trinidad and Tobago know how to fry fish. A dish called bake and shark (also known as shark and bake) takes deep-fried, flaky and surprisingly tender shark meat and nestles it inside a piece of fried puff pastry. You'll find it all over the island, most notably at **Richard's Bake & Shark**. If you're headed to Maracas, the bay on the north coast of Trinidad, you're in the traditional home of the dish. Try it out from any of the bay's beach-side shacks. The food court at **Queen's Park West** in the Port of Trinidad is all about local cuisine.

Most island dishes don't travel well, but spices do. For a real regional experience, you have to go to the market. My pick is the **Scarborough Market** on Wilson Road in Scarborough, Tobago. The market has fresh produce and fish alongside more exotic items like dried sea moss and fresh sassafras root, which is banned in the US. For me, the real draw is the homemade Tobagonian pepper sauce—use an eyedropper to add this hot-and-sour concoction of peppers, vinegar, garlic and spices.

Travel Tip: Travel safety is important throughout all the major cruise ports, and the Port of Spain is no exception. It's a major city as well as a tourist hub, so there is the risk of petty crime like pickpocketing. Stay alert when touring side streets downtown and don't stay out alone after dark.

rain forest of this 14,000-acre reserve. Famed bird authority Sir David Attenborough filmed the documentary series *Trials of Life* on **Little Tobago** (one mile off Tobago's northeast coast).

Port of Spain

Sitting on the northwest side of the island, Trinidad's capital city anchors the Gulf of Paria. It has several sights of interest.

Queen's Park Savannah★★
Off Queen's Park West, city center.
Eat fresh coconut from vendors or sit under shady trees in the capital city's 200-acre centerpiece. The 3-mile jogging track is used by downtown's businesspeople.
The northwest edge of the park is framed by colonial mansions built in the early 1920s. In the northwest corner, the **Botanical Gardens★** (*☎868-622-3530)*, established in 1818 by the British, occupy 62 acres of the park. Modeled on England's Kew Gardens, they are home to 250 species of tropical trees, like acacia, flamboyant and divi-divi.

National Museum and Art Gallery★
117 Frederick St. at Keate St. ☎868-623-5941.
Open Tue–Sat 10am–6pm, Sun 2pm–6pm.
The highlight here is the exhibit of **costumes** from past Carnivals, including elaborate headdresses, concocted from feathers, beads, lace, sequins and other adornments. They share space with Amerindian archaeological pieces and works by local artists, including 19C painter Jean Michel Cazabon.

Laventille★
Suburb east of Port of Spain. Take Wrightson Rd. east to S. Quay Rd., Eastern Main Rd. to Laventille. Take a taxi and some company with you to visit this rather rough neighborhood.
A suburb of Port of Spain is home to the widely known Desperados Panyard, the place to hear steel-pan (steel-drum) bands. The Trinidadian invention has become synonymous with Caribbean music. A month or so before Carnival, the panyard bands are practicing hard for island competitions, which begin the Friday before Lent.

Addresses

For price ranges, see the Legend on the cover flap.

WHERE TO STAY

$ The Pax Guest House – St. Johns Rd., Tunapuna, Trinidad. ☎868-662-4084 or 800-869-0639. www.paxguesthouse.com. *9 rooms.* Serenity-seeking eco-travelers and birdwatchers love this 1916 country inn on the grounds of a monastery, 800ft above sea level. Rooms are modest with views of the forested mountains. Take one of the inn's birding excursions.

$$ Blue Haven Hotel – Bacolet Bay, Scarborough, Tobago. ☎868-660-7400. www.bluehavenhotel.com. *55 rooms.* Movie stars and royalty have sought seclusion here. The Colonial-style villa houses a great restaurant and a terrace bar overlooking Bacolet Bay. In season, calypso music and steel bands entertain guests.

$$ Coblentz Inn – 44 Coblentz Ave., Port of Spain, Trinidad. ☎868-621-0541. www.coblentzinn.com. *16 rooms.* The decor is quite eclectic at this boutique hotel, near Queen's Park Savannah. The rooftop cafe, **Battimamzelle** (**$$**), serves sandwiches with a Creole sauce as well as full-course dinners.

$$$ The Villas at Stonehaven – Stonehaven Bay, Tobago. ☎868-639-0361. www.stonehavenvillas.com. *14 villas.* These 18C French Colonial-style villas offer sea views from hills above the bay. Each villa has three bedrooms, a full kitchen, a veranda and its own pool. Meals can be served on your terrace, or in the on-site restaurant. The common-area infinity pool and low balconies are not suitable for children under 7 years of age.

WHERE TO EAT

$$ Tamnak Thai – 13 Queen's Park East, Port of Spain, Trinidad. ☎868-625-9715. No lunch Sat–Mon. **Thai**. The menu is filled with spicy salads, soups, curries, stir-fries and plenty of fish, duck, lamb, chicken beef and pork dishes. Eat on the patio, or in themed rooms decorated with Asian art.

$$ La Tartaruga – Buccoo Bay Rd., Buccoo Bay, Tobago. Dinner only. Closed Tue, Thu & Sun. ☎868-639-0940. www.latartarugatobago.com. **Italian**. The owner combines Italian olive oils, cheeses and olives with fresh herbs and local fish to re-create the flavors of a great trattoria. Try the homemade pastas or fresh lobster followed by a gelato.

$$$ The Blue Crab – Main and Robinson Sts., Scarborough, Tobago. ☎868-639-2737. www.tobagobluecrab.com. Dinner by reservation only. Closed Sat–Sun. **Caribbean**. This Creole lunch spot is known for its curried crab and dumplings. Try the combination platters of flying fish and shark bites and sip a cool glass of steeped sorrel.

Travel Tip: Trinis don't need New Year's resolutions to get in shape. They have Carnival! Those Carnival costumes are as skimpy as they come. When you sign up with a Carnival band, you don't just get a costume, you can also have a work-out experience. From the end of Christmas to the start of Carnival, bands run Saturday workouts program with music trucks blasting as you do exercise outdoors.

CURAÇAO

Noordpunt
Westpunt
Westpuntbaai
1230
Christoffelberg
Christoffel
National Park
Lagun
Boca Santa
Cruz
Soto
Barber
Boca Santa
Marta
★★ Cas Abao Beach
Sint Willibordus
Salina St. Marie
CURAÇAO
INTERNATIONAL
Bullenbaai
Hato Caves
Santa Catarina
★★★ MUSEUM
KURÁ HULANDA
Sint Michiel
Senior Curaçao
Liqueur Factory
Sint Joris Baai
Curaçao Ostrich
& Game Farm
Otrobanda
Punda
Braakeput
643
★★★ WILLEMSTAD
Curaçao Sea
Aquarium
Caracas
Baai
Den Paradera
Nieuwpoort
Punt Kanon
Curaçao
Underwater Park
KLEIN CURAÇAO

CARIBBEAN
SEA

CARIBBEAN
SEA

ARUBA

BONAIRE

N

0   5   10 mi
0   10 km

Hotels
1 Avila Beach Hotel
2 Hotel Kurá Hulanda

Restaurants
1 Jaanchi's Restaurant

Don't forget your ABCs—Aruba★, Bonaire★ and Curaçao★★★, that is. The westernmost Caribbean islands, part of the Leeward Antilles, run parallel to the northern shore of Venezuela's Península de Paraguná, some 404 miles west of Grenada. The trio shared a history of Dutch ownership dating back to the 17th century. Aruba and Curaçao are now autonomous, self-governing constituent countries of the Kingdom of the Netherlands, while Bonaire is a special municipality of the Netherlands.

Today, Aruba's capital and port of call, Oranjestad, is a thriving hub of casinos, high-rise hotels and shops galore that compete with handsome Dutch-Colonial buildings. Middle island Curaçao, the largest of the three at 38 miles long and 7 miles wide, preserves a taste of Amsterdam in its quaint capital of Willemstad, declared a World Heritage Site for its stunning palette of buildings and stately houses built in characteristic Dutch-style architecture, painted in all hues of pastels. The farthest east is Bonaire, fringed

PETER'S TOP PICKS

SEE

Whether you're a seasoned diver or a first-time snorkeler, Bonaire National Marine Park is one of the best places on the globe to explore the undersea world. Visitors must pay a fee to enter (divers must also participate in an orientation), which awards access to all water sports like snorkeling in the protected coral reef, swimming, boating and kiteboarding. (p **284**)

HISTORY

Museum Kurá Hulanda offers an excellent overview of Curaçao's anthropological history, from ancient artifacts to African art that brings special attention to the slave trade in the Caribbean. In fact, the museum sits on a former slave yard and merchant's home over the St. Anna Bay. (p **286**)

DO

Curaçao Sea Aquarium has a dizzying array of aquatic experiences for all ages. Help feed the sea creatures, swim with dolphins, or simply observe the dazzling spectacle of underwater life in the aquarium hall. (p **289**)

EAT

Skip the tourist restaurants and dine with the locals. Curaçao's Old Market has several stalls cooking up mouthwatering island cuisine. Order the goat stew with a side of plantains, and grab a seat at the communal table. (p **287**)

by a protected coral reef and calm waters that have made it synonymous with world-class diving. Much of the island's industry is centered on the diving industry, with guesthouses doubling as dive centers and schools (including a hotel with a "drive-through" tank-filling station!). Non-divers have their pick of activities both in and out of the water, with exceptional conditions for snorkeling, kiteboarding and hiking.

Situated outside the "hurricane belt," the ABC islands are not susceptible to the violent storms that plague other parts of the Caribbean between June and November. Yet because summer is traditionally the low season in the Caribbean, you can still find off-season deals and discounts. Add in the fact that the weather remains pleasant year-round, and it's a contrarian traveler's dream destination.

Aruba★

Beaches
Palm Beach★★
West coast of Aruba, off J.E. Irausquin Blvd.
Backed by high-rise hotels, this crowd pleaser offers a long stretch of fine, white sand lined with beach bars and water-sports kiosks. It's the haunt of locals on the weekends, when Arubans set up barbecue stands and grill up hot dogs and chicken.

Baby Beach★
South tip of Aruba, east of San Nicolas.
Named for its small size, this beach is a great choice if you have children. The waters are usually lake-calm and no more than four feet deep.

Hadicurari Beach★
Northwest coast of Aruba, off Rte. 1.
Bring your boards, or watch the action at this beach, locally called Fisherman's Hut Beach. Windsurfers love the air movement and choppy surf, so much that an annual windsurfing competition is held here.

Manchebo Beach★
West coast of Aruba, off J.E. Irausquin Blvd., south of Palm Beach.
Also known as Punta Brabo Beach, this long, wide stretch of sand where big surf rules is active with water sports. It's perfectly fine to take off your top at Punta Brabo.

Bonaire★

Bonaire National Marine Park★★
One of the world's top dive destinations, this marine park (*headquarters in Barcadera; ℘5999-717-8444; www.bmp.org*) encompasses the coral reef encircling the island. Most of the 86 designated sites are walk-in dives from the beach; numbers on roadside yellow stones match those on the park's diving map (*available at hotels, tourist offices or online*).
Here are a few great dive sites:
Bari Reef – *Sand Dollar Resort.* Amicable tarpon are the stars of this extremely popular night-dive spot in 20ft to 100ft of water.
Ol' Blue Reef – *Between Columbia and Karpata.* A rocky terrace drops off to 80ft for views of finger sponges and coral, including star, yellow pencil and flower. Watch for turtles in the shallows.

WHEN TO GO

Located outside the hurricane belt, with a hot climate that sees little rain, these islands are year-round sun-and-sea destinations. Average temperatures range from 84°F/29°C in Dec–Feb to 90°F/32°C Jul–Sept. Trade winds cool the beaches. Oct–Feb are rainy, with light showers at night. Expect crowds during the Dec–Apr **peak season**.

GETTING AROUND

BY BUS – Aruba has a modern public bus system. Main terminal is in Oranjestad. Buses circle the island; one-way fare is about US$1.45. Curaçao buses can be confusing for first-timers, but ask locals. Bonaire has no buses; informal vans operate along some routes.

BY TAXI – Taxis are available on islands from the airport, port and major towns. They are unmetered, with rates fixed by the government. Establish the fare (and the currency) before boarding. In Aruba, a ride from the airport to Oranjestad costs about US$9. Taxis have a TX number plate. In Bonaire, a trip from the airport to Kralendijk costs US$9; tours of the island start at US$25/hr. In Curaçao a trip from the airport to Willemstad costs about US$20. Aruba: Pos Abou Taxis (℘297-582-2116), Bonaire: Papi Manuel (℘5999-561-4721).

BY CAR – Major rental car companies operate on all the islands, with offices at the main airports. Rentals start at about US$40/day at local rental firms. Minimum age requirement is 21 years of age, although some companies will not rent to those under 25. Driving is on the right-hand side.

VISITOR INFORMATION

Main tourism offices: Aruba Tourism Authority: LG Smith Blvd., 172 Eagle. ℘297-582-3777. www.aruba.com.
Tourism Corporation Bonaire: Kaya Grandi #2, Kralendijk. ℘599-717-8322. www.infobonaire.com.
Curaçao Tourist Board: Pietermaai 19, Willemstad. ℘5999-434-8200. www.curacao.com
Important numbers
Aruba: Emergency – 911, Police – 100, Fire – 115
Bonaire: Police – 133, Fire – 191, Ambulance – 114
Curaçao: Emergency – 917, Police, Fire – 911, Ambulance – 912
Medical Services:
Aruba: Dr. Horacio E. Oduber Hospitaal, Oranjestad, ℘297-527-4000, www.arubahospital.com
Bonaire: Hospitaal San Francisco, Kaya Soeur Bartola #2, Kralendijk, ℘599-717-8900
Curaçao: St. Elizabeth Hospital, Breedestraat 193, Willemstad, ℘5999-462-4900

MONEY/CURRENCY

The official currency of Aruba is the Aruban florin (Afl), also known as a guilder. Aruban florins and Curaçoan guilders are currently pegged at 1.79 to 1 US dollar. In 2012 Curaçao switches to its own currency. Payment in US dollars is accepted at most major resorts, hotels, restaurants and dive shops. Bonaire uses the US dollar. All major credit cards, most debit cards, and US traveler's checks are widely accepted. ATMs operate 24hrs in main towns and dispense cash in local currency.

1,000 Steps – *South of Ol' Blue Reef*. The 64 steps down to the water lead into a light current, where Hawksbill turtles—and maybe even a whale shark—might be spotted amid colorful sponges and coral. The walk back *up* the steps with gear makes them feel like 1,000 steps.

Curaçao★★★

Willemstad★★★
Museum Kurá Hulanda★★★
At Kurá Hulanda Hotel, Klipstraat. ☎ 5999-434-7700. www.kurahulanda.com. Open daily 10am–5pm. $9.
Exhibits at this first-class museum provide an excellent over view of Curaçao's cultures from the origin of mankind through modern-day Antillean art. The African slave trade, in particula receives in-depth attention. Artifacts include examples of pre Columbian gold and relics from Mesopotamia. Carved mask and tribal drums highlight the superb collection of African art.

Senior Curaçao Liqueur Factory
Mansion Chobolobo, Schottegatweg Oost 129. ☎ 5999-461-3526. www.curacaoliqueur.com. Open Mon–Fri 8am–noon & 1pm–5pm. Free tours include tastings.
For more than a century, the Senior family has mixed aromati oils and exotic spices into the peels of Valencia oranges to pro duce Curaçao's famed liqueur.

Cas Abao Beach★★
Northwest Curaçao. Open Mon–Sun 8am–6pm. $2/car (Sun $3/car).
Coconut palms and chickee huts shade this wide beach, punc tuated on each end by rocky cliffs. The outdoor bar/restauran serves up friendliness and island-brewed Amstel beer.

Klein Curaçao★★
15mi off the southern coast of Curaçao. 2hr one-way boat trip departs Fishermen's Pier Wed, Fri, Sun 6:45am, and returns 4pm. $95 round-trip, including lunch. Mermaid Boat Trips: ☎ 5999-560-1530; www.mermaidboattrips.com.
Some say stepping on the white, powder-fine beaches of thi uninhabited island is a step into paradise. There's a lighthouse to explore, and two underwater dives from the boat.

PORT CITY – CURAÇAO

Although Dutch presence is hard to miss, Curaçao's residents embrace South American, African, Indian and Arabic influences, all of which come together in its markets. The major markets are within walking distance of each other in **Willemstad** on the Punda side of the city (**Otrobanda** is situated on the west side of the **St. Anna Bay**).

Curaçao's arid conditions make growing local produce difficult, but the coastal villages of Venezuela are only 40 miles away. Every morning the **Floating Market** at Willemstad's Punda bustles with brightly colored Venezuelan fishing boats waving their nation's flag, loaded with freshly caught fish and tropical produce. Stalls line up on the walkway along the water where you can pick through the bins piled with exotic fruits and vegetables; watch and learn as the islanders haggle over the day's ingredients.

Not yet a tourist hotspot, the morning market on the dock offers the flavor of "real" Curaçao, where locals congregate each morning, and the fishermen have their own sense of camaraderie. The Venezuelan fisherman don't just shepherd their wares back and forth between countries; they actually live onboard their boats, leaving behind their families for months at a time to sell their goods at the Willemstad port.

Just beyond the **Queen Wilhelmina** footbridge, the **New Market** is a round, covered market where vendors in stalls sell produce, spices, freshly baked bread and local handicrafts. And for a truly local experience, just head down the street to the **Old Market**. Look for the small green building with the sign that says "Plasa Bieu." Follow your nose to the line of stalls where vendors cook homespun island dishes in cast-iron pots, and the locals are sitting at communal tables chatting and laughing over their meals.

Favorites include goat stew and fried kingfish with plantains and *funchi* (a cornmeal side dish, similar to polenta). Don't let someone seat you when you first walk in—that will put you squarely in an area that's designated for just one vendor, meaning your options will be limited. Instead, get your food from various vendors, grab an empty seat and enjoy dining with the locals.

Travel Tip: Most Curaçaoans speak four languages: Dutch, English, Spanish and Papiamento, a Creole language that has evolved over 300 years, spreading from Curaçao to Bonaire and then Aruba. Here's a little Papiamento 101 to get you by: *Bon bini* – Welcome. *Dushi* – Sweetie (used by everyone all of the time). *Bon dia* – Good morning. *Ayo* – Goodbye.

Travel Tip: Curaçao is nowhere near the North Sea!" you might exclaim when you learn of the Curaçao North Sea Jazz Festival. This premier festival is the Caribbean version of a popular Dutch jazz festival. The first event took place in 1975 in The Hague, and brought in major names like Sarah Vaughan and Dizzy Gillespie. The Curaçao version is relatively young, but still brings together some of the biggest names in jazz on the Caribbean island every September. *www.Curacaonorth-seajazz.com.*

Addresses

For price ranges, see the Legend on the cover flap.

WHERE TO STAY

$$$ Avila Beach Hotel – *Penstraat 130, Willemstad, Curaçao. ℘5999-461-4377 or 800 -747-8162. www.avilahotel.com. 108 rooms.* At this colorful beachfront hotel, the lobby occupies an 18C Dutch Colonial mansion that once housed governors. Rooms in the west and east wings are furnished in bamboo and balconies offer sea views. A jazz bar, outdoor restaurant and spa add futher relaxation.

$$$ Hotel Kurá Hulanda Spa and Casino – *Langestraat 8, Willemstad, Curaçao. ℘5999-434- 7700 or 877-264-3106. www.kura hulanda.com. 74 rooms & villas.* At this village of restored, pastel-painted 18C and 19C Dutch-Colonial buildings one-of-a-kind rooms sport hand-carved mahogany and teak furniture, and sculpture dots the grounds. Dine on spicy Indian cuisine at the **Jaipur ($$)**.

$$$$ Harbour Village Beach Club – *Kaya Gobernador N. Debrot 71, Bonaire. ℘599-717- 7500. www.harbourvillage.com. 40 rooms.* Close to the capital and the airport, this upmarket resort has its own marina with the amenities of a PADI dive center. Roomy, well-appointed villas with patios are pricier than the standard rooms. Perks include a pool, spa, restaurant and world-class diving from the shore and by boat.

WHERE TO EAT

$$ Jaanchi's Restaurant – *Westpunt 15, Westpunt, Curaçao. ℘5999-864-0126.* **Caribbean**. Here, Jaanchi, a local character, sings his menu to you and offer recommendations. Combinatio platters might include a Curaçaoan version of conch, shrimp, fish and goat or iguana stew.

$$$ El Gaucho Argentine Grill – *80 Wilheminastreet, Arube ℘297-582-3677. www.elgaucho-aruba.com.* **Argentine**. After 30 years of serving high-quality, grilled-to-perfection beef from the Pampas, this steak house in Aruba is now legendary. If you like it hot, try a Pincho Toro Caliente (a spicy beef shish kabob). The decor is pure macho gaucho, but strolling musicians strum boleros on the guitars. Even the wines are from Argentina.

$$$ Papiamento Restaurant – *Washington 61, Noord, Aruba. Dinner only. Closed Sun. ℘297-594-5504. www.papiamento restaurant.com.* **Continental**. Long ago, this 175-year-old manor was transformed into one of the island's best restaurants. Today the chefs adhere to traditional stone and coal-pot cooking to turn out exceptional flavors. Try Eduardo Seafood Pot, seafood, vegetable and herbs, slow-cooked in a terra-cotta pot. Be sure to take a tour the house before leaving.

KID APPEAL

Maybe it shouldn't be a surprise that islands known as ABC would be kid-friendly. But their westerly location means it's a longer flight from the US than other Caribbean islands; and while Aruba has long welcomed American tourists, Curaçao has only recently been on the US radar due to increased flights. Bonaire's reputation as a diving mecca and its lack of long, white-sand beaches can also be a deterrent for families with young kids. That said, there are plenty of activities and amenities across the islands. In Aruba, look for the **Butterfly Farm** (*J. Irausquin Blvd. Z/ N, Oranjestad; ℘ 297-586-3656; www.thebutterflyfarm.com*), a peaceful sanctuary where butterflies fly freely around the tropical landscape (there are mesh enclosures above). You'll learn about the life cycle of the exotic butterfly and if you're lucky, see one emerging from its cocoon.

Aruba even has the aptly named **Baby Beach**, an out-of-the-way lagoon where the waters are calm and protected. It's so shallow that you can walk out for some time and still touch the sea floor. Farther out into sea the conditions are ideal for snorkeling with brightly colored coral and tropical fish.

The **Curaçao Sea Aquarium** (*Bapor Kibra Z/N, southeast Curaçao; ℘ 5999-461-6666; www.Curacao-sea-aquarium.com; open daily 8:30am–5:30pm; $18.50, children $9.50*) is more than just a tank full of fish. It's a multi-activity park where kids can get hands-on experiences like helping to feed sea turtles, dolphins, nurse-shark pups and other ocean critters. The hall features dozens of tanks filled with colorful underwater creatures, each one representing a different marine ecosystem. The aquarium also has underwater encounters where you can snorkel with sea turtles and reef fish. Next door at the **Dolphin Academy** (*℘ 5999-465-890; www.dolphin-academy.com*) dolphins swim in their natural environment, and children can learn first-hand about these gentle mammals in an assistant trainer course.

Last, but certainly not least, is the **Curaçao Ostrich & Game Farm** (*Groot St. Joris West Z/N, Curaçao. ℘ 5999-747-2566; www.ostrichfarm. net; open daily 8am–2pm; call ahead to reserve*). With 600 ostriches and baby chicks, this farm is a hit with kids. Take a ride on a safari vehicle and get up close and personal with these creatures; grown ups can even ride them! This is the biggest breeding farm outside of Africa, with about 150 resident ostriches, along with a population of emus, black-belly sheep, crocodiles, potbellied pigs and the occasional iguana.

DISCOVERING

MEXICO★★★, BELIZE★★ and HONDURAS★

Hotels

🏨 Hacienda Chichén Resort

🏨 Na Balam

Restaurants

1 Lorenzillo's

2 Yaxché

Where can you find idyllic Caribbean beaches, verdant rain forests, ancient ruins *and* the infrastructure to support visitors of all ages and budgets? Three countries, actually. While Mexico, Belize and Honduras might not be the first countries that come to mind when someone says "Caribbean vacation," these are regions that have the resources to appeal to travelers from all walks of life.

On the Caribbean side of southeastern Mexico is the Yucatán Peninsula, a broad, limestone plank that extends from the State of Chiapas north toward Cuba. The peninsula includes hotspots like Playa del Carmen, Cozumel, and the Riviera Maya, encompassing everything from laid-back beach communities and old

PETER'S TOP PICKS

CULTURE

You'll see the Maya's focus on astronomy and mathematics at Chichén Itzá's Temple of Kukulcán, whose four sides all have 91 steps plus a platform, adding up to a total of 365 steps (the number of days in a year). (p **292**)

GREEN SPACES

Pico Bonito National Park lets you explore or raft through the jungle of Roatán Island. (p **300**)

HISTORY

In Tulum on the Rivera Maya, there are 50 historic structures that date all the way back to 1200 AD and 1501 AD. (p **294**)

SHOP

You'll find European and American chain stores on Fifth Avenue in Yucatán's Playa del Carmen, but if you go off the tourist track, the side streets have some of the best local boutiques. (p **293**)

STAY

Most trips to Belize begin and end in Belize City. The Great House in the historic Fort George district is a good place to get your bearings. (p **302**)

EAT

Elvi's Kitchen in Ambergris Caye is known for Belizean specialties, but go on a Friday night to sample traditional Maya dishes, and a side of homemade pepper sauce. (p **303**)

fishing villages to high-rise hotels and all-night party zones, as well as ancient relics of Maya civilization along the way. Those diverse elements aren't just limited to Mexico. Belize and Honduras also have the gorgeous beaches and lush jungles that draw water enthusiasts and vacationers in search of R&R. And the enduring Maya legacy exists in these countries as well, through exceptionally well-preserved sites like the Caracol Archaeological Reserve and the ancient Classic-period city of Copán.

Of course, with all this natural beauty and strong infrastructure come the tourist trappings of any popular vacation spot: all-inclusive resorts, aggressive vendors and tequila-swilling spring breakers. So how can you see these areas like a local? Arm yourself with information. On Roatán Island, a Bay island of Honduras, know that a short walk or a taxi ride takes you away from the tourist port. In Belize, you can skip the cruise-ship excursions and work with local organizations to visit its national parks. And in Mexico, there's no need to follow the crowds when you can arrange your own private diving or snorkeling excursion. You'll be away from the tour bus and in for a real adventure in no time.

Travel Tip: You might think a trip to Cancún is just a beach vacation, but there's more than just water sports. Few tourists make their way to the Pelopidas Museum in La Isla Shopping Village, which is in the center of the hotel zone. It showcases local and Mexican art, as well as international exhibitions. In the past, works from Picasso, Dali and the Impressionists have been on display.

Mexico's Yucatán Peninsula

Cancún★★ and Area

Cancún is an onshore island, barely cut off from the northeastern tip of the Yucatán Peninsula by a narrow lake, **Laguna Nichupté★**. It was developed for tourism in the 1970s. Soft white sand and gemstone-colored water await you at popular **beaches★★★** like **Linda, Caracol, Ballenas** and **Delfines**, which stretch along Boulevard Kukulcán, from Playa las Perlas south to Punta Nizuc. For many tourists, a lively—even rowdy—club scene and high-fashion shopping heighten the draw.

Accessible by 30min ferry from Cancún (*departs from Playa Tortugas, Hotel Zone; $15US*), **Isla Mujeres★** (Island of Women) is an alluring diving spot, with clear, calm waters. **Garrafon Natural Reef Park** organizes watersports, including swims with dolphins (*☎ 1-866-393-5158; www.garrafon.com.mx*).

Chichén Itzá★★★

*1.5km/2.4 mi west of Pisté village. ☎ 985-851-0137. www.chichenitza.com. Open Tue–Sun 8am–5pm. $10US including Sound and Light Show. Guided tours available. On-site museum and bookstore. Spending the night near the site is highly recommended in order to see the nightly 45min **Sound and Light Show★★★**.*

Rising in the middle of the vast plain between Cancún and Mérida, **Chichén Itzá**—meaning "at the mouth of the water-sorcerer's well"—extends more than 3km/1.9mi amid a clearing in the surrounding low-growth jungle. Once a quiet farming community, then a city of religious import, the site ultimately became the seat of one of the region's greatest powers when a migrant people from central Mexico—dubbed the Itzáes by the Maya-—settled here in the early 10C. Both phases of occupying culture are reflected in the site's architecture. Buildings called **Chichén Viejo** were constructed in the south end of the old city in Classical 9C Puuc style. **Chichén Nuevo**, built from the 10C to the 12C, shows the distinct influence of the Itzá military theocracy, one that practiced ritual human sacrifice. Its centerpiece is the epic **El Castillo★★★**, the three-tiered, 24m/78ft high **Pyramid of Kukulcán**, which dominates the great plaza, and is believed to have had an astronomical function.

The area boasts many **cenotes**—deep well-like sinkholes in limestone—such as **Ik-kil★** (*3km/1.9mi east of Chichén Itzá on Carr. 180; open daily 8am–6pm; $60 pesos*), and **Xkeken★★** (*39km/25mi east of Chichén Itzá on Carr. 180, follow the road to Dzitnup for 2km/1.3mi; open daily 8am–6pm; 35 pesos*), each with a crystal-clear pool of water that makes for a fabulous swim.

Travel Tip: The Maya ruins in Chichén Itzá are accessible throughout the year, but for a real treat, head to the Temple of Kukulcán on the fall or spring equinox. Kukulcán is the Maya serpent deity, and twice a year the temple's design casts shadows that animate the sculpture of the serpent's head at the pyramid's base.

WHEN TO GO

The Yucatán is hot and humid year-round. May temperatures rise above 100°F; Nov–Feb feel slightly cooler. **High season** is mid-Dec–mid-Apr, and always includes Holy Week. In low season (May–mid-Dec), prices may drop 10–30 percent. **Hurricane season**, officially Jun–Nov, can hit the region hard, as it has in recent years.

GETTING AROUND

BY BUS – Travel by bus throughout Yucatán is easy, comfortable, and economic. Look for ADO line terminals and schedules for first class travel. Second class options are widely available, and generally half the price.

BY CAR – Car rentals (998-883-0160; www.cancunrentacar.com) run about $30-$60US/day; offices at the airport and cruise-ship terminal.

BY TAXI – Taxis are widely available and can be flagged down along almost any road. It is a good idea to settle on the fare before embarking.

BY FERRY – Ferries operate between all mainland and island destinations. Magaña Express Service runs from Puerto Juárez in Cancún to Isla Mujeres daily every half hour (35 pesos). For ferry from Playa del Carmen to Cozumel, find ticket booths for two competing companies along 5th Avenue and the dock.

VISITOR INFORMATION

Main tourism office: Mexico Tourist assistance: 01 (800)-903-9200. www.rivieramaya.com.
Important numbers
Emergency (24hrs): 060
Medical Services: Hospital Americano: 998-884-6133 Downtown Cancun (24 hrs)
Hospital Playa Med: 984-879-3145 Playa del Carmen

MONEY/CURRENCY

Mexican currency is the **peso**. Local businesses often charge in US dollars as well as pesos. Current exchange rates hover around 10 to 1 and apply when you pay for a dollar-quoted tour in Mexican pesos. Major credit cards, most debit cards, and internationally recognized traveler's checks in dollar denominations are widely accepted in cities, but generally not in rural areas. You can use your ATM card to withdraw cash, but fees apply.

Riviera Maya★★

68km/42mi south of Cancún via Carr. 307 to Chetumal.
This 120km/75mi stretch of virgin coast on the northeast side of the peninsula has the ingredients for a rewarding vacation: all-inclusive resorts and boutique hotels, coral reefs for diving, beaches for sunning and swimming, eco-adventures and Maya ruins.

Locals refer to it as just "Playa," maybe because not long ago it was little more than soft-sand beachfront, but **Playa del Carmen★★** has since exploded into a bustling cosmopolitan center. The main drag is even called Fifth Avenue (La Quinta), boasting first-class shopping and a hopping nightlife.

Just offshore, **Cozumel★★** *(accessible by boat)* is the largest island in the Mexican Caribbean, and a favorite spot for cruise

ASK PETER...

Q: I want to see wildlife without going on a programmed excursion. What are my options?

A: To make your own getaway, and if you're a bird or animal lover, you should head to Holbox Island. At the intersection of the Caribbean Sea and the Gulf of Mexico, it is home to flamingos, pelicans, whale sharks and a wide variety of marine life. Catch the ferry out there from the port of Chiquilá.

Travel Tip: Choose your beach carefully in Tulum. Yes, you'll find clean Caribbean white-sand beaches up and down the coast, but you'll also find a few surprises. Historically, this area's beaches have welcomed nude bathers. While this used to be a widespread policy, the development of larger resorts has resulted in a crackdown on nudity. Today, you'll still see nude bathers between the Akumal resort zone and the Tulum ruins, especially near the Copal and Azulik resorts.

PORT CITY PLAYA DEL CARMEN

Fifth Avenue in Playa del Carmen is the town's main shopping destination, but it's not necessarily the best place to catch a bargain. Local shopkeepers stand in the doors, trying to urge passersby inside. On the main strip, it's hard to haggle, but you'll have better luck with roadside crafts. Fifth Avenue is also known as restaurant row and you'll find every kind of food like hot dogs, Thai noodles, Argentine steaks and frozen yogurt. But what about local food and local drinks? If you're searching for more authentic eats, head off the strip and go north to 10th Avenue or 15th Avenue. Find a bar that's showing the Mexican Baseball League on TV and you'll have a rowdy local scene.

ships, divers, and bird watchers. Underwater enthusiasts should go to **Palancar★** (*21km/13mi south on the main highway and 1.7km/1mi from the beach of the same name*), whose stunning reef formations and superlative visibility first won Cozumel its world renown as a prime dive spot.

Eco-archaeological park **Xcaret★★★** (*Chetumal-Puerto Juarez Federal Hwy., KM 282; ℰ 800-212-8951; www.xcaret.com; open daily 8:30am–9:30pm; 79 pesos*), 72km/45mi south of Cancún, has sinkholes, a subterranean river and enchanting beaches, where you can swim with dolphins.

You can also explore botanical gardens, aquariums, and a butterfly museum or watch horse shows, Maya ball games and traditional dances.

Tulum★★

60km/37mi south of Playa del Carmen, along Carretera Federal, Federal Highway 370. ℰ 984-206-3150. www.rivieramaya.com; open Mon–Sun 8am–5pm; 51 pesos.

The ruins of this late great Maya city rest on a bluff above the white sands of the Caribbean shore, a location responsible for its original name of Zamá: "sunrise."

Its Late post-Classic (1200-1521 AD) apogee in maritime commerce is reflected in the defensive architecture—a series of outer and inner walls, one 6m/20ft thick—that won it its current name of Tulum, which means "wall" in Mayan.

Large fortified towers are among 50 remaining structures onsite. After exploring the ruins, walk down the bluff and cool off in the turquoise sea. *See Michelin Green Guide Mexico, Guatemala, Belize for additional sights to visit.*

COZUMEL

When cruise ships dock at Cozumel, most passengers head for the water. One-day snorkeling or scuba diving adventures are on offer throughout the area. While many cruise companies or resorts will try to sell you on a package, I find if you call up operators directly, not only do you have more control over your dive experience, but you also might be able to get a better rate.

If you're looking for a wall dive, the Palancar Reef is likely to be your main destination. Palancar is split into a few distinct sections: the Palancar Shallows, The Horseshoe and the Palancar Deep. The coral reef is known for its rainbow of colors as seen, for example, in giant sponges that are orange, yellow and brown. Darting throughout are multicolored parrotfish, iridescent and yellow queen angelfish, red hawkfish and blue damsels. In addition, the reef sometimes attracts turtles, sharks and eagle rays. You can dive down between 15 feet and 100 feet. Or if you're not scuba-certified, it's possible to snorkel in the reef when the current cooperates. You can set up your dive with these any of these companies:

Aqua World: ☎ *877-730-4054 (US), www.aquaworld.com.mx*
Buena Ventura Diving: ☎ *530-889-1174 (US), www.buena venturadiving.net*

Del Mar Aquatics at the Casa del Mar Hotel: ☎ *987-872-5949, www. delmaraquatics.com*

Dive with Martin: ☎ *503-949-5985 (US), www.divewith martin.com*

Sea Robin: ☎ *951-824-9073 (US), www.searobincozumel.com*
Dive Paradise - Playa Villablanca: ☎ *987-872-1007, www.diveparadise.com*

Dive Palancar - Occidental Hotels: ☎ *987-872-5556, www.divepalancar.com*

Scuba Du – At Presidente Intercontinental Resort and Spa: ☎ *310-684-5556 (US), www.scubadu.com*

ISLA HOLBOX

Off the beaten track, **Isla Holbox★★** is a sandy paradise that marks the point where the Caribbean Sea meets the Gulf of Mexico. If you are a bird and animal lover, consider a side trip here to see **flamingos**, and even **swim with whale sharks★★** in the summer. *Access: Carretera 180 LIBRE west toward Mérida to small town of El Ideal at KM 82, continue north on Carr. 5 about 73km/45mi to the port of Chiquilá, where a ferry serves the island 8 times daily, $60 pesos.*

BIRDING IN BELIZE

Divers may urge you spend your time under the sea in Belize's celebrated barrier reef, but that's not the only attraction. Belize is also paradise for birders. The country is home to more than 550 species of birds, many of which are rare or threatened with extinction. Instead of booking yourself on a tour company's nature excursion, head straight to the source—the Belize Audubon Society, which, in conjunction with the government, manages nine conservation areas that were established in 1981 with the National Parks System Act.

In addition to the Audubon staff, the Belize Forest Department, the Fisheries Department and the Institute of Archaeology manage the experience. If birding is your main goal, check out some of these spots:

Cockscomb Basin Wildlife Sanctuary

This is the place to see birds that flock to higher elevations. The park is home to rich forest and deep pine trees, which support forest, pine woodland and savanna species. The park also makes special effort to preserve game birds like the Great Curassow and Crested Guan.

Crooked Tree Wildlife Sanctuary

One of the largest and best-known areas, Crooked Tree is the place to see wetlands and many migratory and non-migratory wetland birds that are drawn to the area. Check out the lagoons in the dry season from February through May when birds head to the water when food is hard to find in other places. Expect to see Sungrebe, Jabiru and Wood Storks, Snail Kites, Bare-throated Tiger and Boat-billed Herons,

and Black-collared Hawks. On land, there are rare endangered Yellow-headed Parrots of the pine savannah.

Caracol Archaeological Reserve

Here is the largest Maya site in Belize, but it's also home to wildlife. Birders watch for the Keel-billed Motmot that nests in the area, as well as colorful toucans, trogons and species of Ocellated Turkey, Crested Guan, and Great Curassow.

Half Moon Caye Natural Monument

First established as a sanctuary in 1928, this historic bird reserve is also the oldest wildlife protection colony in Belize. It's home to the red-footed booby colony that is estimated to have as many as 4,000 birds. You'll also find new species here like the White-throated Sparrow.

WHEN TO GO

Belize has a subtropical climate. Caribbean winds keep **average temperatures** at 79°F/26°C on the coast, rising to 85°F/30°C in May. Average humidity is 85 percent. The **rainy season**, with brief daily downpours, lasts Jun–Oct. **Peak season** is Nov–May. Hurricanes are most common Aug–Oct.

GETTING AROUND

Roads in the region are modern but deteriorate in the rainy season. Car rentals are available in Belize City, costing about $200BZ/day. Water taxis serve offshore sites; $10 to $15US each way (www.cayecaulkerwatertaxi.com).

VISITOR INFORMATION

Main tourism office: Belize Tourism Board, New Horizon Investment Blvd., Mile 3½ Northern Highway, Belize City. 227-2420 or 800-624-0686 (toll-free US & Canada) Mon–Thu 8am–noon & 1pm–5pm, Fri 8am–5:30pm. or www.travelbelize.org.
Important numbers
Emergency (24hrs): 911 or 90
Medical Services:
Universal Health Center: 501-224-5537 Downtown Belize City (24hrs)

MONEY/CURRENCY

The **Belizean dollar** has a fixed exchange rate of BZ$2 per US$1. Major bank branches and gas stations, mostly in Belize City, have ATMs. US currency is widely accepted. Most hotels, restaurants, shops and tour operators take traveler's checks. Only major establishments accept credit cards. Many restaurants add a service charge; otherwise, add a 10 percent or 15 percent tip at your discretion.

Belize★★

Belize City and Area

The country's most populated district is a region of pine savanna, mangrove swamps and Caribbean cays. At its heart lies its largest urban center, Belize City.

Edging the delta where the Belize River joins the Caribbean Sea, this former capital, replaced in 1970 by Belmopan after hurricane damage, remains the center of national life. It is the departure point for most tours.

Day or night, guided tours at nearby **Belize Zoo★★** (*46km/29mi west of Belize City; open daily 8:30am–4:30pm; $15, children $5; 220-8004; www.belizezoo.org*) are a must. Here, 150 animals reside in open spaces on 12ha/29 acres of savannah.

Offshore, the Mesoamerican Reef, which stretches south from Cancún, forms the largest coral **barrier reef★★★** in the Western Hemisphere. It protects diverse marine life and hundreds of cays (small islands) that serve as springboards to world-renowned dive sites.

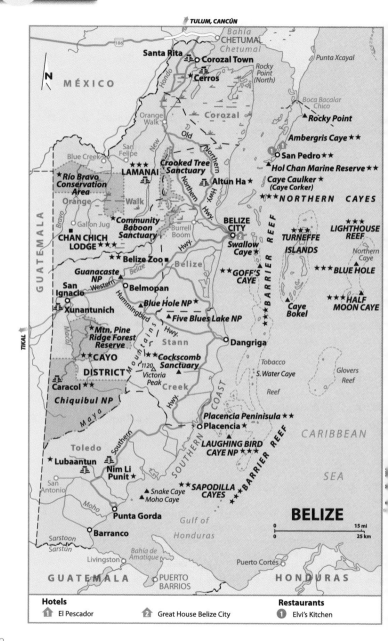

TULUM, CANCÚN

Bahía
CHETUMAL
Chetumal

186

Santa Rita

Corozal Town

Cerros

Punta Xcayal

MÉXICO

N

Rocky
Point
(North)

Corozal

Orange
Walk

Old

Boca Bacalar
Chico

Rocky Point

Ambergris Caye ★★

San Pedro ★★

Hol Chan Marine Reserve ★★

Cave Caulker ★
(Caye Corker)

San
Felipe

Blue Creek

★★★
LAMANAI

★★★
Crooked Tree
Sanctuary

Altún Ha ★

Río Bravo
Conservation
Area

Orange

Walk

Northern Hwy.

★★ NORTHERN CAYES

Gallon Jug

CHAN CHICH
LODGE ★★★

★**Community**
Baboon
Sanctuary

Burrell
Boom

BELIZE
CITY

2

TURNEFFE
★★★ ISLANDS

LIGHTHOUSE
★★★ REEF

GUATEMALA

Bravo

Belize

Belize

Swallow
Caye

Northern
Caye

Hwy.

Belize Zoo ★★

★★ GOFF'S
CAYE

★★★ BLUE HOLE

Guanacaste
NP

Belmopan

Western

★★★ HALF
MOON CAYE

San
Ignacio

Xunantunich

Blue Hole NP ★

Caye
Bokel

Hummingbird

▲ Five Blues Lake NP ★

TIKAL

★★ CAYO

DISTRICT

★**Mtn. Pine**
Ridge Forest
Reserve

Hwy.

Stann

Dangriga

Tobacco

Mountains

1120

★★**Cocksomb**
Sanctuary

Victoria
Peak

S. Water Caye

Glovers
Reef

Caracol ★★

Macal

Maya

Creek

Reef

Chiquibul NP

CARIBBEAN

SEA

Toledo

★ Lubaantun

Placencia Peninsula ★★

Placencia ★

Nim Li
Punit ★

Southern

LAUGHING BIRD
CAYE NP ★★★

BELIZE

San
Antonio

▲ Snake Caye
▲ Moho Caye

★ **SAPODILLA**
CAYES

★★

0   15 mi

0   25 km

Moho

Punta Gorda

Gulf of
Honduras

Barranco

Sarstoon
Sarstún

Livingston

Bahía de
Amatique

Puerto Cortés

GUATEMALA

PUERTO
BARRIOS

HONDURAS

Hotels

🏠 El Pescador

2 Great House Belize City

Restaurants

1 Elvi's Kitchen

Northern Cayes★★★

Northeast of Belize City, offshore 32km/20mi long **Ambergris Caye★★** (*75min by boat from Belize City*) holds the town of **San Pedro★★**, a diving mecca and Belize's main tourist destination. Beginning divers and snorkelers should visit **Hol Chan Marine Reserve★★** (*10min boat ride from San Pedro; open daily 6am–9pm, some sections 24hrs; BZ$20, plus excursion fee; ✆226-2247; www.ambergriscaye.com/holchan*). Home to nurse sharks and giant rays, **Shark Ray Alley★★★** (*20min by boat from San Pedro*) also offers spectacular snorkeling in 6.5ft/2m-shallow waters. The largest of Belize's three atolls, the **Turneffe Islands★★★** (*1hr by boat from San Pedro*)—upwards of 200 cayes surrounding three crystalline lagoons—host hammerheads, mangroves and pristine dive sites.

At **Lighthouse Reef★★★** (*2.5hrs by speedboat from San Pedro*), you can explore five sunken ships and the awesome **Blue Hole★★★** (*open daily 8am–4:30pm; BZ$60; ✆223-4987; www.belizeaudubon.org*), an intensely blue cylindrical cave measuring 1,312ft/400m in diameter and 475ft/145m in depth. **Half Moon Caye Natural Monument★★★** (*on reef's southeastern island; open daily 8am–4:30pm; BZ$20*), the first national park in Belize, is home to 4,000 red-footed boobies and 98 other species. Its waters ensure visibility at great depths.

Community Baboon Sanctuary★

42km/26mi west of Belize City. Take Northern Hwy; turn left after 21.5km/13.5mi through Burrell Boom and west on dirt road 14km/9mi. Open daily 8am–5pm. $10BZ. www.howlermonkeys.org.

In the village of Bermudian Landing, farmers live in harmony with and protect their resident **black howler monkeys**. Entry fee includes a 45min guided walk and a museum visit. Other activities include a canoe tour and an extended walking tour. On-site campsites, lodging and meals are available.

Altun Ha★

54km/34mi northwest of Belize City. Take Northern Hwy 32km/20mi; go right 19km/12mi, then left 3km/2mi. Open daily 9am–5pm. $10BZ. www.howlermonkeys.org.

Jade objects were found in the **Temple of the Green Tomb** of this Classic center, Belize's most heavily excavated Maya site. The **Temple of the Sun God★** (18m/59ft) offers splendid forest views. A 15cm/6in-tall jade head found in 1968 representing sun god, **Kinich Ahau**, is kept in a vault in Belmopan. The 65sq km/25sq mi site was once home to 10,000 people.

Travel Tip: The Centers for Disease Control advises that you should see your doctor or a travel medicine specialist 4 to 6 weeks before a trip to make sure that all your shots are up to date. Typhoid, hepatitis A and malaria have been found in the country, though usually off the tourist paths of Belize City and in the more rural districts of Cayo, Stann Creek and Toledo.

Travel Tip: You might have heard about white-water rafting, but what about "black-water rafting"? Turns out the water isn't black, and you're not actually rafting. Instead, black-water rafting has become the popular term for cave exploration via inner tube. Cave tubing or black-water rafting originated in New Zealand, but is now also offered in Belize. Several tour groups run "black water" expeditions down the Caves Branch River.

Hotels
🏠 Anthony's Key Resort

Restaurants
❶ Palmetto Bay Plantation Restaurant

Honduras★

Roatán Island★★

Safe Way Maritime ferries depart La Ceiba on the mainland daily 9:30am and 4:30pm. $27US.

A blossoming addition to the Caribbean tourist map, idyllic Roatán is the largest of the Bay Islands sitting at the southern-most stretches of the Mesoamerican Reef. All-inclusive resorts dot Caribbean coves, and cruise ships come to port here.

The island's focus is diving; some hotel owners have even installed shipwrecks to provide man-made dive sites. Most resorts have their own dive shops and airport pick-up services that will deliver you to your resort by boat.

West End Village★, Roatán's main urban center, has a decidedly island spirit, but will entertain dedicated shoppers and inspire exacting palates in spite of its laid-back nature. Island tours may include a visit to the oldest Garífuna settlement of **Punta Gorda**. You can also play a round at the brand-new Black Pearl golf course.

WHEN TO GO

Tradewinds keep the tropical Bay Islands comfortable year round. Temperatures average 79°F/26°C on the coast, increasing to 85°F/30°C in May. Average humidity is 75 percent. In the **rainy season** (Aug–Feb), a lightweight coat is recommended. **Peak tourist seasons** are Thanksgiving week and the second half of Dec–Aug. Damaging hurricanes generally do not strike here.

GETTING AROUND

Car rental companies (at the airport) should be contacted before travel: Caribbean Rent-A-Car www. caribbeanroatan.com.

VISITOR INFORMATION

Main tourism office: Roatán Information Center, West Bay Beach, in front of Foster's Resort. ✆011-504-3-336-5597.

Important numbers
Emergency (24hrs): 199 or 399
Medical Services:
Roatán Public Hospital: Coxen Hole,
✆445-1227 or 445-1499
Wood Medical Center: Coxen Hole,
✆445-1080 or 445-1031

MONEY/CURRENCY

The **Lempira** has hovered around 19 to $1US exchange rate for several years, though this year has seen several dives in the strength of the local currency. US dollars are widely accepted on Roatán, though it's advisable to ask in advance. ATMs are available in West End and Coxen Hole. Traveler's checks and credit cards may present problems, so cash is advised. There is a $38 airport exit tax at Roatán's international airport.

ROATÁN ISLAND

Roatán Island's economy is based on tourism. In addition to resorts, this Honduran Island is home to two cruise terminals—Coxen Hole and Mahogany Bay. But guess what, you're not going to have an authentic local experience if you stick to the white-washed area near the docks. Instead, go past the captain of the port's office.

Starting there, you'll be able to find some less crowded and more authentic restaurants and stores (where you should remember to bargain, and you'll usually be able to talk prices down 15 percent). To go deeper into the 26 mile-wide island, you have two options. You can take a taxi (but remember to negotiate the rate ahead of time) or you can take minibuses. Minibuses can be waved down from the street, but you'll also find a staging area in Coxen Hole by Warren's Grocery. Note the bus takes *lempiras*, not US dollars, but you'll be able to change your money at the grocery.

ASK PETER...

Q: I know there are hiking trails and wildlife throughout Pico Bonito National Park, but what if I want more adventure?

A: Río Cangrejal runs through Pico Bonito National Park, which means one thing: whitewater rafting. The river can work for beginners and experts with rapids ranging from Class II to Class IV. On the property, The Lodge at Pico Bonito runs rafting excursions, but you'll also find tours offered through independent companies.

Pico Bonito National Park★

For mainland excursions from Roatán, ferries depart twice daily from Coxen Hole for a 1.5hr ride to La Ceiba; $27US. Flights are also available.

White-water rafting and kayaking on the Class V Río Cangrejal and lush jungle excursions are the main draws of La Ceiba's natural park.

Copán★★

311km/193mi, about 7hrs by car from La Ceiba on CA13 West to CA5 in San Pedro Sula, then CA4 to Copán; 45min flights available from Roatán to San Pedro Sula, where buses or car rental can take you 3hrs to the ruins. Open year-round daily 8am–4pm. $15US ✆ 220-8004.

One of the best-preserved Maya sites, Copán has structures dating from the Classic period that were in use for 2,000 years. A dynasty of 16 kings perpetually devoted their rule to the construction of this once artful city. Represented are architectural styles ranging from Olmec and Teotihuacán to Tikal. Superb stelae honor gods or rulers. Important hieroglyphic messages are etched onto stairways and walls. Many of Copán's outer pyramids are built atop those left by each king's predecessor. While some rulers destroyed what was there, using the rubble as a foundation for the new, others entombed entire structures within a new pyramid, as was the case of **Temple 16**. A life-size **replica★★★** of this inner temple can be found in the on-site museum, entry to which is included in the site fee.

Addresses

For price ranges, see the Legend on the cover flap.

WHERE TO STAY

$$ Anthony's Key Resort – *Sandy Bay, Roatán Island, Honduras. ✆800-227-3483. www.anthonyskey.com. 56 units.* Some wood bungalows stand on stilts above the sea. Rather pedestrian in furnishings, they are nevertheless designed for relaxing—inside or on the balcony—between dives or snorkeling. The leisurely atmosphere is often punctuated with a sense of impending adventure. A pool and gift shop are on-site.

$$ The Great House Belize City – *13 Cork St., Belize City, Belize. ✆501-223-3400. www.greathousebelize.com. 12 rooms.* This imposing inn in the Fort George district is the place to stay if you want to see the zoo or get the lay of the land before setting off on adventure tours. The 4-story wood Colonial mansion is graced with breeze-loving verandas. Rooms with wood floors and ceiling fans are

individually decorated in a traditional style.

$$ Hacienda Chichén Resort – *Carr. 180, KM 120, Chichén Itzá, Mexico.* ☏*985-851-0045. www.haciendachichen.com. 12 cottages.* Cottages come with traditional dark-wood or wrought-iron furnishings and broad ground-level terraces overlooking luxuriant gardens or the pool. The spa specializes in mystic Maya practices.

$$ Na Balam – *Calle Zazil-Ha, 118, Isla Mujeres, Mexico.* ☏*998 -877-0279. www.nabalam.com. 32 rooms.* The somewhat minimalistic but spacious rooms and suites at this Maya retreat don't include TV or telephone, but each has a private balcony and a view of either the Caribbean Sea or the pool. Many come with a hammock as well as beds. Yoga and in-room massage are some of the perks, as well as a swimming pool and restaurant serving three meals a day.

$$$ El Pescador – *Ambergris Caye, Belize District, Belize.* ☏*800-242-2017. www.elpescador.com. 13 rooms, 8 villas.* First acclaimed by fishing enthusiasts, the "Fisherman" resort welcomes guests with comprehensive packages and amenities that include 3 pools and complimentary bike or kayak use. Rooms in the main lodge and oceanfront villas are done in a minimal contemporary style with colorful accents.

WHERE TO EAT

$$ Elvi's Kitchen – *Pescador Dr., San Pedro Town, Belize.* ☏*501-226-2404. www.elviskitchen.com.* **Belizean**. This hopping

Ambergris favorite serves up its famous fried chicken alongside coconut rice and fried plantains, or try the roasted garlic-chipotle lobster. From the Maya buffet, sample fresh chunky salsas blended with spices and seeds like *mole* and *adobo* sauces.

$$ Yaxché – *Calle 8 between 5th and 10th Aves., Playa del Carmen, Mexico.* ☏*984-873-2502.* **Maya**. Taste innovative Maya cuisine in the flower-draped courtyard lined with reproductions of Maya artifacts. Maya recipes range from traditional *tsotobilchay* tamales filled with chaya leaves, boiled egg, and pumpkin seeds to the newly dreamed up Chac Mool, spicy shrimp boiled in tangerine juice with chipotle peppers.

$$$ Lorenzillo's – *Blvd. Kukulcán KM 10.5, Cancún.* ☏*998-883-1254. www.lorenzillos.com.mx.* **Seafood**. This dining spot's sophisticated setting with wood details and nautical accents is eclipsed by delicious fresh lobster and great wine. Its "cava" features carefully selected wines from around the world, including several of the best Mexico has to offer.

$$$ Palmetto Bay Plantation Restaurant – *Palmetto Bay, North Shore, Roatán Island.* ☏*305-851-2581. www.palmettobay plantation.com.* **Seafood**. Catering to clientele of the classy resort of the same name **($$$)**, this restaurant provides an idyllic setting for seafood dishes like crunchy coconut shrimp or conch fritters.

CARTAGENA★★★

It wasn't long ago that, in most people's eyes, Colombia was synonymous with drug cartels and violent crime, but the nation has come a long way in terms of safety and accessibility. Even the U.S. Department of State has altered its stance on travel to Cartagena, noting that security has improved significantly in recent years.

Known officially as Cartagena de Indias, and locally as La Heroica, the city is divided into three sections: the walled Old City that's teeming with historic sights and charming Colonial architecture; bustling, modern downtown; and the casual beaches along the Caribbean Sea, where life moves at a more leisurely pace. Best of all, this city was built for wandering. Take a stroll along the cobblestone streets as musicians, dancers and mimes put on impromptu performances; indulge your tourist side and take a ride in a horse-drawn carriage; enjoy people watching while sipping tropical juice in open-air cafes; peer at the brightly painted Spanish colonial homes where bougainvillea spills out from wooden balconies; explore the formidable Palacio de la Inquisición and the Castillo de San Felipe de Barajas fortress that protected the Spanish city from pirates and foreign invaders; dance until the early morning hours at the eclectic mix of bars and nightclubs.

Outside the walled city, Cartagena is practically surrounded by the Caribbean Sea. The beaches aren't as pristine or secluded as Caribbean islands (think Miami Beach), but they are a part of the city's culture, so make time to see the popular Bocagrande just for the local flavor. Just off the coast is the archipelago of El Rosario, composed of protected coral islands that are easily accessible by sea.

Cartagena has become a mainstay on the cruise-ship route, but has remained off the radar for most American tourists who still harbor concerns of drug-related violence. But that's about to end as the country is poised to welcome even more international travelers by improving its tourism infrastructure.

That includes increasing airlift from US cities, developing cruise ports in addition to Cartagena, and making improvements to intercity roads and the airport in Bogotá. Translation? Cartagena is about to become one of the hottest places for American travelers seeking that ideal combination of modern amenities, colonial flavor and Caribbean influences in one easy-to-reach destination.

PETER'S TOP PICKS

⤳ HISTORY

The sprawling complex of Castillo San Felipe de Barajas tells the story of Cartagena's complicated history as it defended the walled city from pirates and foreign invaders. (p **308**)

⤳ STAY

Although Cartagena is teeming with boutique hotels, Capilla del Mar is worth the splurge for its revolving rooftop bar, 22nd-floor swimming pool and its own private beach. (p **310**)

⤳ SHOP

Forget the touristy trinkets and look for quality jewels on your journey. High-quality emeralds are available all over the city, but stick to reputable dealers like Greenfire Emeralds and Mister Emerald at Pierino Gallo mall. (p **311**)

⤳ EAT

Ceviche is practically a way of life in Cartagena. Get a sample of some of the best in the city at La Cevicheria, prepared by chef/owner Jorge Escandon. (p **306**)

⤳ ENTERTAINMENT

Café Havana is one of the classic nightspots of Cartagena where you can dance the night away to Latin rhythms among locals and tourists alike. (p **309**)

ASK PETER...

Q: What's a typical dish in Cartagena and where are the best places to find it?
A: This is an easy one... ceviche! Cartagenans take their ceviche very seriously, "cooking" raw seafood in a flavorful broth of citrus and spices. Most visitors want to go to **La Cevicheria** (*Calle Stuart 7-14, San Diego*), an off-the-beaten-path little place within the Old City that was put on the map by Anthony Bourdain's *No Reservations*. Another great option is **Peru Mar** (*Calle Santo Domingo 33-41*), which has a slightly more upscale ambiance and exceptional seafood. And if you really want to go local, simply pick up ceviche to-go from one of the many street vendors in the city. For a modern version of this local favorite, simply head to Vera Restaurant inside the very cool Tcherassi Hotel, for a delectable assortment of uniquely prepared seafood carpaccio.

Cartagena★★★ *and Area*

This historic fortified city is a treasure trove of Spanish Colonial-style buildings: cathedrals, convents, palaces, and structures that house interesting museums, eclectic restaurants and unusual shops. Made from hard coral and stone, its brightly painted houses, topped with high roofs, conceal hidden inner courtyards. Narrow calles and carreras wind around breezy plazas, shaded cafes, and ornate churches. Flame-colored bougainvillea cascades from ornate wooden balconies. Walk within and around the walled city and you'll soon appreciate its long and rich history.

Ciudad Amurallada★★★

One of the most impressively preserved examples of 16C Spanish Colonial architecture in South America, the **inner walled town** has been Colombia's eternal tourist destination for more than 40 years. Within the confines of 30-odd square blocks, the old city—or *centro histórico*—San Pedro and San Diego districts hold the nation's best boutique hotels, restaurants and shops. Steeped in history and romance, the cobbled streets of the Ciudad Amurallada are ideal for exploring on foot. Highlights include the **Puerta del Reloj★**, the city's arched main entrance that today shades horse-drawn carriages waiting to offer leisurely tours, and the monumental three-story **Museo Santuario de San Pedro Claver** (*Plaza de San Pedro Claver; ℘ 5-664-4991; open Mon–Fri 8am–5pm, Sat–Sun 8am–4pm; 6,000COP*), which is worth the entrance fee just to admire the central courtyard's colonnade as well as odd museum pieces. Its stone façade is an example of American Baroque style.

Spend some time in the attractive, shaded square dating to 1896, **Plaza de Bolívar★★★**, where a statue of the Great Liberator pays tribute to the plaza's namesake, Venezuelan-born **Simón Bolívar** (1783-1830) Enjoy a cold drink from strolling street vendors before visiting **Palacio de la Inquisición★★** (*Calle 34 3-11; ℘ 5-664-4570; open Mon–Sat 9am–7pm, Sun 10am–4pm; 11,000 COP*). Having arrived in 1610, the Inquisition was expelled in 1810 and reinstalled in 1815 before being finally pushed out of Cartagena in 1821.

The inquisitioners left behind a grim legacy of intolerance and brutality that can be viewed in this museum; several heinous devices of torture are on display.

Under the arches of the **Palacio de Gobierno** are street plaques alongside Plaza de Bolívar denoting all of the **Miss Columbia** winners. Pageants are a megabucks business in Columbia. The televised contest is held each December in Cartagena.

WHEN TO GO

Highs of 32°C/90°F/32°C, lows of 77°F/25°C, and humidity reaching 90 percent in the **rainy season** (Oct–Nov) make the city hot and sticky year-round. Sea breezes cool the beaches. The **dry season** runs Dec–Apr, but tropical downpours can occur any time. The rainiest months coincide with the **hurricane season. Peak tourist season** is in the run-up to Christmas, although the Jan/Feb Hay Festival attracts a literary crowd.

GETTING AROUND

BY BUS – Inexpensive buses serve the old city and beaches of Bocagrande. Destinations are identified on the front of the bus. Minimum fare is about 1,000COP. **Metrocar**, a cheap airport shuttle service in air-conditioned buses (look for green and red signs) drops passengers off at Monumento a la India Catalina, across from the walled city's main entrance.

BY TAXI – A fairly inexpensive way to get to major sights, yellow taxis ply Cartagena's streets. They are unmetered and work on rates fixed by the local government; always agree on the price before getting in. Rates range from about 4,800COP from Bocagrande to the Centro Histórico, 8,000COP from Centro Histórico to the airport, and 13,700COP from the cruise port to the old city. Higher rates apply for air-conditioned cars and at night. Auto Taxi 211 (✆5-677-7087), Rafael Núñez Airport taxi rank, ✆5-666-3709.

BY CAR – Most international rental agencies, Hertz, Avis, operate in Cartagena, but with most attractions in the old city, Bocagrande's beaches, and offshore islands, there is little need to drive unless taking trips outside the city.

VISITOR INFORMATION

Main tourism office: Muelle Turístico La Bodeguita, Piso 2. ✆5-655-0211. www.cartagenadeindias.travel.
Important numbers
Emergency: 123, 112
Police: 112, 156
Fire Brigade: 119
Ambulance: 132
Medical Services:
Hospital Bocagrande, Centro Comercial Bocagrande, Avenida San Martin. ✆5-655-0962. www.hospitalboca grande.com.co
Hospital Naval de Cartagena, Car. 2, Bocagrande. ✆5-665-5360. www. hospitalnavalcartagena.mil.co.

MONEY/CURRENCY

The official currency of Colombia is the peso (COP). At the time of writing the exchange rate was $1 US = 1,947 COP, but check a currency conversion site such as www.xe.com before you arrive. You can change dollars at local banks in the old city on Avenida Venezuela, or exchange houses on Plaza de los Coches, and at most hotels. Avoid moneychangers in the street supposedly offering better rates. You can withdraw cash in pesos with a credit card at ATMs in local banks like Davivienda, Bancolombia and Banco Union Colombiano, but check the symbols first to see if they accept Mastercard or Visa.

ASK PETER...

Q: Can I do a tour of the city that follows the footsteps of Gabriel García Márquez?
A: Colombian novelist Gabriel García Márquez set his iconic magical-realist novel, *Love in the Time of Cholera*, in Cartagena. You can purchase an audio tour that guides you to sights that inspired or influenced the renowned writer, including his home in the Old City at the corner of Calle Zerrezuela and Calle del Curato in the San Diego neighborhood. Plaza Bolívar and Plaza Fernández de Madrid were great inspirations for the author, and you'll pass by El Universal, the newspaper where he honed his journalism skills. The audio tour is available at the **Tierra Magna** office (*San Martín Avenue, CC. Bocagrande, Shop 2-09; ✆ 57-655-1916, www.tierra magna.com*).

Castillo San Felipe de Barajas★★★

Avenida Arévalo, Cerro San Lázaro. ✆ 5-656-0590. www.fortificacionesdecartagena.com. Open daily 8am–6pm. 16,000 COP. Wear comfortable footwear and take a flashlight to illuminate the underground tunnels.

Not to be missed, this formidable **fortress** dominates San Lázaro hill east of the walled city. It was begun in 1536 to protect the city from pirates and marauders. The near indestructible stronghold was built up in earnest from 1639 to 1657 and enlarged in 1762. As the most extensive fortifications in South America, the huge complex was designated a UNESCO Heritage Site in 1984. In the center stands a statue of **Don Blas de Lezo**, who commanded the Spanish forces in the **Battle of Cartagena**, when a sizeable British force was convincingly defeated.

Convento de la Popa★★

Calle Nueva del Toril 21, Cerro de la Popa. ✆ 5-666-2331. Open daily 9am–5pm. 6,000COP.

Located on a hill about 3km/1.8mi east of the old city, this **monastery**, founded in 1607, was used at times as a fortress because of its strategic location. It houses a lovely interior **patio**, a colonial **museum** and a **chapel** dedicated to the Virgen de la Candelaria. But it is most famous for offering unparalleled **views★★** of the old city and the port from the top of its 150m/492ft high hill.

Islas del Rosario★★

46km/28.5mi southwest of Cartagena. Day trips depart from Muelle Turistico in front of the old city; 35-40,000COP. ✆ 5-665-5655. 3,800 COP national park fee.

The beaches of Bocagrande are gray and uninspiring compared to the delights of this archipelago of some 30 **coral islands**, now protected as the **Parque Nacional Natural Corales del Rosario y San Bernardo**. Home to corals, sea grass and colorful fish, these shallow, clear waters are ideal for diving and snorkeling—and a great way to escape the humidity of Cartagena. Boats leave in the morning from the Muelle Turistico (also known as Muelle de los Pegasos) in front of the old city and return late afternoon, stopping at **Isla Grande** for swimming and a fish lunch, and **Isla de San Martín de Pajarales's** opensea aquarium (*10,000COP*).

See Michelin Green Guide Colombia for additional sights to visit.

CARTAGENA MUSIC

Music is the heart and soul of Cartagena. From salsa and reggaeton to *vallenato* and *cumbia*, music spills onto the streets and into the plazas. Head to busy areas like Plaza de Bolívar or Plaza Santo Domingo, a hub for Cartagena's nightlife that is always humming with music and dancing. Sit back at an open-air restaurant and enjoy the sounds of musicians who stroll from table to table, or wander among the cobblestone streets where live performances can surprise you at every corner.

Outside the city walls, several bars and nightclubs are clustered on Calle Arsenal in the Getsemaní area. Also in this neighborhood is the must-see Café Havana, a Cuban-style nightspot that will take you back to old-school Havana with salsa rhythms, moody lighting and dancing into the wee hours of morning (*Calle Media Luna and Calle del Guerrero; ✆ 57-314-519-6745, www.cafehavanacartagena.com*).

Looking for a real celebration? Hop onboard a chiva, a brightly painted, open-air bus that travels through the city's hot spots. By day, it's a mellow sightseeing tour. At night, it's an event like no other. The bus is stocked with plenty of rum (and, if you're lucky, soda and ice) and a live band to keep the party going. At the end of the ride, the revelers meet up at the Old City wall for a rowdy, joyous dance party.

Cartagena's music scene isn't all about Latin rhythms. Tens of thousands of classical music lovers flock to the city every January for the Cartagena International Music Festival. Rather than taking place in a singular concert hall, chamber concerts happen throughout the city's outdoor plazas, churches and theaters.

You haven't experienced classical music until you've heard the sounds of a live orchestra swelling within the walls of an ancient chapel. During the week-long festival, audiences can roam from one venue to another—or even stumble upon live outdoor performances—and participate in expert lectures and discussions.

SIDE TRIPS

You can easily lose yourself in Cartagena's Old City, but there are plenty of side trips that get you out of the urban bustle and into nature. Just about 30 miles northeast of the city lies **Volcán de Lodo El Totumo**, a "mud volcano." This hill is built on top of a vent of an active volcano where you can bathe in pools of natural, heated mud. Just climb a set of rickety steps, wait your turn, and dunk. Don't worry about getting in above your head; the makeup of the thick mud makes you surprisingly buoyant. Attendants linger about offering massages, while you soak in the healing mud. Just be careful as you climb down the steps to a lagoon where women scrub the mud off you. And no, none of these personal services come free.

Although Cartagena has public beaches, the crowds and aggressive vendors can make it a less-than-relaxing afternoon. On the way back from the volcano, make time to stop in the fishing village of **Manzanillo del Mar**. Just a few miles from Cartagena, this little village offers something of a local experience, with a quiet beach and a handful of open-air restaurants where you can relax without contending with overeager vendors.

If you're craving a more idyllic getaway, a day or overnight trip to the coral islands of **El Rosario** is well worth your while. As a protected national park, the islands offer a glimpse into the Caribbean's natural wonders, with mangrove parks and rich coral reefs that are abundant with marine life. El Rosario is just 25 miles off the coast of Cartagena, accessible by high-speed ferry from **Muelle de la Bodeguita** (near the convention center). A popular spot for divers and snorkelers, the park is also home to an open-water aquarium and museum. Most tour operators will also include a stop at **Playa Blanca**, one of the prettier beaches within easy reach from Cartagena.

Addresses

For price ranges, see the Legend on the cover flap.

WHERE TO STAY

$$ Capilla del Mar – *Corner of Carrera 1 and Calle 8, Bocagrande.* ✆*5-650-1500. www.capilladel mar.com. 110 rooms.* This high-class hotel boasts a revolving rooftop bar and a 22nd-floor swimming pool overlooking its own beach area. It's 10 minutes from the airport and 5 minutes from the walled city. Air conditioned rooms have Wi-Fi access and safe deposit boxes.

$$ Casa La Fe – *Calle Segunda de Badillo 36-125, Centro.* ☎*5-664 -0306. www.casalafe.com. 14 rooms.* This friendly B&B in the old city has been tastefully renovated by its English and Colombian owners. Pricier rooms have views of Plaza Fernandez de Madrid. Enjoy breakfast in the lush courtyard.

$$ Casa Relax – *Calle del Pozo 25-105, Barrio Getsemaní.* ☎*5-664-1117. www.cartagenarelax.com. 13 rooms.* Close to the old city, this reasonably priced B&B sits near Trinidad Church in the somewhat down-at-the-heels neighborhood of Getsemaní. The restored colonial property has a large pool, a sunny kitchen and social area. Breakfast is included in the rate.

$$$ Hotel Caribe – *Carrera 12-87, Bocagrande.* ☎*5-665-4042. www.hotelcaribe.com. 363 rooms.* This four-story Spanish Colonial-style hotel on Bocagrande beach dates back to 1941. Renovated rooms in three wings have high-ceilings, some with sea views. Kids will enjoy the swimming pool and miniature golf course.

WHERE TO EAT

$ La Mulata Cartagena – *Calle Cuero 9-52, Barrio San Diego, Centro Histórico.* ☎*5-662-2952. www.restaurantelamulata.com. Lunch only. Closed Sun.* **Colombian**. The appealing set menu at this hip restaurant is a great value, so popular items run out fast. Caribbean cuisine with a Colombian twist, the daily lunch menu lists five entrées and five grilled items. For a refreshing beverage, try an *agua fresca* (fruit juice drink).

$$ 8-18 – *Calle Gastelbondo 2-124 local 8, Centro Histórico.* ☎*5-664-2632. www.restaurante8-18.com. Lunch only.* **International**. Intimate and trendy, 8-18 provides a varied menu of coastal cuisine, including shellfish soup, braised grouper in white wine, and curried chicken. Best to reserve your table in advance.

$$ Club de Pesca – *Manga, Avenida Miramar, Fuerte del Pastelillo.* ☎*5-660-4594. www.clubdepesca.com.* **Seafood**. Affluent gourmands love this chic place inside San Sebastian del Pastellilo Fort, one of the most important forts of the colonial era. You can arrive by land or sea and dine on the deck overlooking the marina. Modern seafood fills the menu, along with a great selection of wine.

$$ El Santísimo – *Calle del Torno 39-62, Barrio San Diego.* ☎*5-660-1531. www.elsantisimo. com.* **Colombian**. This upscale eatery in the Barrio San Diego serves contemporary Colombian fare paired on the menu with a suggested wine for each dish. Use the warm fresh bread to soak up the juices in the *obatala* (marinated beef stew).

Travel Tip: The 1985 Michael Douglas/ Kathleen Turner film, *The Jewel of the Nile*, took place in Cartagena and was centered on an enormous emerald called El Corazon. And for good reason. Cartagena is one of the prime locations for emerald shopping. Beware of synthetic stones and go only to reputable dealers. Hawkers on the street may try to entice you into shady places. The Pierino Gallo mall is a good place to start, where reputable shops include **Greenfire Emeralds** (*Shop #2-1;* ☎*57 5 665-0413*) and **Mister Emerald** (*Shop #2-10,* ☎*57 5 665-0413*)

Travel Tip: Taxis in Cartagena aren't metered, so agree on a price ahead of time. About 5,000 pesos is the minimum to get from major points. Be sure to close taxi doors gently. Taxis are lighter than in the US, and taxi drivers cringe when Americans slam the doors shut!

INDEX

313

INDEX

★★★ **Worth the trip**
★★ **Worth a detour**
★ **Interesting**

MAP LEGEND

Sight Symbols

⊐●━━━━━ Recommended itineraries with departure point

🏠‡🔲 Church, chapel – Synagogue   ▬ Building described

○ Town described   ▭ Other building

AZ B Map co-ordinates locating sights   ▪ Small building, statue

■ ▲ Other points of interest   ○ ⁂ Fountain – Ruins

⚒ ⌒ Mine – Cave   🛈 Visitor information

🌾 🗼 Windmill – Lighthouse   ⛵ ⚓ Ship – Shipwreck

☆ ♠ Fort – Mission   ⁂ ѱ Panorama – View

Other Symbols

🛡 Interstate highway (USA)   ▦ US highway   ⬭ Other route

🍁 Trans-Canada highway   ▦ Canadian highway   ▦ Mexican federal highway

═══ Highway, bridge   ═══ Major city thoroughfare

═●═ Toll highway, interchange   ═══ City street with median

═══ Divided highway   ◄── One-way street

─── Major, minor route   ═══ Pedestrian Street

15 (21) Distance in miles (kilometers)   ⊁⊰⊱ Tunnel

2149/655 Pass, elevation *(feet/meters)*   ┈┈┇ Steps – Gate

△6288(1917) Mtn. peak, elevation *(feet/meters)*   ⊿ ⌁ Drawbridge - Water tower

✈ ✈ Airport – Airfield   🅿 ✉ Parking – Main post office

⛴ Ferry: Cars and passengers   🏫 ✚ University – Hospital

⛴ Ferry: Passengers only   🚆 🚌 Train station – Bus station

◁◄⌐ Waterfall – Lock – Dam   ● ⬤ Subway station

─··─··─ International boundary   ❶ ⬡ Digressions – Observatory

──── State boundary   ▦ ⬌ Cemetery – Swamp

Recreation

●○○○○● Gondola, chairlift   ⟨≡⟩ ⚑ Stadium – Golf course

🚂 Tourist or steam railway   ✺ ▭ ▦ Park, garden – Wooded area

⛴ ◊ Harbor, lake cruise – Marina   🆂 Wildlife reserve

🏄 ◪ Surfing – Windsurfing   ◔ ♈ Wildlife/Safari park, zoo

▦ 🚣 Diving – Kayaking   ────── Walking path, trail

🎿 🎿 Ski area – Cross-country skiing   🚶 Hiking trail

Sight of special interest for children

Abbreviations and special symbols

NP National Park	NMem National Memorial	SP State Park
NM National Monument	NHS National Historic Site	SF State Forest
NWR National Wildlife Refuge	NHP National Historical Park	SR State Reserve
NF National Forest	NVM National Volcanic Monument	SAP State Archeological Park

🛡 National Park   🛡 State Park   🛡 National Forest   🛡 State Forest

All maps are oriented north, unless otherwise indicated by a directional arrow.

MAPS

Michelin Travel and Lifestyle North America
A division of Michelin North America, Inc.
One Parkway South, Greenville, SC 29615, USA

ISBN 978-1-907099-78-6

Printed: February 2012
Printed and bound in Canada

Although the information in this guide was believed by the authors
and publisher to be accurate and current at the time of publication, they
cannot accept responsibility for any inconvenience, loss, or injury sustained
by any person relying on information or advice contained in this guide.
Things change over time and travelers should take steps to verify and confirm
information, especially time-sensitive information related to prices, hours
of operation, and availability.